D0933814

Perinatal Nutrition

Bristol-Myers Nutrition Symposia

Series Editor
JERRY L. MOORE
Nutritional Division
Mead Johnson & Company

1 R. W. Winters and H. L. Greene (Editors):
Nutritional Support of the Seriously Ill Patient, 1983

2 C. E. Butterworth, Jr., and Martha L. Hutchinson (Editors):
Nutritional Factors in the Induction and Maintenance of Malignancy, 1983

3 Morris Green and H. L. Greene (Editors):
The Role of the Gastrointestinal Tract in Nutrient Delivery, 1984

4 Samuel J. Fomon and William C. Heird (Editors):
Energy and Protein Needs during Infancy, 1986

5 Martha L. Hutchinson and Hamish N. Munro (Editors):
Nutrition and Aging, 1986

6 B. S. Lindblad (Editor):
Perinatal Nutrition, 1988

Perinatal Nutrition

Edited by

B. S. Lindblad

Department of Pediatrics
Karolinska Institutet
St. Göran's Children's Hospital
Stockholm, Sweden

ACADEMIC PRESS, INC.

Harcourt Brace Jovanovich, Publishers

San Diego New York Berkeley Boston
London Sydney Tokyo Toronto

ACADEMIC PRESS, INC.
1250 Sixth Avenue, San Diego, California 92101

United Kingdom Edition published by
ACADEMIC PRESS INC. (LONDON) LTD.
24–28 Oval Road, London NW1 7DX

Library of Congress Cataloging in Publication Data

Perinatal nutrition.

(Bristol-Myers nutrition symposia; v. 6)
Papers presented at the Sixth Annual Bristol-Myers Symposium on Nutrition Research, held in Saltsjöbaden, Sweden on Aug. 28-29, 1986.
Includes index.
1. Fetus—Nutrition—Congresses. 2. Fetus—Physiology—Congresses. 3. Maternal-fetal exchange—Congresses. 4. Infants (Newborn)—Nutrition—Congresses. 5. Infants (Newborn)—Diseases—Nutritional aspects—Congresses. 6. Infants (Newborn)—Physiology—Congresses. I. Lindblad, B. S. II. Bristol-Myers Symposium on Nutrition Research (6th : 1986 : Saltsjöbaden, Sweden). III. Series.
[DNLM: 1. Fetal Development—congresses. 2. Infant Nutrition—congresses. W3 BR323F v.6 / WQ 210 P44235 1986]
RG615.P48 1988 612'.647 87-1464
ISBN 0–12–450285–7 (alk. paper)

PRINTED IN THE UNITED STATES OF AMERICA

88 89 90 91 9 8 7 6 5 4 3 2 1

Contents

3 The Handling of Amino Acids by the Fetoplacental Unit

MAUREEN YOUNG

4 Endocrine Control of Fetal Growth?

R. D. G. MILNER

5 The Role of Somatomedins in Fetal Growth

VICKI R. SARA

6 Fetal and Neonatal Skeletal Growth and Mineralization

RICHARDUS ROSS, FRANCIS MIMOUNI, AND REGINALD C. TSANG

7 Discussion: Part I. The Fetus and the Placenta. A. The Need for Animal Models

PETER W. NATHANIELSZ

8 Discussion: Part I. The Fetus and the Placenta. B. Application to Developing Countries

STAFFAN BERGSTRÖM AND JERKER LILJESTRAND

Editor's Comment

B. S. LINDBLAD

Comment on Bergström and Liljestrand's Discussion Paper

R. G. WHITEHEAD

Part II Birth from the Nutritional Point of View

9 Lung Differentiation and Repair in Relation to Vitamin A Status

MILDRED T. STAHLMAN, JAYANT P. SHENAI, MARY E. GRAY, HÅKAN W. SUNDELL, KATHLEEN KENNEDY, AND FRANK CHYTIL

10 Impact of Antimicrobial Agents on the Intestinal Microflora of Newborn Infants

RUTGER BENNET, MARGARETA ERIKSSON, CARL ERIK NORD, AND ROLF ZETTERSTRÖM

11 The Ontogeny of Gut Mucosal Defense

L. Å. HANSON, BARBRO CARLSSON, U. DAHLGREN, FEHMIDA JALIL, SHAUKAT RAZA KHAN, L. MELLANDER, AND A. WOLD

12 Perinatal Development of Liver Enzymes

BIRGITTA STRANDVIK

13 Renal Function and Fluid and Electrolyte Homeostasis in the Neonate

ANITA APERIA AND GIANNI CELSI

14 Metabolic and Endocrine Interrelationships in the Human Fetus and Neonate: An Overview of the Control of the Adaptation to Postnatal Nutrition

ALBERT AYNSLEY-GREEN

15 Discussion: Part II. Birth from the Nutritional Point of View. A. Nutrition in the Postpartum Period

W. ALLAN WALKER

16 Discussion: Part II. Birth from the Nutritional Point of View. B. Birth and Longer Term Well-Being in the Third World

R. G. WHITEHEAD

Part III The First Feed

17 Intestinal Transport of D-Glucose, Bile Salts, Phosphate, and Calcium during Maturation

FAYEZ K. GHISHAN

18 Stable Isotope Probes: Potential for Application in Studies of Amino Acid Utilization in the Neonate

VERNON R. YOUNG, NAOMI K. FUKAGAWA, KENNETH J. STORCH, ROBERT HOERR, THOMAS JAKSIC, AND DENNIS M. BIER

19 The Regulation of Human Milk Flow

MICHAEL W. WOOLRIDGE AND J. DAVID BAUM

20 Digestion and Absorption of Human Milk Lipids

21 Polio and Typhoid Vaccinations of Lactating Women and the Antibody Response in the Milk

22 Discussion: Part III. The First Feed. A. General Comments

23 Discussion: Part III. The First Feed. B. The View from the Third World Countries

OSCAR BRUNSER

Part IV Special Problems Relating to the Preterm and Surgical Newborn Infant

24 Impact of Maternal Blood Glucose Control on Neonatal Morbidity in Diabetic Pregnancies

BENGT PERSSON AND ULF HANSON

25 Trace Elements in the Perinatal Period

BO LÖNNERDAL

26 Parenteral Nutrition and Amino Acid Metabolism in Neonatal Intensive Care

B. S. LINDBLAD, STEFAN HAGELBERG, KENNETH PALMÉR, AND ANDERS LUNDSJÖ

27 Evaluation of a Pediatric Multiple-Vitamin Preparation for Total Parenteral Nutrition: Blood Levels of Vitamins A, D, and E

HARRY L. GREENE, MARY E. COURTNEY MOORE, BARRY PHILLIPS, AND LINDA FRANCK

28 Fortified Human Milk Feeding in the Premature Infant

C. GARZA, R. J. SCHANLER, R. GOLDBLUM, AND A. S. GOLDMAN

Contributors

Numbers in parentheses indicate the pages on which the authors' contributions begin.

Anita Aperia (151), Department of Developmental Physiology, Karolinska Institutet, St. Göran's Children's Hospital, 112 81 Stockholm, Sweden

Albert Aynsley-Green (161), Department of Child Health, University of Newcastle upon Tyne, The Medical School, Newcastle upon Tyne NE2 4HH, England

J. David Baum (243), Department of Child Health, University of Bristol, Royal Hospital for Sick Children, Bristol BS2 8BJ, England

Rutger Bennet (125), Department of Pediatrics, Karolinska Institutet, St. Göran's Children's Hospital, 112 81 Stockholm, Sweden

Staffan Bergström (107), Department of Obstetrics and Gynecology, Central Hospital, 631 88 Eskilstuna, Sweden

Stefan Bernbäck (259), Department of Physiological Chemistry, University of Umeå, 901 85 Umeå, Sweden

Dennis M. Bier (221), Departments of Medicine and Pediatrics, Washington University School of Medicine, St. Louis, Missouri 63110, U.S.A.

Lars Bläckberg (259), Department of Physiological Chemistry, University of Umeå, 901 85 Umeå, Sweden

Oscar Brunser (283), Institute of Nutrition and Food Technology (INTA), University of Chile, Santiago 11, Chile

Barbro Carlsson (133, 273), Department of Pediatrics, and Department of Clinical Immunology, University of Göteborg, 413 46 Göteborg, Sweden

Gianni Celsi (151), Department of Developmental Physiology, Karolinska Institutet, St. Göran's Children's Hospital, 112 81 Stockholm, Sweden

Frank Chytil (117), Department of Biochemistry, Vanderbilt University School of Medicine, Nashville, Tennessee 37232, U.S.A.

U. Dahlgren (133), Department of Clinical Immunology, University of Göteborg, 413 46 Göteborg, Sweden

Margareta Eriksson (125), Department of Pediatrics, Karolinska Institutet, St. Göran's Children's Hospital, 112 81 Stockholm, Sweden

Linda Franck (333), Department of Pediatric Gastroenterology, Oakland Children's Hospital, Oakland, California 94609, U.S.A.

Naomi K. Fukagawa (221), Laboratory of Human Nutrition, Department of Applied Biological Sciences, and Clinical Research Center, Massachusetts Institute of Technology, Cambridge, Massachusetts 02139, U.S.A.

C. Garza (347), USDA/ARS Children's Nutrition Research Center, and Department of Pediatrics, Baylor College of Medicine, and Texas Children's Hospital, Houston, Texas 77030, U.S.A.

Fayez K. Ghishan (209), Department of Pediatric Gastroenterology, Vanderbilt University School of Medicine, Nashville, Tennessee 37232, U.S.A.

R. Goldblum (347), Department of Pediatrics, The University of Texas Medical Branch, Galveston, Texas 77550, U.S.A.

A. S. Goldman (347), Department of Pediatrics, The University of Texas Medical Branch, Galveston, Texas 77550, U.S.A.

Mary E. Gray (117), Department of Pathology, Vanderbilt University School of Medicine, Nashville, Tennessee 37232, U.S.A.

Harry L. Greene, (333), Department of Pediatric Gastroenterology and Nutrition, Vanderbilt University School of Medicine, Nashville, Tennessee 37232, U.S.A.

Stefan Hagelberg (317), Department of Pediatrics, Karolinska Institutet, St. Göran's Children's Hospital, 112 81 Stockholm, Sweden

Mirjana Hahn-Zoric, (273), Department of Pediatrics, and Department of Clinical Immunology, University of Göteborg, 413 46 Göteborg, Sweden

L. Å. Hanson (133, 273), Department of Clinical Immunology, University of Göteborg, 413 46 Göteborg, Sweden

Ulf Hanson (291), Department of Pediatrics, and Department of Obstetrics and Gynecology, Karolinska Institutet, St. Göran's Children's Hospital, and Karolinska Hospital, 112 81 Stockholm, Sweden

Olle Hernell (259), Department of Pediatrics, University of Umeå, 901 85 Umeå, Sweden

E. Hey (3), Department of Child Health, The Princess Mary Maternity Hospital, Newcastle upon Tyne NE2 3BD, England

Robert Hoerr (221), Laboratory of Human Nutrition, Department of Applied Biological Sciences, and Clinical Research Center, Massachusetts Institute of Technology, Cambridge, Massachusetts 02139, U.S.A.

Thomas Jaksic (221), Laboratory of Human Nutrition, Department of Applied Biological Sciences, and Clinical Research Center, Massachusetts Institute of Technology, Cambridge, Massachusetts 02139, U.S.A.

Fehmida Jalil (133, 273), Department of Social and Preventive Pediatrics, King Edward Medical College, Lahore, Pakistan

Kathleen Kennedy (117), Department of Pediatrics, Vanderbilt University School of Medicine, Nashville, Tennessee 37232, U.S.A.

Shaukat Raza Khan (133), Department of Pediatrics, King Edward Medical College, Lahore, Pakistan

Hugo Lagercrantz (367), Nobel Institute for Neurophysiology, Karolinska Institutet, and Department of Pediatrics, Karolinska Hospital, 104 01 Stockholm, Sweden

Jerker Liljestrand (107), Department of Obstetrics and Gynecology, Central Hospital, 371 85 Karlskrona, Sweden

B. S. Lindblad (111, 317), Department of Pediatrics, Karolinska Institutet, St. Göran's Children's Hospital, 112 81 Stockholm, Sweden

Bo Lönnerdal (229), Department of Nutrition, University of California at Davis, Davis, California 95616, U.S.A.

Anders Lundsjö (317), Department of Pediatrics, Karolinska Institutet, St. Göran's Children's Hospital, 112 81 Stockholm, Sweden

N. O. Lunell (15), Department of Obstetrics and Gynecology, Karolinska Institutet, Huddinge University Hospital, 141 86 Huddinge, Sweden

L. Mellander (133), Department of Pediatrics, University of Göteborg, 413 46 Göteborg, Sweden

R. D. G. Milner (45), Department of Pediatrics, University of Sheffield, Children's Hospital, Sheffield S10 2TH, England

Francis Mimouni (75), Division of Neonatology, Department of Pediatrics, University of Cincinnati College of Medicine, Cincinnati, Ohio 45627, U.S.A.

Mary E. Courtney Moore (333), Department of Pediatric Gastroenterology and Nutrition, Vanderbilt University School of Medicine, Nashville, Tennessee 37232, U.S.A.

Peter W. Nathanielsz (103), NYS College of Veterinary Medicine, Cornell University, Ithaca, New York 14850, U.S.A.

Carl Erik Nord (125), Department of Microbiology, Karolinska Institutet, Huddinge University Hospital, 141 86 Huddinge, Sweden

L. Nylund (15), Department of Obstetrics and Gynecology, Karolinska Institutet, Huddinge University Hospital, 141 86 Huddinge, Sweden

Kenneth Palmér (317), Department of Pediatrics, Karolinska Institutet, St. Göran's Children's Hospital, 112 81 Stockholm, Sweden

Bengt Persson (291), Department of Pediatrics, and Department of Obstetrics and Gynecology, Karolinska Institutet, St. Göran's Children's Hospital, and Karolinska Hospital, 112 81 Stockholm, Sweden

Barry Phillips (333), Department of Pediatric Gastroenterology, Oakland Children's Hospital, Oakland, California 94609, U.S.A.

Richardus Ross (75), Division of Neonatology, Department of Pediatrics,

University of Cincinnati College of Medicine, Cincinnati, Ohio 45627, U.S.A.

Vicki R. Sara (63), Department of Psychiatry, Karolinska Institutet, St. Göran's Children's Hospital, 112 81 Stockholm, Sweden

R. J. Schanler (347), USDA/ARS Children's Nutrition Research Center, and Department of Pediatrics, Baylor College of Medicine, and Texas Children's Hospital, Houston, Texas 77030, U.S.A.

Jayant P. Shenai (117), Department of Pediatrics, Vanderbilt University School of Medicine, Nashville, Tennessee 37232, U.S.A.

Gyula Soltész (279), Department of Pediatrics, University Medical School of Pécs, 7623 Pécs, Hungary

D. A. T. Southgate (3), Agriculture and Food Research Council, Institute of Food Research, Norwich Laboratory, Norwich NR4 7UA, England

Mildred T. Stahlman (117), Department of Pediatrics, Vanderbilt University School of Medicine, Nashville, Tennessee 37232, U.S.A.

Kenneth J. Storch (221), Laboratory of Human Nutrition, Department of Applied Biological Sciences, and Clinical Research Center, Massachusetts Institute of Technology, Cambridge, Massachusetts 02139, U.S.A.

Birgitta Strandvik (143), Department of Pediatrics, Karolinska Institutet, Huddinge University Hospital, 171 86 Huddinge, Sweden

Håkan W. Sundell (117), Department of Pediatrics, Vanderbilt University School of Medicine, Nashville, Tennessee 37232, U.S.A.

Nebiat Tafari (371), Department of Pediatrics and Child Health, Addis Ababa University, Addis Ababa, Ethiopia

Reginald C. Tsang (75), Division of Neonatology, Department of Pediatrics, University of Cincinnati College of Medicine, Cincinnati, Ohio 45627, U.S.A.

W. Allan Walker (193), Harvard Medical School, Boston, Massachusetts 02115, U.S.A.

R. G. Whitehead (113, 197), Dunn Nutrition Unit, Medical Research Council, Cambridge CB4 1XJ, England

Elsie M. Widdowson (3), Department of Medicine, Addenbrooke's Hospital, Cambridge CB2 2QQ, England

A. Wold (133), Department of Clinical Immunology, University of Göteborg, 413 46 Göteborg, Sweden

Michael W. Woolridge (243), Department of Child Health, University of Bristol, Royal Hospital for Sick Children, Bristol BS2 8BJ, England

Maureen Young (25), Toft, Cambridge CB3 7RU, England

Vernon R. Young (221), Laboratory of Human Nutrition, Department of Applied Biological Sciences, and Clinical Research Center, Massachusetts Institute of Technology, Cambridge, Massachusetts 02139, U.S.A.

Rolf Zetterström (125), Department of Pediatrics, Karolinska Institutet, St. Göran's Children's Hospital, 112 81 Stockholm, Sweden

Editor's Foreword

Specialization of knowledge and research activity has been the key to much of the dramatic scientific and medical research progress in this century. The key to the clinical application of these basic scientific findings, however, seems increasingly to be the integration of knowledge and practice from many disciplines. This need for integration extends beyond the linking of research in individual disciplines to the exchange of ideas and knowledge across national boundaries.

From that perspective, this symposium on "Perinatal Nutrition" and the proceedings recorded herein present a significant achievement. It was the first symposium to address nutrition concerns spanning the third trimester of pregnancy through the first month of the infant's life—the role of nutrition for mother and child before and after birth. It also provided a significant opportunity for the exchange of views and information between scientists working in both developed and less developed countries. And, in keeping with the theme of international integration, it was the first Bristol-Myers Symposium on Nutrition Research held outside the United States.

Drs. Bo S. Lindblad and Jan-Åke Gustafsson are thus to be commended for envisioning, planning, and, under the auspices of Karolinska Institutet, implementing a unique and highly successful symposium. They insisted on and obtained the highest quality of scientific content, yet they were equally sensitive to providing a meeting environment in beautiful Saltsjöbaden that enhanced cross-disciplinary, multicultural interaction. To them and to the thirty-five scientists who prepared presentations and manuscripts, I extend genuine thanks for their contributions to perinatal nutrition worldwide.

Jerry L. Moore
Series Editor

Foreword

Just 15 years ago, babies born in developed countries who weighed only two pounds at birth had virtually no chance for survival. Today, approximately 70–80% of these tiny babies do survive.

Progress in developing countries has not been as dramatic, yet scientists remain optimistic about improving the survival rate and quality of life of premature infants in these nations as well. This optimism is due in large part to scientists' increased understanding of the crucial role of nutrition for mother and child before and after birth.

The papers on "Perinatal Nutrition" gathered here comprise the proceedings of the sixth annual Bristol-Myers Symposium on Nutrition Research, organized by Karolinska Institutet and held August 28–29, 1986, in Saltsjöbaden, Sweden. "Perinatal Nutrition" was the first international symposium to deal exclusively with nutrition in the critical 4-month period for the mother and child that begins with the third trimester of pregnancy and extends through the first month of life. It was also the first meeting to examine perinatal nutrition from the viewpoint of both developed and developing countries.

Thirty-five scientists from the United States, Sweden, the United Kingdom, Hungary, Chile, India, Pakistan, and Ethiopia presented their latest research on topics ranging from development of the immune system to brain damage in premature infants. Participating researchers represented a number of different disciplines including pediatrics, fetal physiology, nutrition, placentology, chemistry, and obstetrics. The symposium, the first in this series to be held outside the United States, was co-chaired by Drs. Bo S. Lindblad and Jan-Åke Gustafsson of Karolinska Institutet.

When Bristol-Myers and its Mead Johnson subsidiary initiated these symposia in 1980, our goal was to provide a forum where scientists and practitioners from various disciplines could take an in-depth look at leading scientific issues in nutrition.

Symposia are just one part of our program. Our company has committed $3.25 million in unrestricted support of nutrition research. Since the beginning of the program, no-strings-attached grants have been given to fifteen medical research centers—nine in the United States and six in other countries.

Another important element of the Bristol-Myers nutrition program is the annual Bristol-Myers Award for Distinguished Achievement in Nutrition Research. Each year, the $25,000 award is presented to a leading nutrition researcher selected by an independent committee composed of institutions receiving Bristol-Myers' unrestricted grants. The 1986 award was presented to Dr. Arvid Wretlind of Karolinska Institutet for his discovery of the first fat emulsion (Intralipid®) for intravenous feedings of humans.

For more than 70 years, through our Mead Johnson subsidiary, our company has pioneered in developing nutritional products to meet the special needs of infants, children, and adults.

Through symposia, our annual award, and our unrestrictred grant program, we hope to continue to encourage and stimulate scientific exploration in nutrition research. Our commitment to the nutrition grant program remains strong. It is our hope that the knowledge gained through this year's symposium will lead to future advances in the field of perinatal nutrition.

Richard L. Gelb
Chairman of the Board
Bristol-Myers Company

Preface

The papers in this volume were presented, by the persons given in the list of contributors, at the sixth annual Bristol-Myers Symposium on Nutrition Research, "Perinatal Nutrition," held in Saltsjöbaden, Sweden, August 28–29, 1986.

Karolinska Institutet, Stockholm, was entirely responsible for the scientific content of this symposium. We scientists and teachers at the Karolinska Institutet are grateful to Bristol-Myers Company and its Mead Johnson subsidiary for trusting us to arrange the symposium, for the first time outside the United States, and for their generosity and administrative support that made the meeting possible. The chairmanship was shared between Jan-Åke Gustafsson, M.D., Ph.D., Professor and Chairman of the Department of Medical Nutrition, and B. S. Lindblad, M.D., Ph.D, Associate Professor and Head, Unit of Pediatric Gastroenterology and Nutrition, in the Department of Pediatrics, St. Göran's Children's Hospital, Stockholm.

As the first international meeting with this title, this symposium aimed at bringing together fetal physiologists, placentologists, biochemists, nutritionists, obstetricians, and pediatricians to discuss the role of nutrition during the fetal and neonatal periods of life—two important periods of fast growth and development seldom discussed together.

The meeting was designed to provide a series of presentations at the frontiers of research; it was not meant to be a refresher course. There was ample time for informal discussion, but rather limited formal discussions. However, every session was followed by a short presentation by two discussants, one representing relevant research in the industrialized countries and one representing research in less developed countries. This proved to be a successful experiment, and I suggest that the initiative to invite scientists from developing areas to international meetings be practiced more in meetings of this kind, whatever the subject is.

I thank the symposium participants for their willingness to take an active part in the proceedings, for their scholarly contribution, and for sending me the manuscripts in time. I wish to acknowledge the assistance of Ann Wyant, Kathryn Bloom, and Ralph Weaver of the Bristol-Myers Company, New York, and Mr. Bo Ericsson of Bristol-Myers AB, Stockholm, for all their help with the practical arrangements. I also wish to thank Mrs. Gudrun Siegbahn for secretarial services and Ph.D. students Kari Johannsen, Stefan Hagelberg, Jonas Karlén, and Kenneth Palmér for their assistance at the meeting.

B. S. Lindblad

Part I

The Fetus and the Placenta

1

Fetal Growth and Body Composition

Elsie M. Widdowson

Department of Medicine
Addenbrooke's Hospital
Cambridge, England

D. A. T. Southgate

Agricultural and Food Research Council
Institute of Food Research
Norwich Laboratory
Norwich, England

E. Hey

Department of Child Health
The Princess Mary Maternity Hospital
Newcastle upon Tyne, England

I. GROWTH OF THE BODY AS A WHOLE

Since the publication of the paper by Lubchenco *et al.* (1963) on "Intrauterine Growth as Estimated from Birth Weight Data" similar studies have been made in various countries in which the weights of live-born infants of known gestational age have been analyzed and "fetal growth curves" constructed (Gruenwald, 1966; Kloosterman, 1966; Thomson *et al.*, 1968; Usher and McLean, 1969; Babson *et al.*, 1970; Milner and Richards, 1974). Figure 1 shows results of two of the American studies, the original one of Lubchenco *et al.* and that of Gruenwald published three years later. The curves, which are almost identical, are labeled A. The results of the two British studies, that of Thomson *et al.* (1968) and of Milner and Richards (1974), are also almost identical and are represented by curve B. Both curves cover males and females and first and later pregnancies. The British curve is slightly above the American one, and the results of another American study, that of Babson *et al.* (1970), lies between the two. For the present purpose these differences do not matter, for they all show that at about 34 or 35 weeks gestation and 2.4–2.6 kg body weight the rate of gain in weight begins to slow down. This can be interpreted in several ways. It is possible that the placenta is beginning to age at this time and is no longer able to transport the nutrients required for the relatively large fetus to gain weight at the same rate as before. We must remember, however, that these curves are of necessity derived

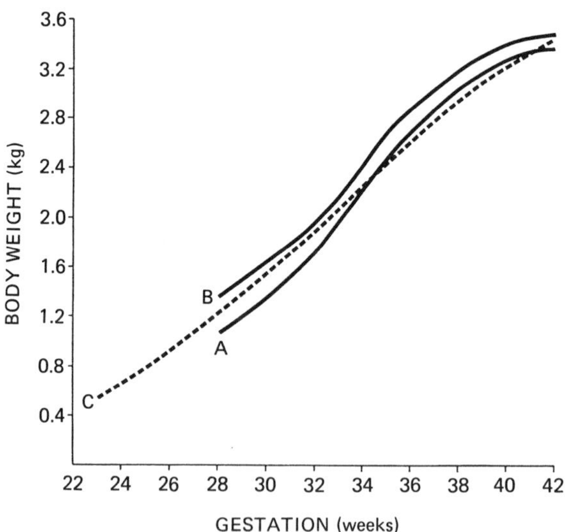

Fig. 1. Fetal birth weights, kg. (A) American (Lubchenco *et al.*, 1963; Gruenwald, 1966). (B) British (Thomson *et al.*, 1968; Milner and Richards, 1974). (C) Present study.

from cross-sectional data, and it may be that it is the slower-growing smaller fetuses that tend to remain in the uterus for the longest time. However, taking the fetal growth curves at their face value, all suggest that there is a decrease in rate of gain in weight toward the end of a normal gestation.

Some years ago we made a study of the chemical composition of 31 fetuses of known gestational age whose weights fell satisfactorily along the published growth curves, indicated as curve C. Even among this small number there is an apparent slowing down in gain of weight from about 240 days or 34 weeks. This is seen more clearly if we express the weights in terms of velocity of gain, that is, gain in weight per unit time—in this case per 10 days (Fig. 2). From the amounts of the various major constituents in the bodies, obtained by chemical analysis, it is possible to see whether all or only some of them participate in the slower gain in weight of the body as a whole.

II. INCORPORATION OF DIFFERENT BODY CONSTITUENTS

The main constituents of the body are water, protein, and fat. At term water accounts for about 69% of the body weight and protein and fat 12–13% each. Bone mineral, as a calcium phosphate–calcium hydroxide salt, makes up much of the remainder. From the values for the amounts of these and other constituents in the fetal bodies, fitted curves were constructed and from them the increments of each constituent over succeeding 10-day periods were calculated. This in fact is how the incremental weight curve was arrived at as shown in Fig. 2.

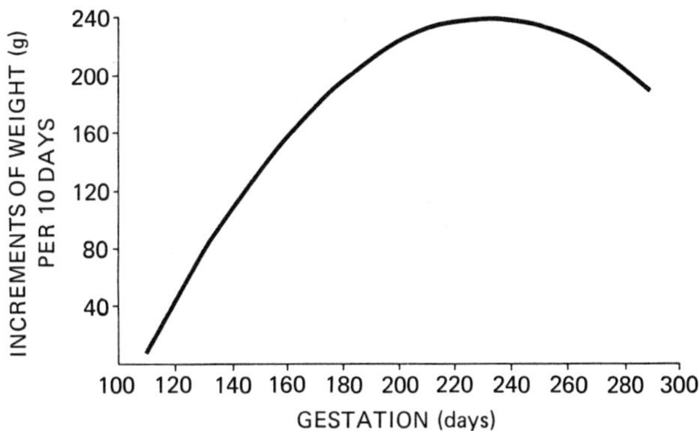

Fig. 2. Velocity of gain in weight *in utero*, g per 10 days. Present study.

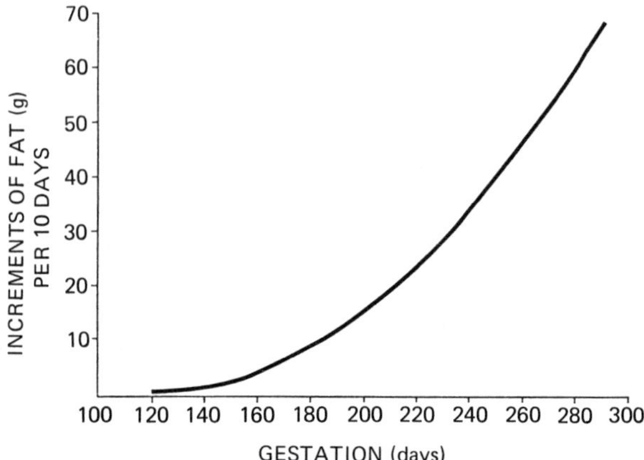

Fig. 3. Increments of fat, g per 10 days.

A. Water, Electrolytes, and Fat

Figure 3 shows that the rate of deposition of fat, far from falling off, goes on increasing. This does not bear out the idea that the fetus is short of nutrients in the form of glucose, the material from which it synthesizes fat. Figure 4 shows the velocity of gain of the nonfat part of the body, the lean body tissue, and, as expected, this is the part of the body that is responsible for the slowing down in growth rate of the body as a whole. The main constituent of lean body tissue is water, and Fig. 4 also shows that there was a considerable falloff in the rate of accumulation of water in the body after 220 days.

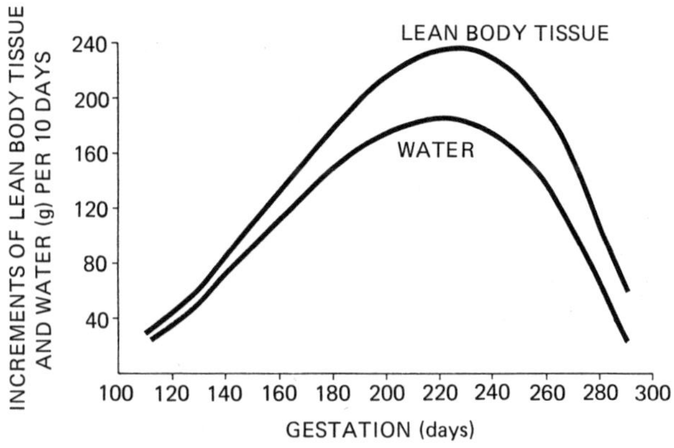

Fig. 4. Increments of lean body tissue and water, g per 10 days.

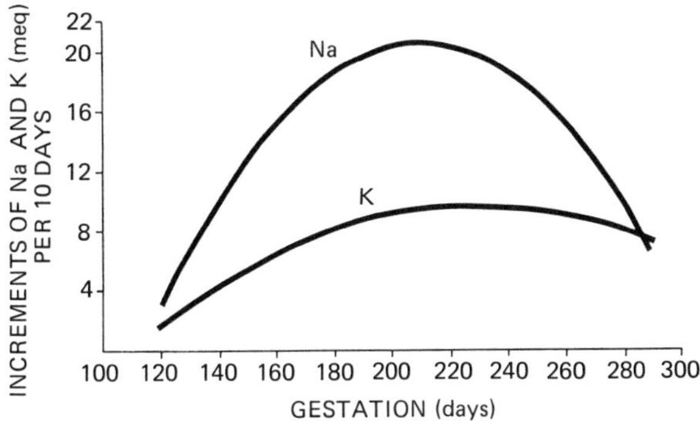

Fig. 5. Increments of Na and K, mEq per 10 days.

There was also a large fall in the rate of gain of sodium by the body from 220 days gestation (Fig. 5), suggesting that extracellular fluid is one important component of the body responsible for the slowing down in rate of gain in weight. In fact we know this already, for one of the characteristics of early development is a fall in the proportion of the body occupied by extracellular fluid. What is more unexpected is that the rate of incorporation of potassium, also shown in Fig. 5, declines as well. Potassium is the characteristic intracellular electrolyte, and the results suggest that the rate of growth of the cell mass of the body slows down toward the end of a normal gestation, though much less markedly than the extracellular fluid. Even at term the body contains twice as much sodium, as milliequivalents, as it does potassium.

B. Protein

Figure 6 shows that, unlike potassium, the rate of accretion of nitrogen continues to increase throughout gestation. However, protein occurs in the body outside as well as inside the cells, and, although intracellular protein is associated with potassium, extracellular protein is not. Extracellular proteins, mainly collagen and elastin, form an important part of skin, cartilage, and the matrix of the bones. The rate of incorporation of extracellular proteins in skin increases during the last weeks of gestation as the stratum corneum and corium begin to thicken (Table I) (Widdowson and Dickerson, 1960). The process continues after birth, and by 3–6 months the skin has almost reached its adult chemical structure.

Extracellular protein also occurs in skeletal muscle and around the individual fibers, the fasciculi, and the bundles of fibers. It increases as a percentage of the total protein when the fibers are increasing in number,

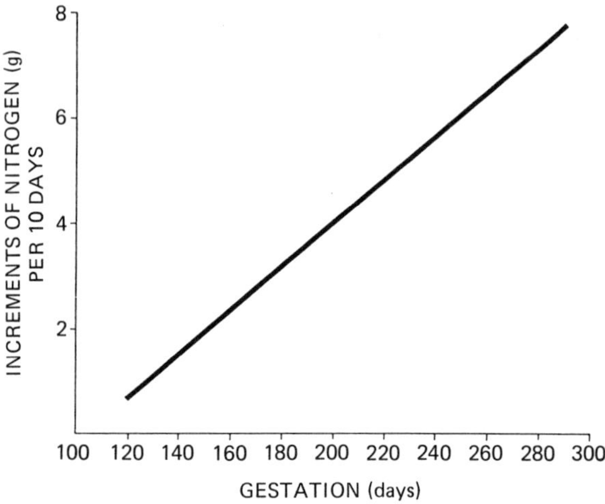

Fig. 6. Increments of N, g per 10 days.

and decreases when they are increasing in size. The full number of muscle fibers is achieved soon after a full-term birth (Montgomery, 1962; Stickland, 1981), and thereafter all growth of muscle is due to increasing fiber size. The contribution of extracellular protein to total protein in muscle reaches its maximum at about 40 weeks gestation (Table II) (Dickerson and Widdowson, 1960). Thus muscle also contributes to the increasing rate of accumulation of extracellular protein in the body as a whole.

We did not measure the total amount of extracellular protein in the whole bodies, so I have calculated the amount of intracellular protein from the measured potassium. Unfortunately the ratio of potassium to intracellular protein is not the same in all tissues, nor is it the same at all ages (Widdowson, 1968). Table III illustrates this for some organs and tissues. We know the approximate contribution of the major tissues to the body weight at different ages, so it is possible to calculate a ratio of

TABLE I

Extracellular Protein in Skin (g/kg)

	Fetus 22 weeks	At term	3–6 Months	Adult
Total protein N	12	27	55	53
Collagen N	2	17	39	46
Collagen N as % total protein N	17	63	71	68

TABLE II

Extracellular Protein in Skeletal Muscle (g/kg)

	Fetus 22 weeks	At term	4–7 Months	Adult
Total protein N	14	18.5	25.8	27.5
Extracellular protein N	1.8	3.8	4.6	1.4
Extracellular protein N as % total protein N	12	21	18	5

potassium to intracellular protein nitrogen which is representative of the body as a whole. I have used this ratio to arrive at the intracellular protein nitrogen from the measured amounts of potassium in the whole body, and I have subtracted this from the total nitrogen to arrive at the amount of extracellular protein nitrogen at different ages. I realize I have made no allowance for nonprotein nitrogen, but this would add only a small error to all the other errors inherent in this type of calculation. However, the results give a general idea of the incorporation of intracellular and extracellular protein into the body during a normal gestation.

Figure 7 shows the result of this arithmetic. It shows the total amounts of intracellular and extracellular protein nitrogen in the body and the results suggest that there is less extracellular than intracellular protein for most of gestation, but by term they are approximately equal. During the last weeks there is a rapid increase in the amount of protein outside the cells. This is seen more clearly in Fig. 8, which shows the increments in the two types of protein, expressed as nitrogen, over successive 10-day periods. Skin is the major contributor to the rapid synthesis of extracellular protein during the last weeks of gestation, but cartilage, muscle, and bones all play their part.

TABLE III

Ratio of Potassium (mEq) to Intracellular Protein Nitrogen (g) at Different Ages

	Fetus 22 weeks	At term	Adult
Skeletal muscle	4.3	3.8	3.4
Heart	7.0	3.4	3.5
Liver	4.2	2.6	2.7
Kidneys	4.6	2.9	2.3
Brain	6.2	6.3	5.0

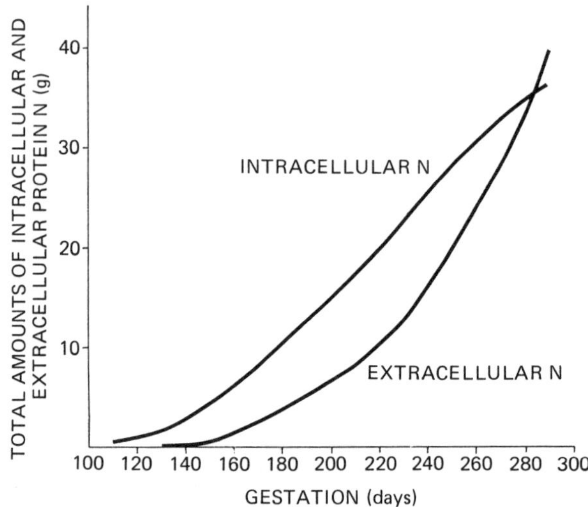

Fig. 7. Total amounts of intracellular and extracellular protein N in body, g.

C. Bone Minerals

Figure 9 shows the increments of calcium and phosphorus in the fetal body over each 10 days of gestational age, and it is clear that the rate of incorporation of bone minerals into the body continues to increase to term. This could be due to an increasing rate of growth of the skeleton, or to an increasing rate of calcification of the bones, or to both.

Studies that have been made on the length of live-born infants at different gestational ages (Lubchenco *et al.*, 1966; Usher and McLean, 1969)

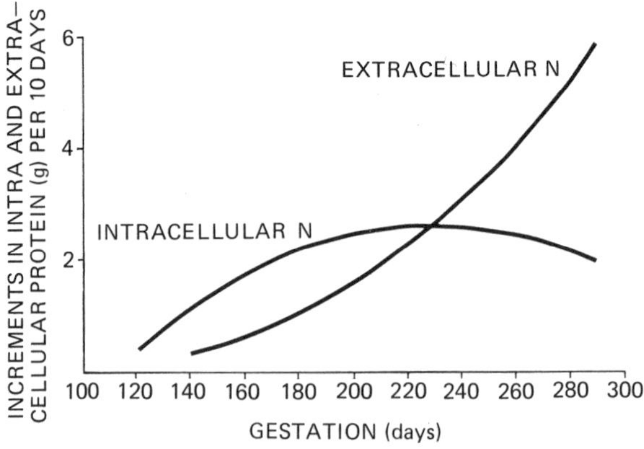

Fig. 8. Increments of intracellular and extracellular protein N, g per 10 days.

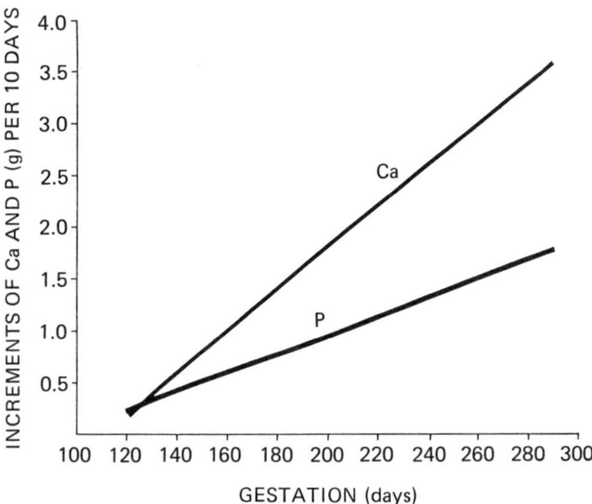

Fig. 9. Increments of Ca and P, g per 10 days.

suggest that the velocity of growth in length of body, that is, the crown–heel length, like the weight, declines from about 34 weeks. This might indicate that the rate of increase in size of the skeleton, like the body weight, declines toward term, and the continued increase in rate of deposition of calcium must therefore be due to some other cause, that is, to an increase in rate of calcification of the matrix of the bone. However, bones grow in width and thickness as well as in length, and this is not apparent in measurements of body length. The velocity of growth in weight of the femur, for example, increases right up to 40 weeks gestation (Dickerson, 1962), and in the last few weeks before term the femur appears to grow in width and thickness of cortex more rapidly than it grows in length. It must be concluded, therefore, that both increasing size and increasing degree of calcification probably contribute to the increase in rate of deposition of calcium in the body as a whole.

Although 99% of the calcium in the body is in the bones, some of the phosphorus is in the soft tissues, as the main anion of the cells as well as in phospholipids and phosphoproteins. The ratio of calcium/phosphorus in bone tissue is constant, 2.3 g per g, so we can separate phosphorus into the fractions forming part of the bones and of the soft tissues, and the total amounts of phosphorus in these two fractions are shown in Fig. 10. The increments per 10 days are shown in Fig. 11. It is the bone and not the soft tissues that accounts for the increasing rate of deposition of phosphorus in the body as a whole, and the rate of accumulation of phosphorus in soft tissues does not appear to change much from 120 days gestation to term. Bone also contains magnesium, which

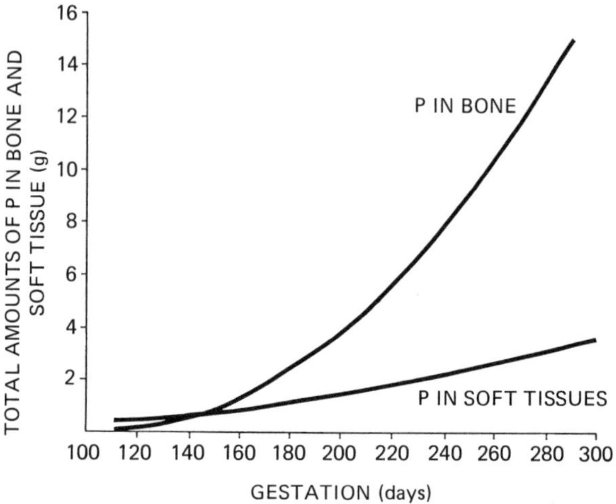

Fig. 10. Total amounts of P in bone and soft tissues, g.

is thought to be adsorbed on the surfaces of the crystals of bone mineral and does not form part of it. The ratio of calcium to magnesium changes with age as the bone crystals enlarge, and we cannot apportion magnesium to hard and soft tissue as we can phosphorus. Most of the magnesium in the body is, however, in the soft tissues, particularly in the cells, and Fig. 12 shows that the rate of accretion of magnesium falls off toward the end of a normal gestation, just as potassium does.

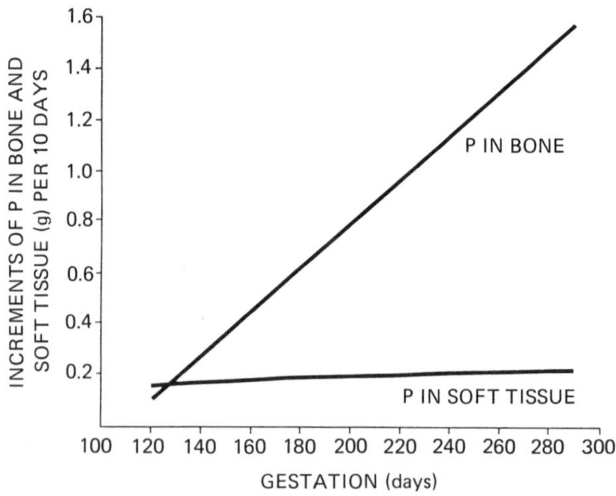

Fig. 11. Increments of P in bone and soft tissues, g per 10 days.

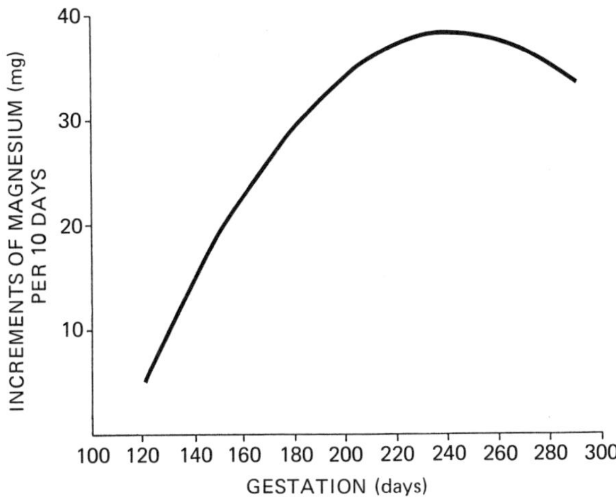

Fig. 12. Increments of Mg, mg per 10 days.

D. Zinc

I am not going to discuss trace elements except to say a word about zinc. In our earlier studies, published in 1951, on the chemical composition of the human fetus (Widdowson and Spray, 1951), we determined zinc by a chemical method which we now know gave values that were much too low. On the basis of these older figures I calculated that the increment of zinc in the fetal body was about 0.36 mg a day from 24 weeks gestation to term (Widdowson, 1981). Our newer, more reliable values confirm our previous observation that the rate of deposition of zinc in the fetal body, like that of phosphorus in the soft tissues, remains fairly constant over the last 3 months of gestation, but the amount incorporated is 0.85 mg a day.

III. SUMMARY

Up to about 34 weeks gestation all major constituents of the body are incorporated at an ever-increasing rate. From 34 weeks onward there seems to be a change. The rate of growth of the weight of the body slows down, and this is due to a decline in the rate at which water, particularly extracellular water, is incorporated, but also to a slowing down of the rate of growth of the cellular component of the body. At the same time fat, extracellular protein as collagen and elastin, and bone mineral are incorporated more and more rapidly up to full term. These changes are not a sign of undernutrition, or indeed are they necessarily suggestive of a shortage of anything. I suggest that they are normal developmental changes, most of which continue after birth.

REFERENCES

Babson, S. G., Behrman, R. E., and Lessel, R. (1970). *Pediatrics* **45,** 937–944.

Dickerson, J. W. T. (1962). *Biochem. J.* **82,** 56–61.

Dickerson, J. W. T., and Widdowson, E. M. (1960). *Biochem. J.* **74,** 247–257.

Gruenwald, P. (1966). *Am. J. Obstet. Gynecol.* **94,** 1112–1119.

Kloosterman, G. J. (1966). *Ned. Tijdschr. Verloskd. Gynaecol.* **66,** 361–379.

Lubchenco, L. O., Hansman, C., Dressler, M., and Boyd, E. (1963). *Pediatrics* **32,** 793–800.

Lubchenco, L. O., Hansman, C., and Boyd, E. (1966). *Pediatrics* **37,** 403–408.

Milner, R. D. G., and Richards, B. (1974). *J. Obstet. Gynaecol. Br. Commonw.* **81,** 956–967.

Montgomery, R. D. (1962). *Nature (London)* **195,** 194–195.

Stickland, N. C. (1981). *J. Anat.* **132,** 557–579.

Thomson, A. M., Billewicz, W. Z., and Hytten, F. E. (1968). *J. Obstet. Gynaecol. Br. Commonw.* **75,** 903–916.

Usher, R., and McLean, F. (1969). *J. Pediat.* **74,** 901–910.

Widdowson, E. M. (1968). "Body Composition in Animals and Man," pp. 71–79. Nat. Acad. Sci., Washington, D.C.

Widdowson, E. M. (1981). *In* "Scientific Foundations of Paediatrics" (J. A. Davis and J. Dobbing, eds.), 2nd Ed., pp. 41–53. Heinemann, London.

Widdowson, E. M., and Dickerson, J. W. T. (1960). *Biochem. J.* **77,** 30–43.

Widdowson, E. M., and Spray, C. M. (1951). *Arch. Dis. Child.* **26,** 205–214.

2

Uteroplacental Blood Flow in Fetal Growth Retardation

N. O. Lunell and L. Nylund
Department of Obstetrics and Gynecology
Karolinska Institutet
Huddinge University Hospital
Huddinge, Sweden

I. INTRODUCTION

Fetal growth rate is determined by a large number of factors. Intrauterine growth retardation (IUGR) can be caused by a lack of normal growth potential in the fetus itself or by a limited substrate availability due to reductions in uteroplacental perfusion, low maternal substrate concentrations, or reduced placental permeability. Several factors may act synergistically and may be difficult to separate, the summation effect being retarded fetal growth.

In this context we will mainly deal with uteroplacental circulation and fetal growth. A substantial part of our knowledge of uteroplacental blood flow is derived from animal experimental models. Information about the maternal placental circulation in the human is still limited because of the complexity of the uterine vascular supply with the inherent difficulty of measuring the blood flow through the uterus.

The uterine vascular supply occurs mainly through the uterine arteries from which arcuate arteries lead to intramyometrial radial and finally spiral arteries that enter the intervillous space. Between 100 to 150 spiral arteries supply the intervillous space (Robertson *et al.*, 1975). The myometrial parts of the arteries are relatively narrow but dilate when they reach the decidua as spiral arteries. During the last part of pregnancy this dilatation also extends to the myometrial segments and forms the structural basis for the increment in maternal placental blood flow that takes place during normal pregnancy (Sheppard and Bonnar, 1974).

Several methods have been tried to measure uteroplacental blood flow in the human. Those giving reasonably good results are isotope clearance techniques with calculation of the disappearance curve of ^{133}Xe (Käär *et al.*, 1980), accumulation rates of iv ^{99m}Tc pertechnetate (Suonio and Olkkonen, 1977) or indium-113m (Nylund *et al.*, 1983a), and ultrasonic measurements using the Doppler principle (Eik-Nes *et al.*, 1980). In this paper we will report about results with the use of indium-113m partly dealt with earlier (Lunell *et al.*, 1979; Nylund *et al.*, 1983b).

II. MATERIAL AND METHODS

A. Material

Seventy-five women participated in the study, which was approved by the local ethical committee. All patients were hospitalized because of pregnancy complications, mainly suspicion of IUGR or vaginal hemorrhage. Thirty-seven women gave birth to infants with weight appropriate for gestational age and served as the control group. Thirty-eight women gave birth to neonates with IUGR defined as a birth weight below the 10th percentile for sex and gestational age (Sterky, 1970). During the first period of the study the women were measured in the supine position. That part comprised 11 control women and 8 women with IUGR. During the latter period all women were in a 30° left lateral position. During this period there were 26 control women with normal weight infants and 30 subjects with IUGR. The clinical data from the two periods are summarized in Tables I and II, respectively. There were no significant differences between the IUGR and the control groups with regard to maternal age, parity, or gestational age at scintigraphy. In the second IUGR group 11 women had coexisting pregnancy-induced hypertension

TABLE I

Clinical Material (Measurements Were Performed in Supine Position, Median and Range)

	Control group	IUGR group
Number	11	8
Gestational age at scintigraphy (weeks)	36 (31–40)	36 (32–39)
Birth weight (g)	3420 (2720–3860)	1915 (625–2530)

defined as a blood pressure of 140/90 mm or more at two occasions. Six of the infants in the latter IUGR group had congenital malformations (Table III).

B. Methods

The uteroplacental blood flow measurements were strictly standardized. After an iv bolus injection of 37 MBq (1 mCi) indium-113m the radiation emanating from the placenta was recorded on a computer-linked gamma camera (General Electric Radicamera 60, Intertechnique CINE 200 or Digital Equipment PDP 11/44) positioned above the uterus. Serial scintigrams with 10-sec intervals were obtained during 240 sec after injection and stored on magnetic disks. After summation of the serial images the placental region could be encircled on the computer screen with a light pen. The computer then calculated a time–activity curve for this region of interest (Fig. 1). The maximum activity (100%) at the curve is proportional to the maternal blood volume of the intervillous space and the rise time defined as the time between 5 and 95% of the maximum activity is proportional to the ratio of this blood volume/

TABLE II

Clinical material (Measurements Were Performed in Left Lateral Position, Median and Range)

	Control group	IUGR group
Number	26	30
Maternal age	25 (18–36)	26 (18–41)
Parity	1 (0–3)	0 (0–7)
Gestational age at scintigraphy (weeks)	36 (32–41)	36 (27–43)
Gestational age at delivery (weeks)	39 (34–42)	38 (29–43)
Birth weight (g)	3000 (1900–4350)	2215 (600–2830)
Fetal length (cm)	50 (43.5–55)	45 (31–51)

TABLE III

Maternal and Fetal Clinical Data in IUGR Pregnancy with Fetal Malformation

	Maternal age	Gestational age at scintigraphy (weeks)	Gestational age at term (weeks)	Birth weight (g)	Fetal length (cm)	Fetal malformation
Case 1	29	43	43	2090	44	Embryopathia alcoholica
Case 2	30	35	35	1185	37.5	Myelomeningocele
Case 3	30	36	36	2140	46	Trisomia 18
Case 4	27	34	35	1230	41	Gastroschisis
Case 5	25	38	38	2380	47	Ventricular septal defect
Case 6	21	36	38	1980	44	Malformation of extremities

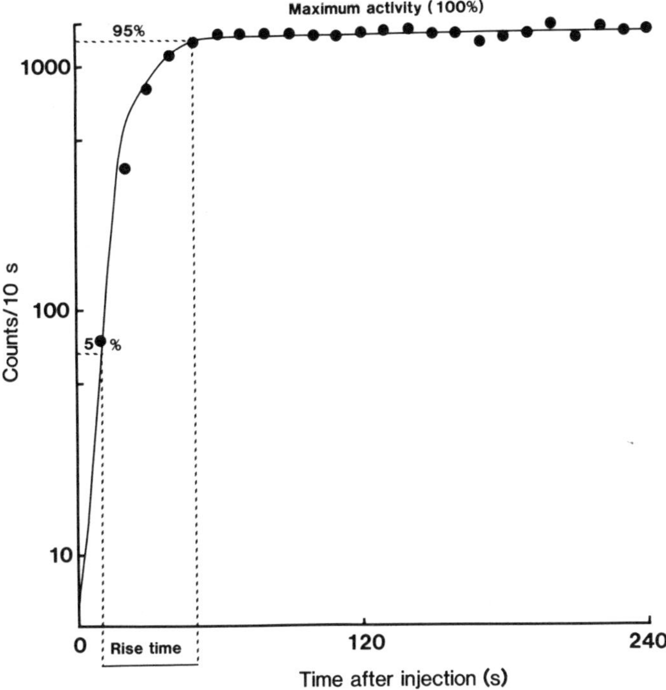

Fig. 1. Time–activity curve recorded by the gamma camera over the placental region after I.V. injection of 37 MBq indium-113m.

uteroplacental blood flow. Subsequently the ratio between maximum activity and rise time is proportional to the uteroplacental blood flow, a measure we denote as uteroplacental blood flow index, which is a relative measure proportional to milliliters per second. The mathematical background for these calculations has been given by us (Nylund *et al.*, 1983a).

Ninety-five percent of injected indium will be bound to maternal transferrin (Hosain *et al.*, 1969). The transfer of indium-113m to the fetus is thus negligible with less than 0.1% of maternal activity recorded in fetal blood (van der Merwe, 1971). Injections of 37 MBq (1 mCi) indium-113m give an absorbed dose of radiation to the mother of 0.10–0.22 mGy and to the fetus of 0.08–0.17 mGy. These figures are equivalent to a natural background radiation of 1–2 months. Most uteroplacental blood flow values were not normally distributed and therefore the nonparametric Mann–Whitney *U* test was used to test hypotheses. Values are given as medians and ranges and correlations were tested with Spearman's rank test.

TABLE IV

Uteroplacental Blood Flow Indices in Control and IUGR Pregnancy Measured in the Supine Position (Median and Range)

	Control group	IUGR group	Significance
Number	11	8	
Rise time (sec)	70 (51–140)	92 (62–142)	n.s.[a]
Maximum activity (counts/10 sec)	590 (345–1392)	260 (95–495)	$p<.01$
Blood flow index (proportional to ml/sec)	9.8 (3.4–20.6)	2.6 (1.5–5.5)	$p<.01$

[a]Not significant.

III. RESULTS

In the first study group with the women examined in the supine position, the median birth weight and placental weight were significantly lower in the IUGR than in the control group ($p<.01$, Table 1). The same gestational age at scintigraphy, 36 weeks, was encountered in both groups. The median rise time was 31% longer and the maximum activity 56% lower in the IUGR group (Table IV). This resulted in a calculated median uteroplacental blood flow index in the IUGR group which was only 27% of that in the control group ($p<.01$).

In the study of the latter period with the measurements performed in the left lateral position, the median birth weight and placental weights in the IUGR group were 2215 and 420 g and in the control group were 3000 and 510 g (Table II). These differences were significant ($p<.001$). The median rise time was prolonged with 40% and the maximum activity reduced with 28% in the IUGR group, resulting in a significantly lower median blood flow index of 44% of that in the control group, that is, 8.3 versus 19.0 ml/sec (Table V).

TABLE V

Uteroplacental Blood Flow Indices in Normal and IUGR Pregnancy Measured in Left Lateral Position (Median and Range)

	Control group	IUGR group	Significance
Number	26	30	
Rise time (sec)	50 (20–84)	70 (30–185)	$p<.001$
Maximum activity (counts/10 sec)	890 (420–1540)	645 (204–1350)	$p<.05$
Blood flow index (proportional to ml/sec)	19.0 (7.4–51.3)	8.3 (2.1–37.5)	$p<.001$

TABLE VI

Comparison between Normotensive IUGR and Control Pregnancies (Measurements in Left Lateral Position, Median and Range)

	Control group	IUGR group	Significance
Number	26	19	
Gestational age at scintigraphy (weeks)	36 (32–41)	36 (32–43)	n.s.[a]
Birth weight (g)	3000 (1900–4350)	2350 (1185–2830)	$p<.01$
Birth length (cm)	50 (44–55)	46 (38–51)	$p<.01$
Rise time (sec)	50 (20–84)	73 (30–125)	$p<.01$
Maximum activity (counts/10 sec)	890 (420–1540)	689 (204–1350)	n.s.
Blood flow index (proportional to ml/sec)	19.0 (7.4–51.3)	8.1 (4.1–37.5)	$p<.001$

[a]Not significant.

Pregnancy-induced hypertension is associated with an impaired uteroplacental blood flow (Lunell *et al.*, 1982). It would thus be of interest to exclude subjects with this complication from the IUGR group. In Table VI normotensive women with IUGR and control subjects were compared. It was found that median blood flow index in this group of IUGR was reduced by 57% in comparison with the control group ($p<.001$).

In the group of 30 IUGR infants delivered during the latter examination period there were 6 who had congenital malformations. The uteroplacental blood flow index was equally low in these two groups (Table VII).

When the clinical data were compared between these IUGR pregnancies with and without fetal malformation no statistically significant differences were found with the exception of the median placental weight, which was 350 g in the group with malformations. The corresponding

TABLE VII

Uteroplacental Blood Flow Indices in IUGR Pregnancy with or without Congenital Malformations

	No malformation	With malformation	Significance
Number	24	6	
Rise time (sec)	65 (30–185)	85 (30–105)	n.s.[a]
Maximum activity (counts/10 sec)	645 (360–1350)	864 (204–1125)	n.s.
Blood flow index (proportional to ml/sec)	8.3 (2.1–21.4)	9.0 (4.1–37.5)	n.s.

[a]Not significant.

TABLE VIII

Comparison between IUGR Pregnancies with Fetal Malformation and IUGR Pregnancies without Fetal Malformation

	Fetal malformation	No malformation	Significance
Number	6	24	
Gestational age at scintigraphy (weeks)	36 (34–43)	36 (27–39)	n.s.[a]
Gestational age at delivery (weeks)	37 (35–43)	38 (29–41)	n.s.
Fetal weight (g)	2035 (1185–2380)	2320 (600–2830)	n.s.
Fetal length (cm)	44 (37.5–47)	45.5 (31–51)	n.s.
Placental weight (g)	350 (300–420)	430 (190–590)	$p<.05$

[a]Not significant.

value in the IUGR pregnancies without malformations was 430 g (Table VIII).

IV. DISCUSSION AND CONCLUSIONS

The present studies showed that there were remarkable reductions in uteroplacental blood flow in IUGR pregnancy. The blood flow was reduced by 56 to 73% depending on the position of the pregnant women during the measurement, the more severe reduction observed in the supine position. The normal control group with the women in the supine position had a median uteroplacental blood flow index of 9.8 while the women in the left lateral position gave a value of 19.0. This is in accordance with a similar comparison we undertook during a study of uteroplacental blood flow in preeclampsia in which we measured normal pregnant women in the supine and in the left lateral position. The women in the latter position had a median blood flow index of 20.6 and those in the supine position had a median index of 13.9. It would seem that it would be more detrimental for the maternal–fetal supply line, especially in IUGR pregnancy, if the mother is lying on her back. This is presumably due to a reduced venous return, caused by pressure of the uterus.

As it is known that IUGR is associated with preeclampsia it would be important to exclude patients with this complication from the analysis. When the cases with preeclampsia were omitted it was found that in IUGR per se a significant reduction of uteroplacental blood flow still was present. An explanation of this impairment in IUGR pregnancy, also without pregnancy-induced hypertension, was given histologically, as spiral arteries in placental bed biopsies were narrower and showed more intimal thickening with fibrinoid degeneration in IUGR than in normal pregnancy (De Wolf *et al.*, 1980). Sheppard and Bonnar (1976) have also described occlusive atheromatous lesions with fibrin deposition in the decidual spiral arteries in IUGR pregnancy without hypertension.

The uteroplacental blood flow index was reduced to a similar extent in IUGR of maternal and of fetal origin (Table VII). This would support the theory that maternal placental blood flow is partly regulated by the fetus (Rankin and McLaughlin, 1979).

The IUGR fetuses with congenital malformations had a lower placental weight than the IUGR fetuses without malformation (Table VIII). No other statistically significant difference between the groups could be detected in this small sample. The pregnancies with fetal malformation had a reduction of fetal weight which was symmetrical to the placental weight reduction. This finding corroborates the hypothesis that these infants had an IUGR of fetal origin.

A reduced uteroplacental blood flow in IUGR has also been observed by several other groups using isotope techniques (Guikovaty *et al.*, 1975; Mund-Hoym *et al.*, 1978) and lately using ultrasound with the Doppler technique (Campbell *et al.*, 1983). With a linear array ultrasound imaging system combined with a pulsed Doppler, the blood flow velocity in a vessel such as the arcuate artery of the uterus can be analyzed. Blood flow velocity in the third trimester of normal pregnancy typically demonstrates low pulsatility and high diastolic velocities, while in women with severe IUGR there often is a flow velocity waveform with high pulsatility and low diastolic velocities.

From the present studies it can be concluded that the applied non-invasive method using indium-113m and calculation of a time–activity curve by a computer-linked gamma camera gives an estimation of the relative maternal placental blood flow, a uteroplacental blood flow index. The radiation to the mother and the fetus is very low compared to 1–2 months of natural exposure. Uteroplacental blood flow in IUGR pregnancy is impaired by more than 50% and is equal in cases with IUGR of both maternal and fetal origin.

ACKNOWLEDGMENT

These investigations were supported by Expressen's Prenatal Research Fund.

REFERENCES

Campbell, S., Griffin, D. R., Pearce, J. M., Diaz-Recasens, J., Cohen-Overbeek, T. E., and Willson, K. (1983). *Lancet* **i,** 675.

De Wolf, F., Brosens, I., and Renaer, M. (1980). *Br. J. Obstet. Gynaecol.* **87,** 678.

Eik-Nes, S. H., Brubakk, A. O., and Ulstein, M. K. (1980). *Br. Med. J.* No. 280, p. 283.

Guikovaty, J. P., Vors, J., Vergnes, R., Truchot, M., and Dellenback, P. (1975). *J. Gynecol. Obstet. Biol. Reprod.* **4,** 671.

Hosain, F., McIntyre, P. A., Poulose, K., Stern, H. S., and Wagner, H. N. (1969). *Clin. Chim. Acta* **24,** 69.

Käär, K., Jouppila, P., Kuikka, J., Luotola, H., Toivanen, J., and Rekonen, A. (1980). *Acta Obstet. Gynecol. Scand.* **59,** 7.

Lunell, N. O., Sarby, B., Lewander, R., and Nylund, L. (1979). *Gynecol. Obstet. Invest.* **10,** 106.

Lunell, N. O., Nylund, L. E., Lewander, R., and Sarby, B., with the technical assistance of Thornström, S. (1982). *Clin. Exp. Hypertens.,* B1(1), 105.

Mund-Hoym, S., Hünermann, B., Stolp, W., and Lang, N. (1978). *Geburtshilfe Frauenheilkd.* **38,** 292.

Nylund, L., Lunell, N. O., Sarby, B., Lewander, R., and Thornström, S. (1983a). *Acta Radiol. Diagn.* **24,** 165.

Nylund, L., Lunell, N. O., Lewander, R., and Sarby, B., with the technical assistance of Thornström, S. (1983b). *Br. J. Obstet. Gynaecol.* **90,** 16.

Rankin, J. H. G., and McLaughlin, M. K. (1979). *J. Dev. Physiol.* **1,** 3.

Robertson, W. B., Brosens, I., and Dixon, G. (1975). *Eur. J. Obstet., Gynecol. Reprod. Biol.* **5,** 47.

Sheppard, B. L., and Bonnar, J. (1974). *J. Obstet. Gynaecol. Br. Commonw.* **81,** 497.

Sheppard, B. L., and Bonnar, J. (1976). *Br. J. Obstet. Gynaecol.* **83,** 948.

Sterky, G. (1970). *Pediatrics* **46,** 7.

Suonio, S., and Olkkonen, H. (1977). *Scand. J. Clin. Lab. Invest.* **37,** 509.

van der Merwe, E. J., Lotter, M. G., van Heerden, P. D. R., Slabber, C. F., and Bester, J. (1971). *J. Nucl. Med.* **11,** 31.

3

The Handling of Amino Acids by the Fetoplacental Unit

Maureen Young
Toft, Cambridge, England

I. INTRODUCTION

Proteins are, after water, the most abundant constituents of all cells; they are the first to be synthesized and, through their enzyme actions, direct the production of the other cellular components. A steady accumulation of protein is the most important feature of growth in all organisms and, in the fetoplacental unit, this is brought about by the symbiosis between the fetal genetic drive for growth and the response of the maternal tissues which should provide an optimal supply of nutrients to meet this metabolic demand. There are many aspects to this accumulation of nitrogen by the fetus, ranging from the activity of the heterogeneous mixture of protein, forming the functional mass of the body, to the metabolic activity of the placenta and the transport processes at the trophoblast membrane, the blood flow on either side of the organ and the changes in maternal metabolism which make some of her tissue stores available to the fetus. This article focuses on the synthetic rate of the placental and fetal proteins and the role this plays in fetal growth, together with the metabolism of the placenta which influences the proportion of the amino acids reaching the fetus. Animals have been used in most of the work to be described because of the experimental procedures necessary, entailing the use of radioactively labeled isotopes in the dynamic situation. Amino acid and protein metabolism is so fundamental to living organisms that a thoughtful application of the results to the human situation may not be out of place.

II. PLACENTAL AND FETAL PROTEIN SYNTHESIS AND TURNOVER

The dependence of protein accumulation on cell number, or DNA units, and the content and activity of the associated RNA has been described very fully by Winick (1974), for fetal and postnatal growth, and the early observations on mixed protein synthetic rate during this period have been reviewed by Young (1981b, 1982, 1983).

The tissue forming the functional mass of the body consists of a heterogeneous mixture of proteins with varying half-lives; this is shown in Table I for the relative proportions of short and long half-lives of proteins in the brain, liver, and kidney of adult mice. Further, breakdown as well as synthesis rates of proteins are rapid in very young animals, so that protein turnover times are short when deposition occurs. During de-

TABLE I

Half-Life of Tissue Proteins in Adult Mice[a]

	Short (hr)	Long (days)	% Long
Brain	15	10	94
Liver	26	—	0
Kidney	18	2.6	60

[a]From Lajtha *et al.* (1976).

velopment synthesis rate decreases more rapidly than breakdown and both are almost equal when the animal is fully grown, with little net accumulation occurring. A high protein turnover rate might have been anticipated to accompany the protein accumulation of growth, to accommodate the differentiation of the tissues during development. The faster average protein turnover is probably due to the higher ribosome content and RNA of the cells and not to a greater proportion of the faster turning over fractions. There may also be less restraint of protein turnover as a result of the immaturity of the developing endocrine systems. Scornick (1982) has written most engagingly on the machinery of protein synthesis and degradation and their relative functions during adult life and in the young animal as body mass increases, focusing on liver and skeletal muscle. He emphasizes the high energy cost of protein turnover and the puzzle that it should be in excess of its necessary roles in the adult of stable weight, namely, scavenging of abnormal polypeptides and obsolete inducible enzymes and the continuous supply of amino acids in the absence of exogenous sources.

A. Measurement of Protein Synthesis and Turnover Rates

The measurement of protein synthetic rate has a relatively short history and Waterlow *et al.* (1978) and Garlick (1980) describe and discuss the various approaches which have been used. These depend, in general, on the uptake by protein of a labeled amino acid in the steady state. The specific activity of the amino acid in the protein is related to that of the precursor pool, plasma or intracellular. In the fetal lamb a constant infusion of 6 hr duration has been used to allow a steady state to be attained, while in the rat a single large dose of a labeled amino acid is employed, for it has been shown that the specific activity in the tissues approximates quickly to that in the plasma. Degradation rate has not been measured directly in the fetus, but is calculated by subtraction of the protein accumulation rate from the synthesis rate.

A modification of the steady-state method, using glycine labeled with the stable isotope ^{15}N, has been used in the newborn infant by Pencharz *et al.* (1977, 1981), Jackson *et al.* (1981), and Catzeflis *et al.* (1985); it is interesting that the method actually preceded those using ^{14}C and ^{3}H labeling of amino acids. A new method which enables repeated measurements in the same animal, and might be suitable for longitudinal studies in the larger growing fetus, has been described by Oddy and Lindsay (1986); indwelling catheters in the hind limb allow the measurement of A–V differences of both cold and labeled leucine which, together with blood flow determinations, provide calculations for both deposition and synthesis rates.

B. Placental Protein Synthesis during Gestation

The human placenta contains about 60 g protein at term, 60% of which is laid down by 20 weeks of gestation, before the acceleration of fetal growth. The DNA content of the organ increases steadily to 35 weeks gestation and Winick *et al.* (1972) maintain that any growth thereafter is due to hypertrophy. However, Sands and Dobbing (1985) subsequently found that the DNA : protein ratio remains constant during gestation and consider that placental mass continues to increase by cellular proliferation to term. Placental RNA content is highest early in gestation during the period of maximum growth of the organ.

The turnover rate of the mixed proteins in the placenta has been measured in two species, with good agreement between the two in spite of the difference in gestational length. In the sheep, during the last trimester, a value of 60%/day was found (Young *et al.*, 1982) (Fig. 2). The same rate was observed for the proteins of the rat placenta at 14 days gestation, but the value fell to 22%/day by 20 days, near term (Fig. 1a). The value in the lamb was comparable with that of other fetal tissues whose synthesis rates are several times greater than the corresponding maternal organs (Figs. 1b and 2). This quick turnover will provide the high priority of the fetoplacental unit in the uterus for available amino acids, as well as other nutrients. The placenta is the major beneficiary of this uptake during the first half of gestation while its weight exceeds that of the fetus. Later, as the fetal cardiac output and placental blood flow increase, the position will gradually be reversed; in the human the placental weight is seven times that of the fetus at 4 weeks gestation, while at term the fetal weight is six times that of the placenta. It would be very interesting to know the part played by the high protein turnover rate of the conceptus in the success of implantation, and whether the placenta directs the inflow of nutrients into the conceptus throughout gestation, as well as maintaining the multicellular membrane and the high free amino acid levels within the syncytium, which determine the final downhill gradient for the supply of amino acids to the fetus. Joseph Barcroft introduced into fetal physiology Child's general hypothesis that the partition of nutrients between the different organs of the body was determined by their metabolic rates. In considering "the relative claims of the fetus and mother to the available nutritive material," the metabolic rate of the placenta might be expected to set the priority of the conceptus within the uterus, particularly in the early stages of gestation; late in gestation there is evidence that both oxygen consumption (Campbell *et al.*, 1966) and glucose utilization (Simmons *et al.*, 1979; Schneider *et al.*, 1981) are high in comparison with the fetus.

There is little information on the control of protein synthesis in the

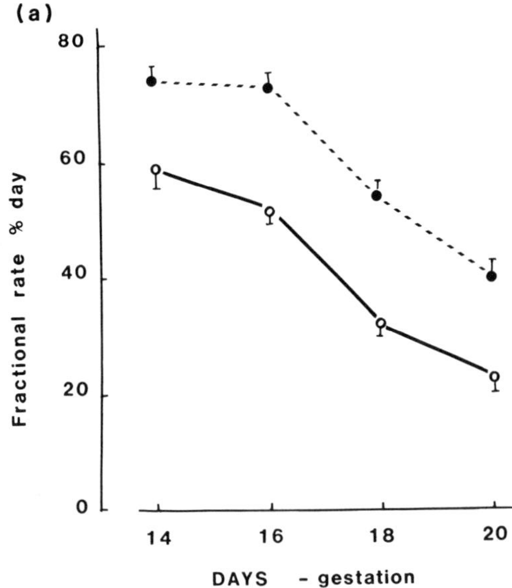

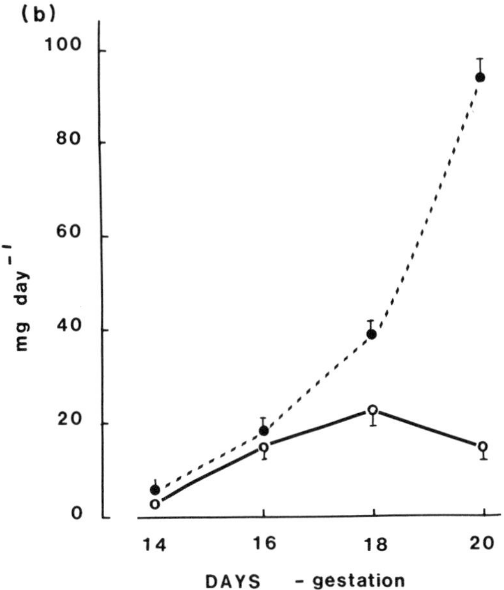

Fig. 1. (a) Protein synthesis rate in the rat fetus (●) is greater than that in the placenta (○), and both decrease during gestation. (b) The accretion of protein by the whole fetus (●) and placenta (○) from 14 to 20 days gestation. (From Morton and Goldspink, 1986.)

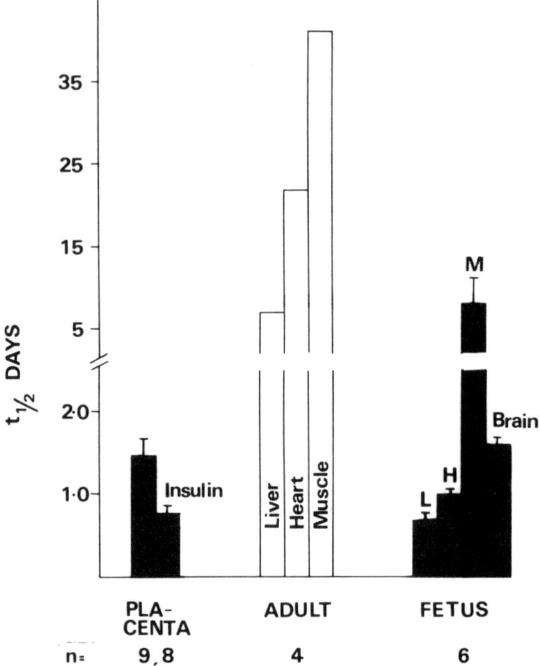

Fig. 2. A comparison of the half-life, $t_{1/2}$, in days, of mixed tissue proteins in the liver, heart, and muscle of the fetal lamb *in utero* during the last trimester and in the adult ewe. (From Young *et al.*, 1979).

placenta *in vivo*. Estrogen and progesterone might be expected to have some direct influence since they are produced *in situ*, but their effect may be indirect through their action on the maternal placental blood flow and, therefore, substrate supply to the organ. It is possible that there is a special relationship between insulin and the human placenta for insulin receptors and degrading capacity are found in the trophoblast of most species (Posner, 1974); the receptors are located in the microvilli on the maternal surface of the human placenta (Whitsett and Lessard, 1978). No role has, so far, been found for insulin in promoting placental transport and the syncytium may just be protecting the fetus from an active maternal hormone. There is preliminary evidence to suggest that raised levels of insulin in the fetal circulation may stimulate placental protein turnover in the ewe (Young *et al.*, 1982) (Fig. 2). If this should also occur in the human subject, it might be responsible for the heavy placentas of diabetic women whose blood sugar is uncontrolled and account for their large functional capacity.

There may be many other stimuli besides the hormonal which can influence placental growth. For instance, the continuous growth of the normal placenta already described means that the organ can still respond to the demands of the fetus at the end of gestation, indicating a reserve capacity to grow and increase in weight. In maternal anemia (Agboola, 1975) and in pregnancies at high altitude (Kruger and Arias-Stella, 1970) the placentas are large and probably represent a physiological response for increasing the transfer potential to compensate for the inadequate supply of oxygen and nutrients from the mother. Further, the small placentas from mothers with toxemia, or bearing small for dates infants, have a very reduced area for exchange (Aherne and Dunhill, 1966), yet the infant's weight is not proportionally reduced, suggesting some adaptive process in the parenchymal metabolic and transport mechanisms. An increased capacity for amino acid uptake in the placentas of small fetuses, born of guinea pigs fed on a low-protein diet but adequate in calories, would support this (Young and Widdowson, 1975).

C. Fetal Protein Synthesis during Growth

The rate at which protein is laid down in the fetus has been measured in a number of species with different in growth rates, and some interesting comparisons have been made by Blaxter (1964). The normal human infant at term contains about 500 g protein, one-seventh of its body weight; most of this is accumulated in a linear fashion from 22 weeks gestation as the fetus increases in weight from 250 g to 3.5 kg (Widdowson *et al.*, 1979). The small embryo contains only 5% protein and the newborn about 12%. The rate of growth and accumulation of protein will vary for each organ during development for a number of reasons, such as the time and rate of onset of cell division, when it finishes, and the rate at which protein is laid down in the cell (Winick *et al.*, 1972). These different relative proportions of tissue will also influence the interorgan fluxes of the free amino acids and their patterns in the body fluids. An understanding of the mechanisms of integration of these processes, the metabolic "harmony of growth" as Widdowson (1970) describes it, is a challenge which the identification of the homeobox containing genes is meeting. Not only can proteins expressed by one gene turn the expression of other genes on, but they can turn them off as well, and so direct them to produce a wing or leg, in *Drosophila* for instance, at the correct time. Homeobox gene clusters are also found in mammalian cells and share many of the features found in *Drosophila*, indicating that the underlying molecular mechanisms for development may be similar across the species (Gehring, 1985).

From evidence for the changes in pattern of cellular and subcellular content of tissues and from the energy requirements at different ages and sizes, Munro (1969) anticipated a three- to fivefold rate of turnover in the newborn human infant in comparison with the young adult, and this was subsequently confirmed experimentally in the tissues of the newborn lamb (Soltesz *et al.*, 1973) and fetal lamb in the last trimester using ^{14}C lysine in chronic preparations with indwelling catheters (Young *et al.*, 1979; Horn *et al.*, 1983). The mean fetal values are compared with those found by Buttery *et al.* (1975) in the yearling ewe in Fig. 2. Fetal organ protein synthesis rates were 38, 72, 40, and 60%/day^{-1} for the brain, liver, cardiac muscle, and placenta; that for skeletal muscle was 6.8%/day. The corresponding half-lives were 2.15, 1.27, 1.8, and 1.42 days, respectively, with 11.3 for skeletal muscle. Very similar values for fetal lamb brain and liver were found by Schaefer and Krishnamurti (1984) using tyrosine, though that for skeletal muscle was faster and that for the small intestine much higher than for either the placenta or fetal liver. Meier *et al.* (1981) found that the turnover rate in the whole fetal body was 20%/day at 110 days gestation and was decreased by 50% at 140 days near term. Morton and Goldspink (1986) have also shown a reduction in whole-body protein synthesis rate from 75%/day at 14 days gestation to 38%/day in the fetal rat by term (Fig. 1a) at a time when total protein was accumulating rapidly (Fig. 1b). These authors also found that the increased accumulation of protein in the uterus during pregnancy is brought about by a decrease in degradation rate and not by an increase in synthesis rate. Fetal rats are more immature than the fetal lamb and this may explain the considerably higher values for the whole-body turnover rate found by Morton and Goldspink in comparison with Meier *et al.;* their use of the intracellular pool as the precurser, which was also used by Young *et al.*, may have enhanced the values calculated.

Bell *et al.* (1985) found that oxygen consumption was 37% higher at midgestation in fetal lambs in comparison with late gestation when expressed per kilogram wet weight but 2.5 times higher at midgestation when calculated per kilogram dry weight. They attribute this to a high viscera : body weight ratio. Such an interpretation may also explain Meier's results, and those of Morton and Goldspink, but the fact remains that turnover rate does decrease in individual organs during development. This has already been pointed out for the placenta and was demonstrated earlier in the cerebrum and cerebellum (Lajtha and Dunlop, 1974) and in the individual proteins of the sarcoplasm and actomysin in skeletal muscle (Waterlow *et al.*, 1978) of growing newborn rats. Recently, the decrease in turnover rate in kidney and liver (Goldspink and Kelly, 1984), in cardiac, in both fast and slow skeletal muscles (Lewis *et al.*, 1984), and in the smooth muscle of the small and large intestine (Goldspink *et al.*, 1984) has been shown from late in intrauterine life to maturity in the rat. The reason for this rapid protein synthesis rate during development is not yet clear; Pardee *et al.* (1985) have evidence for the necessity of maintaining an unstable protein required during the latter half of the G_1 phase of cell division to ensure the later onset of DNA synthesis.

The regulation of fetal body mass and growth is probably determined by the same means as in the adult, by both local trophic factors and hormones secreted by the endocrine organs; before the latter develop, the local, paracrine factors must be the more important in the fetus and accumulating evidence suggests that they are very dependent on the nutritional supply of the cells. Both of these fascinating aspects of fetal growth are dealt with elsewhere in this volume by Milner (Chapter 4) and by Sara (Chapter 5), and the earlier extensive experimental work is reviewed by Liggins (1976) and Gluckman and Liggins (1984). Clinically, the small for gestational age infant, and the large infant born of diabetic mothers whose blood glucose is uncontrolled, has been a great stimulus to investigators, particularly concerning the possible mechanism of action of insulin and its function as a growth hormone *in utero*. The target tissue is not always clearly defined in the growing animal and the interrelationship between skeletal and soft tissue growth must be very important, for skeletal muscle in particular. Horn *et al.* (1983) found that insulin increased protein synthesis rate in one tissue only in the fetal lamb *in utero*, namely, skeletal muscle, and that an increased supply of amino acids was necessary to observe this effect.

III. PLACENTAL TRANSFER AND METABOLISM OF AMINO ACIDS

A. Free Pools

Free amino acids are present in very small quantities in the tissue compartments of the body and must be taken up continually by cells to maintain protein synthesis and other metabolic needs. The transfer process, and placental metabolism, provides this currency between the maternal and fetal plasmas to provide for the growing fetus. Extracellular and intracellular fluid concentrations are very different from each other, and both are greater in the fetus than in the mother. These relationships have been established in human, guinea pig, and sheep pregnancies and have been described fully (Young, 1976, 1981a). There are several interesting features which are familiar in the human subject. First, the maternal plasma concentrations fall during pregnancy, possibly from the influence of the high circulating concentration of steroid hormones. Second, the concentration of free amino acids in the placenta itself is much higher than that in the fetal plasma; this is due to the high turnover rate of the placental protein and to other active metabolic pools. The concentrations of the metabolically labile amino acids, the straight-chain neutral and acidic, are present in very high concentrations in comparison with the neutral branched-chain and basic amino acids; as the former groups are not transferred with ease across the trophoblast, they must be synthesized *de novo* by the tissue. This metabolic activity of the placenta has an important bearing on the delivery of amino acids to the fetus. Finally, the fetal plasma concentration of alanine is particularly high, indicating that gluconeogenesis is not very active *in utero*.

B. Placental Transfer of Amino Acids

This subject has been reviewed thoroughly by Young (1976, 1981a) and by Yudilevich and Sweiry (1985), and the important features will be summarized briefly. Under normal steady-state conditions a close relationship between maternal and fetal plasma levels is found despite the gradients which are held between the compartments. However, big differences between the transfer rates are observed when maternal levels are raised transitorily, and these are related to the transport groups and to the transport rates found in other tissues. The essential, branched-chain neutral amino acids have been shown to cross the placental membrane readily in a number of species. Moreover, they are held in the tissue for a short time, so that the fetal concentration curve is attenuated in comparison with the mother's; the umbilical V–A differences are also increased, showing an increased uptake by the fetus. In contrast, the neutral straight-chain amino acids, such as alanine and glycine, are not transferred readily and the acidic amino acids are probably not transferred across the membrane, as observed in the gut. That much of the non-essential amino acids delivered to the fetus are synthesized in the placenta is shown by comparing their uterine uptake with delivery to the fetus.

C. Umbilical and Uterine A–V Differences and Placental Metabolism

Values for uterine and umbilical A–V differences are obtained in chronic preparations with indwelling catheters in the steady state. Figure 3 shows that all the A–V differences across the uterine circulation in the pregnant ewe are quite small, 10 μM or less. Across the umbilical circulation there is a wide range from 10 to 30 μM with a still larger value for glutamine; the negative difference for glutamic acid indicates that it

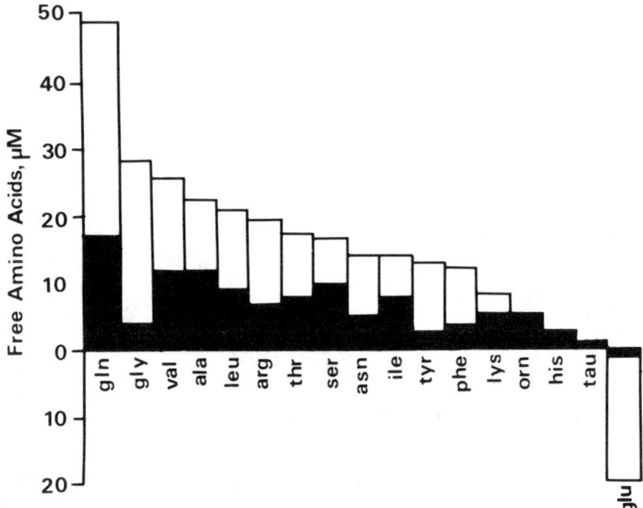

Fig. 3. A comparison of placental uptake of amino acids, uterine A–V (■) differences, release, and umbilical V–A (□) differences, in the pregnant ewe in the third trimester. (From Lemons *et al*, 1976 and Holzman et al, 1979.)

may be taken up by the fetal side of the placenta. An examination of these uterine and umbilical A–V differences shows that they bear no relationship to the rate at which the various amino acids cross the membrane. Moreover, the fetal : maternal A–V difference ratios are not the same; they are particularly large for glutamine ratios and for glycine, indicating again placental synthesis. Lemons *et al.* (1976) and Faichney (1981) calculated that the total output of amino acids from the placenta in the lamb was in excess of fetal requirements and postulated extensive transamination and oxidation in the fetal tissues. Such a situation cannot be extrapolated directly to the human, and it is interesting to note that the pattern of placental to fetal flux is quite different (Fig. 4). A large output of alanine from the trophoblast replaces that of glutamine, indicating a major difference in nitrogen metabolism in the human. This figure also shows that the pattern of umbilical V–A difference changes with gestational age. Most of the amino acids are taken up by the premature infant, but at term the V–A differences are smaller for the essential amino acids and those for the nonessential amino acids join glutamic acid in becoming negative. An understanding of the significance of these observations might prove of great clinical value.

A comparison between uptake and output of amino acids across the mammary gland is interesting in the context of the metabolism of amino acids by an organ whose main function is to provide amino acids for

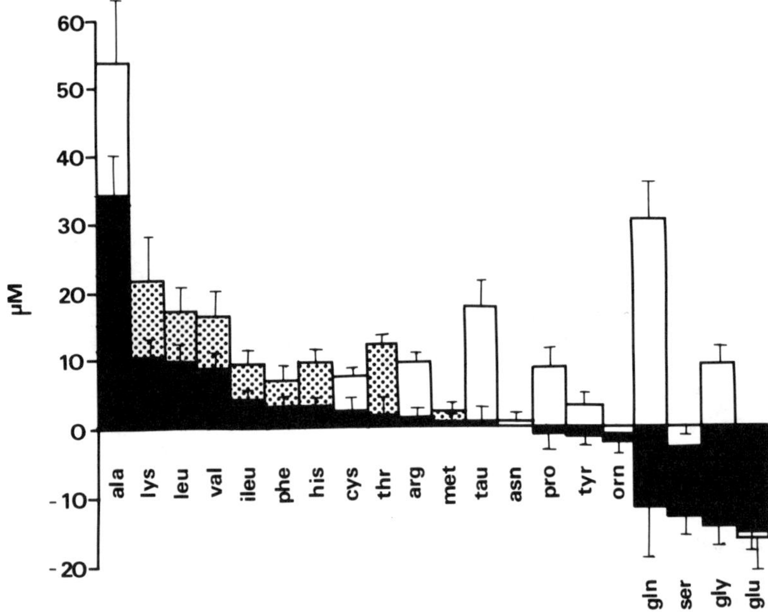

Fig. 4. Umbilical V–A differences in the human subject at vaginal delivery. Most of the amino acids are taken up by the premature infant. At term the V–A differences are smaller for the essential amino acids and those for some of the nonessential are negative, indicating uptake by the placenta from the fetus. □, Premature Infants; ■, mature infants; ⚃, essential amino acids. (From Hayashi and Sanda, 1981.)

the newborn in the form of milk protein, and the balance is easier to measure than for the placenta and fetus. The observations have been made in ruminants and the work is extensively reviewed by Mepham (1982). The essential amino acids, methionine, tryptophan, tyrosine, and phenylalanine, are taken up by the mammary gland in exactly the correct proportion for excretion in the milk protein, while the other essential amino acids, the branched chains, together with arginine, are taken up in excess of their requirement. However, uptake of the straight-chain neutral and acidic amino acids, both nonessential, is insufficient to account for their proportions in milk, and the A–V differences across the mammary gland are also sometimes negative, as for the placenta. Such a balance study is shown for Friesland ewes' milk production in Fig. 5 (Fleet and Mepham, 1985). Direct evidence for the role of the essential amino acids as precursors of the nonessential has been obtained in the perfused guinea pig mammary gland using ^{14}C-labeled branched-chain amino acids. An initial transamination with transfer to nonessential amino acids through the TCA cycle was shown. It is interesting that in the

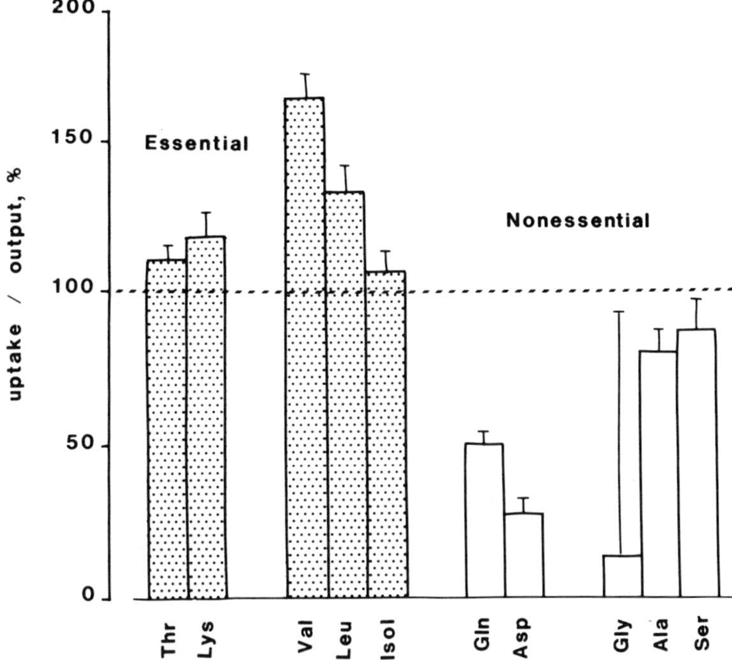

Fig. 5. Mammary gland uptake of certain amino acids related to their output in milk, in the ewe. The excess uptake of some essential amino acids and deficit in uptake of the nonessential acidic and straight-chain neutral amino acids indicate synthesis of the latter within the gland. (From Fleet and Mepham, 1985.)

perfused preparation an approximate doubling of the perfusate concentrations of essential amino acids increased the milk yield by 27%. Clearly, similar experiments need to be carried out on the perfused placenta and these biochemical transformations might also be studied in human placental and mammary gland tissue slices.

D. Essential Amino Acids and Enzyme Development

The differences between the amino acid patterns of the two plasma pools and the tissue pools on either side of the placenta have been emphasized and it remains to stress the difference between the umbilical V–A amino acid patterns and that of the composition of the fetal protein. In Fig. 6 a comparison has been made of the relative proportions of two examples from each of the four main groups of amino acids, acidic, neutral straight chain and branched chain, and basic, in fetal protein (Wid-

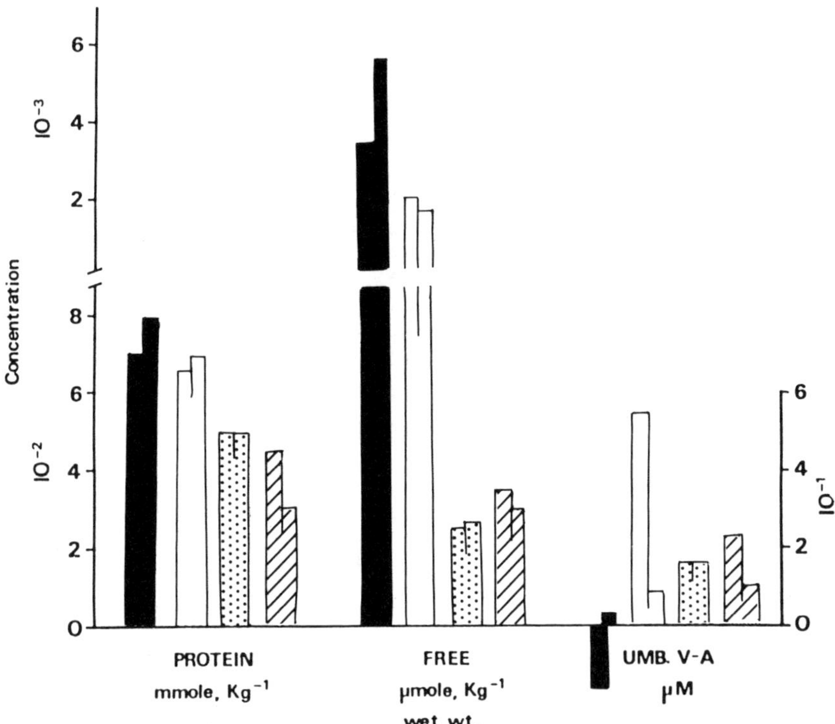

Fig. 6. Amino acids in the human placenta. A comparison of the relative proportions of two examples from each of the four main groups of amino acids, acidic (■), neutral straight chain (□) and neutral branched chain (⊡), and basic (▨), in fetal protein (Widdowson *et al.*, 1979) and the free precursor pool (Phillips *et al.*, 1978), and the umbilical V–A differences (Hayashi *et al.*, 1978).

dowson *et al.*, 1979) and the free intracellular placental pool (Phillips *et al.*, 1978), and the umbilical V–A differences (Hayashi *et al.*, 1978) in the human. A striking difference is observed between the umbilical V–A difference and the proportion of amino acids in protein. The fetal tissues possess a wide variety of transaminases and deaminases, as well as enzymes concerned with intermediary metabolism necessary for the conversion of essential to nonessential amino acids. The subject now has an extensive literature and Jones and Rolph (1985) have reviewed the findings for the liver, heart, lung, brain, and skeletal muscle in a number of species. The time of appearance of the enzymes is genetically controlled, but their activity may be stimulated prematurely, particularly by the adrenal cortical hormones. There are interesting aspects of this enzyme development in the fetus which have a direct bearing on the necessity for the placental transfer of certain amino acids which are not considered essential in the adult. One is the phenylalanine–tyrosine complex and the other the methionine–cystine relationship; the enzymes necessary for these processes do not proceed *in utero* at the adult rate and make the placental transfer of tyrosine and cystine obligatory (Räihä, 1974, 1981; Gaull, 1973).

The term placenta also possesses a wide range of enzymes necessary for intermediary metabolism (Hagerman, 1964), but there is little information on their time of appearance and changes in concentration during development. The study of glutamine and glutamate metabolism in the ovine fetoplacental unit is an exception (Pell *et al.*, 1983). Glutamine concentrations decline in the maternal plasma, while remaining constant in the fetal blood, during the last third of the 147 days of pregnancy, but glutamate concentrations remain constant in maternal blood as those in the fetal blood fall during this period. There were significant activities of glutamate dehydrogenase and glutamic synthetase, and other relevant enzymes in the placental tissue, but no changes in concentration which could account for the increased glutamine production by the placenta which amounted to 50% of the fetal nitrogen requirements at term.

IV. REGULATION OF NITROGEN DISTRIBUTION DURING PREGNANCY

The high protein synthetic rate in the placenta and still higher rate, in the whole-body fetal synthetic rate, which has been shown to exist throughout gestation (Figs. 1a and 2), represent the genetic demand of the conceptus for nutrients. The control of this basic function is dealt with elsewhere in this volume (Chapter 4) and it remains to discuss briefly how the supply of nutrients is controlled. This ultimately depends on both placental blood flows and plasma concentrations on either side of the trophoblast. The role of the steroid hormones in the development and maintenance of the maternal circulation is most familiar, but there is very little quantitative evidence for the influence of alterations in blood flow on nutrient transfer from mother to fetus. It has been shown that the balance of glucose and amino-nitrogen taken up by the gravid bovine uterus remains the same between 1 and 6 months of pregnancy, increasing thirtyfold during this time (Ferrel and Ford, 1980). When calculated on a weight basis, uptake doubled between 3 and 5 months of intrauterine life and declined slowly thereafter. It has also been shown in the perfused guinea pig placenta *in situ* that a 30% reduction in maternal blood flow caused a 20% reduction in the transfer of glucose and amino-nitrogen, but a 50% reduction in the transfer of essential amino acids, indicating that an imbalance as well as a fall in nutrient supply may occur during intrauterine malnutrition (Young, 1974). It would, however, be difficult to relate such findings to the clinical situation where events may take place more slowly and allow time for adaptive changes in metabolism to take place.

The fall in resting levels of the plasma nutrients during pregnancy highlights the importance of the proper development of the uterine and placental circulations to the appropriate blood flow and delivery rate of nutrients. But Freinkel and his colleagues have shown that the daily integrated levels of the plasma constituents must also be considered, for the postprandial profiles of glucose are enhanced during pregnancy as a result of the decreased sensitivity to insulin, though amino acids are not so influenced (Freinkel *et al.*, 1979). Further, well-nourished mothers may be expected to have a higher, and poorly nourished mothers a lower, daily integrated level of nutrients. Nevertheless, there is no consensus whether mothers should eat for two when they are pregnant. Widdowson (1981) suggests that, though the demands of the fetus are relatively small in comparison with her own requirements, she should increase her intake to ensure the maintenance of the supply lines and the necessary hormone production for the maintenance of pregnancy. From studies in rats, Naismith (1981) provides evidence for a cycle of increased anabolism during the first half of pregnancy, followed by one of increased catabolism. This would ensure that the protein cost to the mother is distributed throughout pregnancy and conforms to the dietary practice of most pregnant women. Vincent and Lindsay (1986) have preliminary evidence in the pregnant ewe which indicates that maternal protein metabolism may be modified to enhance the availability of amino acids for fetal growth and lactation. It would be very interesting to know what proportion of maternal endogenous and exogenous nitrogen appears in the fetal body at different stages of gestation. During the second half of a human pregnancy, when the greatest increase in fetal weight occurs, the mother will ingest an average of 9 kg protein. This is equal to that of her own body nitrogen stores, some of which are potentially distributable to the fetal protein, which increases to 500 g at birth. The complex relationship between the placentomaternal unit when, first, hCG then hPL act as tonic anabolic hormones for the protein economy of the mother and, indirectly, that of the fetus has been investigated and analyzed by Kaplan and Grumbach (1974) and Freinkel *et al.* (1979). Maternal growth hormone is suppressed and insulin is regarded as a fluctuating modifier of its action; feeding increases insulin release and restores maternal stores, while in fasting the decrease in effective insulin induces the primary catabolic effects of hPL and so ensures an adequate supply of fetal nutrients. Finally, a good supply of nutrients assures a good production of the paracrine primary growth factors in fetal tissues, which is particularly important in early gestation.

ACKNOWLEDGMENTS

The author and her colleagues carried out their work at St. Thomas's Hospital Medical School, London; she wishes to thank the A.F.R.C., Babraham, Cambridge, for the use of their library.

REFERENCES

Agboola, A. (1975). *J. Obstet. Gynaecol.* **82,** 225–227.

Aherne, W., and Dunnill, M. S. (1966). *J. Pathol. Bacteriol.* **91,** 123–139.

Bell, A. W., Battaglia, F. C., Makowski, E. L., and Meschia, G. (1985). *Biol. Neonate* **47,** 120–123.

Blaxter, K. L. (1964). *In* "Mammalian Protein Metabolism" (H. N. Munro and J. B. Allison, eds.), Vol. 11, pp. 173–223. Academic Press, New York.

Buttery, P. J., Beckerton, A., Mitchell, R. M., Davies, K., and Annison, G. F. (1975). *Proc. Nutr. Soc.* **34,** 91–92A.

Campbell, A. G. M., Dawes, G. S., Mott, J. C., Fishman, A. P., Hyman, H. P., and James, G. B. (1966). *J. Physiol. (London)* **182,** 439–464.

Catzeflis, C., Schulz, Y., Micheli, J-L., Welsch, C., Arnaud, M. J., and Jéquier, E. (1985). *Pediatr. Res.* **19,** 679–687.

Faichney, G. J. (1981). *Proc. Nutr. Soc. Aust.* **6,** 48–53.

Ferrel, C. L., and Ford, S. P. (1980). *J. Anim. Sci.* **50,** 1113–1121.

Fleet, I. R., and Mepham, T. B. (1985). *J. Dairy Res.* **52,** 229–237.

Freinkel, N., Phelps, R. L., and Metzger, B. E. (1979). *In* "Carbohydrate Metabolism in Pregnancy and the Newborn 1978" (H. W. Sutherland and J. M. Stower, eds.), pp. 1–31. Springer-Verlag, Berlin and New York.

Garlick, P. J. (1980). *In* "Protein Deposition in Animals" (P. J. Buttery and D. B. Lindsay, eds.), pp. 51–68. Butterworth, London.

Gaull, G. E. (1973). *In* "Fetal and Neonatal Physiology" (R. S. Comline, K. W. Cross, G. S. Dawes, and P. W. Nathanielsz, eds.), pp. 339–341. Cambridge Univ. Press, London and New York.

Gehring, W. J. (1985). *Sci. Am.* **253**(4), 153–163.

Gluckman, P. D., and Liggins, G. C. (1984). *In* "Fetal Physiology and Medicine" (R. W. Beard and P. W. Nathanielsz, eds.), 2nd Ed., pp. 511–558. Butterworth, London.

Goldspink, D. F., and Kelly, F. J. (1984). *Biochem. J.* **217,** 507–516.

Goldspink, D. F., Lewis, E. M., and Kelly, F. J. (1984). *Biochem. J.* **217,** 527–534.

Hagerman, D. D. (1964). *Fed. Proc., Am. Soc. Exp. Biol.* **23,** 785–790.

Hayashi, S., and Sanda, K. (1981). *In* "Placental Transfer: Methods and Interpretations" (M. Young, R. D. H. Boyd, L. D. Longo, and G. Telegdy, eds.), p. 244. Saunders, Philadelphia, Pennsylvania.

Hayashi, S., Sanda, K., Sagawn, H., Yamada, H., and Kito, C. (1978). *Biol. Neonate* **34,** 11–18.

Holzman, I. R., Lemons, J. A., Meschia, G., and Battaglia, F. C. (1979). *J. Dev. Physiol.* **1,** 137–149.

Horn, J., Stern, M. D. R., Young, M., and Noakes, D. E. (1983). *Res. Vet. Sci.* **35,** 35–41.

Jackson, A. A., Shaw, J. C. L., Barber, A., and Golden, M. H. N. (1981). *Pediatr. Res.* **15,** 1454–1461.

Jones, C. T., and Rolph, T. P. (1985). *Physiol. Rev.* **65,** 357–430.

Kaplan, S. L., and Grumbach, M. M. (1974). *In* "Lactogenic Hormones, Fetal Nutrition and Lactation" (J. B. Josemovich, ed.), pp. 183–192. Wiley, New York.

Kruger, H., and Arias-Stella, J. (1970). *Am. J. Obstet. Gynecol.* **106,** 586–591.

Lajtha, A., and Dunlop, D. (1974). *In* "Advances in Behavioural Biology" (A. Vernadakis and N. Weiner, eds.), Vol. 8, pp. 215–219. Plenum, New York.

Lajtha, A., Latzkowits, L., and Toth, J. (1976). *Biochim. Biophys. Acta* **425,** 511–520.

Lemons, J. A., Adcock, E. W., Jones, D., Naughton, M. A., Meschia, G., and Battaglia, F. C. (1976). *J. Clin. Invest.* **58,** 1428–1434.

Lewis, E. M., Kelly, J. F., and Goldspink, D. F. (1984). *Biochem. J.* **217,** 517–526.

Liggins, G. C. (1976). *In* "Fetal Physiology and Medicine" (R. W. Beard and P. W. Nathanielsz, eds.), pp. 254–270. Saunders, Philadelphia, Pennsylvania.

Meier, P. R., Peterson, R. G., Bonds, D. R., Meschia, G., and Battaglia, F. C. (1981). *Am. J. Physiol.* **240,** 320–324.

Mepham, T. B. (1982). *J. Dairy Sci.* **65,** 287–297.

Morton, A. J., and Goldspink, D. F. (1986). *Am. J. Physiol.* **250,** E114–E120.

Munro, H. N., (ed.) (1969). *In* "Mammalian Protein Metabolism," Vol. 3, p. 133. Academic Press, New York.

Naismith, D. J. (1981). *In* "Maternal Nutrition in Pregnancy. Eating for Two?" (J. Dobbing, ed.), pp. 21–40. Academic Press, New York.

Oddy, V. H., and Lindsay, D. B. (1986). *Biochem. J.* **233,** 417–425.

Pardee, A. B., Campisi, J., and Croy, R. G. (1985). "Cancer Cells, Growth Factors and Transformation," pp. 389–392. Cold Spring Harbor Lab. Cold Spring Harbor, New York.

Pell, J. M., Jeacock, M. J., and Shepherd, D. A. L. (1983). *J. Agric. Sci.* **101,** 275–281.

Pencharz, P. B., Steffe, W., Cochran, W., Schrimshaw, N. S., Rand, W. M., and Young, V. R. (1977). *Clin. Sci.* **52,** 485–498.

Pencharz, P. B., Masson, M., Desgranges, F., and Papageorgiou, A. (1981). *Clin. Sci.* **61,** 207–215.

Phillips, A. F., Holzman, I. R., Teng, C., and Battaglia, F. C. (1978). *Am. J. Obstet. Gynecol.* **131,** 881–887.

Posner, B. I. (1974). *Diabetes* **23,** 209–217.

Räihä, N. C. (1974). *Pediatrics* **53,** 147–156.

Räihä, N. C. R. (1981). *In* "Biology of Normal Human Growth" (M. Ritzén, K. Hall, A. Zetterberg, A. Aperia, A. Larsson, and R. Zetterström, eds.), pp. 203–212. Raven, New York.

Sands, J., and Dobbing, J. (1985). *Placenta* **6,** 13–22.

Schaefer, A. L., and Krishnamurti, C. R. (1984). *Br. J. Nutr.* **52,** 359–369.

Schneider, H., Challier, J. C., and Dancis, J. (1981). *In* "Placental Transfer: Methods and Interpretation" (M. Young, R. D. H. Boyd, L. D. Longo, and G. Telegdy, eds.), pp. 129–138. Saunders, Philadelphia, Pennsylvania.

Scornick, O. A. (1982). *In* "The Biochemical Development of the Fetus and Neonate" (C. T. Jones, ed.), pp. 865–894. Elsevier, New York.

Simmons, M. A., Battaglia, F. C., and Meschia, G. (1979). *J. Dev. Physiol.* **1,** 227–243.

Soltesz, G., Joyce, L., and Young, M. (1973). *Biol. Neonate* **23,** 139–148.

Waterlow, J. C., Garlick, P. J., and Millward, D. J. (1978). "Protein Turnover in Mammalian Tissues and in the Whole Body." North Holland Publishing Company, Amsterdam.

Vincent, R., and Lindsay, D. B. (1986). *Early Hum. Dev.* **13,** 345–346.

Whitsett, J. A., and Lessard, J. L. (1978). *Endocrinology (Baltimore)* **103,** 1458–1486.
Widdowson, E. M. (1970). *Lancet* **1,** 901–905.
Widdowson, E. M. (1981). *In* "Maternal Nutrition in Pregnancy. Eating for Two?" (J. Dobbing, ed.), pp. 1–20. Academic Press, New York.
Widdowson, E. M., Southgate, D. A. T., and Hey, E. M. (1979). *In* "Nutrition and Metabolism of the Fetus and Infant" (H. F. A. Visser, ed.), pp. 169–178. Nijhoff, The Hague.
Winick, M. (1974). "Nutrition and Fetal Development." Wiley, New York.
Winick, M., Brasel, J. A., and Rosso, R. (1972). *In* "Nutrition and Development. Current Concepts in Nutrition" (M. Winick, ed.), pp. 49–89. Wiley, New York.
Young, M. (1974). *Ciba Found. Symp.* No. 27, p. 21.
Young, M. (1976). *In* "Fetal Physiology and Medicine" (R. W. Beard and P. W. Nathanielsz, eds.), pp. 59–79. Saunders, Philadelphia, Pennsylvania.
Young, M. (1981a). *In* "Transfer across the Primate and Non-Primate Placenta" (H. C. S. Wallenberg, B. K. van Kreel, and J. P. van Dyke, eds.), pp. 125–138. Saunders, Philadelphia, Pennsylvania.
Young, M. (1981b). *In* "Fetal Growth Retardation" (F. A. van Assche, W. B. Robertson, and M. Ranaer, eds.), pp. 13–19. Livingstone, Edinburgh.
Young, M. (1982). *Acta Paediatr. Acad. Sci. Hung.* **23,** 99–117.
Young, M. (1983). *In* "Fetal Endocrinology and Metabolism" (L. Martini and V. H. T. James, eds.), Current Topics in Experimental Endocrinology, Vol. 5, pp. 146–177. Academic Press, New York.
Young, M., and Widdowson, E. M. (1975). *Biol. Neonate* **27,** 184–191.
Young, M., Horn, J., and Noakes, D. E. (1979). *In* "Nutrition and Metabolism of the Fetus and Infant" (H. K. A. Visser, ed.), pp. 19–27. Nijhoff, The Hague.
Young, M., Stern, M. D. R., Horn, J., and Noakes, D. F. (1982). *Placenta* **3,** 159–164.
Yudilevich, D. L., and Sweiry, J. H. (1985). *Biochim. Biophys. Acta* **822,** 169–201.

Endocrine Control of Fetal Growth?

R. D. G. Milner
Department of Paediatrics
University of Sheffield, Children's Hospital
Sheffield, England

I. INTRODUCTION

Recent advances in the understanding of fetal growth have had a considerable impact on the concept of endocrine control. Not long ago the fetus was considered to have autonomy of peptide hormone secretion and to be subject, as is the infant postnatally, to the actions of hormones such as growth hormone (GH) and the thyroid hormones which are principally responsible for growth after birth. But growth control in the embryo and fetus is intrinsically more complex than postnatal growth and involves not only cellular multiplication and differentiation, but also planned cell death and tissue and organ modeling. These changes have led the clinician interested in the physiology of human fetal growth to be as impressed by genetic and nutritional control mechanisms as by those which are conventionally called endocrine.

The importance of the classical endocrine concept of a molecule synthesized and secreted in one part of the body passing via the blood stream to exert its action distantly has been much weakened by the realization that in the fetus locally acting peptides called tissue growth factors (GFs) are probably as important if not more so than classical hormones in growth control. Hence the adjective "endocrine" ' has come to be used loosely in the context of fetal growth control, particularly as some of the GFs, the insulinlike growth factors (IGFs), share structural homology with proinsulin (1). Interest in GFs and fetal growth control has also exploded because recent technical advances have permitted the more precise identification of GFs and related molecules and the realization that there is a structural similarity between some of the GFs and proteins expressed by viral oncogenes (2) which has fueled speculation about common control mechanisms for physiological and neoplastic growth.

In this chapter attention will be focused on the IGFs and the following definitions should be understood: the terms somatomedin (SM) and insulinlike growth factor (IGF) are synonymous. SM-C is the same as IGF-I and is a 70-amino acid peptide encoded by a gene on human chromosome 12, whereas IGF-II is a 67-amino acid peptide encoded by a gene mapped to chromosome 11 in close proximity to the insulin gene (3). The equivalent peptide to IGF-II in the rat is called multiplication-stimulating activity (MSA).

Our own interest in fetal growth control has focused on how cells of the fetal lean body mass grow and divide under the influence of traditional hormones, GFs, and nutrition. Each of the three is connected so that acting in unison they provide conditions that optimize fetal cellular development which proceeds under genetic control. Elsewhere we have reviewed fetal growth from different angles: a general review of prenatal growth control in man (4), the contrasting effects of insulin and glucagon on fetal metabolism (5), fetal carbohydrate and fat metabolism (6), insulin as a growth factor before and after birth (7), the role of insulin and related peptides in fetal growth (8), and growth factors in embryogenesis (9). In this chapter the evidence for the prenatal actions of a number of hormones will be reviewed followed by a synthesis of related work which leads to the conclusion that the overall effect of growth-promoting hormones before birth is permissive rather than controlling.

II. ENDOCRINE CONTROL OF FETAL GROWTH?

The endocrine contribution to fetal growth can be considered in three ways, only one of which is explored in detail here. First, there are maternal endocrine changes which, although vital to an optimal pregnancy, are not described fully because they affect fetal growth indirectly by improving the availability of nutrient to the fetus and placental size and blood flow (10). Second, there is the materno-placento-fetal steroid axis; pregnenolene synthesized in the placenta from cholesterol passes to the fetal adrenal where it is converted to dehydroepiandrosterone sulfate, which is then converted in turn to estradiol 17B and estrone by the placenta. These steroids pass into the maternal circulation where they stimulate the renin–angiotensin system causing retention of fluid and expansion of the maternal vascular compartment (11). But it is the third aspect that we will dwell on: the fetus and placenta can be considered to be an autonomous unit insofar as the placenta is functionally impermeable to maternal peptides such as pituitary, pancreatic, or thyroidal hormones. Within the fetoplacental unit the hormones that are important for growth differ quantitatively and qualitatively from those principally responsible for growth after birth. For example, GH and the thyroid hormones have at best a marginal effect prenatally, whereas insulin lack or excess can have dramatic sequelae as seen in the infant with transient neonatal diabetes (12) or the infant of the poorly controlled diabetic mother (13). Some of the evidence for the unimportance of the pituitary and thyroid glands in fetal growth is set out below.

A. Pituitary Hormones

Pituitary GH is essential for normal postnatal linear growth but has little part in growth control before birth. This may seem surprising because GH appears in the fetal pituitary in the first trimester of pregnancy and by the third trimester there are circulating levels that would be associated with acromegaly in the adult (14). The birth weights of infants with congenital pituitary aplasia or hypothalamic hypopituitarism are within the normal range (15). Anencephalics are a heterogeneous collection in which the pituitary may or may not be present but in which there is an absent or abnormal hypothalamo-pituitary link. The birth weight of anencephalics has been reported to be reduced (16) but the topic does not warrant close inspection because fetal growth is further complicated by the fact that those with an absent pituitary may have an abnormally prolonged gestation and thereby end up heavier.

Animal experiments have shown clearly that the pituitary is unimportant in fetal growth control overall and that such contribution as it makes is via the trophic effect of thyroid-stimulating hormone (TSH) on thyroidal development and secretion. This statement does not negate the specific effects of hypophysectomy on the subsequent development of the adrenal and gonads. In the rabbit, rat, and mouse, fetal decapitation or brain aspiration is not associated with a major effect on body weight or length (17,18) although changes in body composition have been recorded. Jost was the first to note increased subcutaneous adipose tissue in decapitated rat fetuses (17), which was confirmed in the rabbit and extended to show alterations in cell size and number in a variety of organs (19). Hill *et al.* (20) demonstrated that decapitation of the fetal rabbit had no effect on growth plate cartilage metabolic activity or circulating somatomedinlike activity.

In species with longer gestation the results are more complex and depend on the contribution of thyroid hormones to prenatal growth. Decapitation of the fetal pig is not associated with a reduction of birth length (21), but in the fetal lamb hypophysectomy has been reported to cause growth retardation (22). This is because of induced pituitary hypothyroidism. If GH deficiency is induced by pituitary stalk section without hypophyseal infarction, fetal growth retardation does not occur (23) and the fetal lamb has lowered circulating levels of GH and thyroid hormones but not to the degree seen when infarction occurs. Similarly, encephalectomy of the monkey fetus which destroys the hypothalamus but not the pituitary results in low circulating GH levels, normal thyroid hormone levels, and no growth retardation (24).

The biological inactivity of GH in the fetus may, in some species, be related to a scarcity of GH receptors in fetal tissues (25) or failure of a biological response to occur following receptor occupancy (26). GH receptors demonstrated on human fetal fibroblasts have a lower affinity and capacity than those on adult-derived fibroblasts (27).

An intriguing and unresolved topic in fetal endocrinology concerns the relationship between the pituitary and the endocrine pancreas. Little was made originally of the observation that decapitated rat fetuses have excess subcutaneous fat (17). We confirmed that decapitation of the rabbit fetus is also followed by fat deposition (19) and asked if this might be the result of increased insulin secretion by the decapitated fetus. The plasma insulin levels of decapitated fetuses were greater than those of litter mate controls and glucose-stimulated insulin secretion *in vitro* from pieces of pancreas of decapitated fetuses was greater than that from controls (28). ACTH injection at the time of decapitation corrected the change in plasma insulin and insulin secretory characteristics of the pancreas. Most recently hGH in pharmacological concentrations has been shown to stimulate DNA replication, insulin release, and IGF-I release from fetal rat islets cultured *in vitro* (29). There is also the serendipitous finding that the pancreatic islet hyperplasia which characterizes the infant of the diabetic mother does not occur if the fetus is anencephalic (30). Taken together these observations are an intellectual irritant; normal histological islet development does not depend on cephalic factors but experimental decapitation may be followed by oversecretion of insulin. The hypothalamo-pituitary axis may be necessary for islet hyperplasia to occur and GH is capable of influencing islet B-cell development. The topic may be of marginal importance to the endocrinology of fetal growth control overall, but it remains like the pea under the princess' mattress.

Within the pituitary family the position of prolactin is complicated by the fact that this peptide is released from the decidua into the amniotic fluid. In both one human (31) and in rat pregnancies (32) where dopamine agonists were given to the mother throughout pregnancy, fetal growth was unaffected despite the suppression of circulating fetal prolactin. Decidual prolactin secretion was unaffected but its role in fetal physiology, if any, is unknown. The potential role of prolactin in mammalian growth merits further study; prolactin is known to stimulate SM-like activity from rat liver perfused *in vitro* (33). Prolactin antiserum administered to neonatal mice inhibited growth (34), but the direct injection of prolactin in hypophysectomized infant rats did not stimulate growth (35). More work is needed.

Alpha melanocyte-stimulating hormone (αMSH) is secreted from the intermediate lobe of the pituitary along with adrenocorticotrophin and B-endorphin. Swaab and colleagues have argued that αMSH may be involved in rat fetal growth. Fetuses injected with αMSH antiserum were growth retarded. A reduction in fetal and placental size caused by encephalectomy was reversed by αMSH administration (36). These observations have not yet been confirmed by other workers.

B. Thyroid Hormones

The contribution of thyroid hormones to fetal growth differs between species. In man athyreosis is characterized by retarded osseous and neuronal development but little or no effect on birth weight and length (37). Experimental hypothyroidism in rodent fetuses toward the end of gestation does not impede growth. This may be because of the short interval between the operation and birth and the relatively long half-life of circulating thyroid hormones (38). Fetal thyroidectomy in species with longer gestation such as the sheep (38) and rhesus monkey (39) is followed by growth retardation. Lambs thyroidectomized between 80 and 115 days gestation were 30% underweight at delivery on day 144 and showed delayed osseous maturation and a failure in the development of skin texture and secondary wool follicles. The effects of thyroidectomy on skin development may be due to a reduction of thyroid hormone-dependent epidermal growth factor (40).

The statement that the placenta is impermeable to thyroid hormones does not entirely exclude a role for maternal thyroid hormones in prenatal development. Obregon *et al.* (41) have measured thyroxine and triiodothyronine levels in rat embryo trophoblasts and in fetuses and placentae from 13–20 days gestation. They found that thyroid hormone concentrations were higher in the embryos at 10–12 days gestation and did not rise in the fetuses until the fetal thyroid became active at day 18. Thyroid hormones could be detected as early as 4 days postconception and presumably at this stage of development were maternal in origin.

III. INTERACTION BETWEEN HORMONES, TISSUE GROWTH FACTORS, AND NUTRITION

In this section the contribution made to fetal growth by the hormones insulin and placental lactogen, by GFs, and by nutrition will be discussed with particular emphasis on the interaction of the three, which has led inevitably to a selective review but more information about GFs and nutritional growth control is provided elsewhere in this volume (Chapter 5).

A. Insulin

Pedersen *et al.* (13) were the first to suggest that the overweight of the infant of the poorly controlled diabetic mother resulted from the sequence: maternal hyperglycemia causes fetal hyperglycemia causes fetal hyperinsulinemia. The metabolic disturbances in diabetic pregnancy are now appreciated to be more complex (42) and other classes of metabolites, notably amino acids, are thought to exert a trophic effect on the development of the fetal B cell as well as being insulin secretagogues (43).

Although insulin is present in the human fetal pancreas from 10 weeks gestation (44), insulin release remains glucose insensitive until approximately 28 weeks gestational age (45) at which time the preadipocyte matures into an insulin-sensitive cell that is capable of accumulating lipid. Most of the excess weight gain seen in the infant of a diabetic mother is fat which is accumulated in the last trimester of pregnancy. The less dramatic but unequivocal increase in somatic growth occurring concurrently suggests that insulin has an additional direct or indirect role in protein synthesis and cellular proliferation. Enhanced fetal somatic development has been described in infants with nesidioblastosis (46) or the Beckwith–Wiedemann syndrome (47), each of which is associated with hypersecretion of insulin. Conversely, the infant with transient neonatal diabetes (12) or pancreatic agenesis (48) is small-for-dates having poor muscle bulk and virtually no adipose tissue.

There are several pathways by which insulin can stimulate fetal growth (7). First, it may promote the uptake and utilization of nutrient at a cellular level. Second, insulin may exert a direct anabolic effect via either the insulin or the type 1 IGF receptor. Third, insulin may modulate the release of IGF or other growth factors from fetal tissue.

There have been numerous studies of the overall association between fetal growth and fetal insulin levels. A direct association between fetal plasma insulin and body weight was reported in both the rat (49) and the rabbit (50). Attempts to produce fetal overgrowth by the injection of exogenous insulin in rodents have been less successful. Rat fetuses injected with insulin showed increased nitrogen retention and body fat but only when pregnancy had been artificially prolonged by treatment of the dam with progesterone (51,52). Induction of hyperinsulinemia in the fetal rat (53) or rabbit (54) either by making the mother mildly diabetic, or treating with tolbutamide (55), or by direct injection of insulin into the fetus (56) led to a rise in circulating IGF levels and increased tissue metabolic activity but did not significantly increase body size.

The effect of fetal hyperinsulinemia in species of longer gestation has been studied by implanting osmotic minipumps in monkey fetuses (57). Three weeks of pharmacological hyperinsulinemia (serum insulin > 20 n*M*) resulted in a 34% increase in fetal body weight associated with enlargement of the heart, liver, and spleen, but not the lung, kidney, or brain. In later experiments less extreme hyperinsulinemia was produced (58). This caused a 23% increase in body weight but the only organ found to be enlarged was the heart, suggesting that most of the weight gain was due to excess adipose tissue which was noted but not quantified. No precocious skeletal development was observed in either group of experimental fetuses. Circulating IGF-I levels were raised in monkey fetuses with gross hyperinsulinemia but not in those with moderately elevated levels. This was in keeping with the observation that concentrations of IGF-I and II in the cord blood of human infants of diabetic mothers did not differ from those of control infants despite raised levels of cord plasma C-peptide (59).

Whereas fetal hyperinsulinemia with or without hyperglycemia causes variable modest body overgrowth, experimental fetal hypoinsulinemia is invariably associated with growth retardation. When hypoglycemia was produced in the rat fetus either by maternal fasting (60) or by ligation of the uterine blood vessels (61), there was pronounced growth retardation accompanied by a lowering of plasma insulin and IGF levels. Since the lack of nutrient availability may have been the major factor in limiting growth, an experimental model in which hypoinsulinemia coexists with euglycemia is particularly relevant. This has been difficult to achieve because chemical agents which damage the B cell may also have direct adverse effects on body growth and operative removal of the pancreas takes away much more than B cells. Nevertheless the observations of Fowden and Comline (62) are interesting. Pancreatectomy of the fetal lamb approximately 3 weeks before term caused an approximate 20% reduction in body weight. A noteworthy clinical observation was that an infant born with transient neonatal diabetes mellitus had low circulating insulin and IGF-I levels but a normal IGF-II. Insulin therapy produced immediate clinical improvement with a delayed rise in serum IGF-I (59).

The ontogeny of insulin and IGF receptors is relevant to the possible mechanisms of action of insulin in prenatal growth. Insulin and IGF receptors were identified in human fetal tissues from at least 15 weeks gestation (63); insulin receptor number increased with age to 25 weeks, after which binding capacity was enhanced by an increase in receptor affinity only. Monocytes from the cord blood of normal babies had five times the insulin-binding capacity of adult cells (64) and that in monocytes from infants of diabetic mothers was even higher (65). Despite the availability of insulin receptors we were unable to demonstrate stimulation of mitosis in cultured human fibroblasts and myoblasts of 12 to 19 weeks gestation by insulin, although the cells did respond to human placental lactogen, SM-C, and MSA activity (66). This finding should not be extrapolated throughout prenatal life since in related experiments using fetal rat myoblasts there was a short period at the end of gestation when physiological concentrations of insulin stimulated incorporation of tritiated thymidine (67). Similar observations on receptor ontogeny have been made in animal studies. At term both the insulin binding and affinity of rat liver membranes exceeded adult values (63). In the chick insulin receptors were demonstrable from the third day of incubation and insulin from the second (68), both antedating the development of pancreatic islets, which occurs at 5 days incubation (69). Receptor density increases in chick muscle cells with increasing embryonic development (70).

The parallel changes in serum insulin and IGF levels, especially those observed during fetal growth retardation, suggest that some of the anabolic actions of insulin *in utero* could be mediated by a change in IGF release. This might be a specific effect on IGF synthesis or an indirect one following an increase of cellular anabolism. The clinical observation of low plasma insulin and IGF-I but normal IGF-II in a neonate with transient diabetes (59) suggests that IGF-II may not be influenced by insulin in the human. This is in keeping with the failure of insulin to affect the release of MSA from fetal rat liver explants (71). The lack of effect of insulin on IGF-I release from cultured fetal rat myoblasts may be an ontogenic phenomenon by analogy with its metabolic action in thymidine uptake (67).

The possibility that insulin could influence IGF synthesis by modulating GH receptors should not be overlooked. Postnatally rat hepatic GH receptors are stimulated by insulin (72).

An interesting and technically novel approach to the effects of insulin on prenatal growth was provided by Cooke *et al.* (73,74), who transplanted paws from 15-day rat fetuses under the kidney capsule of syngeneic young host rats, where the paws continued to grow and undergo limited ossification. When the host rat was diabetic the growth of the transplants was reduced by approximately 40%, but growth was almost completely restored by treatment of the host with insulin but not with GH. Treatment of intact hosts with insulin plus glucose to combat hypoglycemia did not stimulate paw growth. These experiments illustrate several mechanisms involved in fetal limb growth: (1) The continuing growth of the paw at a reduced rate in the totally growth arrested hypophysectomized host illustrates the high endogenous growth capacity of fetal tissues, possibly mediated by endogenous production of tissue growth factors. (2) Likewise in a diabetic, catabolic environment fetal growth continued, but at a suboptimal rate. (3) Excess insulin and glucose could not stimulate fetal tissue growth.

Insulin must also be considered in the context of the placenta and in particular in relation to placental lactogen (PL). The placenta contains insulin receptors from early in gestation that are sited mainly on the maternal surface (75), and the placenta takes up and degrades maternal insulin (76). There are fewer insulin receptors on the fetal side and no evidence of their physiological role (77,78). The concentration of insulin receptors in the placenta overall has been reported to be reduced in pregnancies where there is intrauterine growth retardation (79). Insulin has been reported to stimulate the release of human placental lactogen from isolated cultured trophoblasts (80). If such an effect were to take place within the fetoplacental unit *in utero* it could be an important regulator of PL release into the fetus.

B. Placental Lactogen

This peptide is secreted by the placental trophoblasts into both the maternal and fetal circulation. PL shares amino acid sequence homology with both GH and prolactin. Originally the major physiological role of PL was thought to be the mobilization of maternal metabolites by acting as an insulin antagonist in the mother (81). Then it was appreciated that PL stimulated maternal IGF secretion. In the pregnant hypophysectomized rat circulating IGF levels did not fall until after delivery (82). Ovine PL restored IGF-I levels in nonpregnant hypophysectomized rats (83). In the pregnant ewe there was a positive correlation between PL and IGF-II (84). An intriguing clinical parallel to these animal experiments has been described. A GH-deficient woman became pregnant and at 35 weeks gestation had normal serum levels of IGF-I and II. Following delivery these dropped rapidly in parallel with circulating maternal PL (85). Taken together with the normally elevated maternal IGF-I in late gestation, which declines at parturition (86), this offers plausible evidence favoring the stimulation of maternal IGF by hPL.

Maternal blood levels of hPL are used as a biochemical indicator of fetal well-being in clinical practice. The interpretation of this information has been aided by the work of Hubert *et al.* (87), who prepared RNA from the placentae of control and growth-retarded infants and expressed their protein products *in vitro* in a reticulocyte lysate cell-free system. The capacity to express hPL did not differ with birth weight, suggesting that its concentration in the maternal circulation is a reflection more of placental size than placental cellular function.

Little attention was paid to a possible direct action of hPL in the fetus because of the large maternofetal concentration difference observed at term (81). Maternal levels rise to a plateau of 6000–10,000 ng/ml by 34 weeks, whereas cord blood levels tend to be 100-fold lower, although values of up to 200 ng/ml have been recorded (88). However, fetal PL concentrations are higher earlier in pregnancy. Fetal lamb PL levels prior to 90 days gestation are higher than those in the ewe (89) and we have recently observed that human fetal serum between 12 and 20 weeks gestation may contain in excess of 200 ng hPL/ml.

What then might PL do in the fetus? Most of the published work has involved heterologous systems and must be interpreted cautiously because of the possibility that the PL might have reacted with GH or prolactin receptors rather than PL receptors. Happily the evidence is largely consistent with the idea that PL stimulates anabolism and cellular growth in fetal tissue. Ovine PL stimulated amino acid uptake by fetal rat diaphragm *in vitro* (90). When the experiments were repeated using postnatal fibroblasts both IGF-I and MSA release were stimulated by oPL and hGH (91).

We have concentrated on test systems using only human cells and human hormones. The effects of hPL and hGH on cultured human myoblasts, fibroblasts, and costal cartilage explants from fetuses of 11 to 21 weeks were tested by measurement of [^{3}H]thymidine uptake and SM-C release (92). Incubation with hGH was ineffective but incubation with hPL at concentrations similar to those found in the circulation (50–250 ng/ml) stimulated thymidine uptake by fibroblasts and myoblasts but not by costal cartilage. hPL stimulated SM-C release from all three cell types, most strongly from myoblasts. In another set of experiments the actions of hPL, insulin, SM-C, and MSA on human fetal fibroblasts and myoblasts were studied by measuring [^{3}H]-α-aminoisobutyric acid (AIB) or [^{3}H]thymidine uptake (66). Both AIB and thymidine uptake were stimulated by hPL; incubation in the presence of a monoclonal antibody to SM-C blocked the stimulation of thymidine uptake but had little effect on AIB uptake. The SM-C antibody completely abolished the stimulation of AIB and thymidine uptake by SM-C. These results were interpreted as showing that hPL stimulates anabolism both directly and via SM-C production.

hPL was reported not to stimulate IGF-I release from primary culture of fetal rat hepatocytes (93). This might be the consequence of a heterologous test system for we have found that both hPL and hGH stimulate DNA synthesis by isolated human fetal hepatocytes *in vitro* (94). Both hormones appeared to be equipotent in stimulating cell growth as measured by autoradiography and IGF-I release into the medium. Again it is possible that part of the hPL stimulation was indirect since exogenous IGF-I also stimulated hepatocytic DNA synthesis.

Finally, the possibility that PL stimulates fetal B-cell growth and insulin secretion must be considered. oPL stimulates insulin and DNA synthesis in cultured postnatal rat islets (95) and hGH stimulates DNA synthesis and IGF-I production by fetal rat islets *in vitro* (30). It will be interesting to learn what effect hPL has on human fetal islets.

Although the evidence for PL having an important role in prenatal growth is now very strong, the hormone is not essential. There are two reports of human infants of normal birth size delivered to women apparently devoid of immunoreactive PL during pregnancy. In the better-documented case the child was examined 5 years later, after normal postnatal growth, and was shown to have a gene deletion for PL (96). This raises the possibility that fetal GH or prolactin may be capable of taking over the physiological role of PL or that there may be more than one molecular species of PL in man as has been reported in the rat (97).

C. Tissue Growth Factors and Nutrition

The curious reader may wonder why tissue growth factors and nutrition should feature as headings in a review of the endocrine control of fetal growth. This is because fetal growth control makes sense to the author, if only naively, when it is considered not as a single operational system but as the algebraic sum of different systems. Cellular multiplication is influenced as much by the plane of nutrition and GFs as by hormones acting on the cells.

GFs influence not only cellular multiplication but also differentiation and tissue modeling (9). Within the spectrum of GFs only IGFs will be considered here because they probably have a part in the growth control of most if not all fetal cells. The IGFs are reviewed selectively because of the availability of a comprehensive recent review (98). Postnatally the IGFs are produced mainly in the liver under the influence of GH and act in an endocrine fashion to stimulate chondrogenesis at the epiphyseal growth plate leading to longitudinal skeletal growth. Experimentally IGFs act as mitogens for cells in culture, promote the incorporation of radiolabeled sulfur into cartilage glycosaminoglycans *in vitro,* and have insulin like actions on adipose tissue.

Much of the research on IGFs in the fetus has concentrated on measurements of circulating concentrations, presumably on the premise that they act in an endocrine fashion. But this idea was severely weakened by the discovery that multiple fetal mouse tissue explants all released IGF-I in culture (99). Similar results have been found in human fetal tissues (100). IGF-I was found in all organs or tissues measured, with the highest concentrations in the lung, intestine, kidney, and skin, intermediate levels in pancreas, muscle, and thymus, and the lowest levels in brain, heart, adrenal, and liver. Thus the IGFs may stimulate cellular growth locally, acting on adjacent cells (paracrine) or on the cell that secretes them (autocrine). If this is their major role, measurement of circulating levels may reflect no more than local tissue overflow and thus not be a biologically relevant index.

The control of IGF synthesis and release by fetal cells is incompletely understood. Concentrating on man, we have shown that IGF-I is released from fetal fibroblasts, myoblasts, and costal cartilage when cultured *in vitro* (92). These tissues were chosen as representative of the lean body mass. IGF-I is also present in and released from human fetal pancreatic islets (101) and hepatocytes (94) grown in culture. There is no direct evidence yet that human fetal cells release IGF-II, but this is most likely by analogy with animal experiments and because IGF-II is found in the human fetal circulation. Fetal rat fibroblasts release IGF-II predominantly in culture, whereas postnatal rat fibroblasts release IGF-I (91). Fetal rat myoblasts, on the other hand, release approximately equimolar amounts of IGF-I and IGF-II (102) and both fetal and neonatal rat pancreatic islets release IGF-I only (30,103). Clearly IGF synthesis differs between tissues and possibly also with the stage of development.

Human placental explants and fibroblasts isolated from placenta release

IGF-I (104) and mRNA prepared from either first-trimester or term human placenta translated immunoprecipitable IGF-I-like proteins in a cell-free reticulocyte lysate system (105). While it seems likely that the placenta is a source of IGF as early as the first trimester, there is no evidence that placental IGF stimulates fetal growth in an endocrine manner, the release of IGF from placenta *in vitro* being no greater than that from other fetal cell types. Placental IGF is probably paracrine in effect, but by stimulating placental growth it will have an important indirect effect on fetal development by increasing the potential for nutrient and gaseous transfer.

Both IGF-I and MSA stimulate amino acid uptake and DNA synthesis by isolated human fetal myoblasts and fibroblasts (66). The mean half-maximal effective concentrations for the two peptides were similar. Both IGF-I and IGF-II stimulated the clonal growth of isolated human fetal chondrocytes, but IGF-II was significantly more effective (106). By contrast IGF-I was more potent than IGF-II in stimulating the growth of adult chondrocytes. Neither GH nor insulin influenced fetal or adult chondrocyte growth.

The design of experiments to test whether IGFs are essential for fetal cellular growth is difficult. In the case of IGF-I, antibody blocked AIB or thymidine uptake by cultured fetal fibroblasts stimulated by exogenous IGF-I (92). However, the uptake of each marker persisted at basal levels. This could be interpreted as showing that the cells remained anabolic in the absence of IGF-I or that production of endogenous IGF-I remained adequate to sustain cellular anabolism in the presence of antibody. This dilemma is inevitable when considering a molecule believed to act in a paracrine/autocrine fashion.

The difficulty in dissecting apart interacting variables is also seen when fetal growth is considered from a nutritional viewpoint. First, there is the delivery of substrate to the fetal cell and, second, factors that control cellular uptake of nutrient. In experiments designed to restrict nutrient delivery there are fetal growth retardation, hypoinsulinemia, and a fall in circulating IGF levels. For example, maternal rats fasted for 3 days at the end of pregnancy had offspring that were lighter, had lower plasma glucose, insulin, and IGF levels, and reduced cartilage metabolic activity (60,107). Fetal rat growth retardation induced by uterine artery ligation had similar results and was also associated with lowered concentrations of C-peptide in the amniotic fluid (108). In each case restriction of nutrient availability led to concordant changes in insulin, IGF cellular metabolism, and body growth but the causality of the changes cannot be unraveled. The opposite kind of experiment seeks to increase nutrient supply to the fetus. Chronic glucose infusion in the pregnant rat leads to fetal hyperinsulinemia and raised circulating IGF levels (55) but no increase of body size. Hyperalimentation of pregnant rats by gavage had no effect on body weight or plasma insulin or IGF levels of normal fetuses but interestingly reduced the mortality of fetuses growing in a uterine artery-ligated horn (109). Clearly the interpretation of attempts to influence delivery of nutrient to fetal cells by altering the maternal nutritional plane is as complicated as the approach of increasing fetal cellular nutrition by hyperinsulinemia discussed earlier. There is a consistency among the experimental results, however: increased delivery of fetal nutrient produces predictable hormonal and GF changes but has little effect on somatic growth, suggesting that the normal fetus grows at a near maximum rate. Such effects as are seen in fetal body weight occur in species with prenatal lipogenesis and are mainly due to the laying down of storage fat under the influence of insulin.

IV. CONCLUDING REMARKS

The evidence reviewed here has shown that the endocrinology of fetal growth is very different from that operating postnatally. Pituitary hormones play little part in stimulating growth of the lean body mass or skeleton although GH may be involved, in some as yet ill-defined way in the ontogeny of the fetal pancreatic islet and insulin secretion. Insulin is important because it stimulates fetal cellular anabolism, but acts in a permissive manner: with too little insulin growth is inhibited and with too much growth proceeds at a genetically predetermined rate. Placental lactogen probably acts as a true growth-promoting hormone in the fetus; it stimulates both cellular metabolism and mitosis.

The part played by endocrine control mechanisms in the fetus has been set in context by an appreciation of the importance of locally acting tissue growth factors. Their part in fetal growth control is intimately bound up with the plane of nutrition experienced by the fetus. It is concluded that the simplest analysis that makes biological sense involves a consideration of hormones, tissue growth factors, and nutrition, not hierarchically but as mutually interacting variables.

ACKNOWLEDGMENTS

I am grateful to Dr. D. J. Hill for helpful discussions. Work cited here from the author's laboratory was supported by the Medical Research Council, the Wellcome Trust, the Hawley Trust, the Nuffield Foundation, the British Diabetic Association, and the Yorkshire Cancer Research Campaign.

REFERENCES

1. T. L. Blundell, S. Bedarkar, E. Rinderknecht, and R. E. Humbel, *Proc. Natl. Acad. Sci. U.S.A.* **75,** 180 (1978).
2. M. D. Waterfield, T. Scrace, N. Whittle, P. Stroobant, A. Johnsson, A. Wasteson, B. Westermark, C. H. Heldin, J. S. Huang, and T. Deuel, *Nature (London)* **304,** 35 (1983).
3. J. V. Tricoli, L. B. Rall, J. Scott, G. I. Bell, and T. B. Shows, *Nature (London)* **310,** 784 (1984).
4. R. D. G. Milner, *Nestle Nutr. Workshop, 14th* (J. C. Waterlow, ed.), in press.
5. R. D. G. Milner, *In* "Nutrition and Metabolism of the Fetus and Infant" (H. K. A. Visser, ed.), p. 3. Nijhoff, The Hague, 1979.
6. R. D. G. Milner, *In* "Fetal Physiology and Medicine" (R. W. Beard and P. W. Nathanielsz, eds.) 2nd Ed., p. 153. Dekker, New York, 1984.
7. D. J. Hill and R. D. G. Milner, *Pediatr. Res.* **19,** 879 (1985).
8. D. J. Hill and R. D. G. Milner, *In* "Recent Advances in Perinatal Medicine" (M. L. Chiswick, ed.), No. 2, p. 79. Churchill Livingstone, Edinburgh, 1985.
9. D. J. Hill, A. J. Strain, and R. D. G. Milner, *In* "Oxford Reviews of Reproductive Biology" (J. R. Clarke, ed.), No. 9. Oxford Univ. Press, London and New York, 1987.
10. R. K. Kalkhoff and H.-J. Kim, *In* "Pregnancy, Metabolism, Diabetes and the Fetus" (R. W. Beard and J. J. Hoet, eds.), Ciba Foundation Symposium No. 63, p. 29. Excerpta Med., Amsterdam, 1979.
11. E. Diczfalusy, *Acta Endocrinol. (Copenhagen)* **61,** 649 (1969).
12. D. Schiff, E. Colle, and L. Stern, *N. Engl. J. Med.* **287,** 119 (1972).
13. J. Pedersen, B. Bojsen-Moller, and H. Poulsen, *Acta Endocrinol. (Copenhagen)* **15,** 33 (1954).
14. S. L. Kaplan, M. M. Grumbach, and T. H. Shephard, *J. Clin. Invest.* **51,** 3080 (1972).
15. M. M. Grumbach and S. L. Kaplan, *In* "Foetal and Neonatal Physiology" (R. S. Comline, K. W. Cross, G. S. Dawes, and P. W. Nathanielsz, eds.), p. 462. Cambridge Univ. Press, London and New York, 1973.
16. D. F. Swaab and W. J. Honnebier, *Br. J. Obstet. Gynaecol.* **80,** 589 (1973).
17. A. Jost, *Cold Spring Harbor Symp. Quant. Biol.* **19,** 167 (1954).
18. Y. Eguchi, *Endocrinology (Baltimore)* **68,** 716 (1961).
19. P. M. B. Jack and R. D. G. Milner, *Biol. Neonate* **26,**.195 (1975).
20. D. J. Hill, P. Davidson, and R. D. G. Milner, *J. Endocrinol.* **81,** 93 (1979).
21. B. Colenbrander, C. M. J. E. Van Rossum-Kok, H. W. M. Van Straaten, and C. J. G. Wensing, *Biol. Reprod.* **20,** 198 (1979).
22. G. C. Liggins and P. C. Kennedy, *J. Endocrinol.* **40,** 371 (1968).
23. G. C. Liggins, R. J. Fairclough, S. A. Grieves, T. Z. Kendall, and B. S. Knox, *Recent Prog. Horm. Res.* **29,** 111 (1973).
24. P. D. Gluckman, M. M. Grumbach, and S. L. Kaplan, *Endocr. Rev.* **2,** 363 (1981).
25. B. I. Posner, *Endocrinology (Baltimore)* **98,** 645 (1976).
26. P. D. Gluckman, J. Butler, and T. Elliot, *Endocrinology (Baltimore)* **112,** 1607 (1983).
27. L. J. Murphy, E. Urhovsek, and L. Lazarus, *J. Clin. Endocrinol. Metab.* **57,** 1117 (1983).
28. P. M. B. Jack and R. D. G. Milner, *J. Endocrinol.* **64,** 67 (1975).
29. I. Swenne, D. J. Hill, A. J. Strain, and R. D. G. Milner, *Diabetes* **36,** 288 (1987).
30. F. A. Van Assche, W. Gepts, and M. De Gasparo, *Biol. Neonat.* **14,** 374 (1969).
31. M. Bigazzi, R. Ronga, I. Lancranjan, S. Ferraro, F. Branconi, P. Buzzoni, G. Martorana, G. F. Scarselli, and E. Del Pozo, *J. Clin. Endocrinol. Metab.* **48,** 9 (1979).
32. B. Reusens, E. R. Kuhn, and J. J. Hoet, *Gen. Comp. Endocrinol.* **39,** 118 (1979).
33. M. J. O. Francis and D. J. Hill, *Nature (London)* **255,** 167 (1975).

34. Y. Sinha and W. Vanderlaan, *Endocrinology (Baltimore)* **110,** 1871 (1982).
35. G. F. Glasscock and C. S. Nicoll, *Endocrinology (Baltimore)* **109,** 176 (1981).
36. W. J. Honnebier and D. F. Swaab, *Br. J. Obstet. Gynaecol.* **81,** 439 (1974).
37. H. J. Anderson, *Acta Paediatr. Scand., Suppl.* No. 125, 1 (1961).
38. G. D. Thorburn, *In* "Size at Birth" (K. Elliott and J. Knight eds.), Ciba Foundation Symposium No. 27, p. 185. Elsevier, Amsterdam, 1974.
39. G. R. Kerr, I. B. Tyson, T. R. Allen, J. H. Wallace, and G. Scheffler, *Biol. Neonate* **21,** 285 (1972).
40. G. D. Thorburn, M. J. Waters, M. Dolling, and I. R. Young, *Proc. Aust. Physiol. Pharmacol. Soc.* **12,** 11 (1981).
41. M. J. Obregon, J. Mallol, R. Pastor, G. Morreale de Escobar, and F. Escobar de Rey, *Endocrinology (Baltimore)* **114,** 305 (1984).
42. N. Freinkel and B. E. Metzger, *In* "Pregnancy, Metabolism, Diabetes and the Fetus" (R. W. Beard and J. J. Hoet, eds.), Ciba Foundation Symposium No. 63, p. 3. Excerpta Med. Found., Amsterdam, 1979.
43. R. D. G. Milner, M. de Gasparo, G. R. Milner, and P. K. Wirdnam, *In* "Carbohydrate Metabolism in Pregnancy and the Newborn 1978" (H. W. Sutherland and J. M. Stowers, eds.), p. 132. Springer-Verlag, Berlin and New York, 1979.
44. R. D. G. Milner, *In* "Scientific Foundations of Paediatrics" (J. A. Davis and J. Dobbing, eds.), 2nd Ed., p. 701. Heinemann, London, 1981.
45. R. D. G. Milner and D. J. Hill, *Clin. Endocrinol.* **21,** 415 (1984).
46. P. V. Heitz, G. Kloppel, and W. H. Hacki, *Diabetes* **26,** 362 (1977).
47. G. Filippi and V. A. McKusick, *Medicine (Baltimore)* **49,** 279 (1970).
48. D. E. Hill, *Semin. Perinatol.* **2,** 319 (1978).
49. J. R. Girard, M. Rieutort, A. Kervran, and A. Jost, *In* "Perinatal Medicine" (G. Rooth and L. E. Brateby, eds.), p. 197, Almqvist & Wicksell, Stockholm, 1976.
50. J. M. Fletcher, J. Falconer, and J. M. Bassett, *Diabetologia* **23,** 124 (1982).
51. L. Picon, *Endocrinology (Baltimore)* **81,** 1419 (1967).
52. A. Ktorza, N. Nurjhan, J. R. Girard, and L. Picon, *Diabetologia* **24,** 128 (1983).
53. D. J. Hill, R. A. Sheffrin, and R. D. G. Milner, *Diabetologia* **23,** 270 (1982).
54. A. J. D'Ercole, C. L. Bose, L. E. Underwood, and E. E. Lawson, *Diabetes* **33,** 590 (1984).
55. E. Heinze, C. N. Thi, U. Vetter, and R. D. Fussganger, *Biol. Neonate* **41,** 240 (1982).
56. D. J. Hill and R. D. G. Milner, *Diabetologia* **19,** 143 (1980).
57. J. B. Susa, K. L. McCormick, J. A. Widness, D. B. Singer, W. Oh, K. Adamsons, and R. Schwartz, *Diabetes* **28,** 1058 (1979).
58. J. B. Susa, C. Neave, P. Sehgal, D. B. Singer, W. P. Zeller, and R. Schwartz, *Diabetes* **33,** 656 (1984).
59. S. L. Blethen, N. H. White, J. V. Santiago, and W. H. Daughaday, *J. Clin. Endocrinol. Metab.* **52,** 144 (1981).
60. D. J. Hill, M. Fekete, R. D. G. Milner, F. A. De Prins, and A. Van Assche, *In* "Insulin-Like Growth Factors/Somatomedins. Basic Chemistry, Biology and Clinical Importance" (E. M. Spencer, ed.), p. 345. de Gruyter, Berlin, 1983.
61. F. A. De Prins, D. J. Hill, M. Fekete, D. J. Robsen, N. R. J. Fieller, F. A. Van Assche, and R. D. G. Milner, *Pediatr. Res.* **18,** 1100 (1984).
62. A. L. Fowden and R. S. Comline, *J. Exp. Physiol.* **69,** 319 (1984).
63. V. R. Sara, K. Hall, M. Misaki, L. Fryklund, L. Christensen, and L. Wetteberg, *J. Clin. Invest.* **71,** 1084 (1983).
64. A. V. Thorsson and R. L. Hintz, *N. Engl. J. Med.* **297,** 908 (1977).
65. N. D. Neufeld, S. A. Kaplan, and B. M. Lippe, *J. Clin. Endocrinol. Metab.* **52,** 473 (1981).

66. D. J. Hill, C. J. Crace, A. J. Strain, and R. D. G. Milner, *J. Clin. Endocrinol. Metab.* **62,** 653 (1986).
67. C. J. Crace, D. J. Hill, and R. D. G. Milner, *J. Endocrinol.* **104,** 63 (1984).
68. A. Hendricks, F. De Pablo and J. Roth, *Endocrinology (Baltimore)* **115,** 1315 (1984).
69. C. A. Benzo and T. D. Green, *Anat. Rec.* **180,** 491 (1974).
70. A. Sandra and R. J. Przybylski, *Dev. Biol.* **68,** 546 (1979).
71. I. Fennoy, H. J. Eisen, and R. M. White, *In* "Insulin-Like Growth Factors/Somatomedins. Basic Chemistry, Biology and Clinical Importance" (E. M. Spencer, ed.), p. 357. de Gruyter, Berlin, 1983.
72. M. Maes, R. De Hertogh, P. Watrin-Granger, and J. M. Ketelslegers, *Endocrinology (Baltimore)* **113,** 1325 (1983).
73. P. S. Cooke, S. M. Russel, and C. S. Nicoll, *Endocrinology (Baltimore)* **112,** 806 (1983).
74. P. S. Cooke and C. S. Nicoll, *Endocrinology (Baltimore)* **114,** 638 (1984).
75. B. E. Posner, *Diabetes* **23,** 209 (1974).
76. R B. Steel, J. D. Mosley, and C. H. Smith, *Am. J. Obstet. Gynecol.* **135,** 522 (1979).
77. J. A. Whitsett and J. L. Lessard, *Endocrinology (Baltimore)* **103,** 1458 (1978).
78. J. A. Whitsett, C. L. Johnson, and K. Hawkins, *Am. J. Obstet. Gynecol.* **133,** 204 (1979).
79. N. Potau, E. Riudor, and A. Ballabriga, *Pediatr. Res.* **15,** 798 (1981).
80. Z. Hochberg, R. Perlman, J. M. Brandes, and A. Benderli, *J. Clin. Endocrinol. Metab.* **57,** 1311 (1983).
81. M. M. Grumbach, S. L. Kaplan, J. J. Sciarra, and I. Burr, *Ann. N.Y. Acad. Sci.* **148,** 501 (1968).
82. W. H. Daughaday, B. Trivedi, and M. Kapadia, *Endocrinology (Baltimore)* **105,** 210 (1979).
83. T. W. Hurley, A. J. D'Ercole, S. Handwerger, L. E. Underwood, R. W. Furlanetto, and R. E. Fellows, *Endocrinology (Baltimore)* **101,** 1635 (1977).
84. P. D. Gluckman, J. H. Butler, and T. N. Barry, *Pediatr. Res.* **19,** 620 (1985).
85. T. J. Merimee, J. Zapf, and E. R. Froesch, *J. Clin. Endocrinol. Metab.* **54,** 1101 (1982).
86. R. W. Furlanetto, L. E. Underwood, J. J. Van Wyk, and S. Handwerger, *J. Clin. Endocrinol. Metab.* **47,** 695 (1978).
87. C. Hubert, F. Mondon, and L. Cedard, *Am. J. Obstet. Gynecol.* **144,** 722 (1982).
88. W. N. Spellacy, *Clin. Obstet. Gynecol.* **16,** 298 (1973).
89. P. D. Gluckman, S. L. Kaplan, A. M. Rudolph, and M. M. Grumbach, *Endocrinology (Baltimore)* **104,** 1828 (1979).
90. M. Freemark and S. Handwerger, *Endocrinology (Baltimore)* **112,** 402 (1983).
91. S. O. Adams, S. P. Nissley, S. Handwerger, and M. M. Rechler, *Nature (London)* **302,** 150 (1983).
92. D. J. Hill, C. J. Crace, and R. D. G. Milner, *J. Cell. Physiol.* **125,** 337 (1985).
93. R. A. Richman, M. R. Benedict, J. R. Florini, and B. A. Toly, *Endocrinology (Baltimore)* **116,** 180 (1985).
94. A. J. Strain, D. J. Hill, I. Swenne, and R. D. G. Milner, *J. Endocrinol.* **108,** Suppl., p. 142 (1986).
95. J. Hiriis-Nielsen, *Endocrinology (Baltimore)* **110,** 600 (1982).
96. J. Wurzel, J. Parks, J. Herd, and P. Nielson, *DNA* **1,** 251 (1982).
97. M. C. Robertson, R. E. Owens, J. A. McCoshen, and H. G. Friesen, *Endocrinology (Baltimore)* **114,** 22 (1984).
98. P. D. Gluckman, *In* "Oxford Reviews of Reproductive Biology" (J. R. Clarke, ed.), No. 8, p. 1. Oxford Univ. Press, London and New York, 1986.
99. A. J. D'Ercole, G. T. Applewhite, and L. E. Underwood, *Dev. Biol.* **75,** 315 (1980).
100. A. J. D'Ercole, D. J. Hill, A. J. Strain, and L. E. Underwood, *Pediatr. Res.* **20,** 253 (1986).

101. D. J. Hill, A. Frazer, I. Swenne, P. K. Wirdnam, and R. D. G. Milner, *Diabetes* in press.
102. D. J. Hill, C. J. Crace, S. P. Nissley, D. Morrell, A. T. Holder, and R. D. G. Milner, *Endocrinology (Baltimore)* **117,** 2061 (1985).
103. A. Romanus, A. Rabinovitch, and M. M. Rechler, *Diabetes* **34,** 696 (1985).
104. M. E. Fant, H. N. Munro, and A. C. Moses, *Abstr. Annu. Meet. Endocr. Soc., 67th* Abstr. 66, p. 17 (1985).
105. N. C. Mills, L. E. Underwood, and A. J. D'Ercole, *Abstr. Annu. Meet. Endocr. Soc., 67th* Abstr. 1072, p. 268 (1985).
106. U. Vetter, J. Zapf, W. Heit, G. Helbing, E. Heinze, E. R. Froesch, and W. M. Teller, *J. Clin. Invest.* **77,** 1903 (1986).
107. M. Fekete, D. J. Hill, and R. D. G. Milner, *Biol. Neonate* **44,** 114 (1983).
108. F. De Prins, A. Van Assche, and R. D. G. Milner, *Biol. Neonate* **43,** 181 (1983).
109. F. A. De Prins, Ph.D. Thesis, Univ. of Leuven, Belgium, 1987.

5

The Role of Somatomedins in Fetal Growth

Vicki R. Sara
Department of Psychiatry
Karolinska Institutet
St. Göran's Children's Hospital
Stockholm, Sweden

I. CHARACTERIZATION

The somatomedins are a family of growth-promoting peptide hormones. This term was first introduced by the leading researchers in the field in 1972 (Daughaday *et al.*, 1972) and has been applied broadly to biological activities variously denoted as sulfation factor, thymidine factor, nonsuppressible insulinlike activity, and multiplication-stimulating activity. The first somatomedins to be characterized were isolated by Rinderknecht and Humbel (1978a, b). These peptides, being related to insulin, were called insulinlike growth factors 1 (IGF-1) and 2 (IGF-2). IGF-1 and IGF-2 are homologous single-chain peptides with intrachain disulfide bridges and consist of 70 and 67 amino acids, respectively. They share identical amino acids in 45 of their positions. Homology to proinsulin led Rinderknecht and Humbel (1978a) to propose that insulin and the somatomedins diverged from a common ancestor hormone before the appearance of the vertebrates. Later characterization of somatomedins A (Enberg *et al.*, 1984) and C (Svoboda *et al.*, 1980) revealed both to be identical to IGF-1, if possible deamidation differences are excluded. Several studies have suggested the existence of additional species of somatomedins (Blum *et al.*, 1986). Zumstein *et al.* (1985) characterized a variant form of IGF-2 which has a tripeptide substitution for Ser-33 and a 21-residue extension at the COOH-terminal (Fig. 1). All these peptides have been isolated from human serum or plasma. Carlsson-Skwirut *et al.* (1986) have also characterized IGF-2 as well as a truncated variant IGF-1 in the adult human brain (Fig. 1).

The somatomedins appear to be well conserved between species. Multiplication-stimulating activity (MSA), now termed rat IGF-2, isolated from rat liver cell-conditioned medium is closely homologous to human IGF-2, with five amino acid substitutions in the B and C domains (Marquardt *et al.*, 1981) (Fig. 1). Rat IGF-1 has an amino terminus sequence identical to that of human IGF-1 (Rubin *et al.*, 1982). Similarly, bovine serum contains IGF-1 identical to the human peptide, whereas bovine IGF-2 has three amino acid residues in the C domain which differ from human IGF-2 (Honegger and Humbel, 1986) (Fig. 1). The various forms of IGF-2 characterized are shown in Fig. 1. Differences in amino acid residues are most commonly found in the C domain. Residue 33 of rat IGF-2 sequenced from cDNA differs in two reports (Dull *et al.*, 1984; Whitfield *et al.*, 1984).

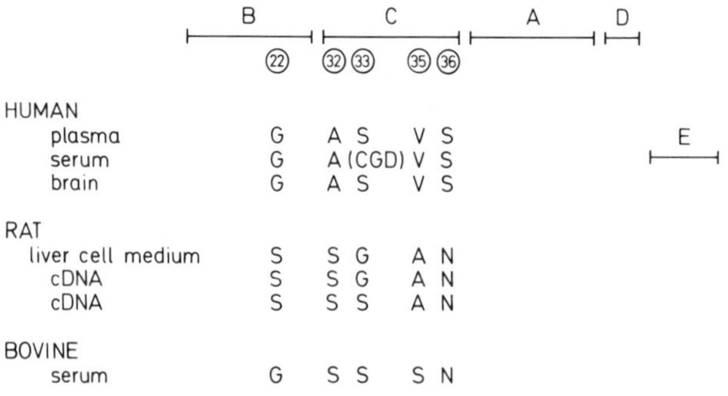

	B	C				A	D	
	22	32	33	35	36			
HUMAN								
plasma	G	A	S	V	S			
serum	G	A	(CGD)	V	S			E
brain	G	A	S	V	S			
RAT								
liver cell medium	S	S	G	A	N			
cDNA	S	S	G	A	N			
cDNA	S	S	S	A	N			
BOVINE								
serum	G	S	S	S	N			

Fig. 1. Amino acid residue differences found in IGF-2 forms isolated from various species. Differences are found in residues 22, 32, 33, 35, and 36. The variant IGF-2 isolated from human serum contains a tripeptide substitution at residue 33 and an E domain extension of 21 residues.

The identity of somatomedins in the human fetus has been a matter of controversy. Elevated somatomedin levels were detected in the human fetal circulation by a fetal receptor assay in spite of low or undetectable immunoreactive IGF-1 and IGF-2 (Sara *et al.*, 1981; Sara and Hall, 1984). These findings led to the proposal of an additional fetal form of somatomedin in the human fetus (Sara *et al.*, 1981). Using a fetal receptor assay to monitor activity during purification, the somatomedins present in the human fetal brain have been isolated and their amino acid sequences determined (Sara *et al.*, 1986). The majority of activity was attributed to a truncated variant of IGF-1. Additionally, IGF-2, which accounted for only a minor part of activity, was identified. These somatomedins appear to be the predominant species in the human fetus since two peptides with different isoelectric points corresponding to the truncated IGF-1 variant and IGF-2 have also been partially purified from human fetal serum (Carlsson-Skwirut *et al.*, 1987).

In other species, forms of both IGF-1 and IGF-2 have been identified prior to birth. In the rat, MSA or rat IGF-2 appears to be the predominant fetal form (Rechler *et al.*, 1979; Moses *et al.*, 1980), although an as yet uncharacterized form of IGF-1 is present in rat (Vileisis and D'Ercole, 1986) and mouse (D'Ercole and Underwood, 1980). While bovine fetal serum contains IGF-1 identical to that found in the adult as well as a variant form of IGF-2 (Honegger and Humbel, 1986), bovine colostrum additionally contains the truncated variant IGF-1 (Francis *et al.*, 1986). An IGF-1-like peptide has also been partially purified from chick embryo liver cells (Haselbacher *et al.*, 1980).

II. BIOSYNTHESIS

As reviewed in Sara and Hall (1984) and Underwood and D'Ercole (1984), all fetal tissues appear to synthesize somatomedins as evidenced by their presence in fetal tissue extracts as well as media harvested from fetal cells and, most elegantly, by the expression of the genes in fetal tissues. The somatomedin biosynthetic pathway is beginning to be elucidated. A single gene locus for IGF-1 and for IGF-2 has been identified on human chromosome 12 and the short arm of human chromosome 11 (11 p 14–11 p 15), respectively (Brissenden *et al.*, 1984; Tricoli *et al.*, 1984). The IGF-2 and insulin genes are contiguous (Bell *et al.*, 1985). The macrosomia of the Beckwith–Wiedeman syndrome is associated with a duplication of the 11 p 15 region which presumably results in overexpression of the IGF-2 gene (Tricoli *et al.*, 1984). Both genes are expressed during fetal life. In the human fetus, for example, Scott *et al.* (1985) reported enhanced expression of the IGF-2 gene in fetal as compared to adult tissues. These authors found abundant expression of IGF-2 transcripts in several fetal tissues including liver, kidney, adrenal, and muscle. Although only single gene loci have been identified, variation in the final protein product may arise from alternative RNA processing. Both tissue-specific as well as developmentally regulated RNA processing is now suggested. Several mRNA forms have been identified for both IGF-1 (Rotwein, 1986) and IGF-2 (Jansen *et al.*, 1985). Multiple mRNA forms occur during development (Rechler *et al.*, 1985; Soares *et al.*, 1985). Alternative RNA splicing pathways in the expression of the single gene confers versatility on the cell and allows for variation in the appearance of different IGF-1 and IGF-2 protein species during development. Tissue-specific expression appears to similarly arise from alternative RNA processing (Soares *et al.*, 1985).

The second possible level of regulation during biosynthesis arises from differential processing of the precursor proteins for IGF-1 and IGF-2 (Fig. 2). Sequence analysis of cDNA clones revealed that IGF-1 is synthesized as a precursor protein of 130 amino acids consisting of a prepeptide region of 25 residues and a COOH-terminal extension peptide of 35 residues (Jansen *et al.*, 1983). Both human and rat prepro IGF-2 consist similarly of a 24-residue presequence and a COOH-terminal extension of 89 residues (Bell *et al.*, 1984; Dull *et al.*, 1984; Whitfield *et al.*, 1984; Rechler *et al.*, 1985). Proteolytic processing at different cleavage sites in the prohormone will result in the generation of different peptides. Differential processing of the precursor proteins during development will provide a mechanism for producing different peptides at various developmental stages. For example, the truncated IGF-1 variant which predominates

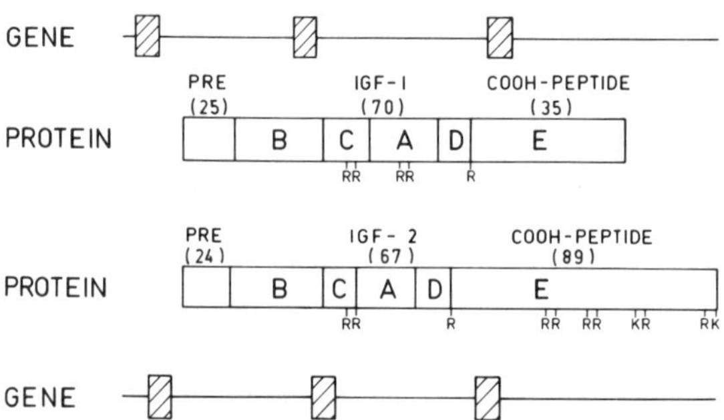

Fig. 2. Proposed regulatory sites in the somatomedin biosynthetic pathway. This schematic presentation of the precursor hormones, prepro IGF-1, and prepro IGF-2 shows possible cleavage sites at basic amino acid residues (R-arginine, K-lysine). The position of introns (▨) in the genes is shown as RNA splicing involves excision of the introns.

during human fetal life is most likely due to posttranslational modification of prepro IGF-1 (Sara *et al.*, 1986). Since there appears to be only a single IGF-1 gene locus, and the amino terminal difference does not correspond to a known intron/exon hinge region, it is likely that during fetal life the prepro IGF-1 is processed to the variant form rather than to IGF-1. Studies of biosynthesis in metabolically labeled cells suggest that the signal peptide is cleaved from the precursor by a microsomal peptidase and that processing of the prohormone occurs at the time of secretion from the cell (Yang *et al.*, 1985). After release from the cell, somatomedins are found coupled to carrier proteins. This has led Sara and Hall (1984) to suggest that the carrier protein may be a transmembranal peptidase which proteolytically processes prosomatomedin to somatomedin to which it remains tightly bound. Figure 2 shows the positions of introns in the genes for IGF-1 and IGF-2 as well as the possible processing sites in the precursor proteins. It is hypothesized that variability in somatomedin species arises at two regulatory levels in the biosynthetic pathway, namely, RNA and precursor protein processing, and that these mechanisms are developmentally regulated.

III. REGULATION

The mechanisms which regulate fetal somatomedin biosynthesis remain to be elucidated (for review see Sara and Hall, 1985). Unlike in the adult, fetal production is independent of growth hormone regulation. This is evidenced by the normal growth and somatomedin levels in human anencephalics (Sara *et al.*, 1981; Ashton *et al.*, 1985), decapitated fetal rabbits (Hill *et al.*, 1979), and hypophysectomized as well as growth hormone-infused fetal sheep (Brinsmead and Liggins, 1979; Parkes and Hill, 1985; Gluckman and Butler, 1985). Growth hormone begins to regulate somatomedin production at the time when growth becomes pituitary dependent, that is, approximately 6 months of postnatal life in man and 20 postnatal days in the rat. At the same time, the growth hormone-regulated large molecular weight somatomedin carrier protein appears (Hall and Sara, 1983). Although the growth hormone homologue, placental lactogen, may regulate fetal somatomedin biosynthesis in some species such as the rat (Adams *et al.*, 1983), this is unlikely to provide a major regulatory pathway in man (Sara and Hall, 1984). Other hormones such as insulin and growth factors such as epidermal growth factor have been implicated. However, in the immature organism, somatomedin biosynthesis may simply depend on substrate availability to the cell (Sara and Hall, 1984; Vileisis and D'Ercole, 1986). Such an elementary regulation of the autocrine and paracrine production of somatomedins during rapid growth early in development would allow a prompt cell response to alterations in nutritional availability.

IV. CIRCULATING FORMS

During or immediately following their secretion from the cell, the somatomedins are bound by carrier proteins and appear as large molecular weight complexes in the circulation (for review see Hintz, 1984). In the adult, the somatomedins occur predominantly as a high molecular weight complex of approximately 150,000 which is stable under neutral conditions (Martin and Baxter, 1985; Enberg, 1986). The 150,000 complex is growth hormone dependent and thus does not appear until toward the end of gestation in man (D'Ercole *et al.*, 1980) and around weaning in the rat (White *et al.*, 1982). During early development, the somatomedins circulate instead as smaller molecular weight complexes of around 40,000. After acidification, the 40,000 complex dissociates to reveal a binding protein of approximately 35,000 and the native 7000 somatomedin. The 35,000 binding protein isolated from human midterm amniotic fluid has been characterized by Póvoa *et al.* (1984a). Using a radioimmunoassay, Póvoa *et al.* (1984b) demonstrated a peak concentration of the 35,000 binding protein in midterm amniotic fluid as well as elevated levels in cord serum.

Although the biological role of the binding protein is not firmly established, its function is presumably to maintain a constant supply of somatomedins available to the cells as well as to regulate cellular responsiveness to the somatomedins. The carrier protein prevents somatomedin degradation and prolongs their half-life in the circulation. Since only cells capable of removing somatomedin from the binding protein may be able to respond, the binding complex may provide a means for selective cell action. The receptors on rapidly growing cells, for example, may display increased affinity for the somatomedins and thereby selectively be able to dissociate the peptide from its binding protein. De Vroede *et al.* (1986) have demonstrated that the release of binding protein from fibroblast monolayers modulates the availability of IGF-1 to the cell receptor. Additionally, binding to carrier proteins may provide a protective mechanism against the potent insulinlike action of the somatomedins (Meuli *et al.*, 1978).

Levels of somatomedins in the fetal circulation are generally measured after dissociation from the binding protein. Although acid–ethanol extraction is often used, this method does not result in complete separation, which may be achieved by acid gel chromatography. In the human fetus, low levels of IGF-1 and IGF-2 have been reported (Bennett *et al.*, 1983; Sara and Hall, 1984; Ashton *et al.*, 1985), whereas elevated levels of the truncated variant IGF-1 are suggested (Carlsson-Skwirut *et al.*, 1987). Both cord and fetal serum levels of IGF-1 correlate to fetal growth (Sara *et al.*, 1981; Ashton *et al.*, 1985). In contrast to man, rat IGF-2 is the major circulating form in the rat during early development (Moses *et al.*, 1980). IGF-2-like peptides also predominate in the fetal sheep circulation (Gluckman and Butler, 1983).

V. RECEPTORS

Somatomedin receptors are classified as Type I or Type II receptors (for review see Nissley and Rechler, 1984; Nissley *et al.*, 1985). The Type I receptor preferentially recognizes IGF-1 rather than IGF-2. At higher concentrations, insulin also cross-reacts in this receptor. The Type I receptor is structurally related to the insulin receptor, consisting of two extracellular α units with a molecular weight of about 130,000 and two transmembranal β units with molecular weight 98,000 joined by disulfide bridges. The Type II receptor preferentially recognizes IGF-2 and insulin does not cross-react in this receptor. The Type II receptor is a single-chain polypeptide with a molecular weight of approximately 250,000. Only the Type I receptor is down-regulated by the ligand. In contrast, the Type II receptor is up-regulated by insulin as a result of redistribution of receptors.

Somatomedin receptors have been demonstrated in a wide variety of fetal cells and tissues from several species (for review see Sara and Hall, 1984). Both Type I and Type II receptors have been identified in the fetus. However, the major receptor type appears to be both tissue and species specific. In the human fetus, for example, Type I receptors predominate in the brain, whereas only Type II receptors are found in the liver (Sara *et al.*, 1983). Similarly, whereas the human placenta contains Type I receptors (Chernausek *et al.*, 1981), mainly type II receptors are found in rat placenta (Perdue *et al.*, 1983). An additional receptor has been proposed to exist during early development in the fetal brain (Sara *et al.*, 1983), human placenta (Jonas and Harrison, 1985), and chick embryonic fibroblasts (Kasuga *et al.*, 1982).

VI. BIOLOGICAL ACTION

As reviewed in Sara and Hall (1984), somatomedins have been demonstrated to have a potent growth-promoting action on a wide variety of fetal cells and tissues *in vitro.* This involves not only their well-documented mitogenic action but also other anabolic effects such as stimulation of protein synthesis and glucose uptake and metabolism. It has also been suggested that the somatomedins may play a role in both initiating and maintaining cell differentiation (Florini and Ewton, 1981; Schmid *et al.,* 1984; Recio-Pinto *et al.,* 1984). McMorris *et al.* (1986), for example, have recently demonstrated IGF-1 to be a potent inducer of oligodendrocyte development and suggested a role in myelination of the nervous system.

The recent availability of biosynthetic IGF-1 has opened new and exciting possibilities for examining the biological actions of somatomedins *in vivo.* We have recently shown that the daily administration of biosynthetic IGF-1 to neonatal rats during their first weeks of postnatal life stimulates their growth and enhances maturation. This study has clearly demonstrated that IGF-1 stimulates growth during early development at a time when growth is independent of growth hormone.

VII. CONCLUSION

The somatomedins are a family of hormones consisting of IGF-1 and IGF-2 as well as their variant forms. A single gene locus has been identified for both IGF-1 and IGF-2. Flexibility in the production of the various somatomedin species resides in differential RNA processing as well as posttranslational modification of the prohormone. Both these mechanisms confer flexibility on the cell and enable the production of different proteins from a single DNA coding sequence. It is suggested that a programmed change in processing at either the RNA or precursor protein level during development determines the prevailing somatomedin peptide produced. In man the predominant species during fetal life appears to be the truncated IGF-1 variant as well as IGF-2. The somatomedins appear to be produced in all fetal tissues, where their primary action occurs presumably at a local level as autocrine or paracrine hormones. The biosynthesis of these peptides may simply be regulated by the availability of substrates to the cell, thus providing a sensitive mechanism for regulation of cellular growth. Whereas the truncated variant IGF-1 may be the major protein from the IGF-1 gene in the fetus, native IGF-1 occurs in the adult. Since only the latter form is growth hormone dependent, induction of the processing change could be triggered by growth hormone.

REFERENCES

Adams, S. O., Nissley, S. P., Handwerger, S., and Rechler, M. M. (1983). Developmental patterns of insulin-like growth factor-I and -II synthesis and regulation in rat fibroblasts. *Nature (London)* **302,** 150–153.

Ashton, I. K., Zapf, J., Einschenk, I., and MacKenzie, I. Z. (1985). Insulin-like growth factors (IGF) 1 and 2 in human foetal plasma and relationship to gestational age and foetal size during midpregnancy. *Acta Endocrinol. (Copenhagen)* **110,** 558–563.

Bell, G. I., Merryweather, J. P., Sanchez-Pescador, R., Stempien, M. M., Priestley, L., Scott, J., and Rall, L. B. (1984). Sequence of a cDNA clone encoding human preproinsulin-like growth factor II. *Nature (London)* **310,** 775–777.

Bell, G. I., Gerhard, D. S., Fong, N. M., Sanchez-Pescador, R., and Rall, L. B. (1985). Isolation of the human insulin-like growth factor genes: Insulin-like growth factor II and insulin genes are contiguous. *Proc. Natl. Acad. Sci. U.S.A.* **82,** 6450–6454.

Bennett, A., Wilson, D. M., Liu, F., Nagashima, R., Rosenfeld, R. G., and Hintz, R. L. (1983). Levels of insulin-like growth factors I and II in human cord blood. *J. Clin. Endocrinol. Metab.* **57,** 609–612.

Blum, W. F., Ranke, M. B., and Bierich, J. R. (1986). Isolation and partial characterization of six somatomedin-like peptides from human plasma Cohn fraction IV. *Acta Endocrinol. (Copenhagen)* **111,** 271–284.

Brinsmead, M. W., and Liggins, G. C. (1979). Serum somatomedin activity after hypophysectomy and during parturition in fetal lambs. *Endocrinology (Baltimore)* **105,** 297–305.

Brissenden, J. E., Ullrich, A., and Francke, U. (1984). Human chromosomal mapping of genes for insulin-like growth factors I and II and epidermal growth factor. *Nature (London)* **310,** 781–784.

Carlsson-Skwirut, C., Jörnvall, H., Holmgren, A., Andersson, C., Bergman, T., Lundquist G., Sjögren, B., and Sara, V. R. (1986). Isolation and characterization of variant IGF-1 as well as IGF-2 from adult human brain. *FEBS Lett.* **201,** 46–50.

Carlsson-Skwirut, C., Andersson, C., and Sara, V. R. (1987). Circulating forms of human fetal somatomedin. *Acta Endocrinol. (Copenhagen)* **114,** 37–40.

Chernausek, S., Jacobs, S., and Van Wyk, J. J. (1981). Structural similarities between human receptors for somatomedin C and insulin: Analysis by affinity labeling. *Biochemistry* **20,** 7345–7350.

Daughaday, W. H., Hall, K., Raben, M. S., Salmon, W. D., Van den Brando, J., and Van Wyk, J. J. (1972). Somatomedin: Proposed designation for sulphation factor. *Nature (London)* **235,** 107.

D'Ercole, A. J., and Underwood, L. E. (1980). Ontogeny of somatomedin during development in the mouse. Serum concentrations, molecular forms, binding proteins, and tissue receptors. *Dev. Biol.* **79,** 33–45.

D'Ercole, J., Wilson, D. F., and Underwood, L. E. (1980). Changes in the circulating form of serum somatomedin C during fetal life. *J. Clin. Endocrinol. Metab.* **51,** 674–676.

De Vroede, M. A., Tseng, L. Y.-H., Katsoyannis, P. G., Nissley, S. P., and Rechler, M. M. (1986). Modulation of insulin-like growth factor I binding to human fibroblast monolayer cultures by insulin-like growth factor carrier proteins released to the incubation media. *J. Clin. Invest.* **77,** 602–613.

Dull, T. J., Gray, A., Hayflick, J. S., and Ullrich, A. (1984). Insulin-like growth factor II precursor gene organization in relation to insulin gene family. *Nature (London)* **310,** 777–780.

Enberg, G. (1986). Purification of a high molecular weight somatomedin binding protein from human plasma. *Biochem. Biophys. Res. Commun.* **135,** 178–182.

Enberg, G., Carlquist, M., Jōrnvall, H., and Hall, K. (1984). The characterization of somatomedin A, isolated by microcomputer controlled chromatography, reveals an apparent identity to insulin-like growth factor I. *Eur. J. Biochem.* **184,** 117–124.

Florini, J. R., and Ewton, D. Z. (1981). Insulin acts as a somatomedin analog in stimulating myoblast growth in serum-free medium. *In Vitro* **17,** 763–768.

Francis, G. L., Read, L. C., Ballard, F. J., Bagley, C. J., Upton, F. M., Gravestock, P. M., and Wallace, J. C. (1986). Purification and partial sequence analysis of insulin-like growth factor-1 from bovine colostrum.*Biochem. J.* **233,** 207–213.

Gluckman, P. D., and Butler, J. H. (1983). "Parturition related changes in insulin-like growth factors I and II in the perinatal lamb. *J. Endocrinol.* **99,** 223–232.

Gluckman, P. D., and Butler, J. H. (1985). Circulating insulin-like growth factor-I and -II concentrations are not dependent on pituitary influences in the midgestation fetal sheep. *J. Dev. Physiol.* **7,** 405–409.

Hall, K., and Sara, V. R. (1983). Growth and somatomedins. *Vitam. Horm. (N.Y.)* **40,** 175–233.

Haselbacher, G. K., Andres, R. Y., and Humbel, R. E. (1980). Evidence for the synthesis of a somatomedin similar to insulin-like growth factor I by chick embryo liver cells. *Eur. J. Biochem.* **111,** 245–250.

Hill, D. J., Davidson, P., and Milner, R. D. G. (1979). Retention of plasma somatomedin activity in the foetal rabbit following decapitation *in utero. J. Endocrinol.* **81,** 93–102.

Hintz, R. L. (1984). Plasma forms of somatomedin and the binding protein phenomenon. *Clin. Endocrinol. Metab.* **13,** 31–42.

Honegger, A., and Humbel, R. E. (1986). Insulin-like growth factors I and II in fetal and adult bovine serum. Purification, primary structures, and immunological cross-reactivities. *J. Biol. Chem.* **261,** 569–575.

Jansen, M., van Schaik, F. M. A., Ricker, A. T., Bullock, B., Woods, D. E., Gabbay, K. H., Nussbaum, A. L., Sussenbach, J. S., and Van den Brande, J. L. (1983). Sequence of cDNA encoding human insulin-like growth factor I precursor. *Nature (London)* **306,** 609–611.

Jansen, M., van Schaik, F. M. A., van Tol, H., Van den Brande, J. L., and Sussenbach, J. S. (1985). Nucleotide sequences of cDNAs encoding precursors of human insulin-like growth factor II (IGF-II) and an IGF-II variant. *FEBS Lett.* **179,** 243–246.

Jonas, H. A., and Harrison, L. C. (1985). The human placenta contains two distinct binding and immunoreactive species of insulin-like growth factor-I receptors. *J. Biol. Chem.* **260,** 2288–2294.

Kasuga, M., Van Obberghen, E., Nissley, S. P., and Rechler, M. M. (1982). Structure of the insulin-like growth factor receptor in chicken embryo fibroblasts. *Proc. Natl. Acad. Sci. U.S.A.* **79,** 1864–1868.

McMorris, F. A., Smith, T. M., DeSalvo, S., and Furlanetto, R. W. (1986). Insulin-like growth factor I/somatomedin C: A potent inducer of oligodendrocyte development. *Proc. Natl. Acad. Sci. U.S.A.* **83,** 822–826.

Marquardt, H., Todaro, G. J., Henderson, L. E., and Oroszlan, S. (1981). Purification and primary structure of a polypeptide with multiplication stimulating activity from rat liver cell cultures. *J. Biol. Chem.* **256,** 6859–6865.

Martin, J. L., and Baxter, R. C. (1985). Antibody against acid-stable insulin-like growth factor binding protein detects 150,000 Mol WT growth hormone-dependent complex in human plasma. *J. Clin. Endocrinol. Metab.* **4,** 799–801.

Meuli, C., Zapf, J., and Froesch, E. R. (1978). NSILA-carrier protein abolishes the action of nonsuppressible insulin-like activity (NSILA-S) on perfused rat heart. *Diabetologia* **14,** 255–259.

Moses, A. C., Nissley, S. P., Short, P. A., Rechler, M. M., White, R. M., Knight, A. B., and Higa, O. Z. (1980). Increased levels of multiplication-stimulating activity, an insulin-like growth factor, in fetal rat serum. *Proc. Natl. Acad. Sci. U.S.A.* **77,** 3649–3653.

Nissley, S. P., and Rechler, M. M. (1984). Insulin-like growth factors: Biosynthesis, receptors and carrier proteins. *Horm. Proteins Pept.* **12,** 128–203.

Nissley, S. P., Haskell, J. F., Sasaki, N., De Vroede, M. A., and Rechler, M. M. (1985). Insulin-like growth factor receptors. *J. Cell Sci.* **3,** 39–51.

Parkes, M. J., and Hill, D. J. (1985). Lack of growth hormone-dependent somatomedins or growth retardation in hypophysectomized fetal lambs. *J. Endocrinol.* **104,** 193–199.

Perdue, J. F., Chan, J. K., Thibault, C., Radaj, P., Mills, B., and Daughaday, W. H. (1983). The biochemical characterization of detergent-solubilized insulin-like growth factor II receptors from rat placenta. *J. Biol. Chem.* **258,** 7800–7811.

Póvoa, G., Enberg, G., Jörnvall, H., and Hall, K. (1984a). Isolation and characterization of a somatomedin-binding protein from mid-term human amniotic fluid. *Eur. J. Biochem.* **144,** 199–204.

Póvoa, G., Roovete, A., and Hall, K. (1984b). Crossreaction of serum somatomedin-binding protein in a radioimmunoassay developed for somatomedin-binding protein isolated from human amniotic fluid. *Acta Endocrinol. (Copenhagen)* **107,** 563–570.

Rechler, M. M., Eisen, H. J., Higa, O. Z., Nissley, S. P., Moses, A. C., Schilling, E. E., Fennoy, I., Bruni, C. B., Phillips, L. S., and Baird, K. L. (1979). Characterization of a somatomedin (insulin-like growth factor) synthesized by fetal rat liver organ cultures. *J. Biol. Chem.* **254,** 7942–7950.

Rechler, M. M., Bruni, C. B., Whitfield, H. J., Yang, Y. W.-H., Frunzio, R., Graham, D. E., Coligan, J. E., Terrell, J. E., Acquaviva, A. M., and Nissley, S. P. (1985). Characterization of the biosynthetic precursor for rat insulin-like growth factor II by biosynthetic labeling, radiosequencing, and nucleotide sequence analysis of a cDNA clone. *Cancer Cells* **3,** 131–138.

Recio-Pinto, E., Lang, F. F., and Ishii, D. N. (1984). Insulin and insulin-like growth factor II permit nerve growth factor binding and the neurite formation response in cultured human neuroblastoma cells. *Proc. Natl. Acad. Sci. U.S.A.* **81,** 2562–2566.

Rinderknecht, E., and Humbel, R. E. (1978a). The amino acid sequence of human insulin-like growth factor I and its structural homology with proinsulin. *J. Biol. Chem.* **253,** 2769–2776.

Rinderknecht, E., and Humbel, R. E. (1978b). Primary structure of human insulin-like growth factor II. *FEBS Lett.* **89,** 283–286.

Rotwein, P. (1986). Two insulin-like growth factor I messenger RNAs are expressed in human liver. *Proc. Natl. Acad. Sci. U.S.A.* **83,** 77–81.

Rubin, J. S., Mariz, I., Jacobs, J. W., Daughaday, W. H., and Bradshaw, R. A. (1982). Isolation and partial sequence analysis of rat basic somatomedin. *Endocrinology (Baltimore)* **110,** 734–740.

Sara, V. R., and Hall, K. (1984). The biosynthesis and regulation of fetal somatomedin. *In* "Fetal Neuroendocrinology" (P. Gluckman and F. Ellendorf, eds.), pp. 213–229. Perinatal Press, New York.

Sara, V. R., Hall, K., Rodeck, C. H., and Wetterberg, L. (1981). Human embryonic somatomedin. *Proc. Natl. Acad. Sci. U.S.A.* **78,** 3175–3179.

Sara, V. R., Hall, K., Mizaki, M., Fryklund, L., Christensen, N., and Wetterberg, L. (1983). The ontogenesis of somatomedin and insulin receptors on the human fetus. *J. Clin. Invest.* **71,** 1084–1094.

Sara, V. R., Carlsson-Skwirut, C., Andersson, C., Hall, E., Sjögren, B., Holmgren, A., and Jörnvall, H. (1986). Characterization of somatomedins from human fetal brain:

Identification of a variant form of insulin-like growth factor I. *Proc. Natl. Acad. Sci. U.S.A.* **83,** 4904–4907.

Schmid, C., Steiner, T., and Froesch, E. R. (1984). Insulin-like growth factor I supports differentiation of cultured osteoblast-like cells. *FEBS Lett.* **173,** 48–52.

Scott, J., Cowell, J., Robertson, M. E., Priestley, L. M., Wadey, R., Hopkins, B., Pritchard, J., Bell, G. I., Rall, L. B., Graham, C. F., and Knott, T. J. (1985). Insulin-like growth factor-II gene expression in Wilms' tumour and embryonic tissues. *Nature (London)* **317,** 260–262.

Soares, M. B., Ishii, D. N., and Efstratiadis, A. (1985). Developmental and tissue-specific expression of a family of transcripts related to rat insulin-like growth factor II mRNA. *Nucl. Acids Res.* **13,** 1119–1134.

Svoboda, M. E., Van Wyk, J. J., Klapper, D. G., Fellows, R. E., Grissom, F. E., and Schleuter, R. J. (1980). Purification of somatomedin-C from human plasma: Chemical and biological properties, partial sequence analysis, and relationship to other somatomedins. *Biochemistry* **19,** 790–797.

Tricoli, J. V., Rall, L. B., Scott, J., Bell, G. I., and Shows, T. B. (1984). Localization of insulin-like growth factor genes to human chromosomes 11 and 12. *Nature (London)* **310,** 784–786.

Underwood, L. E., and D'Ercole, A. J. (1984). Insulin and insulin-like growth factors/somatomedins in fetal and neonatal development. *Clin. Endocrinol. Metab.* **13,** 69–90.

Vileisis, R. A., and D'Ercole, J. (1986). Tissue and serum concentrations of somatomedin-C/insulin-like growth factor I in fetal rats made growth retarded by uterine artery ligation. *Pediatr. Res.* **20,** 126–130.

White, R. M., Nissley, S. P., Short, P. A., Rechler, M. M., and Fennoy, I. (1982). Developmental pattern of a serum binding protein for multiplication stimulating activity in the rat. *J. Clin. Invest.* **69,** 1239–1252.

Whitfield, H. J., Bruni, C. B., Frunzio, R., Terrell, J. E., Nissley, S. P., and Rechler, M. M. (1984). Isolation of a cDNA clone encoding rat insulin-like growth factor-II precursor. *Nature (London)* **312,** 277–280.

Yang, Y. W.-H., Romanus, J. A., Liu, T.-Y., Nissley, S. P., and Rechler, M. M. (1985). Biosynthesis of rat insulin-like growth factor II. I. Immunochemical demonstration of a 20-kilodalton biosynthetic precursor of rat insulin-like growth factor II in metabolically labeled BRL-3A rat liver cells. *J. Biol. Chem.* **260,** 2570–2577.

Zumstein, P. P., Lüthi, C., and Humbel, R. E. (1985). Amino acid sequence of a variant pro-form of insulin-like growth factor II. *Procl. Natl. Acad. Sci. U.S.A.* **82,** 3169–3172.

Fetal and Neonatal Skeletal Growth and Mineralization

Richardus Ross, Francis Mimouni, and Reginald C. Tsang

Division of Neonatology
Department of Pediatrics
University of Cincinnati College of Medicine
Cincinnati, Ohio, U.S.A.

I. INTRODUCTION

The skeleton is one of the first recognizable tissues to develop during embryonic life. Skeletal development continues throughout gestation and on into postnatal life. Bone serves two major functions, namely, mechanical support and protection of the body as well as the maintenance of normal mineral metabolism. The control of these two major functions is referred to as skeletal homeostasis and mineral homeostasis, respectively (1). When growth ceases, bone does not become inert, but is continually remodeled. Both growth and remodeling of bone are dynamic processes brought about by cellular activity which may be influenced by a number of factors.

The processes of skeletal and mineral homeostasis are intimately related and a change in one clearly has effects on the other. Deficiencies of critical hormones at critical times can have an influence on both the structure and the mineral content of the skeleton. This interdependence of skeletal and mineral homeostasis occurs because the process of mineralization results in a mineral phase that is continuous with the matrix phase.

During embryonic life, differentiation of the skeleton is intimately controlled by *cell–matrix interactions* that are no less important later on in determining the pattern of skeletal development as growth proceeds. Disorders in the cellular components of bone as well as in matrix can result in a myriad of skeletal abnormalities. These disorders may be the result of disturbances in the level of critical hormones or inheritable inborn errors of metabolism, as well as teratogens. The mineralization of bone is also critically dependent on provision of appropriate amounts of calcium, phosphorus, and other ions. During intrauterine life, the fetus receives minerals via placental transfer from the maternal blood. Postnatally, bone minerals are obtained from the diet by intestinal absorption. Dietary availability, effective absorption, and appropriate utilization of bone minerals are all necessary prerequisites for normal skeletal and mineral homeostasis. The present report summarizes the pattern of normal skeletal development from embryo to early neonatal life and highlights the physiological basis for selected, representative, pathological disorders in fetal and neonatal bone.

II. EMBRYONIC SKELETAL DEVELOPMENT

The form of the fetal skeleton is determined by *mesenchyme* (both cells and extracellular matrix) that is interposed between the two primary germ layers, the ectoderm and the endoderm. The mesenchymal cells, together with ectodermal cells, secrete a matrix which is primarily composed of collagen and glycosaminoglycans. The composition of the matrix ultimately determines cellular migration and condensation in the early embryo. At the time of gastrulation, there is proliferation of mesoderm that becomes organized to form the somites, which are the first recognizable elements of the embryonic skeleton. They are made up of two types of tissue: first, sclerotome, which forms the vertebral column, and, second, the dermatomyotome, which contributes to the appendicular skeleton.

The extracellular matrix produced by mesenchymal cells has a profound impact on the progress of *cellular migration* and *differentiation* during development. Early on, *collagen* and *hyaluronic acid* are major components of the matrix. Collagen promotes somite organization (2), while hyaluronic acid together with collagen promote somite differentiation (3,4). Increased levels of hyaluronic acid in the extracellular space result in limited cell-to-cell contact and lead to cellular migration of mesenchymal cells (5–7). Later, hyaluronidase levels increase, causing a decrease in the intercellular space, thus limiting cellular migration and increasing cell aggregation; as a result, these mesenchymal cells begin to differentiate (8,9). Disruption in the normal pattern of matrix constituents can result in abnormal skeletal development. For example, persistence of high hyaluronic acid levels results in the inhibition of mesenchymal differentiation (10).

The unique feature of collagen is the polypeptide tertiary structure of its molecular subunit (11). A triple helix (or coil) of three polypeptide alpha chains (alpha 1 and alpha 2) gives the molecule a rodlike form. At least six types of genetically distinct forms of collagen have been identified but types I, II, and III are the most characterized and differ only in respect to the proportions of alpha 1 and alpha 2 chains that make up the triple helix. Type I collagen accounts for 90% of collagen in the body and is the main structural element in skin, tendon, and bone. Type II predominates in hyaline cartilage. Type III is widespread and seems to be the collagenous subunit of reticular fibers abundant in blood vessels, uterus, and synovial membranes.

III. CHONDROGENESIS

Mesenchymal condensation and subsequent differentiation of mesenchymal cells into chondroblasts and then to chondrocytes is a process which is intimately controlled by the temporal appearance of chondroitin sulfate (another glycosaminoglycan) and the disappearance of hyaluronate (12). This condensation and differentiation phase is the first stage in the development of the anlage of the appendicular skeleton.

The differentiated mesenchymal cells that serve as progenitor cells for *chondroblasts* and subsequently *chrondrocytes* (cartilage-forming cells) and also *osteoblasts* (bone-forming cells) are characteristically spindle shaped and have a high DNA, RNA, alkaline phosphatase, and glycogen content (13–15).

IV. OSTEOGENESIS

Osteogenesis is the process of bone formation and involves a specialized group of cells including chondrocytes, chondroclasts, osteoblasts, osteocytes, and osteoclasts. The localization of these various cell types in developing bone is dependent on the anatomical site of osteogenesis as well as the stage in the formation of mineralized bone. Their respective histological appearance and function will become evident in the following description of osteogenesis. Ossification occurs as two distinct processes, depending on the anatomical site. Intramembranous ossification is responsible for the circumferential growth in the cranial and facial bones and for the width of long bones, whereas endochondral ossification is responsible for the longitudinal growth of the long bones. Since these two processes share many similarities, the characteristics of the cells involved, the mineralization process, and the resorption process are dealt with in the following section describing intramembranous ossification.

A. Intramembranous Ossification

1. *Matrix Formation*

Bone is made by *osteoblasts* by a two-stage process involving matrix formation and its subsequent mineralization. The initial event of intramembranous ossification is the condensation of mesenchymal cells and their subsequent differentiation into osteoblasts. The matrix produced by osteoblasts consists of collagen and the proteoglycans, glycoproteins, and other components. Subsequent mineralization of this organic matrix is also controlled by the osteoblasts and involves the deposition of amorphous calcium phosphate in the matrix and its subsequent maturation to hydroxyapatite (see Section IV, A, 3). Osteoblasts are plump-appearing cells that display characteristics of active protein synthesis. These cells contain high levels of calcium and phosphate in mitochondria and intracellular vesicles and high levels of pyrophosphate, ATPase, and alkaline phosphatase.

As matrix is deposited in the extracellular space, some osteoblasts become incorporated into the mineralizing matrix and are termed *osteocytes.* These cells retain connections with osteoblasts lying at the bone surface via cell processes. These connections between cells are in the form of gap junctions (16,17) and allow extensive side-to-side contact for the exchange of various molecules. The appearance of osteocytes is variable depending on their location. On the bone surfaces, early osteocytes resemble osteoblasts, whereas osteocytes that are deeper into the mineralized bone are more flattened and have numerous cytoplasmic extensions that form contacts with other osteocytes as well as with the osteoblasts on the bone surface.

This variable histological appearance of osteocytes is probably a reflection of altering function (18). A variety of functions have been attributed to the osteocyte, including osteolysis; in osteolysis, the osteocyte acts as a bone pump for bone fluid and is important in the long-term mineral exchange of bone with the extracellular space (1). The type of bone that is formed is referred to as *woven bone* and is characterized by the presence of random mineralized collagen fibrils.

2. *Disorders of Matrix Synthesis*

Various disorders arise from deranged matrix synthesis such that the progress of matrix maturation is disturbed leading to ineffective mineralization.

a. Osteogenesis imperfecta. Qualitative or quantitative abnormalities of collagen synthesis result in severe clinical disorders. *Osteogenesis imperfecta* is a typical example of bone collagen abnormality. This condition is probably the commonest of the inherited disorders of connective tissue which primarily affect the skeleton. A recent review of the disease provides a numeric classification correlating with the results of reported morphological, biochemical, and genetic studies of this disorder (19). The main clinical features of osteogenesis imperfecta are fragile bones, dwarfism, blue sclera, dentinogenesis imperfecta, and deafness. In view of the heterogeneity now known to exist in osteogenesis imperfecta, the biochemical studies reported cannot be unequivocally interpreted. However, in recent years specific molecular defects in type I collagen have been defined in a number of different forms of osteogenesis imperfecta. The common abnormality is a quantitative decrease in type I collagen. In type I disease, the total amount of collagen appears to be decreased, whereas in the type II disease, which has been the best defined biochemically, there are structural abnormalities in either the alpha 1 or alpha 2 chains of type I collagen (20,21). In one report, prenatal diagnosis of lethal perinatal osteogenesis imperfecta was made possible by the finding that collagen metabolism in amniotic fluid cells was abnormal: the synthesis of collagen was normal but amniotic fluid cells, in contrast to controls, retained a considerable proportion of the type I procollagen synthesized (22). The constituent pro-alpha chains of the type I procollagen that were secreted into the culture medium had altered electrophoretic mobilities (22). Better definition of the basic molecular defect in the various types of this disorder should be possible within the next few years, resulting in more accurate prenatal diagnosis and genetic counseling.

b. Vitamin C disorders. Ascorbic acid is an essential constituent of culture media for the normal ability of fetal bone to synthesize collagen (23). Ascorbic acid is a necessary cofactor for peptidyl proline and lysyl hydroxylases (24). The function of vitamin C is to provide reducing equivalents for the hydroxylation reaction. In the absence of vitamin C, formation of stable collagen molecules with *cross-linking* does not occur.

In *vitamin C deficiency* (25), because of the failure of normal bone matrix to form, the edges of the metaphyses may be drawn out into small spicules, which point throughout the diaphyses. This spur formation results from separation of the periosteal layer by blood and subsequent mineralization of tissue remnants. In the severest cases, the periosteum becomes almost completely separated from the bone by accumulation of blood as a result of the increased hemorrhagic tendency.

c. Mucopolysaccharidoses. These are rare disorders from the failure of mucopolysaccharide degradation and consequent accumulation in tissues (26). In the *Hurler* syndrome, the nonskeletal manifestations are severe and progressive with mental deterioration and early death; by contrast, in patients with *Morquio* syndrome, skeletal features predominate. Biochemically, the mucopolysaccharidoses differ from the inherited disorders of collagen in that they are disorders of breakdown rather than of synthesis. Indeed, there is lysosomal accumulation of "undigested" or incompletely "digested" mucopolysaccharides in a variety of cells. For example, in Hurler syndrome of autosomal recessive inheritance, which is caused by α-L-hyaluronidase deficiency, there is an intracellular and intralysosomal accumulation of short-chain mucopolysaccharides with L-iduronate at the nonreducing end. The various cells affected include those of fibroblastic origin, those of bone (chondrocytes and osteocytes), the Kupffer and parenchymal cells of the liver, and the nerve cells of the central nervous system. Mucopolysaccharidoses present difficult therapeutic problems. Treatment for symptoms in most cases, particularly in skeletal deformity, is all that is possible. Now that the enzyme defects are recognized in most mucopolysaccharidoses, two problems arise, namely, the possibility of antenatal diagnosis and of enzyme replacement in affected individuals.

3. *The Process of Mineralization of Bone*

It is generally accepted that bone mineral consists primarily of hydroxy apatite (Ca_{10} $(PO4)_6$ $(OH)_2$), probably deriving from octacalcium phosphate (Ca_8H_2 $(PO_4)_6{\cdot}5H_2O$) (27). Electron microscopy studies reveal that the bone mineral is associated with bone collagen in a highly ordered fashion (28). Currently the best model to account for the total crystal volume of fully mineralized bone is that of Smith (29), who proposed that the staggered tropocollagen molecules of collagen are arranged in a pentagonal array to form a five-stranded microfibril. Mineral is said to be deposited within the holes in the quarter-staggered array of the collagen molecules (400 Å long and 15 Å thick), as well as in the central core or cavity formed by the pentagonal array of tropocollagen molecules (see Fig. 1). Because the microfibrils that make up collagen fibrils also are in register, it is likely that the gaps between tropocollagen molecules in adjacent microfibrils are also in register and that these gaps serve as sites for a mineral phase continuous from one microfibril unit to the next. The presence of a continuous matrix and mineral phase in bone may explain the observation that normally mineral and matrix are simultaneously removed during the process of resorption.

The exact nature of the initial interaction between matrix and mineral is debated, but the presence of a layer of unmineralized collagen, or *osteoid,* between the osteoblasts and the underlying calcified bone predicates a lag period during which the unmineralized matrix matures to a form that is calcifiable. Once mature, the matrix rapidly becomes mineralized with amorphous calcium phosphate. Indeed, collagen, even in the absence of other matrix constituents, is calcifiable. It is presently unknown what specific characteristics of bone collagen facilitate calcification. One suggestion is that loss of water by bone collagen decreases the distance between adjacent collagen molecules and chains, allowing the correct spatial arrangement for mineralization (28).

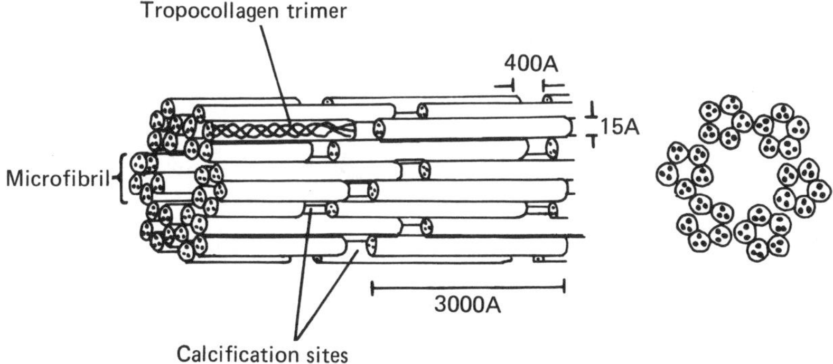

Fig. 1. Diagram to show the proposed three-dimensional structure of collagen. Calcification sites include the 400- by 15-Å holes in the quarter-staggered array of tropocollagen molecules as well as the central core within the microfibril. This model also suggests continuity of mineral from gap to gap contiguous microfibrils and can account for the continuous mineral phase in collagen-free bone. (Adapted from Ref. 34.)

a. Phospholipids and alkaline phosphatase. High levels of phospholipids also are found in the area of the calcification front. The most likely explanation is that the phospholipids are constituents of the membranes of intracellular vesicles which contain calcium and phosphate and which are extruded intact from the osteoblast at the calcification zone (30). Following degradation of the membranes, the released mineral forms the nucleation site for mineralization. In support of a role of matrix vesicles in the mineralization process is the observation that vesicles obtained from the epiphyseal plates contain not only apatite crystals but high levels of alkaline pyrophosphatase and ATPase (31). Hydrolysis of pyrophosphate by pyrophosphatases to inorganic phosphate within the vesicle could be the mechanism by which vesicles accumulate calcium and phosphate. The presence of osteoblast-derived extracellular vesicles is a consistent marker for the mineralization process and emphasizes that the mineralization process is under cellular control.

b. Disorders of alkaline phosphatase. *Hypophosphatasia* is a rare inborn error in bone metabolism occurring in 1 in 100,000 births (32). The severity of this disease is variable. The most severe form, inherited as an autosomal recessive trait, characteristically is apparent *in utero* or at birth. Patients present with severe rickets. Biochemically, there is subnormal circulating alkaline phosphatase activity, reflecting the generalized deficiency in activity of the tissue-nonspecific (bone, liver, kidney) alkaline phosphatase isoenzyme. Hypercalcemia, hypercalciuria, and nephrocalcinosis occur presumably because of the failure of calcium to deposit in bone. To date, there is no established medical therapy for this disease. However, one case of infantile hypophosphatasia has been recently treated successfully by weekly intravenous infusions of pooled normal plasma. Gradual and prolonged normalization of circulating alkaline phosphatase activity occurred. Electrophoretic and heat denaturation studies suggested that the alkaline phosphatase in serum was skeletal in origin. Serial radiographic and histological examination of bone demonstrated skeletal mineralization and the appearance of alkaline phosphatase activity in osteoblasts and chrondrocytes after infusions. It was therefore suggested that in this patient with infantile hypophosphatasia the structural gene for the tissue-nonspecific alkaline phosphatase isoenzyme was intact and could be expressed with marked physiological effect. Infantile hypophosphatasia may therefore result from absence or inactivation of a circulating factor that regulates the expression of the gene for tissue-nonspecific alkaline phosphatase.

Hereditary hyperphosphatasia is a rare disease of childhood resembling adult Paget's disease (33). Usually the first signs and symptoms become apparent in infancy or young childhood, but in one case the disease may have started *in utero*. The mode of inheritance appears to be autosomal recessive. Bowing of long bones and fractures are the most frequent signs. Histologically, the bone tissue shows signs of highly increased remodeling activity as in adult Paget's disease. In the long bones, cortical bone may be replaced by trabecular bone. Serum calcium and phosphate concentrations are normal but alkaline phosphatase is markedly elevated to 20–40 times the normal concentration. The pathogenesis of the disease is unknown but treatment with synthetic human calcitonin has been very promising.

4. *The Process of Bone Resorption*

The woven bone, formed by the action of osteoblasts, is subsequently resorbed by *osteoclasts* and new matrix is deposited by osteoblasts. This matrix is laid down in a polarized fashion and, when mineralized, is referred to as *lamellar bone*. The osteoclasts, responsible for the removal of calcified bone (both mineral and matrix), are short-lived, mobile, multinucleated giant cells which are one of the largest cells in the body (18). They are apposed to the bone surface and are characterized by a ruffled border consisting of numerous cytoplasmic extensions which are seen to infiltrate the disintegrating bone surface. Osteoclasts differentiate from *monocyte-macrophage* cells of the hemopoietic system. It has been suggested that at least on the endosteal surface of bone osteoclasts are *precursors of osteoblasts* (34).

The resorption of bone is necessary for the conversion of woven bone to lamellar bone during growth, a process referred to as *modeling,* as well as in the *remodeling* of bone during later life. The resorption process involves the hydrolysis of collagen as well as the dissolution of bone mineral. The process of bone resorption is under the control of the osteoclast. There is evidence that the ruffled border of the osteoclasts is important in osteoclastic resorption since this border is always in contact with the underlying bone surface (35). There is little information known regarding the chemical composition of the ruffled border because of the difficulties in obtaining sufficient isolated osteoclasts for biochemical metabolic studies. In the same way that, during mineralization, osteoblastic mitochondria are seen to contain electron-dense granules, during states of increased bone resorption osteoclasts appear to specifically accumulate similar granules in the mitochondria adjacent to the ruffled border (36). These observations suggest that the mitochondria are involved in the transport of calcium from the bone to blood by accumulating calcium as it enters the cell from the resorbing surface and discharging it on the opposite side of the cell (34).

Lysosomes are membrane-bound vesicles that are readily observed in osteoclasts and contain numerous hydrolytic enzymes that are active at neutral to acid pH ranges. *In vitro* culture of bone, following stimulation of bone resorption by parathyroid hormone (37), leads to increased release of lysosomal enzymes into the culture medium, though this effect of PTH is likely to be indirect since isolated lysosomes *in vitro* do not respond in this fashion. Since acid proteases will not cleave native collagen but will hydrolyze partially denatured collagen, lysosomes are likely to participate in the final hydrolysis of partially digested collagen (38). A number of collagenases have been partially purified from bone and parathyroid hormone has been shown to increase the release of collagenase activity from bone cells (39–41). Phosphoprotein phosphatase is another enzyme isolated from bone that has been linked to the bone resorptive process (42). This enzyme hydrolyzes phosphate groups from serine and other residues in proteins. Since, during the mineralization process, an early step is the formation of covalent bonds between phosphate groups and matrix, this enzyme could be involved in the initial demineralization process. The enzyme brings about a considerable increase in the rate of bone destruction when incubated along with collagenase *in vitro* (43). A likely model for osteoclastic resorption is that osteoclasts secrete collagenase, carbonic acid, and acid phosphatase, which partially decalcify and hydrolyze the organic matrix. The bone fragments are ingested by the cell and taken up by lysosomes, in which more complete digestion and decalcification takes place (34).

Infantile malignant *osteopetrosis* (44,45) is a rare autosomal recessive disorder characterized by dense sclerotic fragile radiopaque bones and associated hematological and neurological abnormalities. Osteopetrosis is thought to result from dysfunction of osteoclasts, the multinucleated giant cells that resorb bone and mineralized cartilage. Defective bone resorption by osteoclasts, in the presence of normal bone formation by osteoblasts, results in the deposition of excessive mineralized osteoid and cartilage. Encroachment on bone marrow spaces leads to extramedullary hematopoiesis and hypersplenism, resulting in anemia, thrombocytopenia, and leukoerythroblastosis. Encroachment on cranial nerve foramina leads to cranial nerve palsies, optic atrophy and blindness, and deafness. The disorder is lethal, with death usually occurring in infancy or early childhood. Successful bone marrow transplantation has been reported in two cases. Pretransplantation bone histomorphometry reveals small marrow spaces, rare marrow elements, increased number of osteoclasts, and absence of bone resorption. After transplantation, osteoclasts actively resorb bone and medullary cavities contain normal bone marrow. If performed early in the course of the disease, bone marrow transplantation leads to progressively improving vision, hearing, growth, and development.

B. Endochondral Ossification

1. *Normal Physiology*

In contrast to intramembranous ossification, endochondral ossification is the process by which bones grow in length and continues until the epiphyses fuse and growth ceases. The cell types responsible for this process are the same as those involved in intramembranous ossification except for the involvement of *chondroblasts* and *chondrocytes* (cartilage-forming cells). The cycle of woven bone formation followed by lamellar bone formation also occurs in endochondral ossification. Once a cartilagenous anlage of the bone is formed, chondroblasts in the center flatten and proliferate in a polarized fashion parallel to the long axis of the bone. These cells form the *proliferative zone of chondrocytes* or the *active growth plate* (see Figs. 2 and 3). New cells are formed between the proliferative zone and the center of the anlage that synthesize and secrete collagen and mucopolysaccharides. After this synthesis phase, the cells hypertrophy and demonstrate characteristics consistent with increased mem-

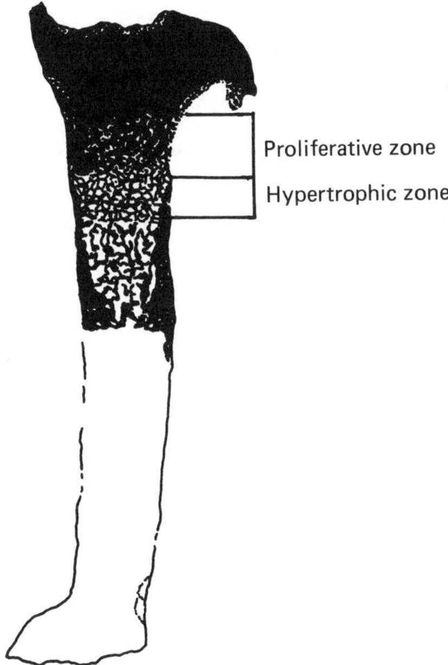

Fig. 2. Schematic diagram of a typical light micrograph of one epiphysis of a 21-day fetal rat tibia. Chondrocytes in the proliferative zone differentiate into hypertrophic chondrocytes in the hypertrophic zone. The cartilage martrix is subsequently resorbed by chondroclasts.

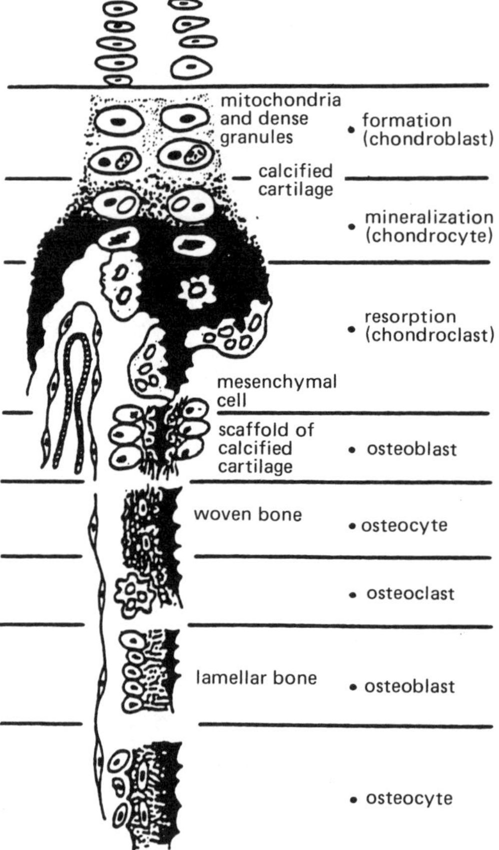

Fig. 3. The sequence of events at the epiphyseal growth plate. (From Ref. 34.)

brane synthesis and accumulation of mitochondrial calcium and phosphate. These cells soon lose their mitochondrial mineral at a time coincident with the appearance of electron-dense membrane-bound vesicles (46) that are rich in the enzymes alkaline phosphatase, pyrophosphatase, and ATPase. Most of the hypertrophic chondrocytes degenerate at the onset of calcification of cartilage but some survive to be transformed into osteoblast cells (47).

As previously described, extracellular vesicles containing calcium and phosphate appear to be the nucleation sites for amorphous calcium phosphate deposition (48). This calcification occurs mainly in the longitudinal cartilagenous septa *(trabeculae)* between the columns of cells rather than in the transverse septa between the cells (this area is referred to as the *zone of provisional calcification*). The next phase of bone formation is initiated by the invasion by capillaries of the spaces between the bars of calcified cartilage. Endothelial cells resorb the nonmineralized transverse septa and these channels are enlarged by the resorptive action of chondroclasts on the mineralized longitudinal septa. The chondroclasts arise from primitive mesenchymal cells on the diaphyseal side of the growth plate and are indistinguishable in appearance from osteoclasts.

Primitive mesenchymal cells also give rise to osteoblasts which lay down woven bone on their surfaces in an entirely random fashion. The trabeculae of calcified cartilage become surrounded by woven bone and constitutes the *primary spongosia*. This is subsequently resorbed by osteoclasts. The primary spongosia is finally replaced by lamellar bone and bone marrow following osteoblast and hemopoietic stem cell infiltration to form the *secondary spongosia*. Growth in length of the long bones continues to occur as a result of endochondral ossification.

2. *Skeletal Dysplasias*

Skeletal dysplasias result from abnormal embryonic skeletal development. Human skeletal dysplasias are a heterogeneous group of disorders that result in disproportionate short stature. There are more than 100 different forms of skeletal dysplasia, primarily classified on the basis of clinical and radiological changes (49). We will consider two distinct types of skeletal dysplasia as illustrative examples of this heterogeneous group of disorders.

In *achondroplastic dwarfism* there is a primary abnormality of endochondral bone growth with apparently normal membranous bone growth (50). The disorder is autosomal dominant. In the majority of individuals with achondroplasia, the growth plates, resting chrondrocytes, and bone appear normal histologically and ultrastructurally. At the periphery of the growth plate, one can see overgrowth of the membranous bone around the endochondral bone, producing the cupped appearance which is seen radiographically (50). There have been some preliminary reports suggesting a molecular abnormality in the type II collagen gene in achondroplasia, but neither qualitative nor quantitative abnormalities of type II collagen in achondroplastic cartilage have yet been described and these molecular studies have not been confirmed by others (51).

Thanatophoric dysplasia occurs in approximately 1 out of 15,000 deliveries (50). Individuals with this disorder have severe short-limbed dwarfism with marked narrowing of the chest. They usually die in the neonatal period with few surviving past a few months of life. Bone biopsy shows a very abnormal growth plate with marked spicule formation at the periphery and disruption with fibrous bands. These fibrous bands appear to be embryonic mesenchymal-like tissue which forms a network around the growth plate. There is a persistence of type III collagen in the growth plate of these individuals, whereas normal cartilage and bone do not contain any type III collagen. Thus, the basic abnormality in thanatophoric dysplasia may be the persistence of embryonic mesenchyme interrupting normal endochondral ossification (50).

C. Comparison of Intramembranous and Endochondral Ossification

The preceding discussion demonstrates that intramembranous and endochondral ossification are similar in all respects except that in endochondral ossification there is a prior stage of calcified cartilage whereas there is none in intramembranous ossification. In endochondral bone growth, there appears to be a close "coupling" between chondrocyte proliferation and differentiation to hypertrophic chondrocytes and the resorption of the mineralized cartilage. This coupling ensures that the epiphyseal growth plate does not widen during active growth.

Growth in width of long bones occurs by apposition of new bone at the periosteal surface by osteoblasts and resorption of the endosteal surface by osteoclasts in a fashion similar to the process of intramembranous ossification. The modeling of bone by endosteal resorption and periosteal apposition is *not* a coupled process and differs from remodeling in that the appositional rate is much faster during growth than that found in the adult. This leads to an extremely high bone turnover rate in growing animals.

To summarize, woven bone is laid down directly in matrix during intramembranous ossification or as a replacement of mineralized cartilage in endochondral ossification (see Section IV,B) by the nonpolarized and uncoordinated action of osteoblasts and occurs rapidly and diffusely. Woven bone is the bone that is produced at all locations where bone did not previously exist and resembles mineralization of cartilage. Lamellar bone, however, is only formed following osteoclastic resorption of previously laid down woven bone and is characterized by a regular and symmetrical alignment of collagen fibrils. Embryonic bone is almost entirely woven in character. Woven bone is the only form of bone that can be maintained in tissue culture. This type of bone is subject to chemical and physical influences (see Section V) but is relatively *refractory* to hormonal regulation. Differences in the type of bone and its responsiveness to hormonal regulation lead to a confusion in the interpretation of factors which influence bone formation.

V. CONTROL OF SKELETAL HOMEOSTASIS

Adult bone is continually "remodeled," in contrast to the "modeling" described earlier, by the processes of resorption by osteoclasts and bone formation by osteoblasts. Since the net rate at which skeletal mass is gained or lost is slow compared to absolute rates of the formation and resorption, these processes must, therefore, be closely coupled (52). The mechanism by which coupling is achieved is thought to involve factors elaborated by bone cells that have a stimulatory or inhibitory effect on other bone cell types. For example, during bone resorption by osteoclasts, a factor is released that causes chemotaxis (unidirectional migration) of osteoblastlike cells (53). However, during growth, bone formation exceeds resorption, resulting in an increase in skeletal mass, but nothing is known of the mechanism for this "uncoupled" state.

There is little direct evidence of the roles of fetal/maternal hormones in skeletal development *in utero*. However, most *in vitro* methods used to study bone formation have utilized fetal or neonatal tissue explants that are predominantly woven bone. As a result, a number of factors, both systemic and local, have been shown to influence bone growth and it is likely that fetal and neonatal bone growth is regulated by the interaction among a wide variety of these factors.

A. Parathyroid Hormone

There is much evidence that parathyroid hormone (PTH) increases bone resorption by stimulating the activity of osteoclasts and possibly osteocytes. However, there is also evidence that PTH influences the activity of the osteoblasts and stimulates bone formation (34).

The parathyroid glands develop during embryonic life from the third and fourth branchial pouches around the eighth week of intrauterine life in the human. Secretion of bioactive parathyroid hormone does not occur until after the tenth week of intrauterine life (54). However, there is very little information regarding the role of the parathyroid hormone in either skeletal growth or calcium homeostasis *in utero*. Fetal guinea pig parathyroid glands secrete PTH that can resorb adjacent bone (55) and injections of parathyroid extract cause hypercalcemia and hyperphosphatemia to develop in fetal dogs (56).

In adult bone, PTH stimulates bone resorption, and a phase of bone resorption always precedes a phase of new bone formation. PTH increases bone formation *in vivo* (57), and enhanced rates of bone formation have also been shown in patients with hyperparathyroidism (58,59). In contrast, cultured bone, which is primarily woven bone, responds to parathyroid hormone with a decrease in bone collagen synthesis (60). Despite the apparent inhibitory effects of PTH on collagen synthesis by osteoblasts, it is possible that, *in vivo*, PTH has an indirect effect that is modulated by coupling factors that are released in response to osteoclastic bone resorption. The apparent discrepency between *in vitro* and *in vivo* effects may be the result of variable populations of active bone cell types in each situation studied, since PTH stimulates lysosomal activity in osteoclastlike cells and inhibits collagen synthesis and alkaline phosphatase in cultured osteoblasts (61).

The major resulting osteoclastic action of PTH on bone explains the finding of diffuse demineralization, subperiosteal resorption of the phalanges, and occasionally osteitis fibrosa and spontaneous fractures that are found in *neonatal hyperparathyroidism* (62). This condition may be transient, or primary, with occasional familial patterns compatible with autosomal recessive inheritance. It is usually due to chief-cell hyperplasia rather than parathyroid adenoma. Laboratory findings include hypercalcemia, hypophosphatemia, hyperphosphatasia, hypercalciuria, and phosphaturia. Interestingly, neonatal hyperparathyroidism may be secondary to maternal hypoparathyroidism or to other causes of chronic maternal hypocalcemia (63). In such cases, neonatal hypercalcemia is an inconstant finding, the etiology of which is poorly understood.

B. Mineral Ions

Many years ago, it was found that phosphate lowers plasma calcium concentration when administered to humans with hyperparathyroidism (64). Subsequent work in animals and humans has shown that phosphate stimulates osteoblastic activity, new bone collagen synthesis, and deposition of calcium in sites of new bone formation (65–67). *In vitro* studies have also shown the importance of phosphate in bone formation in culture. Phosphate stimulates bone collagen synthesis and bone mineralization (68) but inhibits bone resorption. Using hypophosphatemic rats, high *in vivo* concentrations of phosphate were related to rapid rates of skeletal growth during development. Conversely, low phosphate concentrations were associated with impaired bone formation (69). Since renal synthesis of $1,25(OH)_2D$ is inversely related to plasma phosphate concentrations, this impaired bone formation may have been the result of increased resorption by $1,25(OH)_2D$. The principal effect of phosphate is on the synthesis and secretion of bone collagen. It has little direct effect on cartilage (70). In addition, phosphate is an *obligatory constituent* of hydroxyapatite, whereas calcium can be replaced by other ions (28). These results are consistent with a primary role of phosphate in the initiation of mineralization of collagen, and phosphorus deficiency has been shown to play an important role in the pathogenesis of rickets.

In vitro, decreasing medium calcium concentrations results in decreased growth and mineralization of the shaft of the bone. Cartilage growth is only slightly inhibited. These results suggest that adequate provision of calcium locally is important for chondroclast maturity (see Section V, C, 2). A low-calcium diet in many species leads to osteopenia. In humans, the effects of calcium deficiency on bone metabolism are uncertain. In adults, dietary calcium deficiency is associated with increased secretion of parathyroid hormone and increased bone resorption. In children, calcium deficiency has been described in rural black populations in South Africa (71). These children have radiological, clinical, biochemical, and histological features of rickets with normal serum concentration of 25-hydroxyvitamin D. A calcium-supplemented diet without vitamin D therapy heals the rickets of these children (72). This, associated with the very low dietary calcium intake in these patients (about 125 mg of calcium per day), supports the thesis that dietary calcium deficiency may lead to osteomalacia in humans.

C. Vitamin D

1. *Physiology*

It has long been known that vitamin D is necessary for both the growth and mineralization of the skeleton. During the last two decades, considerable advances have been made in understanding vitamin D metabolism. It is now clear that for vitamin D to exert its biological activity, it first undergoes a series of biotransformations, first in the liver to form 25-hydroxyvitamin D (25(OHD)), the major circulating form, and thereafter in the kidney to 1,25-dihydroxyvitamin D (1,25$(OH)_2$D) or to 24,25-dihydroxyvitamin D (24,25$(OH)_2$D). A myriad of other metabolites subsequently are produced by side-chain cleavage and these additional pathways are regarded as steps in the inactivation and elimination of the hormone.

1,25$(OH)_2$D is the most active metabolite in assays of intestinal calcium transport and bone calcium mobilization, and its synthesis is tightly regulated by calcium, phosphate, and PTH (for review see Ref. 73). The molecular basis for 1,25$(OH)_2$D action is now partly understood. Available evidence suggests that 1,25$(OH)_2$D acts in a fashion analogous to other steroid hormones, in that it is bound to an intracellular "receptor" protein which is involved in the translocation of the steroid to the nucleus. Subsequently, messenger RNAs are induced that code for specific functional proteins, for example, calcium-binding protein (CaBP). These intracellular receptor proteins have now been demonstrated in a variety of tissues including bone cells. Receptors for $1,25(OH)_2D$ have been found in bone cells (74) as well as in osteosarcoma cells (75). In cloned osteosarcoma cells, which demonstrate osteoblastlike activity, $1,25(OH)_2D_3$ has been shown to increase alkaline phosphatase activity (76) as well as production of osteocalcin, the major noncollagenous bone protein (77) (see Section V,D). In contrast, in bone culture, 1,25-dihydroxyvitamin D appears to act like parathyroid hormone in inhibiting collagen synthesis (78). What is currently unknown is whether vitamin D, by one of its active metabolites, has a direct effect on osteoblast function or whether vitamin D affects bone mineralization essentially by maintaining appropriate serum calcium and phosphate concentrations.

2. *Rickets*

A striking derangement of the growth plate occurs in vitamin D deficiency. Here chondroclasts fail to resorb the calcified cartilage matrix. As a result, the normal pattern of osteoblast infiltration, bone matrix deposition, and subsequent calcification to form woven bone does not occur. The width of the growth plate therefore enlarges. When vitamin D-deficient animals are given calcium and phosphate but no vitamin D, normal mineralization of the cartilage occurs followed by chondroclastic resorption of the mineralized matrix. It is thought that these derangements result from the requirement for vitamin D in maintaining local calcium ion concentrations at the growth plate which are necessary for *chondroclast maturation*. Therefore, the actions of vitamin D may be summarized by the regulation of the transport of calcium and phosphate in a manner which aims to maintain normal concentrations of these ions in body fluids and to make possible maximal availability of these ions from dietary sources. Failure of these functions, in particular failure of maintenance of inorganic phosphate concentrations because of impaired renal tubular conservation of phosphate, results in formation of unmineralized cartilage and bone matrix collagen. *Rickets* can therefore result not only from vitamin D deficiency but also from other physiological disturbances which interfere with calcium and phosphate transport despite an adequate presence of vitamin D (79). Rickets may be caused by the following factors.

a. Vitamin D deficiency (79,80). Poor sunlight exposure without vitamin D supplementation is still the major cause for rickets in infancy. Schematically, there are three stages in the progression of the disease. In stage 1, serum calcium concentrations are low (due to decreased intestinal absorption) and serum phosphorus concentrations are normal.

In stage 2, serum calcium concentrations are restored to normal because of compensatory hyperparathyroidism. However, serum phosphorus concentrations are low with hyperphosphaturia and hyperaminoaciduria from hyperparathyroidism. Typical rachitic bone features are present. In stage 3, both serum calcium and phosphorus concentrations are low and bone disease is florid because of the combined effect of mineral deficiency and hyperparathyroidism.

b. Rickets associated with hepatic disease (79–81). Decreased plasma 25-hydroxyvitamin D concentration and rickets may occur in liver disease presumably from vitamin D malabsorption (secondary to deficient bile salt secretion), decreased 25-hydroxylation of vitamin D, and decreased enterohepatic circulation of 25-hydroxyvitamin D.

c. Anticonvulsant osteomalacia (82). Phenobarbital and phenylhydantoin increase the hepatic catabolism of vitamin D and its metabolites; epileptic patients treated with these drugs may develop osteomalacia in the absence of appropriate D supplementation.

d. Rickets of prematurity. More than 30% of very low birth weight preterm infants may develop radiological signs of rickets (83). Infants most at risk are very immature and sick. Vitamin D deficiency does not seem to be the cause in most cases, and 25(OH)D concentrations (the best indicator of vitamin D status) usually are within the normal range (84). It is likely that mineral deficiency is the most important etiological factor (85,86). Indeed, calculated intakes of calcium and phosphorus in these infants are much lower than the fetal intrauterine requirements (normally up to 150 mg calcium/kg/day and 75 mg phosphorus/kg/day in the last trimester of pregnancy), particularly if the infants have been on total parenteral nutrition for extended periods. Using photon absorptiometry (which allows measurement of bone mineral content (BMC)) it has been shown that undermineralized bones occur when these infants receive standard proprietary formula (85,86). However, with adequate mineral supply, reduced BMC can be prevented. Other etiological factors in rickets of prematurity have been suggested, among them total parenteral nutrition-induced cholestasis (87) and hypersulfatemia (88), aluminum intoxication (89), and urinary calcium losses due to chronic furosemide therapy (90). Some preterm infants of low birth weight fed human milk may develop a very particular hypophosphatemic type of rickets (91). The mechanism of this rickets is believed to be due to the low phosphorus concentration in human milk, which in some very preterm infants may be insufficient. Phosphorus deficiency theoretically leads to increased 1,25$(OH)_2$D production and subsequent increased bone resorption leading to hypercalcemia, hypercalciuria, and rickets. The condition is reversible with phosphorus supplementation.

e. Hypophosphatemic rickets (92). Primary hypophosphatemic rickets occurs by X-linked dominant inheritance or may be sporadic. It is accepted that hypophosphatemia is caused by a primary defect in renal transport of phosphate. Rickets can be diagnosed in the first weeks of life, supporting the probable effect of vitamin D in fetal bone growth. Clinical features are similar to those of vitamin D deficiency rickets. Treatment of this disease consists primarily in phosphate supplementation; since phosphate administration may result in hypocalcemia and hyperparathyroidism, the addition of 1,25$(OH)_2$D has been shown to be useful by improving phosphorus and calcium absorption and by preventing secondary hyperparathyroidism.

f. Vitamin D-dependent rickets (93–97). Vitamin D-dependent rickets (VDDR) is a syndrome in which patients have clinical and biochemical features of vitamin D deficiency rickets but do not have vitamin D deficiency. It is often hereditary with autosomal recessive transmission. VDDR type I is characterized by low serum concentration of 1,25$(OH)_2$D and probably is a result of defective renal 1-α-hydroxylation of 25(OH)D. There is a prompt clinical and biochemical response to physiological amounts of 1-α-hydroxyvitamin D, an analog of 1,25$(OH)_2$D or of 1,25$(OH)_2$D therapy. In VDDR type II (or vitamin D-"resistant" rickets) the renal 1-α-hydroxylation is intact and biological rickets persists in spite of a supranormal concentration of 1,25$(OH)_2$D. Some of these kindreds also have total alopecia present from birth. In these patients, there is a defective nuclear uptake of 1,25$(OH)_2$D in cultured skin fibroblasts, suggesting a cellular defect in 1,25$(OH)_2$D receptors. Rickets is extremely difficult to treat in VDDR type II because of absent or diminished response to vitamin D metabolites. Recently, it has been shown that long-term parenteral calcium and phosphate infusions can cure rickets and promote normal mineralization in hereditary resistance to 1,25-dihydroxyvitamin D. This demonstrates that even in the absence of a normal 1,25$(OH)_2D_3$ receptor–effector system in bone cells, normal mineralization can be achieved in humans if adequate serum calcium and phosphate concentrations are maintained.

g. Renal osteodystrophy (98,99). Disordered mineral metabolism in renal failure may result in osteopenia, fractures, ectopic calcifications, and sustained secondary hyperparathyroidism. Renal osteodystrophy subsequently becomes resistant to vitamin D therapy in that the requirement of the vitamin to produce an effective sustained biological response is increased when compared to the usual dosage. It is likely that renal osteodystrophy is multifactorial. Indeed, there is coexistence of decreased intestinal calcium absorption which may be secondary to decreased $1,25(OH)_2D$ production in the kidney, secondary hyperparathyroidism, and acidosis.

D. Vitamin K and Osteocalcin

Between 10 and 20% of the noncollagenous protein in adult bone consists of a small molecular weight protein referred to as osteocalcin or bone gla protein (BGP). In common with the clotting factors, osteocalcin contains α-carboxyglutamic acid residues which are vitamin K dependent. Osteocalcin is detectable in embryonic bone and its appearance coincides with the onset of mineralization (100). This protein contains hydroxyproline and is produced by osteosarcoma cells in culture, suggesting that osteocalcin is a synthesis product of the osteoblast in normal bone. The precise function of osteocalcin is not known but certain characteristics, such as its ability to bind to hydroxyapatite but not amorphous calcium phosphate, suggest that it is involved in the mineralization process. The synthesis of osteocalcin in bone is modulated by vitamin n D (101), and osteosarcoma cells in culture have been shown to respond to 1,25-dihydroxyvitamin D with increased synthesis of osteocalcin (77). Both intracellular and serum osteocalcin concentrations are increased by $1,25(OH)_2D$ administration to rachitic animals. The bone levels of osteocalcin are dependent on the degree of mineralization. For example, during repletion of rachitic chicks with vitamin D, osteocalcin deposition precedes the deposition of mineral.

To date, there are no proven skeletal disorders due to acquired or inherited abnormalities of osteocalcin. However, in the human fetus, serious bone defects have been described in the so-called fetal "warfarin" syndrome (102), in which women taking the anti-vitamin K drug warfarin as an anticoagulant during the first trimester of pregnancy may give birth to fetuses with defective bone development such as stippled epiphyses, punctate calcifications, saddle nose, frontal bossing, and other bone anomalies. From a review of 24 cases, it has been concluded that the teratogenic window for warfarin occurs between weeks 6 and 9 and results in one abnormal fetus for every three pregnancies. This window corresponds to a time when embryonic bone tissue (presumably involving osteocalcin) develops even before the vitamin K-dependent blood coagulation system. Therefore, early vitamin K antagonism could result in bone defects without the concurrent development of an acute hemorrhagic state. It has also been hypothesized that the fetal warfarin syndrome may result partly from inhibition of vitamin K-dependent protein carboxylation in the placenta. Indeed, it has been shown that certain placental transport processes also may be vitamin K dependent (103).

VI. CONCLUSION

Skeletal development begins in the early embryo as a result of migration and subsequent differentiation of mesenchymal cells. These cells provide the matrix necessary for cellular stability. In addition, cell–matrix interactions have a critical influence on the function of the differentiated cells, and disturbances in the normal pattern of matrix constituents lead to abnormal skeletal development. Bone cells are also influenced by the hormones, PTH, and $1,25(OH)_2D_3$, as well as local concentrations of mineral ions. Failure to provide appropriate amounts of these minerals also has a deleterious influence on the progress of skeletal development. Genetic disturbances, such as vitamin D-dependent rickets type II, are now better understood as a result of continuing research on the molecular action of $1,25(OH)_2D_3$.

An attempt has been made to provide a brief and cogent description of fetal skeletal growth and mineralization as a basis for understanding clinically relevant skeletal abnormalities.

While much is yet to be learned regarding the factors controlling skeletal development, future research will undoubtedly lead to new relevant information that will provide a rational approach to prenatal diagnosis and hopefully treatment of skeletal abnormalities.

ACKNOWLEDGMENTS

This work was supported in part by Grants HD-11725, HD-20748, and AM-36487 from the National Institutes of Health and a Trustees Grant from Children's Hospital Research Foundation, Cincinnati, Ohio.

REFERENCES

1. Vaughan, J. "The Physiology of Bone," 2nd Ed. Oxford Univ. Press (Clarendon), London and New York, 1975.
2. Cohen, A. M., and Hay, E. D. Secretion of collagen by embryonic neuroepithelium at the time of spinal cord–somite interaction. *Dev. Biol.* **26,** 578–605 (1971).
3. Hall, B. K. Chondrogenesis of the somatic mesoderm. *Adv. Anat., Embryol. Cell Biol.* **53,** 1–50 (1977).
4. Hall, B. K. Intracellular and extracellular control of the differentiation of cartilage and bone. *Histochem. J.* **13,** 599–614 (1981).

5. Toole, B. P. Hyaluronate and hyaluronidase in morphogenesis and differentiation. *Am. Zool.* **13,** 1061–1077 (1973).
6. Pratt, R. M., Larsen, M. A. and Johnston, M. C. Migration of cranial neural crest cells in a cell-free hyaluronate-rich matrix. *Dev. Biol.* **44,** 298–305 (1975).
7. Fisher, M., and Solush, M. Glycosaminoglycan localization and role in maintenance of tissue spaces in the early chick embryo. *J. Embryol. Exp. Morphol.* **42,** 195–207 (1977).
8. Toole, B. P. Hyaluronate turnover during chondrogenesis in the developing chick limb and axial skeleton. *Dev. Biol.* **29,** 321–329 (1972).
9. Toole, B. P., and Trelstad, R. L. Hyaluronate production and removal during corneal development in the chick. *Dev. Biol.* **26,** 28–35 (1971).
10. Toole, B. P., Jackson, G., and Gross, J. Hyaluronate in morphogenesis: Inhibition of chondrogenesis *in vitro*. *Proc. Natl. Acad. Sci. U.S.A.* **69,** 1384–1386 (1972).
11. Eyre, D. R. Concepts in collagen. *Clin. Orthop. Relat. Res.* **159,** 97–107 (1981).
12. Kvist, T. N., and Finnegan, C. V. The distribution of glycosaminoglycans in the axial regions of the developing chick embryo. II. Histochemical analysis. *J. Exp. Zool.* **175,** 221–225 (1970).
13. Scott, B. L., and Glimcher, M. J. Distribution of glycogen in osteoblasts of fetal rat. *J. Ultrastruct. Res.* **36,** 565–586 (1971).
14. Hall, B. K. "Developmental and Cellular Skeletal Biology." Academic Press, New York, 1978.
15. Linsenmayer, T. F., Toole, B. P., and Trelstad, R. L. Temporal and spatial transitions in collagen types during embryonic chick limb development. *Dev. Biol.* **35,** 232–239 (1973).
16. Holtrop, M. E., and Weinger, J. M. Ultrastructural evidence for a transport system in bone. *In* "Calcium, Parathyroid Hormone and the Calcitonins" (R. V. Talmage and P. L. Munson, eds.), p. 365. Exerpta Med. Found., Amsterdam, 1971.
17. Doty, S. B. Morphological evidence of gap junctions between bone cells. *Calcif. Tissue Int.* **33,** 509–512 (1981).
18. Aaron, J. E. Histology and microanatomy of bone. *In* "Calcium, Phosphate and Magnesium Metabolism" (B. E. C. Nordin, ed.), pp. 298–356. Churchill Livingstone, Edinburgh, 1976.
19. Sillence, D. O. Osteogenesis imperfecta: An expanding panorama of variants. *Clin. Orthop. Relat. Res.* **159,** 11–25 (1981).
20. Prockop, K. J., and Vivirikko, K. I. Heritable diseases of collagen. *N. Engl. J. Med.* **311,** 376–386 (1984).
21. Rimoin, D. L. Prenatal abnormal bone growth: A perspective. *In* "Normal and Abnormal Bone Growth: Basic and Clinical Research" (A. D. Dixon and B. G. Sarnat, eds.), pp. 131–140. Alan R. Liss, New York, 1985.
22. Shapiro, J. E., Phillips, J. A., and Byers, P. H. Prenatal diagnosis of lethal perinatal osteogenesis imperfecta (OI type II). *J. Pediatr.* **100,** 127–133 (1982).
23. Chen, T. L., and Raisz, L. G. The effects of ascorbic acid deficiency on calcium and collagen metabolism in cultured fetal rat bones. *Calcif. Tissue Res.* **17,** 113–127 (1975).
24. Kivirikko, K. I., and Prockop, D. J. Enzymatic hydroxylation of proline and lysine in proto collagen. *Proc. Natl. Acad. Sci. U.S.A.* **57,** 782–789 (1967).
25. Hutton, J. J., Tappel, A. L., and Udenfriend, S. Cofactor and substrate requirements of collagen proline hydroxylase. *Arch. Biochem.* **118,** 231–240 (1967).
26. Spranger, J. W. Catabolic disorders of complex carbohydrates. *Postgrad. Med. J.* **53,** 441–448 (1977).
27. Brown, W. E. Crystal growth and bone mineral. *Clin. Orthop. Relat. Res.* **44,** 205–220 (1966).

28. Glimcher, M. J., and Krane, S. M. The organization and structure of bone, and the mechanism of calcification. *In* "A Treatise on Collagen. II" (B. S. Gould and G. N. Ramachardra, eds.). Academic Press, New York, 1968.
29. Smith, J. W. Molecular pattern in native collagen. *Nature (London)* **219,** 157–158 (1968).
30. Bonnucci, E. The locus of initial calcification in cartilage and bone. *Clin. Orthop. Relat. Res.* **78,** 108–138 (1970).
31. Matsuzawa, T., and Anderson, H. C. Phosphatases of epiphyseal cartilage studied by electron microscopic cytochemical methods. *J. Histochem. Cytochem.* **19,** 801–808 (1971).
32. Whyte, N. P., Magill, H. L., Fallon, M. D., and Herrod, H. D. Infantile hypophosphatasia: Normalization of circulating bone alkaline phosphatase activity followed by skeletal remineralization. *J. Pediatr.* **108,** 82–88 (1986).
33. Woodhouse, N. J. Y., Fisher, M. D., and Sigurdsson, G. Paget's disease in a 5-year-old: Acute response to human calcitonin. *Br. Med. J.* **iv,** 267–271 (1972).
34. Rasmussen, H., and Bordier, P. "The Physiological and Cellular Basis of Metabolic Bone Disease." Williams & Wilkins. Baltimore, Maryland, 1975.
35. Hancox, N. M., and Boothroyd, B. Electron microscopy of the early stages of osteogenesis. *Clin. Orthop. Relat. Res.* **40,** 153–161 (1965).
36. Matthews, J. L., and Martin, J. H. Intracellular calcium in connective tissues in immunopathology of inflammation. *Exerpta Med. Int. Congr. Ser.* No. 229, 216–224 (1970).
37. Vaes, G. Excretion of acid and of lysosomal hydrolytic enzymes during bone resorption induced in tissue culture by parathyroid extract. *Exp. Cell Res.* **39,** 470–474 (1965).
38. Laitiner, O. The metabolism of collagen: Its hormonal control in the rat. *Acta Endocrinol. (Copenhagen), Suppl.* No. 120, 5–86 (1967).
39. Wood, J. F., and Nichols, G. Collagenolytic activity in rat bone cells. *J. Cell Biol.* **26,** 747–757 (1965).
40. Walker, D. G., Lapiere, C. M., and Gross, J. A collagenolytic factor in rat bone produced by parathyroid extract. *Biochem. Biophys. Res. Commun.* **15,** 397–402 (1964).
41. Kaufman, E. J., Glimcher, M. J., Mechanic, G. C., and Goldhaber, P. Collagenolytic activity during active bone resorption in tissue culture. *Proc. Soc. Exp. Biol. Med.* **120,** 632–637 (1965).
42. Vaes, G., and Vreven, J. Acid pyrophosphatase phosphoproteinphosphatase and phosphomonoesterase activities in bone tissue. *Isr. J. Med. Sci.* **7,** 401–402 (1971).
43. Kreitzman, S. N., and Fritz, M. E. Demineralization of bone by phosphoprotein phosphatase. *J. Dent. Res.* **49,** 1509–1512 (1970).
44. Coccia, B. F., Krivit, W., Cervenka, J., Clawson, C., Kersey, J. H., Kim, T. H., Nesbit, M. E., Ramsay, N. K. C., Warkentin, P. I., Teitelbaum, S. L., and Brown, D. M. Successful bone-marrow transplantation for infantile malignant osteopetrosis. *N. Engl. J. Med.* **302,** 701–708 (1980).
45. Ballet, J. J., Griscelli, C., Coutris, C., Milhand, G., and Maroteaux, P. Bone marrow transplantation in osteopetrosis. *Lancet* **ii.,** 1137 (1977).
46. Matthews, J. L. Ultrastructure of calcifying tissues. *J. Anat.* **129,** 451–452 (1970).
47. Holtrop, M. E. The ultrastructure of the epiphyseal plate. I. The flattened chondrocyte. *Calcif. Tissue Res.* **9,** 131–139 (1972).
48. Anderson, H. C. An electron microscopy study of induced cartilage development and calcification. *J. Cell Biol.* **35,** 81–101 (1967).
49. Rimoin, E. L., and Sillence, D. O. The skeletal dysplasias, nomenclature, classification and clinical evaluation. *In* "Heritable Disorders of Connective Tissue" (W. H. Akeson, P. Bornstein, and M. J. Glimscher, eds.), pp. 3–4. Mosby, St. Louis, Missouri.
50. Rimoin, E. L. Prenatal abnormal bone growth: A perspective. *In* "Normal and Abnormal Bone Growth: Basic and Clinical Research" (A. D. Dixon and B. G. Sarnat, eds.), pp. 131–140. Alan R. Liss, New York, 19

51. Strom, C. N. Achondraplasia due to DNA insertion into the type II collagen gene. *Pediatr. Res.* **18,** 226A (1984).
52. Harris, W. H., and Heaney, R. P. Skeletal renewal and metabolic bone disease. *N. Engl. J. Med.* **280,** 193–311 (1969).
53. Mundy, G. R., Rodan, G. A., Rodan, S., Majeska, R. J., and DeMartino, S. D. Unidirectional movement of bone forming cells in response to a factor derived from resorbing bones and collagen *in vitro*. *Clin. Res.* **28,** 892A (1980).
54. Leroyer-Alizon, E., David, L., Anast, C. S., and Dubois, P. M. Immunocytological evidence for parathyroid hormone in human fetal parathyroid glands. *J. Clin. Endocrinol. Metab.* **52,** 513–516 (1981).
55. Graham, R. W., and Scothorne, R. J. The onset of functional capacity in fetal guinea-pig parathyroid glands. *Q. J. Exp. Physiol. Cogn. Med. Sci.* **56,** 41–52 (1971).
56. Hoskins, F. M., and Snyder, F. F. Calcium content of maternal and foetal blood serum following injection of parathyroid extract in foetuses *in utero*. *Proc. Soc. Exp. Biol. Med.* **25,** 264–266 (1928).
57. Kalu, D. N., Pennock, J., Doyle, F. H., and Foster, G. V. Parathyroid hormone and experimental osteosclerosis. *Lancet* **1,** 1363–1366 (1970).
58. Flanagan, B., and Nichols, G. Metabolic studies of human bone *in vitro*. II. Change in hyperparathyroidism. *J. Clin. Invest.* **44,** 1795–1804 (1965).
59. Jowsey, J. Quantitative microradiography. A new approach in the evaluation of metabolic bone disease. *Am. J. Med.* **40,** 485–491 (1966).
60. Dietrich, J. W., Canalis, E. M., Maira, D. M., and Raisz, L. G. Hormonal control of bone collagen synthesis *in vitro:* Effects of parathyroid hormone and calcitonin. *Endocrinology (Baltimore)* **98,** 943–949 (1976).
61. Rodan, G. A., and Martin, T. J. Role of the osteoblast in hormonal control of bone resorption—A hypothesis. *Calcif. Tissue Int.* **33,** 349–351 (1981).
62. Goldbloom, R. B., Gillis, D. A., and Prasad, M. Heriditary parathyroid hyperplasia, a surgical emergency of early infancy. *Pediatrics* **49,** 514–523 (1972).
63. Harrisson, H. E., and Harrison, H. E. "Disorders of Calcium and Phosphate Metabolism in Childhood and Adolescence." Saunders, Philadelphia, Pennsylvania, 1979.
64. Albright, F., and Reifenstein, E. C., Jr. "The Parathyroid Glands and Metabolic Bone Disease." Williams & Wilkins, Baltimore, Maryland, 1948.
65. Feinblatt, J., Belanger, L. E., and Rasmussen, H. Effect of phosphate infusion on bone metabolism and parathyroid hormone action. *Am. J. Physiol.* **218,** 1624–1631 (1970).
66. Goldsmith, R. S., Richards, R., Dube, W. J., Hulley, S. B., Holdsworth, D., and Ingbar, S. H. Metabolic effects and action of phosphate supplements. *In* "Phosphate et Metabolisme Phosphocalcique" (D. J. Hioco, ed.), pp. 275–292. Edition Sandor, Paris, 1971.
67. Krane, S. M., Munoz, A. J., and Harris, E. D., Jr. Collagen-like fragments: Excretion in urine of patients with Paget's disease of bone. *Science* **157,** 713–716 (1967).
68. Bingham, P. J., and Raisz, L. G. Bone growth in organ culture: Effects of phosphate and other nutrients on bone and cartilage. *Calcif. Tissue Res.* **14,** 31–48 (1974).
69. Baylink, D., Wergedal, J., and Stauffer, M. Formation, mineralization and resorption of bone in hypophosphatemic rats. *J. Clin. Invest.* **50,** 2519–2530 (1971).
70. Simmons, , H. A., and Raisz, L. G. Effect of phosphate on growth and mineralization of rat tibia in organ culture. *Calcif. Tissue Res.* 11A, Abstr. (1981).
71. Pettifor, J. M., Ross, F. E., Travers, R., Glorieux, F. H., and DeLuca, H. F. Dietary calcium deficiency, a syndrome associated with bone deformities and elevated serum 1,25-dihydroxyvitamin D concentrations. *Metab. Bone Dis. Relat. Res.* **2,** 301–305 (1981).
72. Marie, P. J., Pettifor, J. M., Ross, F. P., and Glorieux, F. H. Histological osteomalacia due to dietary calcium deficiency in children. *N. Engl. J. Med.* **307,** 584–588 (1982).

73. DeLuca, H. F., and Schnoes, H. K. Vitamin D: Recent advances. *Annu. Rev. Biochem.* **52,** 411–439 (1983).
74. Chen, T. L., Hirst, M. A., and Feldman, D. A receptor-like binding macromolecule for 1,25-dihydroxycholecalciferol in cultured mouse bone cells. *J. Biol. Chem.* **254,** 7491–7494 (1976).
75. Manolagas, S. C., Haussler, M. R., and Deftos, L. J. 1,25-Dihydroxyvitamin D_3 receptor-like macromolecule in rat osteogenic sarcoma cell lines. *J. Biol. Chem.* **225,** 4414–4417 (1980).
76. Manolagas, S. C., Burton, P., and Deftos, L. J. 1,25-Dihydroxyvitamin D_3 stimulates alkaline phosphatase activity of osteoblast-like cells. *J. Biol. Chem.* **256,** 7115–7117 (1981).
77. Price, P. A., and Baukol, S. A. 1,25 Dihydroxyvitamin D_3 increases synthesis of the vitamin K-dependent bone protein by osteosarcoma cells. *J. Biol. Chem.* **255,** 11660–11663 (1980).
78. Kream, B. E., and Rowe, D. W. Regulation of collagen synthesis in fetal rat calvaria by 1,25-dihydroxyvitamin D3. *Proc. Annu. Sci. Meet. Am. Soc. Bone Miner. Res., 3rd* p. 51A (1981).
79. Harrison, H. E., and Harrison, H. C. Rickets, then and now. *J. Pediatr.* **87,** 1144–1151 (1975).
80. Haussler, M. R., and McCain, T. A. Basic and clinical concepts related to vitamin D metabolism and action. *N. Engl. J. Med.* **297,** 1041–1050 (1977).
81. Kooh, S. W., Jones, G., and Reilly, B. J. Pathogenesis of rickets in chronic hepatobiliary disease in children. *J. Pediatr.* **94,** 870–874 (1979).
82. Hahn, T. J., Hendin, B. A., Scharp, C. R., and Haddad, J. G. Serum 25-hydroxycholecalciferol levels and bone mass in children on anticonvulsant therapy. *N. Engl. J. Med.* **292,** 550–554 (1975).
83. Callerbach, J. C., Sheehan, M. B., Abramson, S. J., and Hall, R. T. Etiologic factors in rickets of very low birth weight infants. *J. Pediatr.* **98,** 800–805 (1981).
84. Steichen, J. J., Tsang, R. C., and Greer, F. R. Elevated serum 1,25-dihydroxyvitamin D concentrations in rickets of very low birth weight infants. *J. Pediatr.* **99,** 293–298 (1981).
85. Steichen, J. J., Gratton, T. L., and Tsang, R. C. Osteopenia of prematurity: The cause and possible treatment. *J. Pediatr.* **96,** 528–534 (1980).
86. Greer, F. R., Steichen, J. J., and Tsang, R. C. Effects of increased calcium, phosphorus and vitamin D intake on bone mineralization in very low birth weight infants fed formulas with Polycose and medium-chain triglycerides. *J. Pediatr.* **100,** 951–955 (1982).
87. Pereira, G. R., Sherman, M. S., and DiGucoma, J. Hyperalimentation cholestasis. *Am. J. Dis. Child.* **135,** 842–845 (1981).
88. Cole, D. E. C., and Zlotkin, S. H. Increased sulfate as an etiological factor in the hypercalciuria associated with total parenteral nutrition. *Am. J. Clin. Nutr.* **37,** 108–113 (1983).
89. Sedman, A. B., Klein, G. L., Merritt, R. J., Miller, N. L., Weber, K. O., Gill, W. L., Anand, H., and Alfrey, A. C. Evidence of aluminum loading in infants receiving intravenous therapy. *N. Engl. J. Med.* **312,** 1337–1343 (1985).
90. Venkataraman, P. S., Han, B. K., Tsang, R. C., and Daugherty, C. C. Secondary hyperparathyroidism and bone disease in infants receiving long term furosemide therapy. *Am. J. Dis. Child.* **137,** 1157–1161 (1983).
91. Greer, F. R., Steichen, J. J., and Tsang, R. C. Calcium and phosphate supplementation in breast milk related rickets. *Am. J. Dis. Child.* **136,** 581–583 (1982).
92. Glorieux, F. H., Marie, P. J., Pettifor, J. M., and Delvin, E. E. Bone response to phosphate salts ergocalciferol and calcitriol in hypophosphatemic vitamin D-resident rickets. *N. Engl. J. Med.* **303,** 1023–1031 (1980).

93. Hirst, M. A., Hochman, H. I., and Feldman, D. Vitamin D resistance and alopecia: A kindred with normal 1,25-dihydroxyvitamin D binding, but decreased receptor affinity for deoxyribonucleic acid. *J. Clin. Endocrinol. Metab.* **60,** 490–495 (1985).
94. Silver, J., Landau, H., Bab, I., Shvil, Y., Friedlander, M. M., Rubinger, P., and Popovtzer, M. M. Vitamin D-dependent rickets type I and II: Diagnosis and response to therapy. *Isr. J. Med. Sci.* **21,** 53–56 (1985).
95. Feldman, D., Chen, T., Cone, C., Hirst, M., Shani, S., Benderli, A., and Hochberg, Z. Vitamin D resistant rickets with alopecia: Cultured skin fibroblasts exhibit defective cytoplasmic receptors and unresponsiveness to $1,25(OH)_2D_3$. *J. Clin. Endocrinol. Metab.* **55,** 1020–1022 (1982).
96. Balsan, S., Garabedian, M., Larchet, M., Gorski, A. M., Cournot, G., Tau, C., Bourdeau, A., Silve, C., and Ricour, C. Long-term maternal calcium infusions can cure rickets and promote normal mineralization in hereditary resistance to 1,25-dihyrdroxyvitamin D. *J. Clin. Invest.* **77,** 1661–1667 (1986).
97. Fraser, D., Kooh, S. W., Kind, H. B., Holick, M. F., Tanaka, Y., and DeLuca, H. F. Pathogenesis of hereditary vitamin D-dependent rickets: An inborn error of vitamin D metabolism involving defective conversion of 25-hydroxyvitamin D to 1-alpha, 25-dihyroxyvitamin D. *N. Engl. J. Med.* **289,** 817–822 (1973).
98. Avioli, L. V. Renal osteodystrophy. *In* "Metabolic Bone Disease" (L. V. Avioli and S. M. Crane, eds.), Vol. 2, pp. 149–215. Academic Press, New York, 1978.
99. Mankin, H. J. Rickets, osteomalacia, and renal osteodystrophy, part II. *J. Bone Joint Surg.* **56,** 352–380 (1974).
100. Hauschka, P. V., and Reid, M. Time appearance of a calcium binding protein containing y-carboxyglutamic acid in developing chick bone. *Dev. Biol.* **65,** 426–434 (1978).
101. Lian, J. B., Glimcher, M. J., Roufosse, A. H., Hauschka, P. V., Gallop, P. M., Cohen-Sdal, L., and Reit, B. Alterations of the y-carboxyglutamic acid and osteocalcin concentrations in vitamin D deficient chick bone. *J. Biol Chem.* **257,** 4999–5003 (1982).
102. Hall, J. G., Pauli, R., and Wilson, K. Maternal and fetal sequelae of anticoagulation during pregnancy. A review. *Am. J. Med.* **68,** 117–140 (1980).
103. Friedman, P. A., Hauschka, P. V., Shia, M. A., and Wallace, J. K. Characteristics of the vitamin K-dependent carboxylation system in human placenta. *Biochim. Biophys. Acta* **583,** 261–265 (1979).

7

Discussion: Part I. The Fetus and the Placenta A. The Need for Animal Models

Peter W. Nathanielsz
NYS College of Veterinary Medicine
Cornell University
Ithaca, New York, U.S.A.

Much of the firm, established information discussed today comes from the chronically instrumented fetal sheep model. Other animal models have also been used. These various models permit careful control of the different nutritional, endocrine, cardiovascular, and other physiological systems under study. Several of these models have been described in considerable detail together with their strengths and limitations (6–11).

After listening to this morning's papers several major questions arose. First, is there a slowing of the rate of fetal growth toward the end of gestation? Cross-sectional data from experimental animals as well as human infants suggest that there is a slowing of the rate of growth (1). Longitudinal data are required from experimental animal models. One view of this slowing in growth rate is that during the later stages of gestation the fetus is maturing and differentiating many important tissue and organ systems, for example, the lungs, the liver, and the brain. Metabolic activity is channeled into differentiation rather than growth.

This competition or incompatibility between growth and differentiation is exemplified by the different effects of transforming growth factor-β (TGF-β). TGF-β may be involved in the terminal differentiation of cell types, thus precluding further proliferation. For example, the proliferative effects of insulin and hydrocortisone on renal epithelial cells are inhibited by TFG-β. In contrast the protein synthesis stimulated by these hormones is not inhibited by TGF-β (2).

A corollary of this competition between growth and maturation is the appreciation that size may not be the only important factor in assessing the degree of risks to which the newborn is exposed. Many growth-retarded babies and experimental animals show accelerated maturation of vital organ systems. The intrauterine growth-retarded (IUGR) baby is often more mature than appropriate for a gestational-age baby of the same size as the IUGR baby but born at an earlier stage of gestation.

Experimental studies with fetal sheep have shown that the fetal hypothalamo-pituitary-adrenocortical axis plays an important role in initiating labor and delivery (3,4). The rise in fetal plasma cortisol that plays a central role in this process begins about 15–20 days before delivery (5). Cortisol and other endocrine, paracrine, and autocrine messengers probably play important roles in the slowing of fetal growth rate that precedes parturition.

The second major question raised follows from the independent suggestion by Drs. Milner, Sara, and Tsang that the rate of supply of nutrients plays an important role in the regulation of fetal growth. Is this effect direct or is it indirect via the effect of nutrients on the production and release of growth-promoting factors? Unpublished data from Dr. Peter Gluckman's laboratory suggest that, in the sheep at least, fetal plasma IGF-11 (the fetal somatomedin in this species) falls when the availability of glucose to the fetus falls. Dr. Sara's data suggest that amino acid availability may play a similar role in regulating growth factor production in the newborn rat.

Professor Lunell provided data in the human to show that IUGR is associated with a fall in placental blood flow. To what extent is this decreased uterine perfusion the cause and to what extent is it the effect of the decreased fetal growth and hence decreased demand? More data are required from animal studies in several species including nonhuman primates. In my laboratory we have recently been successful in maintaining the chronically instrumented pregnant rhesus monkey on a swivel and tether system that permits relatively free movement and opens the way to long-term studies in the nonhuman primate regarding long-term nutritional alteration to fetal growth (12).

Professor Young's interesting paper showed the importance of measuring dynamic features of protein metabolism rather than the overall tissue content. These studies and many other excellent investigations were conducted in the fetal sheep. Nonhuman primate experimental data are badly needed to highlight similarities and differences between the sheep and primates. I am sure this symposium will be a stimulus to us all to find ways of answering these questions.

When we have these answers, further questions will remain. If we can improve fetal weight gain—should it be done? Perhaps fetal weight will increase at the expense of differentiation. What are the critical metabolites and are there any critical times at which they need to be administered and other times at which it would be better not to administer them? Perhaps these questions will be answered at the next symposium.

ACKNOWLEDGMENTS

I should like to thank Susan Shell for her help with this manuscript. Our studies referred to were supported by Grants HD 17129 and HD 18870 from the NIH.

REFERENCES

1. Battaglia, F. C., and Lubchenco, L. C. *J. Pediatr.* **71,** 159 (1967).
2. Fine, L. G., Holley, R. W., Nasri, H., and Badie-Dezfooley, B. *Proc. Natl. Acad. Sci. U.S.A.* **82,** 6163 (1985).
3. Liggins, G. C., Fairclough, R. J., Grieves, S. A., Kendall, J. Z., and Knox, B. S. *Recent Prog. Horm. Res.* **29,** 111–159 (1973).
4. Liggins, G. C., Nathanielsz, P. W., and Silver, M. *In* "Animal Models in Fetal Medicine" (P. W. Nathanielsz, ed.), Vol. 2, pp. 1–23. Perinatology Press, Ithaca, New York, 1982.
5. Magyar, D. M., Fridshal, D., Elsner, C. W., Glatz, T., Eliot, J., Klein, A. H., Lowe, K. C., Buster, J. E., and Nathanielsz, P. W. *Endocrinology (Baltimore)* **107,** 155–159 (1980).
6. Nathanielsz, P. W. "Animal Models in Fetal Medicine," Vol. 1. Perinatology Press, Ithaca, New York, 1980.
7. Nathanielsz, P. W. "Animal Models in Fetal Medicine," Vol. 2. Perinatology Press, Ithaca, New York, 1982.
8. Nathanielsz, P. W. "Animal Models in Fetal Medicine," Vol. 3. Perinatology Press, Ithaca, New York, 1984.
9. Nathanielsz, P. W. "Animal Models in Fetal Medicine, Vol. 4, Intrauterine Growth." Perinatology Press, Ithaca, New York, 1984.
10. Nathanielsz, P. W. "Animal Models in Fetal Medicine, Vol. 5, Parturition." Perinatology Press, Ithaca, New York, 1985.
11. Nathanielsz, P. W. "Animal Models in Fetal Medicine, Vol. 6, Metabolism." Perinatology Press, Ithaca, New York, 1987. In press.
12. Nathanielsz, P. W., Poore, E. R., Brodie, A., Taylor, N. F., Pimentel, G., Figueroa, J. P., and Frank, D. *In* "Research in Perinatal Medicine" (P. W. Nathanielsz and J. T. Parer, eds.), Vol. 1, pp. 87–111. Perinatology Press, Ithaca, New York, 1984.

Discussion: Part I. The Fetus and the Placenta B. Application to Developing Countries

Staffan Bergström
Department of Obstetrics and Gynecology
Central Hospital
Eskilstuna, Sweden

Jerker Liljestrand
Department of Obstetrics and Gynecology
Central Hospital
Karlskrona, Sweden

Not infrequently the grim realities of advanced impoverishment in the hard, down-to-earth sense of this word are beyond the comprehension of research workers without Third World experience of their own. Let us therefore begin a discussion on the possible applications of the preceding six contributions by reminding ourselves of these realities and contemplate three slides from a Third World cemetery, where only small children are buried. Nowhere in the world is the brutal challenge of lacking maternal and child health more concretely exposed than here. They appear as pictures from a post-World War I cemetery with vast fields crowded by dead infants and small children. It is less easy to overlook the individual tragedies when considering these fields than when looking at vital statistics. The number of deaths remains extremely high and new graves are constantly dug. Up to 80% of all deaths in some African countries occur among children under five. This is, indeed, a veritable perinatal and pediatric challenge.

Perinatal nutrition is in this context a pressing priority for obstetricians and pediatricians in the Third World and extensive research efforts are needed.

We find it an outstanding feature of this symposium to invite a number of speakers to comment on topics from the angle of "developing" countries. It is important to stress this, since one of the key expressions of disturbances in the perinatal nutrition, the low birth weight, is one of the most dramatic challenges facing Third World obstetricians today. This can be put more concretely by repeating the well-known figures on the annual incidence of low birth weight (LBW) in the world today: of roughly 22 million newborns with LBW, 21 million cases occur in "developing" countries, that is, 95% of the LBW problem in the world resides in the Third World.

When offering our comments on the preceding six presentations we must confess that we have read them from a particular point of view, namely, as obstetricians with recent responsibility for maternities in Mozambique taking care of very large numbers of severally ill obstetric patients. Of our stillbirths roughly 60% were LBW cases, which is the greatest overall problem and a common denominator. This was our number one perinatal challenge both clinically and scientifically.

It must be recognized immediately that much of the basic research effort presently carried out in perinatal medicine in general has very little direct application to developing countries. This may appear nihilistic and blasphemic but is, we think, a correct description. Having said that we would like to stress that this symposium may not be expected to deviate too much from the general pattern of sophistication. Handling of amino acids by the fetoplacental unit or perfusion studies of the uteroplacental unit using indium-113m are research fields—though important in our world—very far away from the realities in the world where 95% of the LBW problem resides. Somatomedins, hormonal regulation of fetal growth, and preterm infant bone mineralization are, unfortunately, topics equally far from the pressing research priorities in a Third World country. If our primary reaction, honestly and frankly, is almost blasphemic in the sense that we find little application to developing countries, we feel that this conclusion must be made more concrete and substantial to be considered minimally credible. We recognize two dangers here: one *problem-oriented* and one *method-oriented*.

The *problem-oriented* danger emanates from the lack of down-to-earth experience of the nature of the scientific challenge in Third World perinatal nutrition: few research workers from developed countries with scientific interest in problems of developing countries have that kind of hard experience. The heavy clinical and organizational burden soon creates a clear insight into the limitations of the time accessible to "research." The key deficiencies are, obviously, time and manpower.

Research priorities created or at least formulated outside this reality always run the risk of being counterproductive—even if basically sound from a scientific point of view. The potential collision between "expert" aspirations imported to a poor country on a consultant basis from a scientific community in a developed country is a real danger related to the formulation of the problem labeled as "priority." Its counterproductive character, which we have witnessed several times in practice, emanates both from the wrong orientation of the starting point in itself and from the fact that such a research effort diverts scientific attention from more relevant and action-oriented perinatal research.

The *method-oriented* danger is related to the problem-oriented one: the problem solving assumes a methodology. The risk of overlooking fundamental research priorities creates the risk of accepting sophisticated technology that is empirically a temptation and a fascination far from an appropriate technology. Many expensive adventures in advanced methodology may illustrate this kind of risk.

What, then, is the alternative?

In the obstetrical field of perinatal nutrition our experience is that simple anthropometric studies should have the highest priority. We are referring, for example, to studies on the positive and negative predictive values of maternal upper-arm circumference, symphysis–fundus distance, and other potentially useful parameters. There are still today many conflicting results regarding the value of anthropometry. One important example is the fundal height. In the absence of any kind of instruments in maternal health care, fundal measurements remain one of the cornerstones in Third World obstetrics. Another example of our own concerns maternal mid-upper-arm circumference and maternal height, which were shown to correlate to maternal malnutrition and perinatal outcome, respectively. An arm circumference of the mother less than 25 cm had a sensitivity of 75% in detecting women with weight for height below 85% of standard and a specificity of 85%. The predictive value of an arm circumference below 25 cm was 46% regarding weight for height below 85% of standard. We could conclude that a mid-upper-arm circumference of less than 25 cm is a warning of malnutrition and less than 23 cm is strong evidence of malnutrition (1).

We think these examples, together with food supplementation studies on pregnant women, indicate possible ways out of the ivory tower.

REFERENCES

1. Liljestrand, J., and Bergström, S. Value of single anthropometric measurements in Mozambican antenatal care. *Proc. Br.–Scand. Joint Meet. Trop. Med. Parasitol., Copenhagen, 1985 (September).*

Editor's Comment

B. S. Lindblad

The discussion paper by Drs. Bergström and Liljestrand aroused some controversy. Scientists representing both industrialized countries as well as teaching institutions in the Third World contributed to a lively discussion. For example, delegates from India and Chile expressed doubts as to the validity of the concept "developing countries" in this particular context as the degree of development in medical care varies considerably from country to country. One delegate from Chile opposed the expression "the Third World" and proposed that they be called "less developed countries" instead. One could then discuss "least developed countries." Dr. R. G. Whitehead from the Dunn Nutrition Unit, MRC, Cambridge, England, with long research experience in Uganda and Gambia, has kindly agreed to summarize his views in the following comment.

Comment on Bergström and Liljestrand's Discussion Paper

R. G. Whitehead
Dunn Nutrition Unit
Medical Research Council
Cambridge, England

The appropriateness of yet more fundamental scientific research in the Third World vis-à-vis the application of already existing scientific knowledge is always a difficult priority to resolve. One commonly hears, however, a statement to the effect that we now have sufficient basic knowledge and we should proceed, without further ado, in its application. I believe that in many circumstances this is unfortunately a gross oversimplification; it fails to recognize the inexact quality of much of the scientific data from the Third World collected so far. The facts of life are that we cannot, with any degree of certainty, provide firm health advice, based on sound science, even on topics so elementary as the amounts of extra dietary energy a pregnant or a lactating woman needs to consume each day, and the same is true for both protein intake as well as for calcium.

These comments will surprise many people. The underlying reason has been a major shortcoming in investigative design. There has been a lack of appropriate scientific technologies to study how *free-living* people perform under circumstances in which they are living on a nutritional knife-edge. We have little or no concept of the extent to which the body can adapt physiologically or behaviorally to accommodate key environmental deficiencies. In the wealthier areas of the world, such considerations tend not to be of any major practical significance as we conveniently include in our recommended nutritional allowances a significant safety margin. We, however, can afford this luxury, but to achieve the same in most Third World countries would place an impossible burden on that country's financial resources. In such circumstances it is all too often necessary to ask how little we can get away with rather than what is ideal.

The current status of our knowledge really does not enable us to answer such questions with any degree of scientific exactitude and it is for this reason that scientists will have to do more fundamental research in maternal and perinatal physiology if they are to provide safe practical advice to health planners that is compatible with the prevailing economic circumstances of most of the Third World.

Having made this basic comment, which is intended to soften the somewhat extreme statement of Bergström and Liljestrand, I would like to join the latter participants in making a plea to the scientific community, that when they are planning their fundamental research to always have in firm focus the ultimate responsibility to apply any useful new-found knowledge to solve real health issues. Investigators working in the biomedical sciences quite clearly have a duty to use their science for the benefit of the community; but there is no point in trying to apply poor or oversimplified science. The health problems of the Third World are complex and if we underestimate this complexity it is unlikely that any substantial practical benefit will accrue.

Part II

Birth from the Nutritional Point of View

Lung Differentiation and Repair in Relation to Vitamin A Status

Mildred T. Stahlman,* Jayant P. Shenai,* Mary E. Gray,† Håkan W. Sundell,* Kathleen Kennedy,* and Frank Chytil‡
*Departments of *Pediatrics, †Pathology, and ‡Biochemistry*
Vanderbilt University School of Medicine
Nashville, Tennessee, U.S.A.

I. INTRODUCTION

A. Vitamin A Deficiency

Vitamin A is a fat-soluble vitamin and is largely transferred from mother to fetus in the third trimester of pregnancy. Its role in fetal development has been shown to be one of pro-

Perinatal Nutrition

moting differentiation of various epithelial populations, including skin, gut, bladder, and pulmonary conducting airways.

Severe vitamin A deficiency results in a predictable sequence of changes in the epithelial lining of pulmonary conducting airways (Wolbach and Howe 1925; Wolbach and Howe 1933; Wong and Buck 1971). In those proximal airways where basal cells exist as stem cells for replacement of lining cells following natural attrition and for relining damaged epithelial surfaces following airway injury, basal cell proliferation is stimulated. As these normally discontinuous basal cells become confluent, the columnar ciliated and nonciliated secretory cells become displaced from their basement membrane footing. They are separated thereby from their nutritional blood supply and become necrotic, resulting in what is described pathologically as necrotizing tracheobronchitis. With continued proliferation, basal cells, apparently in the absence of the stimulus to differentiate into ciliated and nonciliated columnar epithelium, lose their phenotypic future and develop as layers of stratified squamous epithelium similar to skin or esophagus.

The physiological results of this series of events are (1) loss of the mucous secretions of goblet cells and of the less viscous secretions of other populations of nonciliated secretory cells; (2) the loss of cilia with their ability to move the mucous blanket, in which bacteria or foreign inhaled particles may be trapped, upward in the airways; (3) loss of normal water homeostasis across the tracheobronchial epithelium, which is dependent on active chloride transfer across normal lining cells; and (4) probably some loss of distensibility of airways now lined with what amounts to multilayered skin, which would be especially important in infants with small conducting airways. Since resistance to airflow varies with the radius to the fourth power, a small decrease in diameter might result in a profound increase in airway resistance.

If the conducting airways are injured, either by trauma or disease, the stimulus to epithelial regeneration is triggered. We have reasoned that, if simultaneous with injury, vitamin A deficiency of such proportion as to preclude normal differentiation of proliferating basal (stem) cells were present, normal healing will not occur. The replacement with new cells, if under the stimulus of differentiating vitamin A, would result in new ciliated and nonciliated columnar cells, possessing all their important functions. Without adequate vitamin A influence on differentiation, basal cell proliferation followed by squamous metaplasia would result.

B. Bronchopulmonary Dysplasia

If one examines the tracheobronchial tree of premature infants who, following neonatal pulmonary insults such as hyaline membrane disease, undergo an abnormally protracted healing phase and die subsequently, the sequential changes classically described as bronchopulmonary dysplasia (BPD) are seen. These consist of early phase (1–2 weeks) necrotizing tracheobronchitis followed by squamous metaplasia (Stahlman, 1984). BPD is thought to be a multifactorial process, resulting from lung injury from prolonged and high concentrations of oxygen and from the use of high mean and peak airway pressures, including air dissection, often with secondary infection common with prolonged tracheal intubation, all occurring on the background of lung immaturity (Stahlman *et al.*, 1979).

C. Hypothesis

It is a common occurrence that very low birth weight infants who require ventilatory assistance for prolonged periods of time cannot be fed enterally. Parenteral alimentation is given, often inadequate in amounts of total calories and vitamins, and enteral feedings may be delayed for many weeks. We have hypothesized that very low birth weight infants, having been deprived of much of their vitamin A transplacental transfer because of their early delivery at a low gestational age, and also being succeptible candidates for acute pulmonary injury such as HMD or iatrogenic trauma or injury from intubation, ventilator dependency, and oxygen use, have the healing phase of their acute lung injury prolonged and that their vitamin A status at birth and during subsequent weeks may greatly influence their normal healing process.

II. EPIDERMAL GROWTH FACTOR AND VITAMIN A TO FETAL LAMB

In an attempt to model the effects of vitamin A supplementation on the immature lung, we have used 10 twin pairs of fetal lambs ranging in gestational age from 120 to 134 days. Vitamin A levels in lambs at this fetal age are quite comparable to those in human premature infants and are significantly lower than those of term lambs, which are lower than those of ewes. One lamb of each pair served as a control. One pair was given epidermal growth factor (EGF) or normal saline. Three pair were given vitamin A or normal saline, four pair were given either EGF alone or vitamin A plus EGF, and two pair were given either vitamin A alone or vitamin A plus EGF. Serum levels of vitamin A were sampled daily and at sacrifice on day 5 or 6 of treatment. Serum, liver, and lung vitamin A levels were obtained from both twins and the ewe. Daily arterial blood gases and pH were used to assess the well-being of both fetuses. Large doses of EGF were used to assure clear-cut proliferative changes within 4 days, and large amounts of vitamin A were also given in an effort to rapidly differentiate the basal cell proliferation. Vitamin A was given po *in utero* beginning 1 day before EGF iv administration. EGF alone caused marked proliferation of basal cells of trachea and bronchi with undermining of surface columnar epithelium and beginning necrosis. Vitamin A alone had no effect on tracheobronchial epithelium. Vitamin A given along with EGF had no demonstrable effects on basal cell proliferation, but differentiation into ciliated and goblet cells appeared to be stimulated and surface characteristics of more normal ciliated and nonciliated cells were preserved rather than progressive surface necrosis followed by squamous metaplasia (Stahlman *et al.*, 1986).

III. VITAMIN A STATUS OF NEWBORN INFANTS

Several years ago we embarked on a systematic evaluation of the vitamin A status of newborn infants, especially those of very low birth weight. The results of these initial studies have been published previously. They can be summarized as follows: We first demonstrated a direct relationship between cord serum vitamin A and retinol-binding protein levels with gestational age in a series of premature and term infants (Shenai *et al.*, 1981a). We then assessed the liver concentration of vitamin A in a group of 25 infants of less than 1500 g birth weight who died within 24 hr of birth. Since the liver is the primary site of vitamin A storage, liver levels reflect vitamin A reserves available to the infant at birth better than serum concentrations do and probably represent the need for vitamin A intake in the neonatal period quite accurately (Shenai *et al.*, 1985a). Serum vitamin A and retinol-binding protein were also measured in 16 of these very low birth weight infants. In children, liver concentrations below 40 μg/g are generally considered to be indicative of low vitamin A reserve. Four-fifths of these levels were below 40 μg/g. Only one serum vitamin A was above 20 μg/dl and only one RBP was above 3 mg/dl, values below these levels being thought to represent suboptimal vitamin A status.

We then looked at the efficiency of vitamin A administration in TPN solution in an *in vitro* system. Vitamin A is photodegradable and also binds to polyethylene tubing, both potential sources of loss in transit from solution bottle to infant. We showed that, with the combined loss from both photodegradation and adsorption into tubing, even under optimal conditions, less than 38% of the expected amount of vitamin A was actually being delivered through the iv route (Shenai *et al.*, 1981b).

IV. SERUM VITAMIN A LEVELS IN BRONCHOPULMONARY DYSPLASIA

We next prospectively assessed and compared vitamin A status of two groups of preterm neonates (<1500 g birth weight, <32 weeks gestation), one that developed clinical and radiological evidence of bronchopulmonary dysplasia ($n=10$) and one (control) that developed no significant lung disease ($n=8$) (Shenai *et al.*, 1985b). Infants who developed BPD had significantly lower mean plasma vitamin A concentrations than those of controls at four sampling times in the first postnatal month, beginning at 4 days after birth. In contrast to controls without lung disease, infants with BPD showed a substantial decline in their plasma vitamin A concentrations from their initial values, and a high percentage of individual values in these infants were less than 10 μg/dl during the 8-week postnatal period of observation. Delayed establishment of gastrointestinal feedings and a lower vitamin A intake may have accounted for this decline. During the initial phase of declining plasma vitamin A concentrations in these infants, the average daily vitamin A intake was <700 IU/kg/day and the mode of feeding was predominantly intravenous. During the subsequent phase of increasing plasma vitamin A concentrations, the average daily intake was >1500 IU/kg/day and the mode of feeding was predominantly by the gastrointestinal route.

V. VITAMIN A SUPPLEMENTATION IN HIGH-RISK INFANTS

Encouraged by these results and by our animal model, we recently completed a randomized double-blind trial of vitamin A supplementation in very low birth weight infants who were considered to be at high risk for developing BPD. Forty infants of <1500 g birth weight were entered if they met the following criteria: they were appropriately grown for gestational age and were oxygen dependent and ventilator dependent on the fourth day of life. Parental consent was obtained in every instance. On a blinded randomized basis, half the infants received a vitamin A supplementation of 2000 IU intramuscularly every other day for the next 28 days and half received a saline placebo. Vitamin A and retinol-binding protein levels in serum were drawn on day of entry and at weekly intervals thereafter for 4 weeks. Routine vitamin A intake was administered to both groups in accordance with the usual intensive care nursery protocol. Infants in each group were judged to be comparable in birth weight, gestational age, and by a wide variety of perinatal and neonatal variables, including the diagnosis of hyaline membrane disease and ventilatory and oxygen requirements on admission to the study.

Values for such variables as average inspired O_2 level by week of study, positive end expiratory pressure, mean added airway pressure, and mean ventilatory index, which were comparable at day of entry, all diverged progressively, reaching statistically different values at 4 weeks, with the vitamin A-supplemented infants having the lower values. The average BPD score for each group was also highly statistically different at 4 weeks ($p = .008$).

The average vitamin A blood levels for control and supplemented infants were identical at entry, but by day 7 of the study and progressively thereafter became highly statistically significantly different, with levels falling in the control group from 19.0 to 14.1 μg/dl and rising in the treated group from 19.7 to 33.2 μg/dl ($p < .005$). One vitamin A-supplemented infant died on the 13th day of study with massive air dissection and grade IV intraventricular hemorrhage, and worse case values were assigned to this infant thereafter.

VI. CONCLUSION

We conclude that vitamin A supplementation in very low birth weight infants can (1) raise their serum levels to those of normal adults; (2) serum levels of retinol-binding protein are likewise increased in response to increased vitamin A blood levels; (3) if infants susceptible to lung injury from such insults as hyaline membrane disease, high inspired oxygen concentrations, and barotrauma from mechanical ventilators also have low vitamin A stores, a prolonged healing phase may occur, contributed to by their vitamin A status; and (4) that such infants, if supplemented with adequate vitamin A intake, may have a more normal regenerative healing phase to their lung injury.

REFERENCES

Shenai, J. P., Chytil, F., Jhaveri, A., and Stahlman, M. T. (1981a). Plasma vitamin A and retinol-binding protein in premature and term neonates. *J. Pediatr.* **99,** 302–305.

Shenai, J. P., Stahlman, M. T., and Chytil, F. (1981b). Vitamin A delivery from parenteral alimentation solution. *J. Pediatr.* **99,** 661–663.

Shenai, J. P., Chytil, F., and Stahlman, M. T. (1985a). Liver vitamin A reserves of very low birth weight neonates. *Pediatr. Res.* **19,** 892–893.

Shenai, J. P., Chytil, F., and Stahlman, M. T. (1985b). Vitamin A status of neonates with bronchopulmonary dysplasia. *Pediatr. Res.* **19,** 185–188.

Stahlman, M. T. (1984). Les maladies respiratoires chroniques du nouveau-ni. *In* "Medecine

Neonatale" (P. Vert and L. Stern, eds.), pp. 450–470. Masson Publishing Company, New York.

Stahlman, M. T., Cheatham, W., and Gray, M. E. (1979). The role of air dissection in bronchopulmonary dysplasia. *J. Pediatr.* **95,** 878–882.

Stahlman, M. T. Gray, M. E., Sundell, H. W., and Chytil, F. (1986). The effects of EGF and retinol on fetal airways. *Pediatr. Res.* **20,** 442A (Abstract).

Wolbach, S. B., and Howe, P. R. (1925). Tissue changes following deprivation of fat-soluble A vitamin. *J. Exp. Med.* **42,** 753–784.

Wolbach, S. B., and Howe, P. R. (1933). Epithelial repair in recovery from vitamin A deficiency. An experimental study. *J. Exp. Med.* **57,** 511–526.

Wong, Y. C., and Buck, R. C. (1971) An electron microscopic study of metaplasia of the rat tracheal epithelium in vitamin A deficiency. *Lab. Invest.* **24,** 55–66.

10

Impact of Antimicrobial Agents on the Intestinal Microflora of Newborn Infants

Rutger Bennet, Margareta Eriksson, and Rolf Zetterström
Department of Pediatrics
Karolinska Institutet
St. Göran's Children's Hospital
Stockholm, Sweden

Carl Erik Nord
Department of Microbiology
Karolinska Institutet
Huddinge University Hospital
Huddinge, Sweden

I. INTRODUCTION

The most common and significant cause of disturbances in the normal intestinal microflora is the administration of antimicrobial agents (1). The microflora can be influenced by antimicrobial agents as a result of incomplete absorption of an orally administered antimicrobial agent, secretion of an agent into the saliva or in the bile, or secretion from the intestinal mucosa. Parenteral agents secreted into the bile or from the intestinal mucosa also cause significant changes in the intestinal microflora. Antimicrobial agents that influence the normal microflora promote emergence of antimicrobial-resistant bacteria. The potential of an antimicrobial agent to affect the colonization is related to its dose and pharmacological properties. Many antimicrobial agents can cause changes in the intestinal microflora, the severity of which depends on the agent's spectrum and concentration in the intestinal contents.

The anaerobic microflora has an inhibitory effect on potentially pathogenic aerobic microorganisms and may act as a resistance factor against new colonization (2). If the anaerobic flora is disturbed, for example, by administration of an antimicrobial agent, the resistance to colonization by new microorganisms is decreased and subsequent overgrowth or new colonization with antimicrobial-resistant bacteria or fungi may occur.

Several investigations have shown that antimicrobial agents have a considerable influence on both the aerobic and anaerobic intestinal flora in children and adults (3). The infant's intestinal microflora is more susceptible to different exogenous factors and therefore the impact of antimicrobial treatment on the flora in newborns may be much greater than that in children and adults.

This chapter summarizes our experience concerning the influence of different antimicrobial agents on the intestinal microflora in newborn infants (4,5).

II. MATERIAL AND METHODS

During the years 1978–1984 we studied the intestinal microflora of newborn infants in the neonatal and intermediate care nurseries of St. Göran's Children's Hospital, Karolinska Institute, Stockholm, Sweden. The hospital is a referral center for pediatric surgery and cardiology for a large area covering the eastern part of middle Sweden. The neonatal intensive and intermediate care units also receive all newborn infants requiring intensive observation and treatment from a local maternity ward with about 1500 births per year. In addition, newborn infants with life-threatening complications are referred from the other four neonatal wards in Stockholm. All aspects of neonatal disease are therefore seen, amounting to approximately 600 patients per year.

One hundred and sixty-four newborn infants of all categories were studied. Of these, 106 were treated with one of the following antimicrobial regimens: gentamicin + ampicillin, gentamicin + ampicillin + cloxacillin, benzylpenicillin + cloxacillin, cefoxitin alone, cefuroxime alone, or flucloxacillin alone. The following doses (in mg/kg/24 hr) were used: benzylpenicillin 100, cloxacillin 100, flucloxacillin 50 (per os), ampicillin 200, gentamicin 5–7.5, cefoxitin 100, and cefuroxime 150. All antimicrobial agents except flucloxacillin were given intravenously.

The first fecal specimen was taken after 4 days of treatment and then every second week during the stay at the hospital. The specimen was collected from the napkin and transported anaerobically to the microbiological laboratory where cultivation and identification was carried out.

III. RESULTS

Anaerobic bacteria disappeared from 90% of the infants during antimicrobial treatment, regardless of regimen used (Fig. 1). Colonization with *Klebsiella* on *Enterobacter* occurred in 60% of the treated infants as opposed to 20% of untreated vaginally delivered infants in the same

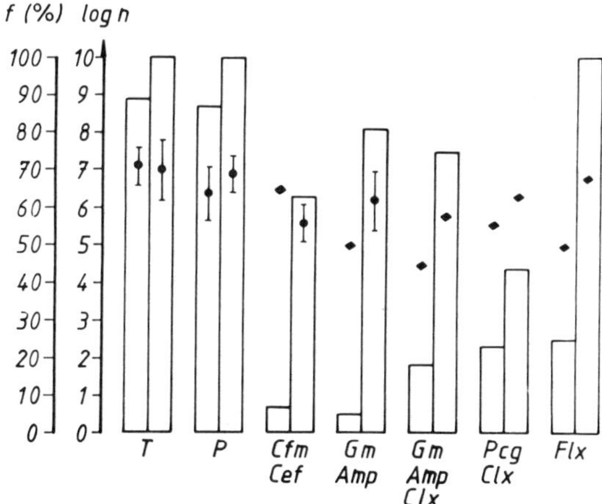

Fig. 1. Influence of preterm birth and antibiotic treatment on rates of colonization and counts of all anaerobic bacteria. Colonization rates are given as percentages of the number of infants showing growth of a given species one or more times (open bars). Counts are presented as mean $\log_{10}$ when there are sufficient numbers of values with 95% confidence interval. T denotes full term and P denotes preterm infants without antibiotic treatment. The other groups were treated with cefuroxime (cfm), cefoxitin (cef), flucloxacillin (flx), or combinations of gentamicin (gm), ampicillin (amp), cloxacillin (clx), and benzylpenicillin (pcG). For the T and P groups, the values to the left signify results for the first 2 weeks of life and to the right for 3–10 weeks. For the treatment groups the left values were obtained *during* antibiotic treatment and the right ones 0–10 weeks *after* treatment.

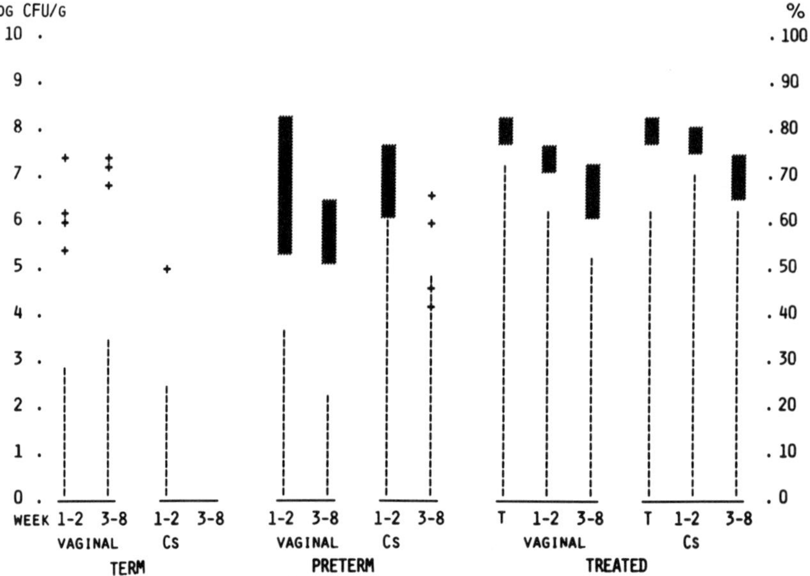

Fig. 2. *Klebsiella* colonization. Percentages of infants colonized by *Klebsiella/Enterobacter* (bars). When there are more than five positive cultures in one group, 95% confidence limits of the mean counts (log *n*/g wet weight) are given (shaded areas). There are three groups of infants: term untreated, preterm untreated, and treated infants (median gestational ages for the two last groups were both 34 weeks.) In each group, infants delivered vaginally are separated from those delivered by cesarean section. Week numbers signify postnatal age for the untreated infants and weeks after termination of antibiotic therapy for the treated ones. T denotes during treatment. Treatment was withdrawn at a median age of 10 days.

ward (Fig. 2). During the 2 weeks following withdrawal of antimicrobial therapy, anaerobic bacteria reappeared in the intestinal tract but the appearance was slower than normal colonization after birth. During the same period *Klebsiella/Enterobacter* decreased, but did not reach the same low levels as in the control infants. The *Klebsiella/Enterobacter* group was partly replaced by *Escherichia coli*. High counts of *Klebsiella/Enterobacter* were found to coincide with low counts of bifidobacteria, lactobacilli, and bacteroides (Fig. 3). During cephalosporin treatment, there was an overgrowth of enterococci, whereas the enterococci were suppressed by the other regimens. *Escherichia coli* was also suppressed by all regimens, except those including only benzylpenicillin, cloxacillin, or flucloxacillin.

An influence of mode of delivery was also observed during the study. Thus, *Bacteroides* species were rarely isolated after cesarean section (Fig. 4), and there was a significant colonization with *Klebsiella/Enterobacter* to levels similar to those seen during antimicrobial treatment (Fig. 2). There

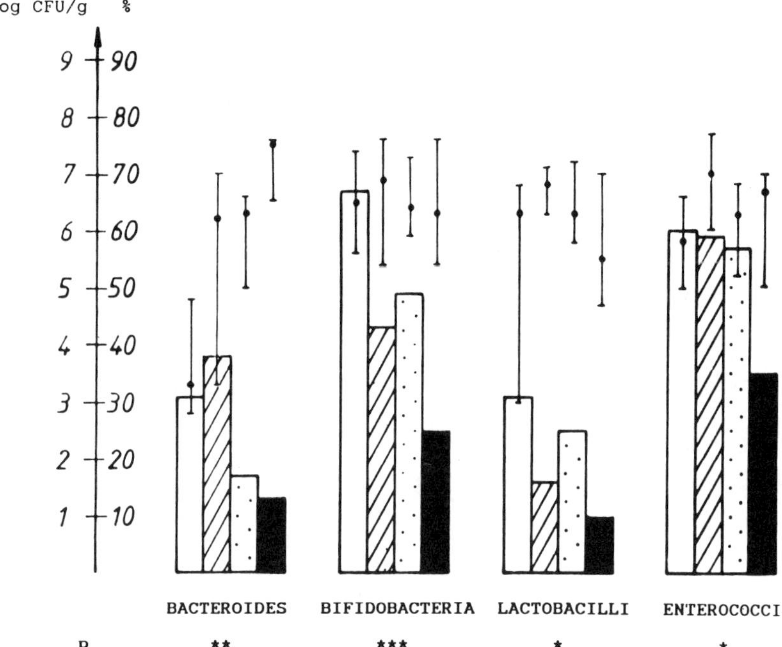

Fig. 3. Fecal growth of *Bacteroides, Bifidobacterium,* and *Lactobacillus* species and of group D streptococci in the presence of various amounts of enterobacteria. All cultures showing growth of *E. coli* or *Klebsiella* were divided into four groups according to counts (log CFU/g wet weight). The isolation rates (%) of anaerobic bacteria and enterococci in each of these four groups were represented by bars as follows: *E. coli* <7.0, open bars; *E. coli* >7.5, hatched bars; *Klebsiella* <7.0, dotted bars; *Klebsiella* >7.5, solid bars. Counts of anaerobic bacteria and enterococci are given as median values with 25th and 75th percentiles as measures of distribution. The *p* values were obtained by chi-square analysis of the colonization frequencies. $^{*}p < .05$; $^{**}\ p < .01$; $^{***}\ p < .001$.

was a slightly lower detection rate of bifidobacteria after cesarean section. Interestingly, this difference relating to mode of delivery persisted when anaerobic bacteria reappeared after antimicrobial treatment (Fig. 5).

IV. DISCUSSION

When antimicrobial agents act on a mixed bacterial population, suppression of susceptible bacterial species and overgrowth of resistant microorganisms can be expected. This has usually also been the case when intestinal microflora has been studied during antimicrobial therapy. However, there are examples of persistence of sensitive bacterial species in spite of high antimicrobial concentrations in feces (6). Several expla-

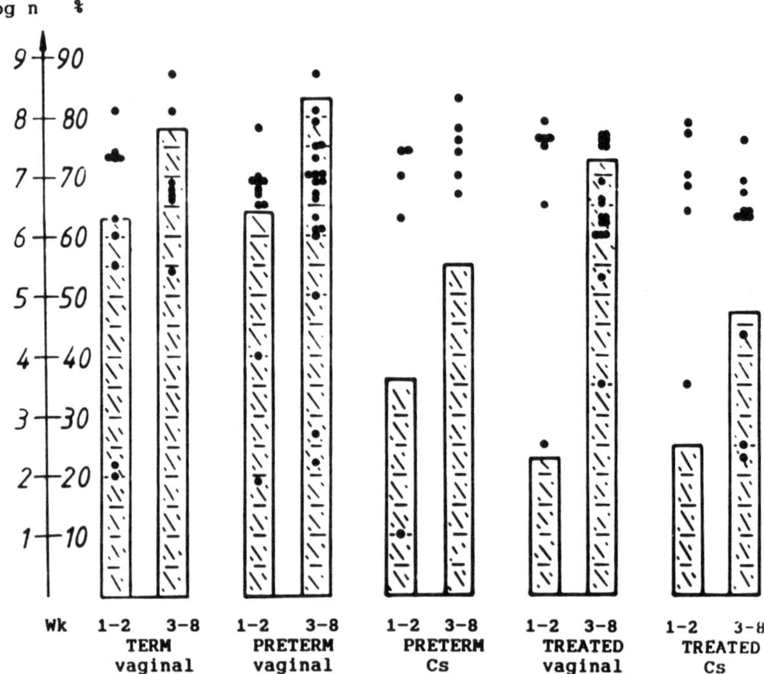

Fig. 4. Isolation rates (%) and counts (log CFU/*g* feces) of *Bifidobacterium* species in newborn, breast milk-fed infants. There are five groups of infants: (1, 2) full term of preterm, vaginally delivered, and healthy; (3) preterm, cesarean section-delivered, and healthy. (4, 5) vaginally or cesarean section-delivered infants treated with the broad-spectrum antibiotic regimens outlined in the legend to Fig. 1. Median gestational age 34 weeks. Treatment was withdrawn at a median age of 10 days. Week numbers signify postnatal age for the untreated infants and weeks after termination of antibiotic therapy for the treated ones.

nations for this inhibition of antimicrobial activity have been suggested, such as binding of antimicrobials to food residues or other fecal constituents (7), enzymatic inactivation, and inaccessible microbial sites (8).

Similar mechanisms could perhaps explain why the impact of parenteral antimicrobial agents on intestinal microflora is less pronounced in adults and older children than in newborn infants. The relative antimicrobial doses used in newborn infants are frequently higher than those given to adults. It is therefore possible that fecal concentrations of antimicrobial agents are higher in newborns. Also, excretion patterns may be different, especially in preterm infants because of immaturity of the kidneys, the biliary system, and the intestinal mucosa. Fecal concentrations of antimicrobial agents in newborn infants are presently being investigated at our hospital.

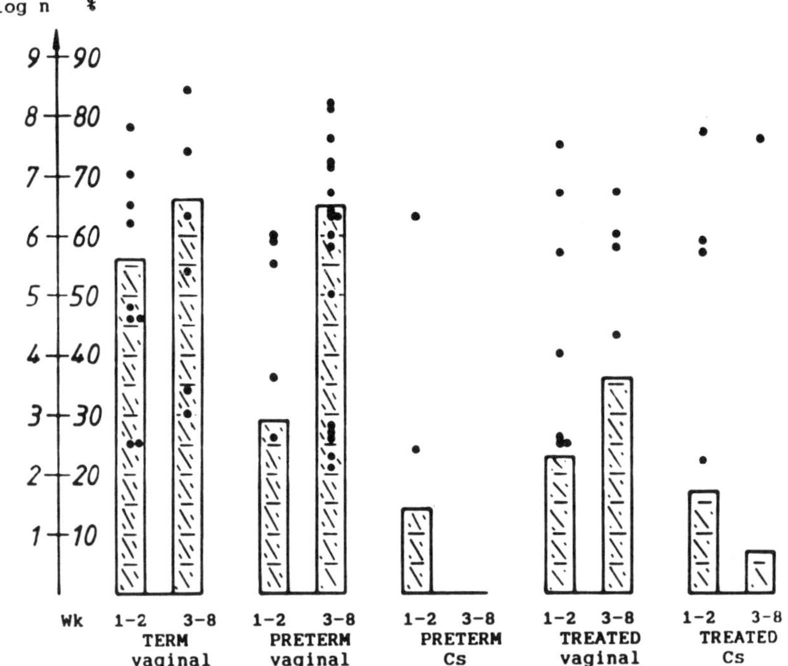

Fig. 5. Isolation rates and counts of *Bacteroides* species in newborn, breast milk-fed infants. For explanation of symbols, see legend to Fig. 4.

Changes of intestinal microflora are probably of consequence, at least for the high-risk infant. The anaerobic intestinal flora is thought to maintain a resistance to colonization and overgrowth of microorganisms from the environment (2). Both colonization and overgrowth are common steps in the pathogenesis of nosocomial infection (9,10) and heavy colonization with gram-negative aerobic bacteria increases the risk of nosocomial infections (1). The immunological systems of breast milk and the host must also be overcome before infection can occur. The host defense systems are probably strengthened by modern methods of general neonatal care, including such major progress as parenteral nutrition. This might explain why the proportion of neonatal septic infections caused by gram-negative bacteria is diminishing despite the increasing survival of high-risk newborns and the frequent use of antimicrobial agents in these patients (11).

In one study, increase of fecal loss of carbohydrates was shown to occur in formula-fed infants during antimicrobial therapy (12). The explanation for this is proposed to be impairment of microbial "colonic salvage" of undigested lactose (13). By this mechanism, lactose is supposed to be degraded by colonic microflora to short-chain fatty acids that are subsequently absorbed and utilized by the newborn infant as an accessory energy source. The suppression of lactose-fermenting bacteria by antimicrobial treatment demonstrated by us fits this hypothesis. It can be concluded that the relationship between antimicrobial treatment and infant nutrition merits further studies.

REFERENCES

1. C. E. Nord, L. Kager, and A. Heimdahl, *Am. J. Med.* **76,** 99 (1984).
2. D. van der Waaij, *J. Antimicrob. Chemother.* **10,** 263 (1982).
3. C. E. Nord, A. Heimdahl, and L. Kager, *Scand. J. Infect. Dis.* **49,** 64 (1986).
4. R. Bennet, M. Eriksson, C. E. Nord, and R. Zetterström, *Pediatr. Infect. Dis.* **5,** 533 (1986).
5. R. Bennet, and C. E. Nord, *Infection* in press.
6. M. J. Butel, and Y. Boussougant, *Pathol. Biol.* **34,** 591 (1986).
7. E. M. Veringa and D. van der Waaij, *J. Antimicrob. Chemother.* **14,** 605 (1984).
8. M. Mulligan, D. Citron, E. Gabay, B. D. Kirby, W. L. George, and S. M. Finegold. *Antimicrob. Agents Chemother.* **26,** 343 (1984).
9. D. Goldmann, J. Leclair, and A. Macone, *J. Pediatr.* **93,** 288 (1978).
10. T. D. Chugh, M. B. Ghaffoor, and A. C. Kuruvilla. *J. Trop. Pediatr.* **31,** 200 (1985).
11. R. Bennet, M. Eriksson, B. Melen, and R. Zetterström, *Acta Paediatr. Scand.* **74,** 687 (1985).
12. J. Bhatia, A. R. Prihoda, and J. C. Richardson, *Am. J. Dis. Child.* **140,** 111 (1986).
13. J. D. Johnson, *Am. J. Dis. Child.* **140,** 101 (1986).

11

The Ontogeny of Gut Mucosal Defense

L. Å. Hanson,* Barbro Carlsson,*,† U. Dahlgren,* L. Mellander,† and A. Wold*

*Department of Clinical Immunology
†Department of Pediatrics
University of Göteborg
Göteborg, Sweden

Fehmida Jalil* and Shaukat Raza Khan†

*Department of Social and Preventive Pediatrics
†Deparment of Pediatrics
King Edward Medical College
Lahore, Pakistan

I. INTRODUCTION

Man cannot live without host defense, but the defense against infections is more important in some organs than in others. This is clearly illustrated by the central nervous system, in which few, if any, cells involved in defense, such as lymphocytes and phagocytes, are seen. In contrast, the intestinal mucosa contains more than half of the lymphoid system as well as many phagocytes and a number of other cells which also can be enhanced by lymphocytes, such as mucosal mast cells and goblet cells. The explanation for this discrepancy is of course the striking difference in antigenic exposure. Few if any microbes and little other antigenic material pass the blood–brain barrier, whereas the gut is constantly exposed to large numbers of microbes—half the weight of the stool is said to consist of live or dead bacteria. In addition, the intestine has the task of absorbing food, small amounts of which are later found in the circulation still in antigenic form. Clearly the intestine has a very difficult task: to react with and keep out potentially harmful microorganisms and at the same time accept and not react with food antigens.

II. HOST DEFENSE IN THE GUT

A. Specific Immunity

There are as many as 10^{10} lymphocytes per meter in the intestine. Most of these produce IgA dimers which carry J chain and can bind to special receptors present on the basal portion of certain epithelial cells. Receptor-carrying epithelium is found in submucosal glands of the gut as well as in most other mucosae and also in exocrine organs, such as the mammary gland. The extramural part of this receptor structure is called the secretory component. Once it has combined with the J chain–IgA dimer the complex is transported through the epithelial cell cytoplasm and appears on the mucosal surface as stable secretory IgA (sIgA) antibodies. These antibodies can be induced by antigenic exposure in central lymphoid organs in the gut, the Peyer's patches. The patches consist of aggregates of lymphocytes and antigen-presenting macrophages covered by a specialized epithelium, the M cells, which are pinocytotically active and seem to "sample" intestinal content and bring it into contact with the macrophages-lymphocytes. The B lymphocytes in the patches are mostly committed to IgA production and leave after antigen exposure via the lymph through the blood-circulation. They home to exocrine glands, the sites where they finally propagate and produce the J chain–IgA dimer antibodies. After being transported onto the mucosa the sIgA antibodies are found as an "antiseptic paint" throughout the intestine. These antibodies were originally found in human milk, where they are present in large amounts (Hanson, 1961).

In addition to sIgA much IgG is present in the mucosa. Immunocytes producing not only IgG but also IgM and IgD are found there (Hanson and Brandtzaeg, 1987). IgE antibodies are not synthesized in the intestinal mucosa, but are mainly carried into it by mast cells.

If IgG and IgM antibodies are allowed to react with their antigens in the mucosa, they activate complement, bring in granulocytes, and inflammation follows. IgE antibodies enact inflammation in the form of an immediate type of hypersensitivity. The mucosa is also rich in T lymphocytes, which can turn into cytotoxic killer cells or, via lymphokine production and activation of macrophages, release an inflammation seen as a delayed type of hypersensitivity reaction. About 5–20% of the epithelium consists of intraepithelial lymphocytes of the T and/or NK (natural killer) lymphocyte cell lineage. It has been shown that sIgA antibodies together with intraepithelial lymphocytes or mononuclear cells from the lamina propria can kill *Salmonella* bacteria via an antibody-dependent cellular cytotoxicity (ADCC) reaction (Tagliabue *et al.*, 1984). It is obvious that the intestine is very well equipped for specific immune defense.

Recent data suggest that there may be a close cooperation between hormones and the immune system of the gut. Freier *et al.* (1983) have shown that secretin as well as pancreozymin can increase the amount of immunoglobulin in the lumen. It is also becoming obvious that neurotransmitters can specifically influence lymphocytes from the intestinal lymphoid tissue. Thus VIP as well as substance P can enhance production of IgA from such cells (Stanitz *et al.*, 1986). The gut is very rich in nervous tissue and it seems likely that neurotransmitters can interfere positively, or negatively, with the intestinal immune mechanisms.

B. Nonspecific Defense

Increased peristalsis and diarrhea is part of the host defense of the gut and so is production of mucus. In this connection it is of interest that the proliferation of mucus-producing goblet cells in mucosal membranes seems to be T-cell dependent in man, as well as in experimental animals (Karlsson *et al.*, 1985). The phagocytes in the gut mucosa must be important for the defense through their capacity to respond to chemotaxis induced via complement, lymphokines, and mediators from mast cells. The capacity of granulocytes and lymphokine-activated macrophages is crucial for engulfing and killing microorganisms via the content of, for example, lactoferrin and free radicals.

III. THE ONTOGENY OF HOST DEFENSE IN THE GUT

A. Specific Defense

After this brief review of the normal defense of the gut it would be interesting to describe when and how this develops in the fetus and neonate. Unfortunately, our specific knowledge concerning this aspect of the ontogeny of the human gut is very limited. A recent study by Spencer *et al.*, (1986) showed that indications of development of Peyer's patches occurred first in an 11-week fetus. At 14–16 weeks gestation there were macrophages as well as T and B lymphocytes in this gut-associated lymphoid tissue. Only at 19 weeks was an architecture similar to that of Peyer's patches noted. At that time the B cells had surface IgM, IgD, and C3b receptors.

In a recent, preliminary study, large numbers of IgM-positive cells were detected in the liver and spleen, with small numbers in the small intestine and stomach, in fetuses of 16 weeks gestational age. Only a few IgA-positive cells appeared in the bone marrow by 25 weeks and at 26–28 weeks in salivary glands and small intestine (Takashi and Moro, 1987). J chain-positive cells were also noted early and at 25 weeks of fetal age secretory component could be found in the small intestine. Early studies showed the presence of plasma cells in the gut of infants at the age of 3 weeks (Bridges *et al.*, 1959). The number of such cells between the ages 3 months and 2 years was at about 80% of the level seen in older children (Savilathi, 1972). A more recent study by Perkkiö and Savilathi (1980) of 46 intestinal biopsies taken from infants 2 hr to 6 months of age showed that only occasional IgM-producing cells could be seen between 6 and 12 days of age. From 12 days on, IgA- as well as IgM-containing cells were observed. Up to about 1 month of age the IgM cells predominated, but later the IgA cells took over. The number of IgM and IgA producers continued to increase up to 2 years of age after having remained at about the same level during the age 1–6 months.

IgG was seen intercellularly in the mucosa in the neonates. Presumably it was of maternal origin (Perkkiö and Savilathi, 1980). There were few IgG-producing cells the first 6 months, then there was an increase up to 2 years of age, but still the IgA-containing cells dominated, followed by the IgM-containing cells.

The findings of Takashi and Moro (1987) are in agreement with our recent studies of sIgA and IgM antibodies in the saliva of neonates and the findings of Petit *et al.* (1973) of sIgA and IgM in the gut wall and gut contents from some fetuses. The salivary antibodies result from local production in labial salivary glands and antigenic stimuli in the Peyer's patches, followed by homing of IgA-committed cells to the salivary glands (Hanson and Brandtzaeg, 1987). Therefore the salivary antibodies should be expected to reflect the intestinal responsiveness. sIgA antibodies to *Escherichia coli* O antigens and poliovirus type I antigen were found in the newborn and remained at the same low level for the first several months of life in Swedish infants (Mellander *et al.*, 1984). In Pakistani infants with a heavier microbial exposure, a significant increase of sIgA antibodies to the *E.coli* lipopolysaccharide (LPS) was seen at a few weeks of age (Mellander *et al.*, 1985). In the Swedish infants the sIgM remained at the same level as long as their salivary sIgA was low; when the increase of sIgA anti-*E.coli* LPS occurred in the Pakistani infants a parallel decrease of the sIgM was noted. Thus IgM antibodies to *E.coli* were obviously transferred into the saliva via the secretory components as long as the local production of IgA was limited. It may be useful for the infant to have the early produced IgM appear not only in the circulation but also on mucosal membranes, in effect waiting for the sIgA antibodies to be produced. Once the local IgA synthesis increases, the secretory component-dependent transfer mechanism may be fully utilized and no more IgM can be transferred via its J- chain, which may form the ligand for the receptor consisting of the secretory component.

Neonatal breast milk (witch's milk) contains sIgA. Recent studies by Roberton *et al.* (1986) showed sIgA antibodies in the neonatal milk against β-lactoglobulin during the second week of life in infants who were given cow's milk formula. No such antibodies were seen in babies not given cow's milk, arguing against a transfer of sIgA antibodies from the mother. Also in agreement with this is the continuous increase of IgA in feces during the first weeks of life (Haneberg and Aarskog, 1975).

It seems that the response of salivary sIgA antibodies to *E. coli* adhesins in the form of pili or fimbriae comes later than the response to *E.coli* LPS antigens. The difference could be due to the fact that the infants are less exposed to the adhesins than the LPS, but it could also relate to the mitogenic effect of LPS.

Another possibility is suggested by recent studies in the rat showing that IgA-committed cells from the Peyer's patches of different specificity may home differently (Dahlgren *et al.*, 1987). Immunization of rats in the Peyer's patches with *E. coli* 06 carrying type 1 pili results in IgA antibodies to the pilus and the LPS found, for example, in milk and bile. It was noted, however, that the IgA antibody activity to the pilus antigen was higher in the milk than in the bile, whereas the IgA anti-LPS antibody activity was higher in the bile than in the milk (Fig. 1). If a similar diversity includes salivary antibodies, sIgA antibodies to LPS may for this reason come earlier than antibodies to pili.

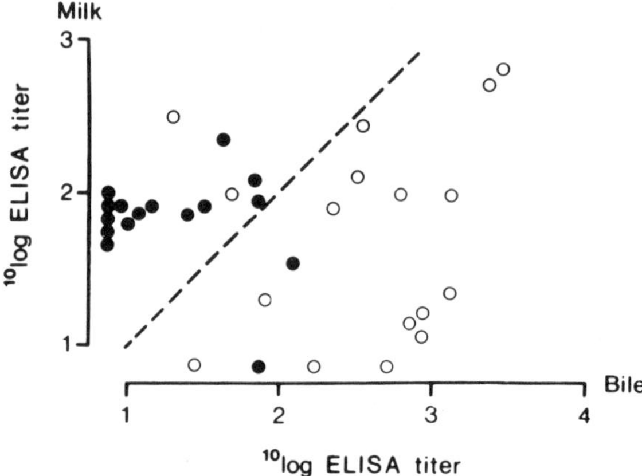

Fig. 1. Plot of IgA anti-type 1 pili (•) and IgA anti-06 LPS (○) antibody titers in milk versus bile 8 days after immunization in the Peyer's patches with *E. coli* 06 carrying type 1 pili. Each dot represents one rat.

It was a surprising observation that sIgA and sIgM antibodies occurred in the saliva of the neonates, not only against *E.coli* but also against poliovirus. The latter finding may be especially relevant, since neither wild nor vaccine strains of polioviruses occur in Sweden after many years of efficient immunization with inactivated vaccine. Therefore no exposure of the fetus to poliovirus antigen should have taken place, as could have happened with the commonly present *E.coli* LPS. Transfer of sIgA and IgM antibodies from mother to fetus is not known to occur (Roberton *et al.*, 1986). Such antibodies were noted in amniotic fluid and in meconium of newborns, as well as in the saliva and meconium of a healthy newborn of a hypogammaglobulinemia mother who lacked IgA and IgM, but had IgG after intravenous immunoglobulin prophylaxis (Mellander *et al.*, 1986). In this instance the fetus must have produced the IgA and IgM, but the question is where the antigen came from. Since no poliovirus antigen presumably is around, we have assumed that the stimulus might have consisted of IgG anti-anti-polio antibodies transferred from the mother. If this is correct, infants may be born primed by anti-idiotypic antibodies of many specificities from the mother. Many immune responses of the neonate may therefore be booster responses coming faster and reaching higher levels than in primary responses.

The young infant is deficient in T-helper cell activity and also in various functions of phagocytes (Hayward, 1983). It is not clear in what way this may influence intestinal defense. However, the early onset of the sIgA production in the human suggests that the Peyer's patches may be functional early and that sufficient T-cell help is available, since sIgA production is clearly dependent on the T-cell system (Hanson and Brandtzaeg, 1987).

B. Influence of Maternal Food Intake on the Immune Responsiveness of the Offspring

Rat pups nursed by dams fed ovalbumin-substitued rat- chow did not show any altered immune response to ovalbumin after a subcutaneous injection at adult age if they were only exposed to ovalbumin *in utero* or via the milk the first 2 weeks of the lactation period. On the other hand, if the pups were allowed access to the food the last week of their nursing period as well, they showed a marked decrease in the activity of their antibody response to ovalbumin. This was in sharp contrast to the effect on the dams, who did not show any tolerance to ovalbumin despite the fact that they had been eating the food for 5 weeks. It is probable that these findings are also relevant for the immune response to food in the human infant.

C. Nonspecific Defense in the Gut

Little is known about the maturation of the mucosa from the host defense point of view, including when the epithelial cell receptors occur, to which microorganisms can bind in the initiation of infection (Svanborg Edén *et al.*, 1980). It was demonstrated that human milk, in addition to being a rich source of sIgA antibodies, also contains nonimmunoglobulin components which inhibit the attachment of pneumococci to pharyngeal cells (Andersson *et al.*, 1986) and presumably enterobacterial toxins to intestinal epithelium (Otnaess *et al.*, 1983). These receptor analogues can be low molecular weight oligosaccharides, as for pneumococci, or high molecular weight structures, as for *Haemophilus influenzae* (Andersson *et al.*, 1986). It is likely that the oligosaccharides in meconium contain a number of analogues for microbial receptors. It could be that they are important in helping to prevent infections from occurring in the newborn during the early intestinal colonization with many bacterial species, including potentially pathogenic *E.coli* (Hanson *et al.*, 1983).

IV. CONCLUSION

Clearly our knowledge concerning the ontogeny of gut defense is very limited. Still, it seems clear that the capacity to produce secretory IgA and IgM antibodies may be present much earlier than previously realized. These antibodies may be important for host defense in the gut. Analogues for microbial receptors on gut epithelium may also be important. Such receptor analogues are found, for example, in milk.

ACKNOWLEDGMENTS

The skillful technical assistance of Eva Nisshagen, Helena Kahu, and Eva Ågren is much appreciated. The studies were supported by grants from the Swedish Medical Research Council (No. 215), the Swedish Agency for Research Cooperation with Developing Countries, the Ellen, Walter, and Lennart Hesselman Foundation for Research, and the Swedish National Bank Fund.

REFERENCES

Andersson, B., Ponas, O., Hanson, L. Å., Lagergård, T., and Svanborg Edén, C. (1986). *J. Infect. Dis.* **153,** 232–237.

Bridges, R. A., Condie, R. M., Zak, S. J., and Good, R. A. (1959). *J. Lab. Clin. Med.* **53,** 331–357.

Dahlgren, U., Ahlstedt, S., and Hanson, L. Å. (1987). *J. Immunol.* **138,** 1397–1402.

Freier, S., Lebenthal, E., Freier, M., Shah, P. C., Park, B. H., and Lee, P. C. (1983). *Immunology* **49,** 69–75.

Haneberg, B., and Aarskog, D. (1975). *Clin. Exp. Immunol.* **22,** 210–222.

Hanson, L. Å. (1961). *Int. Arch. Allergy Appl. Immunol.* **18,** 241–267.

Hanson, L. Å., and Brandtzaeg, P. (1987). *In* "Immunological Diseases in Infants and Children" (R. T. Stiehm, ed.), 3rd Ed. Saunders, Philadelphia, Pennsylvania. In press.

Hayward, A. R. (1983). *In* "Pediatric Immunology" (J. F. Soothill, A. R. Hayward, and C. B. S. Wood, eds.), pp. 48–55. Blackwell, Oxford.

Karlsson, G., Hanson, H. A., Petruson, B., Björkander, J., and Hanson, L. Å. (1985). *Int. Archs. Allergy Appl. Immunol.* **78,** 86–91.

Mellander, L., Carlsson, B., and Hanson, L. Å. (1984). *J. Pediatr.* **104,** 564–568.

Mellander, L., Carlsson, B., Jahil, F., Söderström, T., and Hanson, L. Å. (1985). *J. Pediatr.* **107,** 430–433.

Mellander, L., Carlsson, B., and Hanson, L. Å. (1986). *Clin. Exp. Immunol.* **63,** 551–561.

Otnaess, A. B., Laegreid, A., and Ertesväg, K. (1983). *Infect. Immun.* **40,** 563–569.

Perkkiö, M., and Savilathi, E. (1980). *Pediatr. Res.* **14,** 953–955.

Petit, J. C., Galinha, A., and Salomon, J. C. (1973). *Eur. J. Immunol.* **3,** 373–375.

Roberton, D. M., Forrest, P. J., Frangonlis, E., Jones, C. L., and Mermelstein, N. (1986). *Arch. Dis. Child.* **3,** 489–494.

Savilathi, E. (1972). *Clin. Exp. Immunol.* **11,** 415–425.

Spencer, J., MacDonald, T. T., Finn, T., and Isaacson, P. G. (1986). *Clin. Exp. Immunol.* **64,** 536–543.

Stanitz, A. M., Befus, D., and Bienenstock, J. (1986). *J. Immunol.* **136,** 152–156.

Svanborg Edén, C., Hagberg, L., Hanson, L. Å., Korhonen, T., Leffler, H., and Olling,

S. (1980). *In* "Adhesion and Microorganism Pathogenicity," Ciba Foundation Symposium No. 80, pp. 161–187. Pitman, London.

Tagliabue, A., Boraschi, D., Villa, L., Keren, D. F., Lonell, G. H., Rappuoli, R., and Neucioni, L. (1984). *J. Immunol.* **133,** 988–992.

Takashi, I., and Moro, I. (1987). *Proc. Int. Congr. Mucosal Immun.* Abstr. In press.

12

Perinatal Development of Liver Enzymes

Birgitta Strandvik

Department of Pediatrics
Karolinska Institutet
Huddinge University Hospital
Huddinge, Sweden

I. PHYLOGENESIS

In comparative physiology the liver is considered a unique organ found only in vertebrates (for review see Cornelius, 1985). A limited homophyly is found in the midgut glands in invertebrates. These midgut glands have sometimes been referred to as the hepatopancreas, a criticized term because of the limited structural and functional similarities with the pancreas and the still fewer identical properties of the vertebrate liver.

The liver originates as a digestive gland and is embryologically similar to the midgut gland but with addition of new functions involving excretion of specific compounds, metabolism and storage of nutrients, and regulating homeostasis of the internal environment of the organism. Some of these functions, whether identical or similar, can be found in the invertebrates, but not always in the midgut gland; for example, chloragogen cells surrounding the intestines of earthworms perform metabolic functions similar to the vertebrate liver and store lipids and glycogen. Microsomal cytochrome *P*-450 is known in the midgut gland of the lobster; UDP-glucosyltransferase and UDP-glucoronyltransferase conjugations occur in the midgut homogenates of sea urchin, and aromatic acids can be metabolized and excreted by insects. Crustaceans lack the ability to synthesize cholesterol but can synthesize a detergent taurine compound, which is essential for intestinal micellization of ingested sterols, a function similar to that of bile acids in vertebrates.

The abrupt change from a simple midgut gland in *Amphioxus,* which for invertebrates has a unique portal vein system (Buchsbaum, 1955), to a separate liver and pancreas in vertebrates remains a mystery. These developmental aspects have more than historical interest, since phylogenesis is usually reflected in the ontogenesis of an organ, and remembering this old truth can help us understand the human development.

II. ONTOGENESIS

A. Enzymatic Pattern during Development

The regulatory function of the liver in the neonatal period has been extensively investigated. In the 1950s and 1960s important contributions regarding carbohydrate and protein metabolism were made (for reviews see Dawkins, 1966; Kretchmer, 1959). The immaturity of bilirubin metabolism in the neonatal period was recognized and with the development of clinical pharmacology special attention was given to drug metabolism. A rapid extension of our knowledge has occurred in the last 10 years, since investigations in rats have shown that the various enzymes in the developing rat liver tend to change in the same direction as they do in the human (Greengard, 1977). Because of the sparse data on human liver enzyme concentrations and activities during development, the animal model can give us information about the quality of the immaturity of the human liver. The trigger mechanisms for development of enzymatic activity at the time of birth are possibly similar and less species specific.

During study of tyrosine metabolism, Kretchmer (1959) recognized different patterns of enzymatic activity during development. The phenylalanine transaminase activity increased before birth to adult levels and after birth exceeded this level for about 2 weeks (Fig. 1,I). In contrast, the activity of phenylalanine hydroxylase remained low for the first days

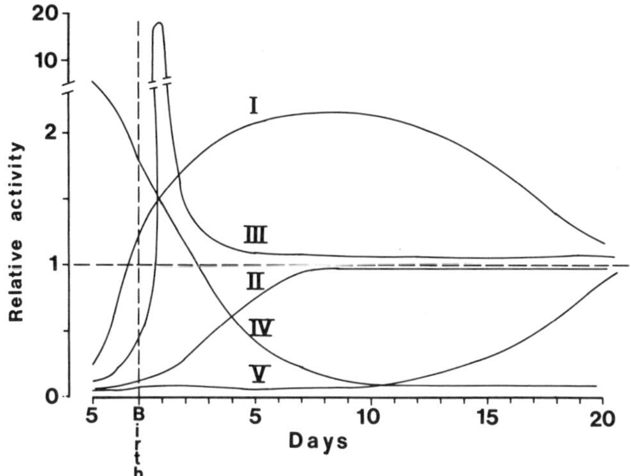

Fig. 1. Developmental patterns of enzymatic activity. I: gradual increase around time of birth, II: gradual increase after birth; III: sharp increase after birth; IV: decrease of activity around time of birth; V: gradual increase around time of weaning. Relative activity in comparison to that in adults.

of life and only slowly reached the activity in the adult (Fig. 1,II). A third pattern was represented by tyrosine transaminase, which suddenly exhibited activity a few hours postnatally and had a maximum activity 12 hr after birth, which was up to 10 times that of the adult liver, and within 24 hr the activity returned to that found in adults (Fig. 1,III). These different patterns have now been recognized in most hepatic enzymes studied, although a few enzyme activities decrease at time of, or after, birth (Fig. 1,IV). The 12-hydroxylating activity to bile acids shown in the mitochondrial fraction of fetal human liver is one interesting example (Gustafsson, 1985), since this activity is only found in the microsomal fraction in adults. Sometimes this decrease of enzyme is due to the development of isoenzymes which take over a function, and which may be species specific (Herzfeld *et al.*, 1976). Still another enzymatic pattern is represented by enzymes whose activity develops more slowly after birth, as in rats at or after weaning (Fig. 1,V). This fifth pattern is found in alcohol dehydrogenase (Pikkarainen and Räihä, 1967), ornithine aminotransferase (Herzfeld and Greengard, 1969), and cystine dioxygenase and cysteinsulfinate decarboxylase (Sturman *et al.*, 1977).

B. Mechanisms of Enzymatic Differentiation

Different known mechanisms of enzymatic differentiation in the perinatal period are shown in Table I. The central determinant of synthesis

TABLE I

Regulation of Enzymatic Development

Gene expression	
Activators/inhibitors	Vitamins Minerals
Hormones	ACTH Corticosteroids Thyroxine Gonadal Glucagon
Membrane fluidity	Ratio of phospholipids/cholesterol Ratio of phosphatidylcholine/sphingomyelin Ratio of saturated/unsaturated fatty acids
Nutrition	Starvation Cholesterol Fat content Protein

of enzymes *de novo* is the gene expression and this is therefore the main regulator of the changing profile of specific enzymes of proteins in embryonic or fetal development. The lack of the production of a protein, or protein portion, of a specific enzyme is one possible mechanism that can lead to lack of enzymatic activity. If the appropriate gene locus exists there must also be a trigger which starts enzyme activity at the crucial time of development. This would be an activation or loss of inhibitor, a classical example being the activation of *p*-OH-phenylpyruvate oxidase by vitamin C in tyrosine metabolism.

The induction of several enzyme activities at delivery has mainly been considered to be controlled by endocrine events. The pituitary (ACTH) regulates the glycogen storage in the liver at birth, which was first shown in the rabbit (Jost and Jacquot, 1955). Cortisone and thyroxine are other important regulators (Greengard, 1970). Administration of corticosteroids to fetuses causes precocious rises in the levels and activities of several enzymes (Greengard, 1971) or in products, suggesting a stimulatory effect on, for instance, cholesterol synthesis (Carr and Simpson, 1984), glycine conjugation of bile acids (Haber *et al.*, 1978), and bile acid pool size (Watkins *et al.*, 1975). In a study of albumin synthesis performed on fetal rat hepatocyte cultures, it has been shown that the effect of corticosteroids on albumin synthesis was mediated by an effect of mRNA levels (Yeoh *et al.*, 1985). The experiments did not clarify if the dexamethasone led to a stabilization of the message and/or an increased rate of transcription of the gene. The present development of molecular biology will probably further elucidate the modes of the corticosteroid effects in stimulation of enzyme activity.

Other important influences are exerted by the gonadal hormones, which have been shown to influence the hepatic bile salt sulfotransferase activity (Kane *et al.*, 1984; Kirkpatrick *et al.*, 1985). The bile salt sulfotransferase activity is very low in the human fetus (Chen *et al.*, 1978) but increases after birth (Chen *et al.*, 1982; S.-I. Niijima, Å. Ellin, and B. Strandvik, unpublished observations) (Fig. 2). The difference in activity in sexes is due to the influence of estrogen on one of two isoenzymes, which have different activities for different monohydroxy bile acids. Whether the postnatal development of bile salt sulfotransferase activity is due to one or both of the isoenzymes is not known, but could be of great importance in relation to neonatal cholestasis. Preliminary results in our laboratory indicate that adrenalectomy also influences the postnatal development of this enzyme activity (Fig. 2).

Other hormones that regulate gene expression at the time of birth are glucagon, which in both man and rat increases in plasma at birth (Assan and Girard, 1975; Girard *et al.*, 1972). Both tyrosine aminotransferase and phosphoenolpyruvate carboxykinase can be evoked by glucagon administration or premature delivery (Greengard, 1977; Yeung and Oliver, 1968).

Membrane-bound enzymes are also influenced by the physical properties of the membranes, mainly the lipid microviscosity. It has been

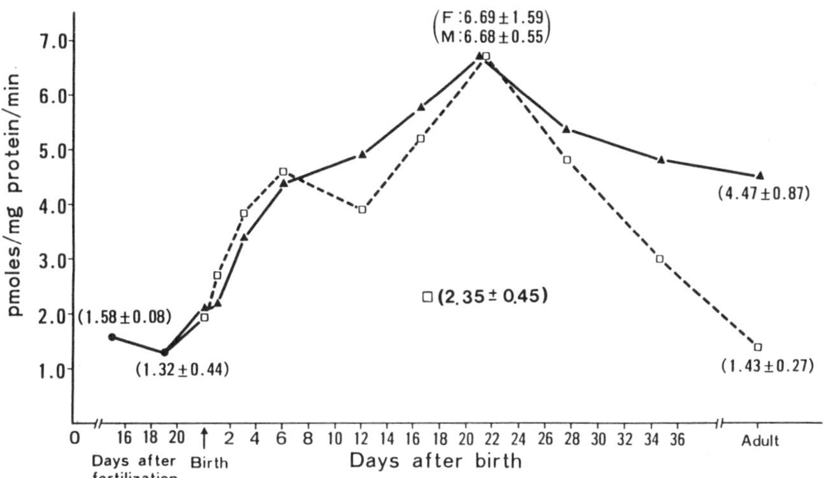

Fig. 2. Bile salt sulfotransferase activity in rat liver during development in fetus (●) and in female (▲) and male (□) animals. Single square represents mean of six animals adrenalectomized after birth (S.-I. Niijima *et al.*, unpublished observations.).

shown that rat liver microsomal membranes undergo a remarkable perinatal fluidization (Kapitulnik *et al.*, 1979; Delpech *et al.*, 1984). The microviscosity of lipids decreased 30–40% at days around birth, which was paralleled by an increase in the phospholipid content of the liver, giving a twofold rise in the phospholipid–cholesterol molar ratio. Other factors influencing the microviscosity are the degree of unsaturation of the phospholipid acyl chains and the molar ratio of phosphatidylcholine to sphingomyelin. This has been shown by Feuer (1978), who reported a significant perinatal increase in the production of liver microsomal phosphatidylcholine with an increasingly higher proportion of unsaturated fatty acids. The development in the piglet liver of Δ5-desaturase—a fatty acid elongation and desaturation enzyme—shows a 23-fold increase of the activity during the second part of gestation (Clandinin *et al.*, 1985).

Nutrition, qualitatively and quantitatively, is probably also of great importance (Goldsmith, 1981) and has potential long-term effects. Starvation of newborn rats has been shown to increase the lipoprotein lipase activity in the liver. The triacylglycerol content, as well as circulating triacylglycerol and ketone bodies, was not increased progressively as seen in fed animals. The actual mechanism of the rapid induction of the enzyme was not established (Grinberg *et al.*, 1985).

Effects of early cholesterol feeding have generated great interest because of the possible association with atherosclerosis in adults. Feeding newborn chicks with 2% cholesterol showed an increase in the cholesterol–phospholipid molar ratio of hepatic microsomes, which in relation to what has been said above might influence other enzyme activities as well (Alejandre *et al.*, 1985a). One example is the inhibition of 3-hydroxy-3-methylglutaryl-CoA reductase (HMG-CoA reductase), the rate-limiting enzyme of cholesterol synthesis, which was found in both short-term (Ramirez *et al.*, 1984) and long-term studies (Alejandre *et al.*, 1985b). Recently, a factor (not cholesterol) has been found in breast milk which stimulates cholesterol 7-hydroxylase, the rate-limiting enzyme of bile acid biosynthesis (Subbiah and Yunker, 1985). This could be related to earlier observations that premature weaning in animals to solid diets causes changes in cholesterol homeostatic mechanisms, some of which persist into adult life (Hahn *et al.*, 1978; Kris-Etherton *et al.*, 1979).

There have also been studies indicating that perinatal changes in the dietary fat intake (35% of calories versus 5%) give no immediate effect on drug-metabolizing enzymes, but regulate the pattern of microsomal mixed-function oxidases in adult life (Sonawane *et al.*, 1983). It has been known for a long time that protein intake stimulates the hydroxylating microsomal enzymes.

III. PRACTICAL IMPLICATIONS

Knowledge about enzyme development in the perinatal period is important for the understanding of normal development and diseases in the neonatal period. Many studies show that it is important not to interfere with, for instance, nutritional changes before animal studies, including long-term effects, have been performed. Knowledge about different hepatic enzymes might also be of value for classifying or identifying different neoplasms and may make it possible to interfere with their growth and thus their malignancy. I support the suggestion by Greengard (1977) that a more extensive study of enzymes in biopsies and postmortem examinations would greatly extend the resolving power of the usual diagnostic procedures. When morphology is normal, only deviation from the organ-characteristic quantitative pattern of gene products would provide sensitive enough indicators of metabolic lesions and the aberrant aspects of differentiation that were responsible for them. Collaboration between pediatricians and molecular biogeneticists would probably open new fields and rapidly extend our present knowledge.

ACKNOWLEDGMENT

This work was supported by grants from the Swedish Medical Research Council (4995).

REFERENCES

Alejandre, M. J., Zafra, M. F., Ramirez, H., Segovia, J. L., and Garcia-Peregrin, E. (1985a). *Int. J. Biochem.* **17,** 835–838.

Alejandre, M. J., Ramirez, H., Segovia, J. L., and Garcia-Peregrin, E. G. (1985b). *Ann. Nutr. Metab.* **29,** 111–118.

Assan, R., and Girard, J. R. (1975). *In* "Early Diabetes in Early Life" (R. A. Camerini-Davalos and H. S. Cole, eds.), pp. 115–136. Academic Press, New York.

Buchsbaum, R. (1955). "Animals without Backbones," Vol. 2, pp. 338–347. Penguin Books, Middlesex, England.

Carr, B. R., and Simpson, E. R. (1984). *J. Clin. Endocrinol. Metab.* **58,** 1111–1116.

Chen, L. J., Thaler, M. M., Bolt, R. J., and Golbus, M. S. (1978). *Life Sci.* **22,** 1817–1820.

Chen L. J., Kane, B., Bujanover, Y., and Thaler, M. M. (1982). *Biochim. Biophys. Acta* **713,** 358–364.

Clandinin, M. T., Wong, K., and Hacker, R. R. (1985). *Biochem. J.* **227,** 1021–1023.

Cornelius, C. E. (1985). *Hepatology* **5,** 1213–1221.

Dawkins, M. J. R. (1966). *Adv. Reprod. Physiol.* **1,** 217–264.

Delpech, I., Kiffel, L., Magdalon, J., Siest, G., Martin, P., Bouchy, M., and Andreé, J.-C. (1984). *Biochem. Biophys. Res. Commun.* **119,** 29–34.

Feuer, G. (1978). *Res. Comm. Chem. Pathol. Pharmacol.* **22,** 549–56.

Girard, J., Bal, D., and Assan, R. (1972). *Horm. Metab. Res.* **4,** 168–170.
Goldsmith, P. K. (1981). *Biochim. Biophys. Acta* **672,** 45–56.
Greengard, O. (1970). *In* "Biochemical Actions of Hormones" (G. Litwack, ed.), Vol. 1, pp. 53–87, Academic Press, New York.
Greengard, O. (1971). *Essays Biochem.* **7,** 159–205.
Greengard, O. (1977). *Pediatr. Res.* **11,** 669–676.
Grinberg, D. R., Ramirez, I., Viraró, S., Reina, M., Llobera, M., and Herrera, E. (1985). *Biochim. Biophys. Acta* **833,** 217–222.
Gustafsson, J. (1985). *J. Clin. Invest.* **75,** 604–606.
Haber, L. R., Vaupshas, V., Vitullo, B. B., Seemayer, T. A., and De Belle, R. C. (1978). *Gastroenterology* **74,** 1214–1223.
Hahn, P., Girard, J., Assan, A., Kenvran, A., and Koldovsky, O. (1978). *J. Nutr.* **108,** 1783–1789.
Herzfeld, A., and Greengard, O. (1969). *J. Biol. Chem.* **244,** 4894–4898.
Herzfeld, A., Rosenoer, V. M., and Raper, S. M. (1976). *Pediatr. Res.* **10,** 960–963.
Jost, A., and Jacquot, R. (1955). *Ann. Endocrinol.* **16,** 849–872.
Kane, R. E., Chen, L. J., and Thaler, M. M. (1984). *Hepatology* **4,** 1195–1199.
Kapitulnik, J., Tshershedsky, M., and Barenholz, Y. (1979). *Science* **206,** 843–844.
Kirkpatrick, R. B., Wildermann, N. M., and Killenberg, P. G. (1985). *Am. J. Physiol.* **248,** G639–G642.
Kretchmer, N. (1959). *Pediatrics* **23,** 606–617.
Kris-Etherton, P. M., Layman, D. K., York, P. V., and Frantz, I. D., Jr. (1979). *J. Nutr.* **109,** 1244–1257.
Pikkarainen, P. H., and Räihä, N. C. R. (1967). *Pediatr. Res.* **1,** 165–168.
Ramirez, H., Alejandre, M. J., Zafra, M. F., Segovia, J. L., and Gracia-Peregrin, E. (1984). *Int. J. Biochem.* **16,** 291–295.
Sonawane, B. R., Coates, P. M., Yaffe, S. J., and Koldovsky, O. (1983). *Dev. Pharmacol. Ther.* **6,** 323–332.
Sturman, J. A., Rassin, D. K., and Gaull, G. E. (1977). *Life Sci.* **21,** 1–22.
Subbiah, M. T. R., and Yunker, R. L. (1985). *Biochem. Biophys. Res. Commun.* **28,** 1133–1137.
Watkins, J. B., Szczepanik, P., Gould, J. B., Klein, P., and Lester, R. (1975). *Gastroenterology* **69,** 706–713.
Yeoh, G. C. T., Brighton, V. J., Angus, D. A., and Kraemer, M. (1985). *Eur. J. Cell Biol.* **38,** 157–164.
Yeung, D., and Oliver, I. I. (1968). *Biochem. J.* **108,** 325–331.

13

Renal Function and Fluid and Electrolyte Homeostasis in the Neonate

Anita Aperia and Gianni Celsi
Department of Developmental Physiology
Karolinska Institutet
St. Göran's Children's Hospital
Stockholm, Sweden

I. PHYSIOLOGY OF THE IMMATURE KIDNEY

The kidney is structurally and biochemically immature at birth. Most parameters of renal function are lower in the neonatal than in the adult kidney (12). Animal studies have given us a mechanistic insight into the ontogeny of renal function. Most such studies have been performed in rats. In 1- week-old rats, the maturation of the kidney corresponds to the maturation of the kidney in very preterm infants. Glomerular filtration rate (GFR) is low in the immature kidney (4,9,25) (Fig. 1). GFR is restricted by the small capillary area for fil-

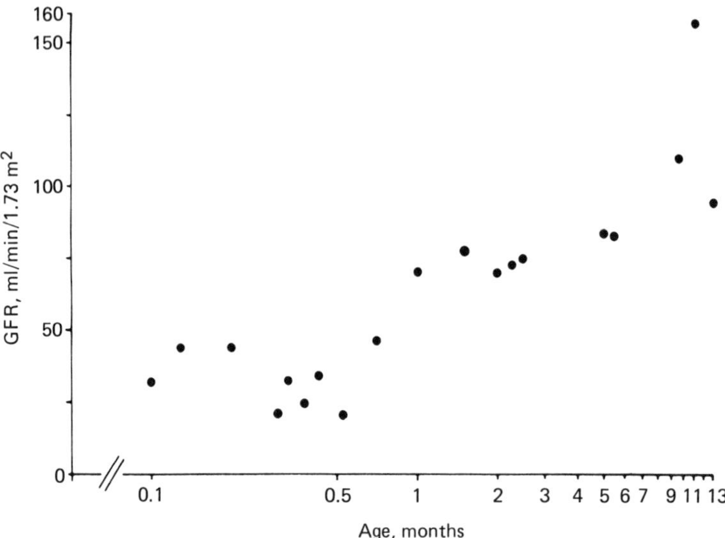

Fig. 1. Glomerular filtration rate (GFR) during the first year of life. (Age is on a logarithmic scale.)

tration and by a low renal blood flow (5,28,32). The renal blood flow can, however, be increased by active vasodilation (22,34). Increased renal blood flow will increase the GFR. In full-term infants there is a rapid increase in GFR during the first 4 days of life which is probably due to renal vasodilation (24). Are there any advantages with renal vasoconstriction that maintains GFR at a low level? The tubular transport systems in the neonatal kidney are not fully developed (6,10). The transporting area of the tubular cell is relatively small and the number of transporting sites per cell is low (8). The tubules are probably working at their maximal capacity in the neonatal kidney. Any increase in GFR would therefore result in an increase in filtered load that would exceed the tubular reabsorptive capacity. This would result in inappropriate losses of electrolyte and other solutes. The healthy term infant is generally capable of maintaining glomerular–tubular balance, but in the preterm infant there might sometimes be signs and symptoms of glomerular preponderance (see below).

The immature tubular cell has a low concentration of NaKATPase (11,41), the enzyme that yields energy to active sodium transport (29). This restricts the sodium-transporting capacity of the tubular cell. Several electrolytes and other solutes are cotransported with sodium. The capacity to reabsorb, for instance, bicarbonate, glucose, and phosphate will therefore be restricted in the very immature kidney (14,30,42) (Fig.

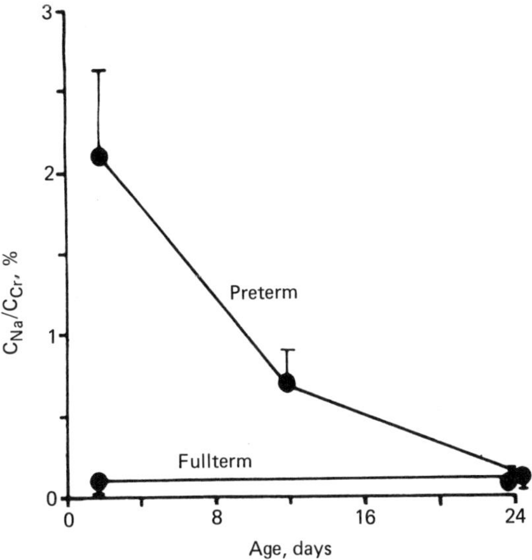

Fig. 2. Fractional Na excretion in preterm and full-term newborn during the first month of life.

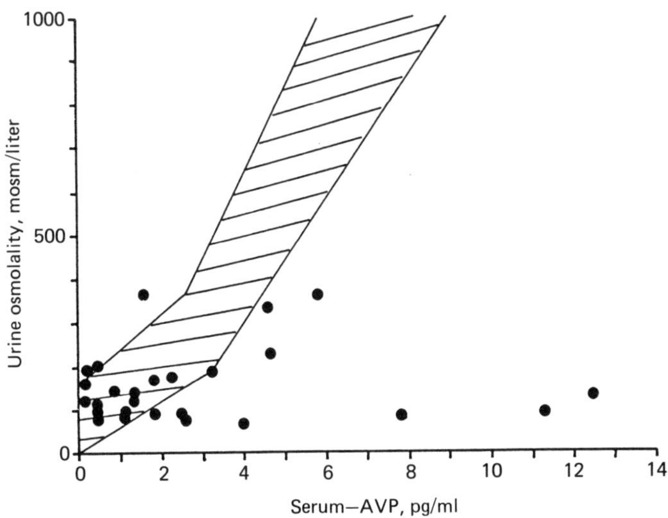

Fig. 3. Effect of AVP on urine osmolality in newborn infants. (Hatched area is normal range in adults.)

2). The immature tubular cell also has a smaller number of Na permeability units (33) and of the Na^+/H^+ exchanger. This results in a restricted capacity to secrete hydrogen ions (45).

One of the most important tasks of the kidney is to concentrate the urine. The process of urinary concentration requires well-developed loops of Henle, high capacity to reabsorb sodium against a gradient in the thick ascending limb of Henle, intact medullary circulation, and intact collecting tubule cells with a good end-organ response to the antidiuretic hormone. Several of these parameters are not fully developed in a neonatal kidney (13,20,38). The renal concentrating capacity is therefore low and urine osmolality is rarely hypertonic in the neonate (46) despite the fact that the serum concentration of antidiuretic hormone is often very high (35,37) (Fig. 3).

II. RENAL FUNCTION AND COMMON FLUID AND ELECTROLYTE PROBLEMS IN THE NEONATE

If we measure GFR in terms of ml/1.73 m^2 body surface area or ml/kg, the values that we record in the neonate will be approximatly 25% of the value in the healthy young adult. This implies that the neonatal kidney is borderline insufficient. It is therefore not surprising that acute renal failure is a common complication in all sick neonates. The infant with acute renal failure typically shows signs of both glomerular and tubular insufficiency. The most common sign of tubular insufficiency is excessive salt losses. Hyponatremia is therefore characteristic for renal failure in the neonate (39). What is the immediate cause of acute renal failure? It is most often poor renal perfusion. It has recently been demonstrated that dopamine has a beneficial effect on renal circulation in sick preterm infants and dopamine is now used successfully to prevent and treat acute renal failure in these infants (43,44).

In preterm infants with gestational age lower than 34 weeks, the glomerular–tubular imbalance described above will result in inadequate losses of sodium, phosphate, and peptides. If preterm infants are given a daily sodium intake less than 2 mmol/kg, the urinary sodium losses during the first 2 weeks of life will generally exceed the sodium intake (1,7). This results in negative sodium balance. Extrauterine life seems to accelerate renal maturation. Even in infants with gestational age less than 30 weeks, inadequate urinary sodium losses are uncommon after the second week of life (9), provided the infant does not have severe respiratory problems or renal disease (16,39). It is therefore questionable if salt supplementation is needed in preterm infants with relatively uncomplicated postnatal course.

Is it harmless to give the infant more salt than what breast milk would provide? Several reports have demonstrated that short-term sodium supplementation resulting in a daily sodium intake of 3–4 mmol/kg will not result in any serious side effects such as hypernatremia (19,23). However, the infant kidney has a restricted capacity to increase sodium excretion in case of positive salt balance (2,3,18) (Fig. 4). We would therefore not recommend sodium supplementation for a prolonged period such as 2–3 months since it is still controversial whether a moderately positive salt balance during a prolonged period in infancy will predispose to hypertension later in life (26).

The urinary concentrating capacity is very low in the neonate (36,38) and develops slowly during the first year of life (36). The capacity of the tubular cell to transport sodium is probably not fully developed until the first to second year of life. These expressions of renal immaturity will, during the entire first year of life, have clinical consequences in situations of abnormal fluid and electrolyte losses. The infant with diarrheal disease will have difficulties in retaining both water and sodium. In very young infants (less than 4 months of ages) the low urinary concentrating capacity is generally the dominant problem. Although young dehydrated infants are in severe negative water balance, water will still be lost from the kidney. In most cases water losses exceed sodium losses (15,36). This will predispose the young infant to hypernatremic dehydration. The risk for hypernatremic dehydration decreases with increasing age (31,40). In infants older than 4 months of age, hyponatremic

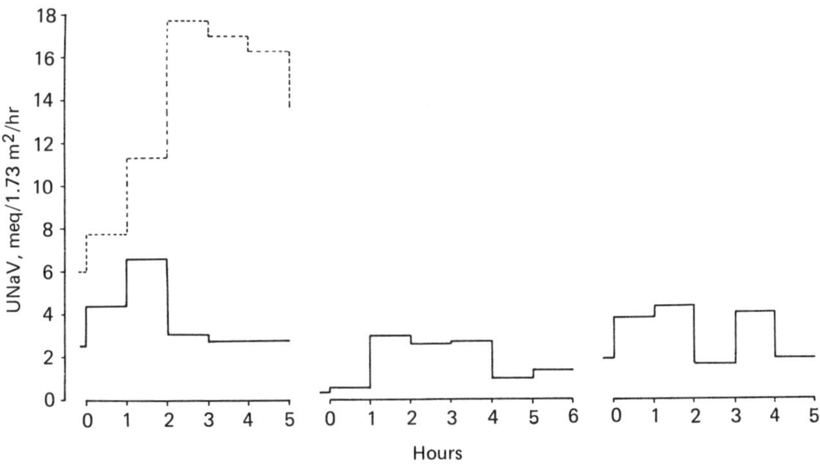

Fig. 4. Natriuretic response to an oral salt load in three different preterm infants. (Dotted line is natriuretic response in older children.)

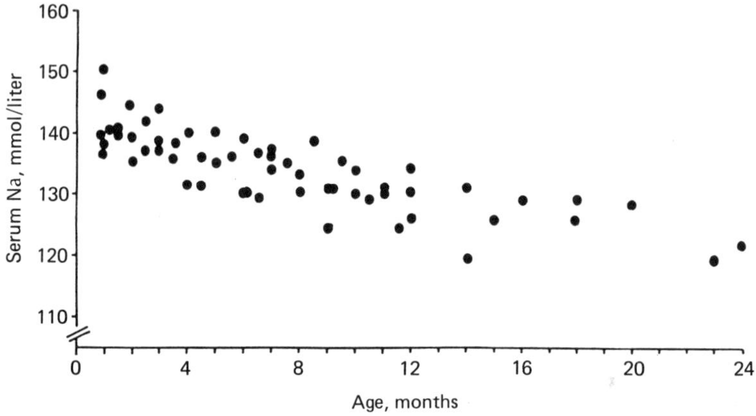

Fig. 5. Serum Na concentration in dehydrated children with acute gastroenteritis at admission.

dehydration is a more common problem (Fig. 5). Renal immaturity will also contribute to this condition, since in the immature kidney the capacity to reabsorb sodium is restricted and, in the situation of severe and extra renal salt losses, sodium will not be adequately retained (39).

III. INFLUENCE OF ENVIRONMENTAL FACTORS ON RENAL MATURATION

Edelmann and collaborators (1960) reported more than 20 years ago that high protein intake would accelerate renal functional development in 2- to 6-month-old infants (21). In a recently completed experimental study we found that renal functional development as well as renal growth was highly dependent on the protein intake (27). High protein intake will in fact stimulate kidney growth out of proportion to body growth. Low protein intake will retard kidney growth (47). It remains to be elucidated to what extent low protein intake will retard kidney growth and renal functional development in the human infant.

IV. ONTOGENY OF CELLULAR ELECTROLYTE HOMEOSTASIS

We have demonstrated that in tubular cells from young rats, both Na influx and pump-mediated Na out-transport are lower than in tubular cells from adult rats (17,33). This implies that the control of cell electrolyte homeostasis is not as well developed in infancy as later in life. Several clinical observations support this statement. It is unlikely that the hyponatremia that is commonly observed in newborn preterm infants is only due to inappropriate Na losses. Hyponatremia in infants is often associated with hyperkalemia, indicating that there is a disturbance in the distribution of the electrolytes between the intracellular and extracellular spaces. NaKATPase, present in virtually all cell membranes, pumps Na out of the cell and K into the cell. Insufficient function of the Na pump would result in an increase in extracellular K and redistribution of Na from the extracellular to the intracellular space.

In a collaborative study in Pakistan, it was observed that the most common electrolyte disturbances in severely dehydrated infants were hyponatremia, hyperkalemia, hypocalcemia, and hypophosphatemia. Hypocalcemia was found to be the main cause of convulsions. Hypocalcemia was significantly correlated to hypophosphatemia and hyperkalemia was significantly correlated to acidosis. During oral rehydration therapy, all electrolyte disturbances were spontaneously corrected. These findings suggest that in severely dehydrated infants phosphate and potassium are redistributed from the intracellular to the extracellular space, and calcium is redistributed from the extracellular to the intracellular space.

REFERENCES

1. Al-Dahhan, J., Haycock, G. B., Chantler, C., and Stimmler, L. (1983). Sodium homeostatis in term and preterm neonates. I. Renal aspects. *Arch. Dis. Child.* **58,** 335.
2. Aperia, A., Broberger, O., Thodenius, K., and Zetterström, R. (1972). Renal response to an oral sodium load in newborn fullterm infants. *Acta Paediatr. Scand.* **61,** 670.
3. Aperia, A., Broberger, O., Thodenius, K., and Zetterström, R. (1974). Development study of the renal response to an oral salt load in preterm infants. *Acta Paediatr. Scand.* **63,** 517.
4. Aperia, A., Broberger, O., Thodenius, K., Zetterström, R. (1975). Development of renal control of salt and fluid homeostasis during the first year of life. *Acta Paediatr. Scand.* **64,** 393.
5. Aperia, A., and Herin, P. (1975). Development of glomerular perfusion rate and nephron filtration rate in rats 17–60 days old. *Am J. Physiol.* **228,** 1319.
6. Aperia, A., and Broberger, U. (1979). Beta-2 microglobulin, an indicator of renal tubular maturation and dysfunction in the newborn. *Acta Paediatr. Scand.* **68,** 669.
7. Aperia, A., Broberger, O., Herin, P., and Zetterström, R. (1979). Sodium excretion in relation to sodium intake and aldosterone excretion in newborn pre-term and full-term infants. *Acta Paediatr. Scand.* **68,** 813.
8. Aperia, A., and Larsson, L. (1979). Correlation between fluid reabsorption and proximal tubule ultrastructure during development of the rat kidney. *Acta Physiol. Scand.* **105,** 11.

9. Aperia, A., Broberger, O., Elinder, G., Herin, P., and Zetterström, R. (1981). Postnatal development of renal function in pre-term and full-term infants. *Acta Paediatr. Scand.* **70,** 183.
10. Aperia, A., and Elinder, G. (1981). Distal tubular Na reabsorption in the developing rat kidney. *Am. J. Physiol.* **240,** F487.
11. Aperia, A., Larsson, L., and Zetterström, R. (1981). Hormonal induction of NaKATPase in developing proximal tubular cells. *Am. J. Physiol.* **10,** F356.
12. Aperia, A. (1983). Salt and water metabolism in the perinatal period. *In "Pediatrics, Vol. 2, Perinatal* Medicine" (F. C. Battaglia and R. D. H. Boyd, eds.), pp. 113–130. Butterworth, London.
13. Aperia, A., Herin, P., Lundin, S., Melin, P., and Zetterström, R. (1984). Regulation of renal water excretion in newborn fullterm infants. *Acta Paediatr. scand.* **73,** 717.
14. Arant, B. S., Jr. (1978). Developmental patterns of renal functional maturation compared in the human neonate. *J. Pediatr.* **92,** 705.
15. Arneil, G. C., and Chin, K. C. (1979). Lower-solute milks and reduction of hypernatraemia in young Glasgow infants. *Lancet* **8147,** 840.
16. Broberger, U., and Aperia, A. (1978). Renal function in idiopathic respiratory distress syndrome. *Acta Paediatr. Scand.* **67,** 313.
17. Celsi, G., Larsson, L., and Aperia, A. (1986). Proximal tubular fluid reabsorption and NaKATPase activity in young unilaterally nephrectomized rats. *Am. J. Physiol.* **251,** F588.
18. Clarke, T. A., Markarian, M., Griswold, W., and Mendoza, S. (1979). Hypernatremic dehydration resulting from inadequate breast-feeding. *Pediatrics* **63,** 931.
19. Day, G. M., Radde, I. C., Balfe, J. W., and Chance, G. W. (1976). Electrolyte abnormalities in very low birth weight infants. *Pediatr. Res.* **10,** 522.
20. Edelmann, C. M., Jr., and Barnett, H. L. (1960). Role of the kidney in water metabolism in young infants. . *J. Pediatr.* **56,** 154.
21. Edelmann, C. M., Jr., Barnett, H. L., and Troupkou, V. (1960). Renal concentrating mechanisms in newborn infants. Effect of dietary protein and water content, role of urea, and responsiveness to antidiuretic hormone. *J. Clin. Invest.* **39,** 1062.
22. Elinder, G., Aperia, A., Herin, P., Källskog, Ö. (1980). Effect of isotonic volume expansion on glomerular filtration rate and renal hemodynamics in the developing rat kidney. *Acta Physiol. Scand.* **108,** 411.
23. Engelke, S. C., Shah, B. L., Vasan, U., and Raye, J. R. (1973). Sodium balance in very low-birth-weight infants. *J. Pediatr.* **93,** 837.
24. Fawer, C. L., Torrado, A., and Guignard, J. P. (1979). Maturation of renal function in full-term and premature neonates. *Helv. Paediatr. Acta* **34,** 11.
25. Guignard, J. P., Torrado, A., and Gautier, E. (1975). Glomerular filtration rate in the first three weeks of life. *J. Pediatr.* **87,** 268.
26. Hofman, A., Hazebroek, A., and Valkenburg, H. A. (1983). A randomized trial of sodium intake and blood pressure in newborn infants. *JAMA, J. Am. Med. Assoc.* **250,** 370.
27. Jakobsson, B., Celsi, G., Lindblad, B. S., and Aperia, A. (1987). Influence of different protein intake on renal growth in young rats. *Acta Paediatr. Scand.* **76,** 293.
28. John, E., Goldsmith, D. I., and Spitzer, A. (1981). Quantitative changes in the canine glomerular vasculature during development: Physiological implications. *Kidney Int.* **20,** 223.
29. Jörgenssen, P. L. (1980). Sodium and potassium pump in kidney tubules. *Physiol. Rev.* **60,** 864.
30. Karlén, J., Aperia, A., and Zetterström, R. (1985). Renal excretion of calcium and phosphate in preterm and fullterm infants. *J. Pediatr.* **106,** 814.

31. Khuffash, F. A., and Majeed, H. A. (1984). Hypernatremic dehydration in infants with gastroenteritis. *Clin. Pediatr.* **23,** 255.
32. Larsson, L., and Maunsbach, A. B. (1980). The ultrastructural development of the glomerular filtration barrier in the rat kidney: A morphometric analysis. *J. Ultrastruct. Res.* **72,** 392.
33. Larsson, S., Aperia, A., and Lechene, C. (1986). Studies of final differentiation of rat renal proximal tubular cells in culture. Cellular membrane Na and K effective permeability. *Am. J. Physiol.* **251,** C455.
34. Leake, R. D., Zakauddin, S., Trygstad, C. W., Fu, P., and Oh, W. (1976). The effects of large volume intravenous fluid infusion on neonatal renal function. *J. Pediatr.* **89,** 968.
35. Pohjavuori, M., and Fyhrquist, F. (1980). Hemodynamic significance of vasopressin in the newborn infant. *J. Pediatr.* **97,** 462.
36. Polácek, E., Vocel, J., Neugebauerová, L., Sebková, M., and Véchetová, E. (1965). The osmotic concentrating ability in healthy infants and children. *Arch. Dis. Child.* **40,** 291.
37. Polin, R. A., Husain, M. K., James, L. S., and Frantz, A. G. (1977). High vasopressin concentrations in human umbilical cord blood, lack of correlation with stress. *J. Perinat. Med.* **5,** 114.
38. Rane, S., and Aperia, A. (1985). Ontogeny of NaKATPase activity in the thick ascending limb of Henle and of the urinary concentrating capacity in rats. *Am. J. Physiol.* **249,** F723.
39. Reimold, E. W., Don, T. D., and Worthen, H. G. (1977). Renal failure during the first year of life. *Pediatrics* **59,** 987.
40. Samadi, A. R., Wahed, M. A., Islam, M. R., and Ahmed, S. M. (1983). Consequences of hyponatraemia and hypernatraemia in children with acute diarrhoea in Bangladesh. *Br. Med. J.* No. 286, p. 671.
41. Schmidt, U., and Horster, M. (1977). Na–K-activated ATPase: Activity maturation in rabbit nephron segments dissected *in vitro. Am. J. Physiol.* **233,** F55.
42. Schwartz, G. J., and Evan, A. P. (1983). Development of solute transport in rabbit proximal tubule. I. HCO^3 and glucose absorption. *Am. J. Physiol.* **245,** F382.
43. Seri, I., Tulassay, T., Kiszel, J., Machay, T., and Csömör, S. (1984). Cardiovascular response to dopamine in hypotensive preterm neonates with severe hyaline membrane disease. *Eur. J. Pediatr.* **142,** 3.
44. Seri, I., Tulassay, T., Kiszel, J., and Csömör, S. (1984). The use of dopamine for the prevention of the renal side effects of indomethacin in premature infants with patent ductus arteriosus. *Int. J. Pediatr. Nephrol.* **5,** 209.
45. Sulyok, E., Heim, T., Soltész, G., and Jászai, V. (1972). The influence of maturity on renal control of acidosis in newborn infants. *Biol. Neonate* **21,** 418.
46. Svenningsen, N. W., and Aronson, A. S. (1974). Postnatal development of renal concentration capacity as estimated by DDAVP-test in normal and asphyxiated neonates. *Biol. Neonate* **25,** 230.
47. Winick, M., Fish, I., and Rosso, P. (1968). Cellular recovery in rat tissue after a brief period of neonatal malnutrition. *J. Nutr.* **95,** 623.

14

Metabolic and Endocrine Interrelationships in the Human Fetus and Neonate: An Overview of the Control of the Adaptation to Postnatal Nutrition

Albert Aynsley-Green
Department of Child Health
University of Newcastle upon Tyne
The Medical School
Newcastle upon Tyne, England

I. INTRODUCTION

The cutting of the umbilical cord at birth is an event of immense psychological and physiological importance. The survival of the newborn infant in the hostile extrauterine environment depends crucially on successful adaptive changes occurring in a number of the body's physiological systems. Events occurring in the cardiovascular and respiratory systems are evident immediately after birth, but other adaptive changes at least as complex in nature and as important in terms of survival occur during the process of adaptation to extrauterine metabolism and nutrition.

Before birth the fetus is fed largely by transplacental transfer of nutrients into the umbilical vein, the enteral assimilation of amniotic fluid being of considerably less importance in terms of nutritive value. Maternal metabolism clearly has an important regulatory influence on fetal metabolism through controlling the delivery of substrates across the placenta. After birth, the infant has to be metabolically independent and needs, moreover, to adapt to a totally new form of nutrition, namely, the intermittent delivery of enteral milk into the gut. During the postnatal period major changes occur in gastrointestinal structure, motility, and digestive and absorptive function, together with critically important adjustments in intermediary metabolism. A number of publications have appeared that document evidence for these changes in both experimental animals and man (1–4) and it would seem that some of these postnatal adaptive changes are urgent, for instance, the need to maintain glucose homeostasis following the sudden cessation of the maternal supply, whereas others occur more gradually over a period of hours or days as the enteral feeding is introduced.

We have suggested from collaborative work performed during the last 10 years that the adaptation to postnatal nutrition depends on the secretion of chemical messengers, or regulatory peptides, released from specialized cells in the gut together with those products of the more classical endocrine organs of the pancreas, thyroid, pituitary, and adrenal gland. We have also suggested that it is important to examine the interrelations of the concentrations of these regulatory peptides with those of metabolic fuels to obtain a true perspective of the endocrine influences on metabolism and vice versa.

This review will not attempt to consider all the papers written by our own group or those of others, but will address itself to five issues to illustrate some important concepts. To understand the significance and importance of postnatal adaptive changes it is necessary to begin with a brief review of the control of utilization of food in the adult. This will be followed by a description of some of the structural and functional changes which occur in the neonate after birth before considering the relevance of prenatal preparation for successful postnatal adaptation. Metabolic and endocrine events at the time of birth will be assessed, and this will be followed, finally, by a few illustrative examples of the postnatal events which occur in relation to food intake.

II. REGULATION OF FOOD UTILIZATION IN THE ADULT

The efficient utilization of food in the human adult depends on the integration of the functions of several physiological systems. Thus, food has to be propelled through the gut, and this requires coordination of gut motor activities to ensure the orderly transit of the foodstuffs through the different regions of the alimentary tract. The passage of food leads to local trauma, necessitating a continuous process of regeneration of the gut mucosa. Digestive secretions have to be introduced into the gut lumen at the appropriate times, and coordinated with this is redistribution of blood flow to carry the products of digestion and absorption through the visceral and then the systemic circulations. The influx of nutrients leads to changes in metabolic hormone secretion to ensure postprandial metabolic homeostasis and this in turn has to be integrated with other adaptive metabolic changes as the individual enters into the interprandial starvation period.

The integration and coordination of these facets of physiology clearly requires a complex and efficient regulatory system; it is equally obvious that many factors are likely to be involved. Recent evidence, however, has suggested that the secretion of hormones and regulatory peptides from the gut and from the classical endocrine organs has a key role to play in this process.

The whole science of modern endocrinology is, of course, based on the observations of Bayliss and Starling in 1902, who suggested that the gut secreted a chemical messenger which circulated in the bloodstream to influence the activity of the pancreas. They called their postulated messenger secretin. Two further hormones, gastrin and cholecystokinin, were identifed in 1906 and 1928, respectively, but little progress was made in the field of gastrointestinal endocrinology for the next 40 years, largely because of methodological difficulties in identifying and characterizing the peptides produced from cells dispersed throughout the gastrointestinal tract. The diffuse nature of the gut endocrine system precluded the rapid advances which occurred in understanding the physiology of the discrete organs such as the pituitary, thyroid, and adrenal glands, where it is possible to remove the gland, identify the consequences of the hormone deficiency, extract the hormone, and then replace it to restore physiological normality. These experiments are not possible where the endocrine cells are scattered throughout the whole length of the gut.

However, during the past 10 years or so there has been an explosion of knowledge on the manufacture, secretion, and regulation of peptides secreted by the gut and it is clear that all the aspects of the utilization of food listed above can be influenced by these substances (5,6). Table I shows a list of some of the peptides with their principal actions, linked with the effects of hormones from the pancreas, pituitary, adrenal, and thyroid glands, which are also involved in the regulation of food utilization.

There is an immediate problem of terminology since the peptides exert their effects in at least three different ways. Some substances act as true circulating hormones, and this is exemplified best by the classical hormones, namely, glucagon, insulin, growth hormone, cortisol, and thyroxine. However, some gut peptides are also secreted into the bloodstream and act on target tissue distally. The anatomical localization of the cells secreting these hormones in the adult is shown in Fig. 1. Other peptides, for example, somatostatin, act as paracrine substances, which means that the peptide-secreting cell acts locally to influence the activity of surrounding cells. Thus, Larson (7) has shown that the somatostatin cell appears to have long cell processes which extend to influence cells

TABLE I

Regulatory Peptides and Hormones Involved in Food Utilization

Peptide/hormone	Function
Gastrin	Gastric acid secretion, growth of the gut
Secretin	Pancreatic exocrine secretion
Cholecystokinin	Gallbladder contractility
GIP	Modulation of insulin secretion
VIP	Intestinal secretions, blood flow
Motilin	Intestinal tract and gastric motility
Neurotensin	Intestinal tract and gastric motility
Enteroglucagon	Gut growth, gut transit time
Glucagon	Glucose homeostasis
Insulin	Glucose homeostasis
Pancreatic polypeptide	Pancreatic growth, exocrine function, intestinal absorption
Somatostatin	Insular hormone release, intestinal absorption
Growth hormone	Fuel utilization
Cortisol	Gut enzyme activity
Thyroxine, T_3	Gut development, hormone receptor activity, metabolic rate

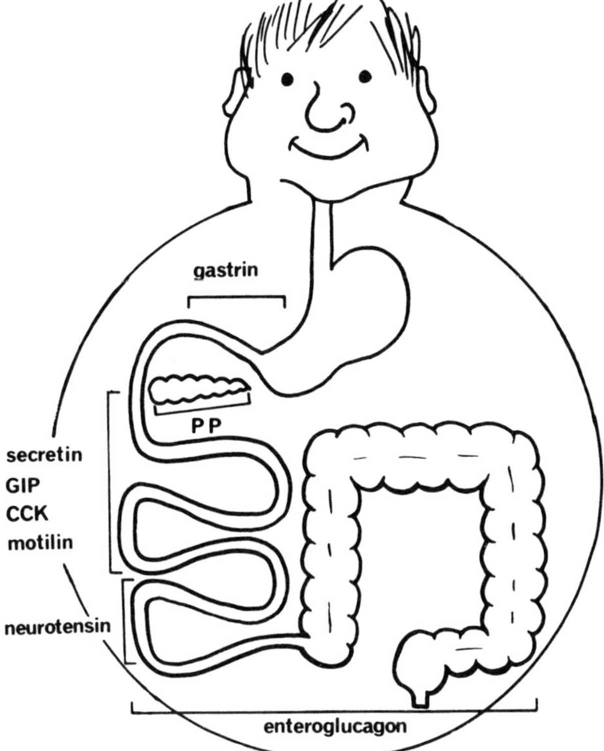

Fig. 1. Schematic diagram showing the distribution of endocrine cells in the gut which secrete true circulating hormones.

some distance from the main body of the cell manufacturing the peptide. Finally, other peptides, for example, VIP, act as neurocrine substances, in other words as neurotransmitters, the peptides being produced by nerve endings (7). It will be many years before the precise interrelation and interregulation of these different substances will be elucidated with certainty. Nonetheless, there is now substantial literature both on the measurement of circulating and local concentrations of the peptides and on their physiological and pharmacological effects. Recent reviews are to be found relating to studies in the human adult and in the experimental animal (5,6). Measurement of circulating levels may not reflect accurately events occurring within the gut mucosa, but nonetheless it is a useful starting point in attempting to determine the role of the individual peptides. This is particularly true for the physiology of those substances which are acting as true circulating hormones.

Gut peptides are likely to have arisen early in vertebrate evolution (5);

indeed, these peptides may have appeared before the evolution of structures which have been regarded until now as the traditional target organs in man and other mammals. There is evidence that these peptide "hormones" have fundamental biological roles independent of those described initially in relation to digestive physiology. One such role is discussed in Section III concerning the regulation of gut development.

III. THE SIGNIFICANCE OF POSTNATAL ADAPTATION TO FEEDING

During fetal life an orderly sequence of developmental changes occurs in the gut in terms of structure and function, which prepares it for postnatal nutrition. Structural development precedes that of function, which is limited before 26 weeks of gestation in the human fetus (2,3,8). Lebenthal has emphasized the importance of the "biological time clock" in the regulation of these changes, but it is evident that this natural rate of development can be influenced profoundly by environmental triggers, as suggested by the fact that prematurely born infants may adapt to enteral feeding as much as 12 weeks "too soon" in biological terms. There is a substantial body of evidence from studies in experimental animals to suggest that extragastrointestinal hormones, notably cortisol and thyroxine, influence gastrointestinal development (3).

Enteral feeding itself may be such a key environmental trigger, and this contention is supported by animal studies. Thus, in piglets (9,10) and rats (11) oral feeding after birth results in marked structural changes and in the growth of the digestive tract; these changes are not seen in animals deprived of enteral feeding. Moreover, oral feeding enhances gut enzyme activity (9) and initiates important changes in intermediary metabolism, for example, the increased responsiveness to glucose by pancreatic insulin-secreting cells which is seen in enterally fed newborn piglets (12,13).

The fetus swallows amniotic fluid containing a significant protein content, but when milk feeds commence after birth the gut is exposed for the first time to a diet containing high concentrations of fat and lactose as well as protein. Moreover, microorganisms enter the gut lumen for the first time. These intraluminal factors have a significant effect on the development of gut function (3). For example, lactase activity and pancreatic lipase and trypsinogen activities are induced by feeding and occur much earlier than normal in infants born prematurely.

Intraluminal secretions themselves may have an essential role to play in gut development, evidence for this being the bile activation of enter-

TABLE II

Hormones Reported in Breast Milk

Steroids	Prolactin
Thyroxine	Erythropoietin
Gonadotrophins	Melatonin
LHRH	Epidermal growth factor
TRH	Prostaglandins
TSH	Calcitonin
ACTH	

opeptidase (14) and the increased turnover of brush border proteins by pancreatic proteases (15). Finally, it has been shown that milk itself contains high concentrations of hormones and growth factors (Table II). Thus, concentrations of calcitonin, epidermal growth factor, prostaglandins E and F, neurotensin, and melatonin, as well as classical pituitary, thyroid, and adrenal hormones, are all detectable in milk. These ingested hormones could exert their effects "topically" on the gut or may even be absorbed intact to affect the body systemically (16–19).

However, we have suggested previously in a number of publications that the major contribution to the regulation of postnatal gut development may be through the endogenous secretion of regulatory peptides in response to food in the gut. Our working hypothesis suggests that enteral feeding triggers the secretion of gut regulatory peptides, and through their endocrine, paracrine, and neurocrine effects, a cascade of developmental changes affecting gut growth, gut motility, development of intestinal secretions and transport mechanisms, initiation of the enteroinsular axis, the modulation of pancreatic endocrine function, and hence the development of hepatic metabolism are all stimulated. The validation of this hypothesis requires a number of conditions to be met: the gut endocrine cell lines for these peptides should be present in the fetus; postnatally, gut hormones should be released by enteral feeding and not released in neonates deprived of nutrition by this route; gut peptide receptors should be responsive in the neonatal period; there should be a temporal relationship between postnatal gut hormone secretion and the adaptive changes proposed to be influenced by them; and, finally, there should be direct experimental evidence that either inhibition of endogenous hormone release or exogenous hormone administration would inhibit or induce, respectively, their proposed actions. The evidence to conclusively prove this hypothesis is as yet incomplete. Nevertheless, the body of data considered in the following sections is strongly supportive of the basic postulate.

IV. THE PRENATAL METABOLIC AND ENDOCRINE MILIEU OF THE HUMAN FETUS

The study of fetal metabolism in experimental animals has advanced rapidly following the development of new biochemical and physiological techniques. Of particular relevance is the development of the chronically catheterized fetal lamb preparation, which allows frequent sampling of fetal blood vessels without manipulation and stress. These studies have provided many new data and have also challenged many old dogmas. However, the applicability of most of the data derived from animals to man still awaits confirmation because, as yet, it has not been possible to sample both fetal umbilical vessels simultaneously, let alone measure blood flow under unstressed conditions. Most of the information which is available on circulating concentrations of fetal fuels in man is based on measurements in blood samples drawn at delivery or during hysterotomy under circumstances which cannot be regarded as physiological. Nonetheless, a number of publications have appeared using these data, and a good review is Girard (20).

Through collaboration with Mr. I. Z. Mackenzie, an obstetrician skilled in the technique of fetoscopy, we have taken advantage of this skill to obtain blood samples from the mother, fetal artery, and fetal vein together with amniotic fluid samples under the circumstance of termination of pregnancy for therapeutic reasons. Opportunity has been taken to study

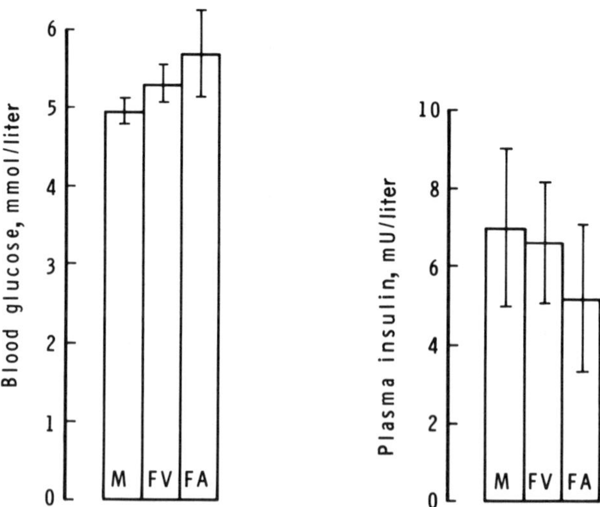

Fig. 2. Concentrations of blood glucose and plasma insulin (mean ±SEM) in maternal vein, fetal artery, and fetal vein, the latter samples being obtained at fetoscopy.

mothers and their fetuses between 16 and 20 weeks of gestation, with the mother being starved overnight before the procedure first thing in the morning and conscious throughout the fetoscopy procedure, although sedated with diazepam and opioid.

Figure 2 shows the mean blood glucose concentrations in maternal vein, fetal umbilical artery, and fetal umbilical vein. No significant differences were to be found between these concentrations, although in 10 fetuses the fetal artery concentration was higher than that in the maternal blood, whereas it was lower in 6 fetuses. There was no correlation of cross-sectional data between maternal and fetal blood glucose levels. From the analysis of paired data the umbilical venous arterial concentration difference for blood glucose was negative in six and positive in four cases, and there was a significant inverse correlation between umbilical artery levels and umbilical venous arterial concentration differences. (Fig. 3)

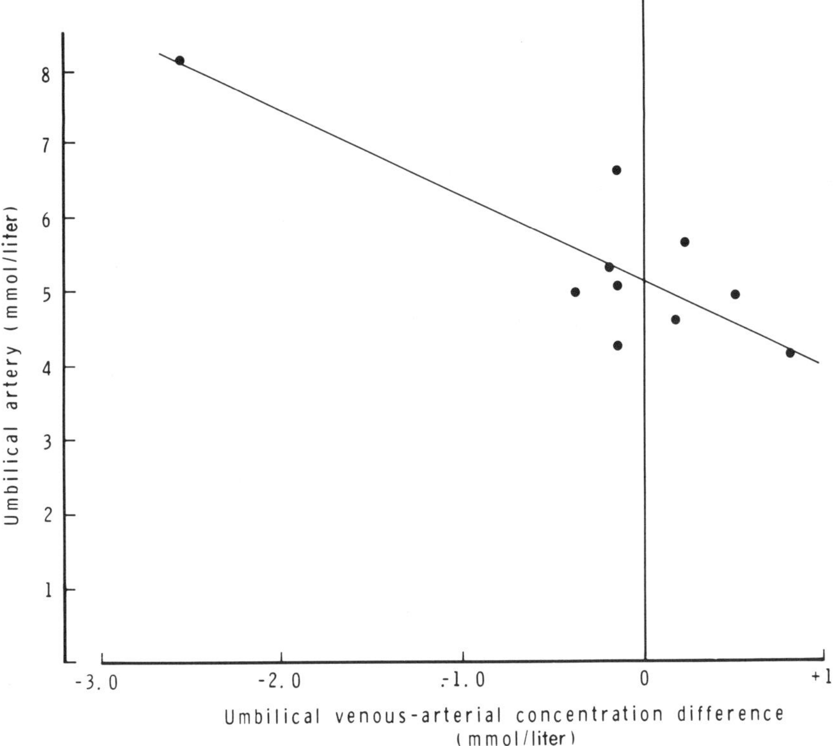

Fig. 3. Fetal umbilical artery concentrations of blood glucose and umbilical venous–arterial concentration differences in the human fetus during the second trimester of pregnancy.

Mean blood lactate and pyruvate concentrations were similar in maternal vein, umbilical artery, and umbilical vein with no correlation between maternal and fetal concentrations in cross-sectional or in paired data (Fig. 4). The umbilical venous arterial concentration difference was negative in seven and positive in three cases, and, as with blood glucose concentrations, there was a significant inverse relationship between umbilical artery levels and umbilical venous arterial concentration differences (Fig. 5).

The mean total blood ketone body concentration (the sum of acetoacetate and 3-hydroxybutyrate) in the maternal vein was more than twice the level found in both the fetal umbilical artery and umbilical vein (Table III). From analysis of the paired data, there was a significant positive correlation between maternal and fetal levels (Fig. 6) but there was no significant difference between mean umbilical artery and umbilical vein levels of ketone bodies.

Glucose is the major metabolic fuel for the fetus supplied by the mother (21–23). Blood glucose concentrations in the fetus of a number of animal species studied have been found to be lower than those in the mother (22). The results from most human studies have also demonstrated a maternal–fetal glucose gradient in cord blood samples at term (24–26). Thus, the existence of both the maternal–fetal gradient for glucose and that of net umbilical uptake of glucose appears to be well established. Moreover, it has also been shown that the maternal–fetal glucose gradient does not change with gestational age (27). Our results seem to be at variance with these findings, and since it would seem unlikely that glucose transport and glucose uptake of the midterm human fetus are fundamentally different from either those of the full-term fetus or those of

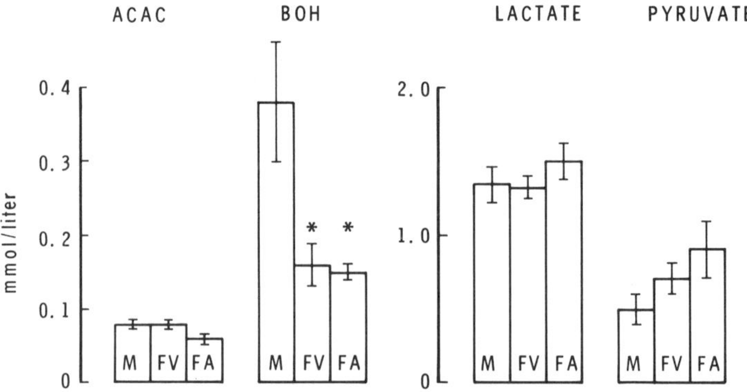

Fig. 4. Concentrations of blood lactate, pyruvate, acetoacetate, and hydroxybutyrate concentrations (mean ±SEM) in maternal vein, umbilical vein, and umbilical artery during the second trimester of human pregnancy. Asterisk indicates $p < .05$.

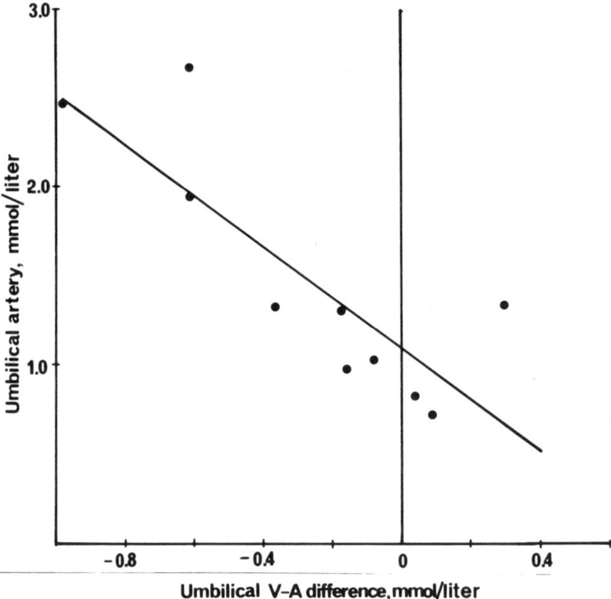

Fig. 5. Umbilical artery concentration of blood lactate and umbilical vein–artery differences during the second trimester of human pregnancy.

TABLE III

Blood Glucose, Lactate, Pyruvate, and Total Blood Ketone Body Levels in Maternal Vein (MV), Fetal Umbilical Vein (UV), and Fetal Umbilical Artery (UA) (mmol/Liter; Mean ± SEM)

				Significance		
	MV	UV	UA	MV vs. UV	MV vs. UA	UV vs. UA
Blood glucose	4.83±0.10	5.14±0.18	5.35±3.4	NS[a]	NS	NS
n	16	15	11			
Blood lactate	1.23±0.16	1.25±0.10	1.43±0.20	NS	NS	NS
n	16	15	11			
Blood pyruvate	0.05±0.01	0.07±0.01	0.08±0.01	NS	NS	NS
n	16	16	11			
Blood total ketone bodies	0.49±0.06	0.25±0.03	0.22±0.03	$p<.01$	$p<.01$	NS
n	16	15	10			

[a]NS = Not significant

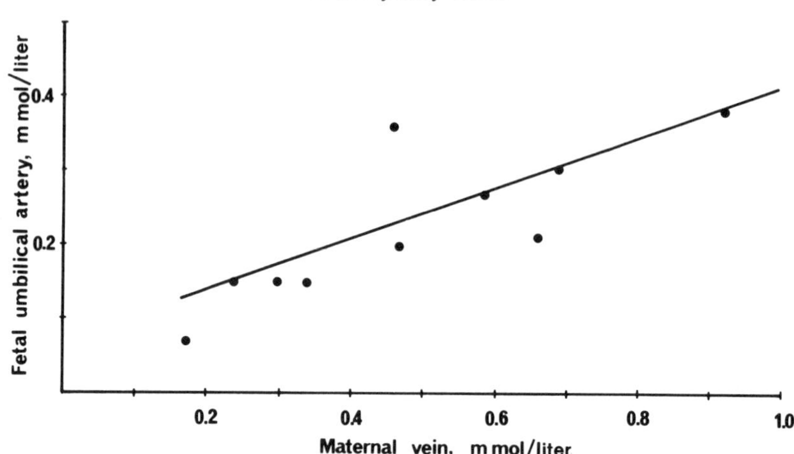

Fig. 6. Maternal vein and fetal umbilical artery concentrations of total ketone bodies (acetoacetate and hydroxybutyrate) during the second trimester of human pregnancy. $y = 0.05 + 0.36\,x$, $r = 0.82$, $p < .01$.

the fetus of other mammalian species, it is more likely that the absence of these gradients in our study is due to artifacts introduced by the methods used for sampling. Thus, it is impossible to withdraw blood from both the fetal umbilical artery and umbilical vein simultaneously and there is, inevitably, an interval of one to three minutes between the two samplings. The umbilical venous and arterial blood glucose levels presented are, therefore, not true paired samples. Moreover, stress, albeit minimal, from the procedure before sampling might have been sufficient to increase fetal blood glucose levels, although the evidence for substantial stress is not present insofar as measurement of counter regulatory hormones is concerned (see below).

Whatever the precise explanation for the observations on blood glucose concentrations, it is suggested that at lower fetal umbilical artery glucose levels the fetus is a glucose "consumer" (positive venous arterial concentration difference), whereas at higher, "stressed" fetal umbilical artery blood glucose levels, the umbilical arterial blood leaving the fetus has higher blood glucose concentrations than the umbilical venous blood entering the fetal circulation, suggesting, for the first time, that the human fetus at this stage in gestation can be a glucose producer. Similar arguments apply to the measurements of blood lactate concentrations.

The data on maternal and fetal blood ketone body levels confirm the presence of a maternal–fetal gradient for this fuel (28,29), but the very low concentrations in both fetal vessels suggest that ketone bodies do not contribute substantially to fetal energy requirements in early gestation. The close positive relationship between maternal and fetal levels (Fig. 6) suggests that the fetal concentration is influenced by maternal concentration.

Until now, no human data have been available on the uptake of amino acids and information on the circulating concentrations of amino acids during early gestation is scarce (30–32).

Maternal and fetal plasma amino acid levels in another group of mothers and fetuses at a similar gestational period are shown in Table IV. It is apparent that all amino acids had a significantly higher concentration in fetal than in the maternal plasma, but there was considerable variation, with a range of the fetal–maternal ratio from 1.4 to 4. Nonetheless, the total molar concentration of the 17 amino acids measured in the study was 2.4 times greater in fetal than in maternal plasma (2.26 versus 0.96 mmol/liter).

There was a significant direct linear relationship between maternal and fetal levels for 14 amino acids, the slope of the regression line being similar for most amino acids (Table V).

TABLE IV

Maternal and Fetal Plasma Amino Acid Levels at 18–21 Weeks of Gestation (mmol/Liter; Mean ± SEM)[a]

Amino acid	MV	UA	UV	MV vs. UA (p)	MV vs. UV (p)
Taurine	22.4±1.7	85.4±5.6	81.8±3.7	<.001	<.001
Threonine	115.2±7.7	237.6±20.1	258.7±18.2	<.001	<.001
Serine	48.3±3.4	85.5±7.1	92.8±7.5	<.01	<.001
Glycine	84.0±4.5	126.5±9.3	151.8±8.6	<.001	<.001
Alanine	161.6±9.2	225.8±13.6	283.0±19.6	<.005	<.005
Citrulline	16.5±1.5	23.2±1.9	25.4±1.8	<.05	<.005
α-Amino isobutyric acid	9.9±1.2	23.4±2.2	26.7±2.6	<.001	<.001
Valine	122.3±7.2	251.7±14.2	277.2±14.2	<.01	<.005
Methionine	10.5±0.8	18.3±2.9	19.8±2.5	<.001	<.001
Isoleucine	36.4±2.6	63.1±5	72.9±4.1	<.001	<.001
Leucine	66.1±3.9	120.9±6.3	137.8±6.1	<.001	<.001
Tyrosine	23.0±1.6	64.1±5.4	64.6±4.4	<.001	<.001
Phenylalanine	29.2±2.5	55.9±4.3	69.6±5.2	<.001	<.001
Ornithine	19.7±1.1	78.9±6.6	82.6±6.6	<.001	<.001
Lysine	106.2±7.1	376.1±45	418.2±33.5	<.001	<.001
Histidine	54.5±3.6	81.6±6.5	96.4±5.4	<.005	<.001
Arginine	30.2±1.9	90.1±5.7	99.5±6.5	<.001	<.001

[a]Abbreviations: MV, maternal vein; UA, umbilical artery; UV, umbilical vein.

TABLE V

The Relationship between Maternal and Fetal Plasma Amino Acid Levels and Correlation Coefficients (MV vs. FA)

Amino acid	*r*	*p*
Alanine	0.66	<.05
Valine	0.80	<.01
Threonine	0.77	<.01
Lysine	0.86	<.01
Glycine	0.66	<.05
Leucine	0.71	<.05
Histidine	0.66	<.05
Serine	0.73	<.05
Isoleucine	0.77	<.01
Arginine	0.71	<.05
Phenylalanine	0.84	<.01
Tyrosine	0.73	<.05
Ornithine	0.71	<.05
Methionine	0.84	<.01

The mean umbilical V–A concentration differences are ordered according to magnitude in Fig. 7. The majority of V–A concentration differences were positive for most amino acids.

The existence of a higher fetal than maternal α-amino-nitrogen concentration has been described previously in all species studied, including man during both early and late gestation (for review see Ref. 33). However, the validity of the observations for early human pregnancy obtained at hysterotomy has been questioned because of the unphysiological conditions of sampling. The results of our study confirm the existence of a fetomaternal gradient for amino acids at midterm gestation in human pregnancy. Moreover, the present results show that there are important quantitative and qualitative differences between our data and those derived from previous hysterotomy studies (30,32), suggesting that the latter have been artifactually elevated due to the circumstances of the sampling. It is also noteworthy that our data confirm substantial differences in the profiles of the concentrations of amino acids between the human and the sheep fetus (34,35).

Of particular significance is the largest significant positive V–A concentration difference for alanine implying that there is a high uptake of this nonessential amino acid and making it the major source of fetal nitrogen as well as being possibly an important source of nonglucose

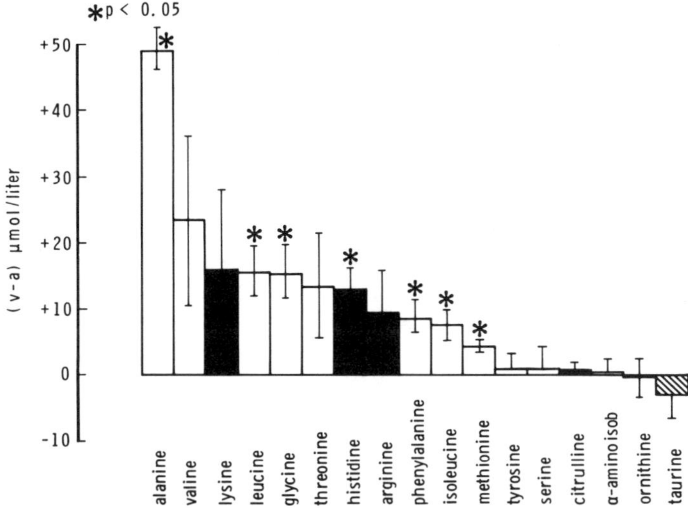

Fig. 7. Differences in umbilical vein and artery concentrations of plasma amino acids in the midterm human fetus. $n = 10$, mean ± SEM. Asterisk indicates $p < .05$. □, Neutral amino acids; ■, basic amino acids; ▧, acidic amino acids.

carbon supplied by the mother (36,37). This appears to be in contrast to the fetal lamb, where the greatest umbilical V–A difference is found for glutamine (34). These data emphasize that it is not possible to extrapolate data derived from the sheep fetus to man.

It is also of interest that despite the substantially elevated concentrations of insulinogenic amino acids (alanine, arginine, and leucine), plasma insulin concentrations were not significantly higher in the fetal circulation than in the maternal circulation (Fig. 2). No significant differences were to be found in the case of pancreatic glucagon.

Regulatory peptides, together with their corresponding cell lines, have been identified in the human fetal gut from 6 to 16 weeks after conception (38–41). For most of the peptides examined to date, the gut tissue concentrations rise to values found in the last 10 weeks of gestation that are at least as high as those seen in adults (39), and, as the gut is relatively large in the perinatal period, this may indicate a correspondingly larger gut endocrine cell mass for some lines in this period of development. Moreover, there is a changing spectrum of molecular forms during fetal life and indeed certain peptides appear and disappear from different regions of the gut during development. These observations suggest that regulatory peptides may have a key role as local inducing agents regulating the growth and functional development of the fetal intestine.

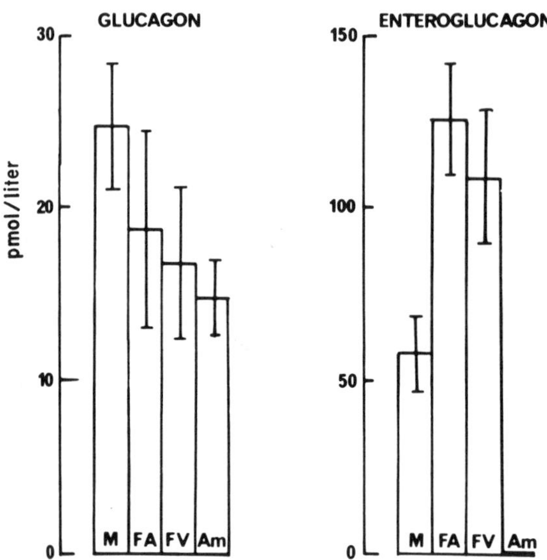

Fig. 8. Maternal, fetal, and amniotic fluid concentrations (mean ± SEM) of glucagon and enteroglucagon.

Figures 8 and 9 show the concentrations of enteroglucagon, gastrin, gastric inhibitory polypeptide, and pancreatic polypeptide concentrations in the maternal and fetal circulations, together with values from amniotic fluid assay.

In contrast to the absence of significant differences between the ma-

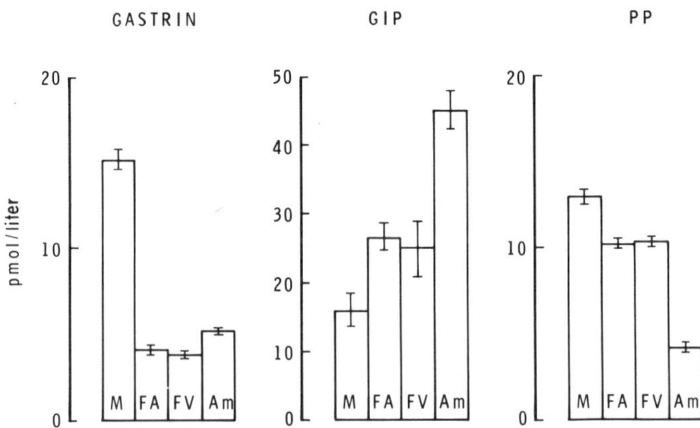

Fig. 9. Maternal, fetal, and amniotic fluid concentrations (mean ± SEM) of gastrin, GIP, and PP. (M = Maternal vein, FA = fetal artery, FV = fetal vein, Am = amniotic fluid.)

ternal and fetal concentrations of glucagon, there are substantially elevated concentrations of enteroglucagon in the fetal circulation. On the other hand, gastrin concentrations are much higher in the maternal circulation than in the fetal circulation, as are the concentrations of pancreatic polypeptide. Fetal concentrations of GIP, on the other hand, are higher than those in the maternal circulation, the highest levels of this peptide being found in amniotic fluid.

Several questions follow from these observations. First, why are some hormones present in lower concentrations in the fetus than in the mother, whereas others are present in higher concentrations? What is the significance of the very high amniotic concentrations of GIP and the absent

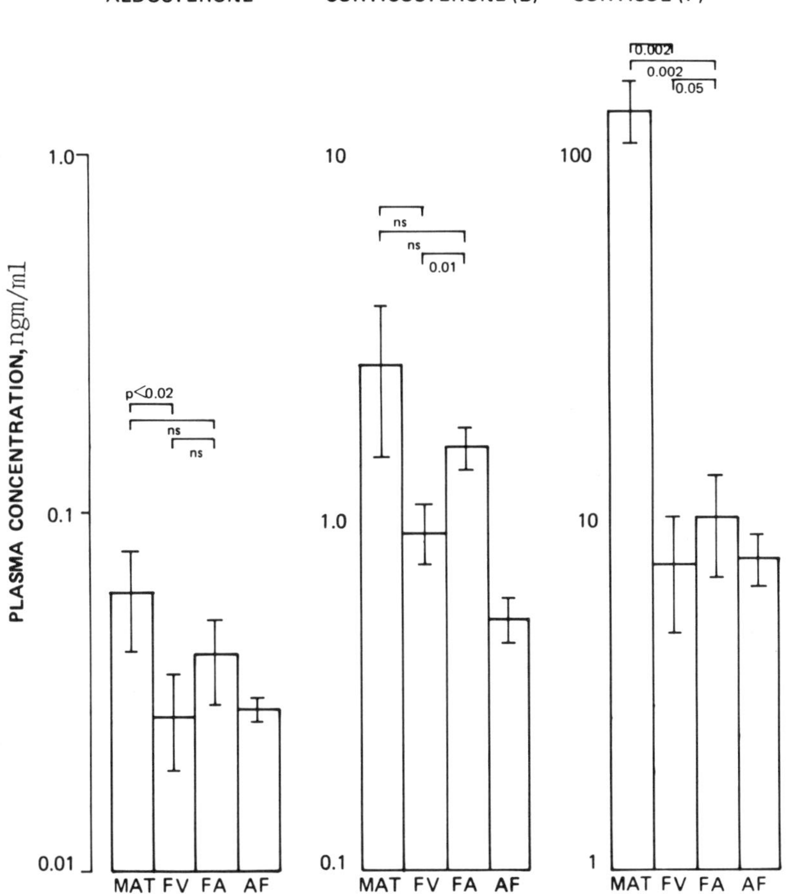

Fig. 10. Maternal vein, fetal vein, fetal artery, and amniotic fluid concentrations of aldosterone, corticosterone, and cortisol during the second trimester of human pregnancy.

concentration of enteroglucagon in amniotic fluid? From where do amniotic concentrations arise? Are the molecular forms of the hormone similar in mother, amniotic fluid, and fetus?

It is known that the fetus swallows and can utilize the constituents of amniotic fluid (42) and, moreover, amniotic fluid is in continuous circulation with the fetal lung. Could these peptides have an important role to play as local inducing agents in the development of the fetal lung as well as the alimentary tract? Whatever the final answers to these questions are, the observations listed above suggest that the study of the ontogeny and the control of the fetal secretion of hormones and regulatory peptides may well throw further light on the orderly sequence

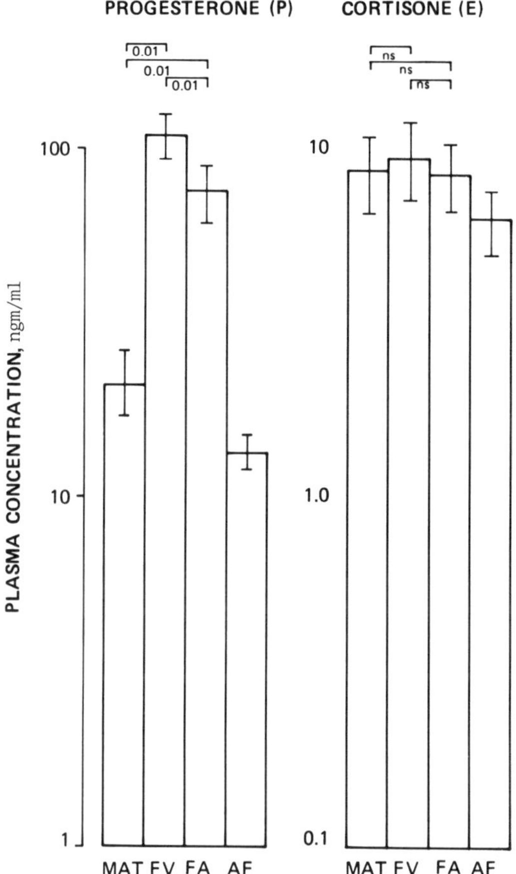

Fig. 11. Maternal vein, fetal vein, fetal artery, and amniotic fluid concentrations of progesterone and cortisone during the second trimester of human pregnancy.

of development of the lung and gut as well as on pathological development.

We have also taken the opportunity to measure with Professor W. Sippell the concentrations of adrenal steroid hormones and their precursors in the maternal and fetal circulations. The preliminary results of the study are shown in Fig. 10, 11, and 12.

The data confirm that the fetal adrenal gland is functionally active at this stage in human pregnancy and works independently of that of the mother. Moreover, since the concentrations in amniotic fluid are lower than those reported previously from mothers undergoing routine amniocentesis without leading to termination of pregnancy, it suggests that

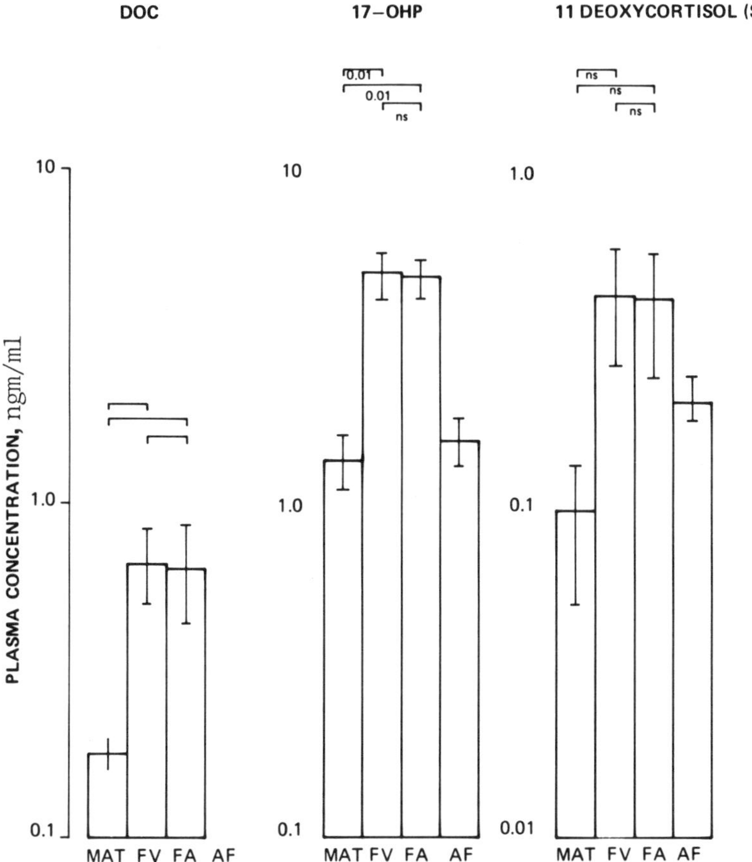

Fig. 12. Maternal vein, fetal vein, fetal artery, and amniotic fluid concentrations of DOC, 17-hydroxyprogesterone, and 11-deoxycortisol during the second trimester of human pregnancy.

the maternal sedation given to our mothers has an effect in decreasing stress hormone secretion by the fetus.

These studies emphasize the power of the fetoscopy model in investigating the maternal and fetal milieu during the second trimester of human pregnancy. Other studies are in progress that document the concentrations of other variables, but the data to date already raise important questions which need to be answered in the near future.

V. THE ENDOCRINE MILIEU AT BIRTH

Gastrointestinal peptides are found in significant concentrations in venous cord blood at birth in infants delivered by the normal vaginal route (Table VI). It is interesting that most of the measured hormone concentrations at birth are similar to those seen in healthy fasting adults (see Fig. 14 for comparison), but it is particularly noteworthy that the concentrations of gastrin and VIP are significantly higher than fasting adult values. Hypergastrinemia at birth has been reported by others (43), who suggested that gastrin might be released by vagal stimuli at delivery and this accords with our own data which show that plasma gastrin concentrations fall sharply toward adult fasting levels in the early hours postnatally prior to the commencement of enteral feeding (44,45).

The observations implying that gut peptide-releasing mechanisms may operate at birth are further supported by our observations that full-term

TABLE VI

Enteroinsular Hormone Concentrations in Venous Cord Plasma from Normal Deliveries Compared with Those from Infants Showing Fetal Distress (pmol/Liter; Mean ± SE).

Hormone	Normal deliveries $n = 20$	Fetal distress $n = 8$	p^a
Motilin	34±4	127±24	<.001
GIP	10±2	28±6	<.01
Pancreatic polypeptide	13±3	44±10	<.01
Pancreatic glucagon	4±2	14±4	<.05
Neurotensin	33±3	48±4	<.01
Enteroglucagon	77±5	107±10	<.05
Gastrin	42±5	39±3	NS[b]
Secretin	6±1	5±1	NS

[a]Mann–Whitney rank sum test.
[b]NS = Not significant.

infants born following fetal distress show a selective venous cord plasma elevation of motilin, VIP, pancreatic polypeptide, pancreatic glucagon, neurotensin, and enteroglucagon (46). The rise in plasma motilin in fetal distress is especially marked, and we have suggested this might account for the passage of meconium, an event pathognomonic of this condition. The elevation in plasma glucagon occurring in infants suffering fetal dis-

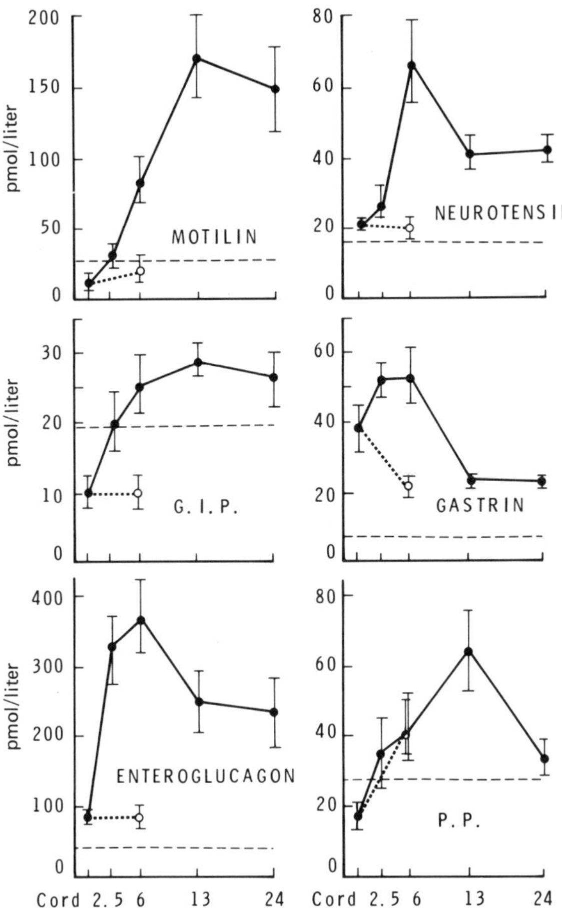

Fig. 13. Plasma concentrations of motilin, neurotensin, GIP, gastrin, enteroglucagon, and PP in cord blood and at 2.5, 6, 13 and 24 days of age (sample drawn immediately before a milk feed) in healthy pre-term infants. The dotted line represents the mean fasting value for the hormone in normal adult subjects. The open circles on day 6 represent the values obtained in preterm infants who received only intravenous fluids during the first 6 days.

tress would account for the rapid mobilization of glycogen which occurs under hypoxic conditions, with the consequent induction of hypoglycemia after the asphyxia has been resolved. The significance of the changes in plasma VIP, PP, and neurotensin is uncertain at the present time, but collectively the peptides may be having effects on redistributing the visceral blood flow of the distressed fetuses.

It is also worth emphasizing that the metabolic milieu at delivery is profoundly influenced by the administration of glucose to mothers during labor. We have shown in retrospective analysis of plasma insulin concentrations in cord blood of infants born after normal delivery that mothers given "routine" dextrose infusions during labor produce neonates with hyperinsulinism in cord blood. That the magnitude of the hyperinsulinism is related to the amount of glucose given to mothers during delivery demonstrates that transplacental passage of glucose is a potent stimulus to insulin at this time. Others (47) have confirmed this finding and have demonstrated that high cord plasma insulin concentrations may be accompanied by rebound hypoglycemia during the first hours after delivery. It is a curious belief among obstetricians that maternal ketosis during delivery is unsatisfactory, and this belief can lead on occasions to a totally uncritical approach to the administration of glucose during parturition. This policy may be totally inappropriate, not only in the context of the induction of postnatal hypoglycemia, but it would also be particularly disadvantageous for an infant who was hypoxic to be experiencing a massive influx of glucose from the mother, since this would almost certainly exacerbate a lactic acidosis.

Cord concentrations of regulatory peptides in preterm infants are shown in Fig. 13, and in comparing these values with those in Table VI, which outline the concentrations in normal infants at term, it can be seen that plasma GIP, gastrin, and enteroglucagon concentrations are similar in both groups of infants, whereas there are some differences in the cord levels of PP, motilin, and neurotensin.

VI. THE METABOLIC AND ENDOCRINE MILIEU IN RELATION TO POSTNATAL FEEDING

After preparation of the fetal gut for postnatal feeding, an important physiological event which occurs immediately after birth is the first feed of milk. This is an event of considerable physiological significance, since it is the first time that the alimentary tract has been challenged by an exogenous foodstuff. Rogers *et al.* (48) showed that gastrin and enteroglucagon increased in the plasma of human neonates during the first 4 days, and Lichtenberger and Johnson (11) confirmed that the early postnatal elevation in gastrin in rats was due to enteral feeding. Von Berger *et al.* (49) demonstrated that gastrin rose in the plasma after the first feed in the human neonate. In a rather more extensive study we have also demonstrated that the first feed of human milk given to full-term infants caused a significant increase in blood glucose concentrations, together with increases in insulin, growth hormone, gastrin, and enteroglucagon, but not in GIP nor in pancreatic glucagon (45). The lack of GIP response accords with the findings of King *et al.* (50) who failed to identify an active enteroinsular axis in the immediate postpartum period. This, together with the absent feed response for pancreatic glucagon in our studies, supports the view that the glucagon surge after birth (4) is of importance in the initiation of glycogenolysis and gluconeogenesis independently of enteral feeding. It would seem to be particularly appropriate for the newborn infant to achieve rapid regulation of blood glucose immediately after birth independently of the precise timing of the initiation of enteral feeding and to ensure that insulin dominance does not occur at a time of glucose instability.

The consequences of abnormal pancreatic endocrine development at this time of life are vividly revealed in considering the consequences of infants born with nesidioblastosis of the pancreas. It has been demonstrated by our own group and by others that normal pancreatic islet cell hormone control is of major importance in preventing hypoglycemia and its consequent risk of neonatal death or brain damage. The investigation and management of this most difficult neonatal problem is beyond the scope of this review, but the interested reader is referred to Soltesz and Aynsley-Green (51,52) for further information. What is clear from these experiments of nature, however, is that the endocrine pancreas has a crucial role to play in the stabilization of blood glucose levels during the first hours after birth and in the maintenance of normoglycemia until enteral feeding is established.

It is concluded from these studies that the infant born at term is prepared for enteral feeding and that within hours of birth demonstrable postprandial changes occur in intermediary metabolism together with changes in the secretion of hormones from the gut, pancreas, and pituitary gland. However, in contrast to these impressive changes in the infant born at term, when the same study was repeated in infants born prematurely it was found that no change occurred after the first feed in the concentration of any metabolite or hormone that was measured (53). This implies that developmental changes occur during the last few weeks of gestation which prepare the infant born at term to respond immediately.

A series of papers has now been published that documents the development of postnatal hormone concentrations in preterm infants, and some of the more important conclusions from these studies are summarized in the following paragraphs.

It should be obvious to the informed reader that a number of different feeding practices are used routinely in newborn nurseries. Prematurely born infants may receive milk directly into the stomach or into the small bowel, the milk may be given continuously or intermittently, and the composition of the milk may vary widely from "drip" breast milk to expressed breast milk or to a variety of specially designed formulae for the low birth weight infant. There is evidence that the mode of delivery and the composition of the feed have important influences on the development of the metabolic and endocrine milieu of the newborn infant. Indeed, the effects of different feed composition can be documented in the infant born at term as early as the very first feed after birth. Thus the gut appears to have the ability to respond to milk with an increase in enteroglucagon concentrations, but not in response to dextrose (54).

With particular reference to the prematurely born infant, we have shown that infants who are given milk feeds by regular boluses directly into the stomach experience multiple gut hormonal surges during the first postnatal days (55). Thus, although no demonstrable change occurred after the first feed, within 2 1/2 days of being born preprandial hormone concentrations had increased markedly in six of the peptides measured (Fig. 13) and by the sixth day there had been a highly significant threefold to fourfold rise above the levels at birth in, for example, the basal plasma concentrations of neurotensin and enteroglucagon. By 13 days of age, the basal plasma motilin concentration had risen 13-fold and PP threefold. Plasma concentrations of all these substances rose significantly above adult values, in the case of enteroglucagon by a factor of 10.

In addition to the rise in basal hormone concentration, during the postnatal period in preterm infants there are progressive changes in the effect of a feed on postprandial plasma concentrations of motilin, neurotensin, GIP, enteroglucagon, gastrin, secretin, glucose, and insulin. In the early neonatal days the responses to a feed are small or absent, whereas by 24 days the responses are marked (55,56) (Fig. 14).

More limited data from the term breast-fed infant show that significant postnatal hormonal surges do occur in preprandial blood samples but are smaller than those seen in preterm infants (57,58). There are several explanations for this difference between premature and term infants which is rather contrary to expectations. It may, for example, be explained by the fact that lactation takes some days to become established in breast-fed infants and that enteral feed volumes are lower on a body weight per kilogram basis in term infants than those given to preterm neonates.

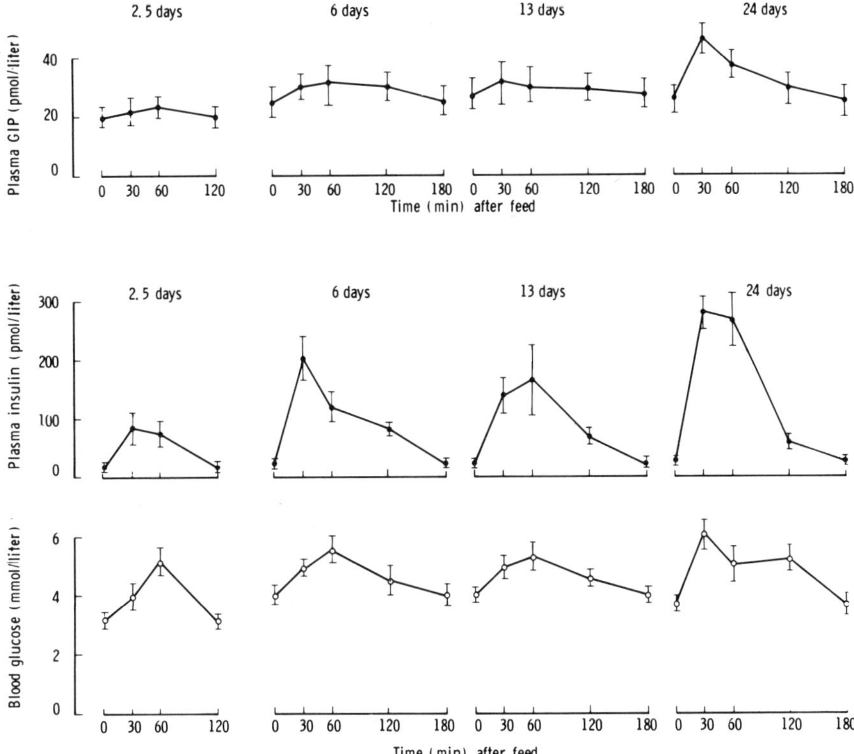

Fig. 14. Plasma concentrations of GIP and insulin and of blood glucose in healthy preterm infants after milk feeds at a mean age of 2.5, 6, 13, and 24 days after birth (cross-sectional data, each infant contributing only one blood sample to the study).

The precise mechanism for the unexpectedly high concentrations of peptides in preterm infants still requires further exploration.

That it is enteral feeding which has triggered these postnatal surges is confirmed by Fig. 13, which also shows basal concentrations of six substances in preterm infants who had received regular boluses of milk into the stomach compared with another group of infants who had received no enteral feeds. With the exception of the change in PP, none of the other five hormones increased in concentration after birth, suggesting that food introduced into the gut in the form of milk is indeed a powerful stimulus to the secretion of gut hormones and that these changes do not occur in infants who have never been fed (59).

More recently Dr. Alan Lucas has analyzed how much milk has to be given to induce gut hormone secretion (60). Figure 15 shows the relationship between plasma enteroglucagon concentrations and the volume

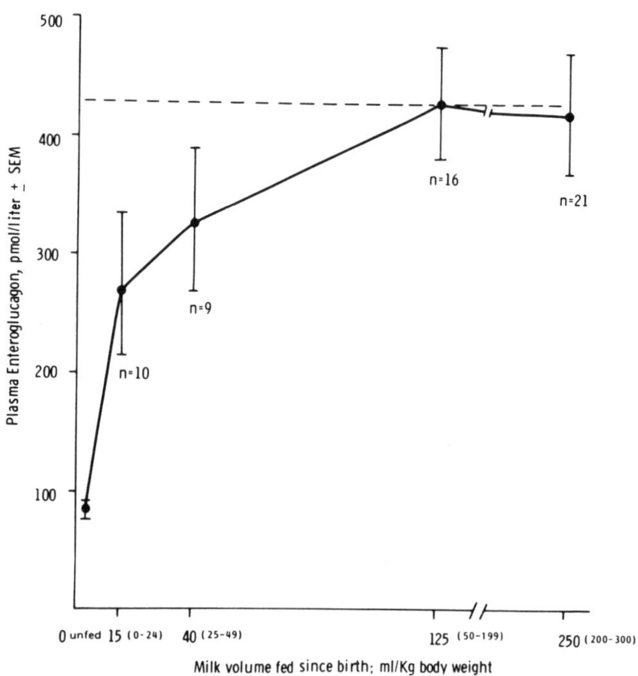

Fig. 15. Plasma enteroglucagon concentrations in preterm infants in relation to milk volume fed since birth.

of milk consumed since birth in preterm infants. It is evident that a highly significant increase in enteroglucagon concentrations occurs after a volume of milk as low as 15 ml/kg has been given.

These data can be used to question current policy of routinely feeding small premature infants entirely by the intravenous route. These infants are deprived not only of enteral milk but also of the amniotic fluid they should be swallowing *in utero*. Experimental deprivation of enteral feeding is known to result in delay in gut development (9). Furthermore, in animal studies (61) total parenteral nutrition results in rapid changes in the gut within 3 days, including marked mucosal hypotrophy, decrease in brush border enzyme activities, and reduction in absorptive surface as evidenced by diminished xylose absorption; indeed xylose absorption is reduced also in human neonates fed parenterally. In neonatal clinical practice, enteral feeds are usually tolerated within a few days after reintroduction of food after short periods of total parenteral nutrition. However, in certain circumstances, for instance, in extreme immaturity and, in particular, following surgery for congenital abnormalities in the gut, it may be necessary to employ parenteral nutrition for prolonged periods after birth. The above data suggest that the use of milk should be considered not only as a nutrient but also as a pharmacological agent to maintain the stimulus to gut development. It needs to be proved conclusively that this practice of "minimal enteral feeding" has a beneficial effect on gut development and tolerance to enteral feeding in seriously ill neonatal patients.

A further interesting issue concerns the effects of continuous intragastric infusions of milk compared with regular intermittent bolus administration of the same total daily food volume. We have performed a study examining the endocrine milieu induced by these practices, and it is evident that the continuously fed infant, although demonstrating an increase in basal concentrations of several peptides, does not experience the regular cyclical responses of hormones, particularly the anabolic hormones insulin and growth hormone, which are seen in babies given regular boluses of milk (62). While it could be argued that feed-induced surges of anabolic hormones in relation to bolus feeding might stimulate faster growth (and this has yet to be proved), it could be postulated equally that postprandial hormone changes after bolus feeding could be deleterious by inducing changes in blood pressure and cerebral blood flow which might predispose to further problems, such as intraventricular hemorrhage (63,64). Some preliminary data have been published suggesting that the bolus-fed infant grows faster than the continuously fed infant, but again this needs to be proved conclusively.

The composition of the milk given to premature infants also appears to have effects on the milieu during the first 3 to 4 weeks after birth. Infants fed on a proprietary formula for premature babies have higher plasma GIP concentrations around the second week after birth, whereas pancreatic polypeptide concentrations are higher in human milk-fed infants around 3 weeks after birth (65). The mechanism and significance of these differences are unclear, but it does suggest that not only the method of feeding but also the composition of the feed may influence the development of postnatal hormone concentrations for some of the peptides.

The concept of differences induced by feed composition is more vividly exemplified in the context of the full-term infant in the first week after birth. We have documented impressive differences between the breast-fed and formula-fed infant on the sixth postnatal day. There is a greater insulin response to the feed at this age in formula-fed infants than in the breast-fed infants, and this appears to be related to differences in GIP secretion (66). There are also differences in the responses of the motor hormones of the gut, motilin and neurotensin, together with a tendency to a greater growth hormone secretion (66). The functional and long-term consequences of these differences remain to be clarified. One obvious area of immediate relevance concerns the stool frequency of normal term neonates. It has been known for a long time that the breast-fed infant has his bowels open less frequently than the formula-fed infant, this difference having been attributed to differences in the residue of the two milks. However, our observations of differences in motor hormone secretion suggest that they may be more relevant in this context.

It is also fascinating to deliberate whether or not these endocrine differences could have an effect on the programming of the central nervous system in relation to satiety and food intake in later life. It should be remembered that the premature infant, born at a time when it should be receiving only amniotic fluid into its gut, is given routinely in most newborn nurseries volumes of milk on the order of 150 to 200 ml/kg/24 hr. These volumes of milk, if given to an adult, would amount to volumes on the order of 20 liters per day! It would be an extremely interesting study to determine whether or not the food intake, feeding pattern, and satiety of infants in the first 1 to 5 years after birth are different in relation to the mode of neonatal nutrition.

Finally, it should be emphasized that other hormones may have important effects on postnatal adaptation. These include cortisol secretion and prolactin and thyroxine release. The latter may be particularly important in view of the suggestion that it is relevant in the induction of hepatic receptors for the metabolic hormones.

VII. PHYSIOLOGICAL SIGNIFICANCE OF THE METABOLIC AND ENDOCRINE MILIEU OF THE FETUS AND NEONATE

The factors regulating the ontogeny of the intestinal tract have been reviewed recently (3). Many factors are known to be involved in this process, including the genetic endowment, the existence of a biological clock regulating developmental chronology, and other endogenous mechanisms and environmental influences. The expression of the genetic endowment at various stages of fetal gastrointestinal development is accomplished by way of regulatory mechanisms and although most of those postulated mechanisms have been studied in experimental animals, the above evidence suggests that parallelism exists for the human fetus and that regulatory peptides and hormones in general may be of fundamental importance.

The interaction of environmental influences on the ontogeny of the gut appears to be well exemplified by the adaptation of the premature infant to postnatal feeding. One unexplained point relates to why preterm infants, and to a lesser extent, the infant at term, have concentrations of peptides that are considerably above those seen in the adult. It is possible that they could relate to deficient plasma clearance mechanisms in the immature infant or, alternatively, could result from the relatively large endocrine cell mass of the developing gut. Whatever the mechanism, it is possible that high concentrations of hormones and regulatory peptides are needed in both preterm and term neonates to induce receptor activity and hence the functional effects in target tissues. This raises a whole new issue of further work to be performed. The data reported represent "phenomenology," and there is an urgent need to relate these observations to data demonstrating the actual functional development of gut activity.

Of greater practical significance are the implications of these data for the feeding practices currently employed in newborn nurseries. It is evident that differences in practice which may seem at first glance to be innocuous may indeed have fundamental effects on the metabolic and endocrine milieu.

It is clear that further work is needed to determine the control of the development of gut function after birth, and answers to some of the questions posed in this review may be of practical importance both in defining more scientifically the nutritional management of different groups of newborn infants and in the investigation and treatment of disorders interfering with normal adaptation to postnatal nutrition.

ACKNOWLEDGMENTS

The extensive collaboration over many years of Professor S. R. Bloom and his team at the Hammersmith Hospital in the measurement of regulatory peptides is gratefully acknowledged. Dr. A. Lucas and Dr. G. Soltesz were responsible for the development of many of the experimental models and results presented in this review. The collaboration of Mr. I. Z. Mackenzie and of Professor W. Sippell are also gratefully acknowledged.

The editors of *Acta Paediatrica Scandinavica*, *Archives of Disease in Childhood*, and *Lancet* are thanked for permission to reproduce some of the figures.

REFERENCES.

1. R. J. Grand, J. B. Watkins, and F. M. Torti, *Gastroenterology* **70,** 790 (1976).
2. E. Lebenthal, *Monogr. Paediatr.* **16,** 17 (1982).
3. E. Lebenthal and P. C. Lee, *Pediatr. Res.* **17,** 19 (1983).
4. M. A. Sperling, *Monogr. Paediatr.* **16,** 39 (1982).
5. S. R. Bloom, ed., "Gut Hormones." Churchill-Livingstone, Edinburgh, 1978.
6. S. R. Bloom and J. M. Polak, eds., "Gut Hormones." Churchill-Livingstone, Edinburgh, 1981.
7. L.-L. Larson, *Clin. Gastroenterol.* **9,** 485 (1980).

8. R. J. Milla, *in* "Neonatal Gastroenterology" (M. S. Tanner and R. J. Stocks, eds.), p. 1. Intercept, Newcastle upon Tyne, England, 1984.
9. R. W. Stoddart and E. M. Widdowson, *Biol. Neonate* **29,** 18 (1976).
10. E. M. Widdowson, V. E. Colombo, and C. A. Artavanis, *Biol. Neonate* **28,** 272 (1976).
11. L. Lichtenberger and L. R. Johnson, *Am. J. Physiol.* **227,** 390 (1977).
12. J. Gentz, B. Persson, M. Kellum, G. Bengtsson, and J. Thorell, *Life Sci.* **10,** 137 (1971).
13. K. Asplund, *Diabetologia* **8,** 152 (1972).
14. G. M. Green and E. S. Nasset, *Gastroenterology* **79,** 695 (1980).
15. D. H. Alpers and F. J. Tedesco, *Biochim. Biophys. Acta* **401,** 28 (1975).
16. R. H. Starkey and D. N. Orth, *J. Clin. Endocrinol. Metab. 45,* 1144 (1977).
17. A. Lucas and M. D. Mitchell, *Arch. Dis. Child.* **55,** 950 (1980).
18. J. Sack, *in* "Human Milk, Its Biological and Social Value" (S. Frier and A. I. Eidelman, eds.), p. 56. Excerpta Med. Found., Amsterdam, 1980.
19. S. Werner A.-M. Widstrom, V. Wahlberg, P. Eneroth, and J. Winberg, *Early Hum. Dev.* **6,** 77 (1982).
20. J. Girard, *in* "Pediatric Nutrition" (G. C. Arneil and J. Metcoff, eds.), p. 3. Butterworth, London, 1985.
21. F. C. Battaglia and G. Meschia, *Physiol. Rev.* **58,** 499 (1978).
22. W. W. Hay, *Semin. Perinatol.* **3,** 157 (1979).
23. W. W. Hay, J. W. Sparls, B. J. Quissell, F. C. Battaglia, and G. Meschia, *Am. J. Physiol.* **240,** E662 (1981).
24. K. O. Raivio and K. Teramo, *Acta Paediatr. Scand.* **57,** 512 (1968).
25. F. M. Morris, E. L. Makowski, G. Meschia, and F. C. Battaglia, *Biol. Neonate* **25,** 44 (1975).
26. T. M. Coltart, R. . W. Beard, R. C. Turner, and N. W. Oakley, *Br. Med. J.* **iv,** 17 (1969).
27. R. D. H. Boyd, F. H. Morris, Jr., G. Meschia, E. L. Makowski, and F. C. Battaglia, *Am. J. Physiol.* **225,** 897 (1973).
28. F. H. Morris, R. D. H. Boyd, E. L. Makowski, G. Meschia, and F. C. Battaglia, *Proc. Soc. Exp. Biol. Med.* **145,** 875 (1974).
29. A. F. Phillips, J. W. Dubin, P. J. Motty, and J. R. Raye, *Pediatr. Res.* **17,** 51 (1983).
30. F. Cockburn, S. P. Robins, and J. O. Forfar, *Br. Med. J.* **ii,** 747 (1970).
31. N. McIntosh, C. H. Rodeck, and R. Heath, *Biol. Neonate* **45,** 218 (1984).
32. M. Young and M. A. Prenton, *J. Obstet. Gynaecol. Br. Commonw.* **76,** 333 (1969).
33. F. C. Battaglia and G. Meschia, *Physiol. Rev.* **58,** 499 (1978).
34. J. A. Lemons, E. W. Adcock, M. Douglas Jones, M. A. Naughton, G. Meschia, and F. C. Battaglia, *J. Clin. Invest.* **58,** 1428 (1976).
35. M. Young, G. Soltesz, D. Noakes, J. Joyce, I. R. MacFadyen, and B. V. Lewis, *J. Perinat. Med.* **3,** 180 (1973).
36. S. Hayashi, K. Sanada, N. Sagawa, N. Yamada, and K. Kido, *Biol. Neonate* **34,** 11 (1978).
37. M. Young, *Placenta* **125,** Suppl. 11.
38. L.-I. Larsson and L. M. Jorgensen, *Cell Tissue Res.* **194,** 79 (1978).
39. A. M. J. Buchan, M. G. Bryant, J. M. Polak, M. Gregor, M. A. Ghatei, and S. R. Bloom, *in* "Gut Hormones" (S. R. Bloom and J. M. Polak, eds.), p. 119. Churchill-Livingstone, Edinburgh, 1981.
40. T. Lehy and M. L. Christina, *Cell Tissue Res.* **203,** 415 (1979).
41. J. A. Chayvialle, C. Paulin, and M. P. Dubois, *Gastroenterology* **76,** 1112 (1979).
42. T. M. Abbas and J. E. Tovey, *Br. Med. J.* **1,** 476 (1960).
43. A. R. Euler, W. J. Byrne, L. M. Cousins, M. E. Ament, R. D. Leake, and J. D. Walsh, *Gastroenterology* **72,** 1271 (1974).

44. A. Lucas, T. E. Adrian, N. D. Christofides, S. R. Bloom, and A. Aynsley-Green, *Arch. Dis. Child.* **55,** 673 (1980).
45. A. Aynsley-Green, S. R. Bloom, D. H. Williamson, and R. C. Turner, *Arch. Dis. Child.* **52,** 291 (1977).
46. A. Lucas, T. E. Adrian, A. Aynsley-Green, and S. R. Bloom, *Lancet* **ii,** 968 (1979).
47. J. Mediola, L. J. Grylack, and J. W. Scanlon, *Anesth. Analg. (Cleveland)* **61,** 32 (1982).
48. I. M. Rogers, D. C. Davidson, J. Lawrence, J. Ardill, and K. D. Buchanan, *Arch. Dis. Child.* **49,** 796 (1974).
49. L. Von Berger, I. Henrichs, S. Raptis, E. Heinze, W. Jonathan, W. M. Teller, and E. F. Pfeiffer, *Pediatrics* **58,** 264 (1976).
50. K. C. King, R. Schwartz, K. Yamaguchi, and P. J. Adam, *J. Pediatr.* **91,** 783 (1977).
51. G. Soltesz and A. Aynsley-Green, *Adv. Intern. Med. Padiatr.* **51,** 152 (1984).
52. A. Aynsley-Green and G. Soltesz, "Hypoglycaemia in Infancy and Childhood." Churchill-Livingstone, Edinburgh, 1985.
53. A. Lucas, S. R. Bloom, and A. Aynsley-Green, *Arch. Dis. Child.* **53,** 731 (1978).
54. A. Aynsley-Green, A. Lucas, and S. R. Bloom, *Acta Paediatr. Scand.* **68,** 265 (1979).
55. A. Lucas, T. E. Adrian, S. R. Bloom, and A. Aynsley-Green, *Acta Paediatr. Scand.* **69,** 205 (1980).
56. A. Lucas, S. R. Bloom, and A. Aynsley-Green, *Arch. Dis. Child.* **55,** 678 (1980).
57. A. Lucas, S. R. Bloom, and A. Aynsley-Green, *Biol. Neonate* **41,** 63 (1982).
58. A. Lucas, S. R. Bloom, and A. Aynsley-Green, *Acta Paediatr. Scand.* **71,** 71 (1982).
59. A. Lucas, S. R. Bloom, and A. Aynsley-Green, *Acta Paediatr. Scand.* **72,** 245 (1983).
60. A. Lucas, S. R. Bloom, and Aynsley-Green, *Acta Paediatr. Scand.* **75,** 719 (1986).
61. C. A. Hughes, *in* "Neonatal Gastroenterology" (M. S. Tanner and R. J. Stocks, eds.), p. 69. Intercept, Newcastle upon Tyne, England, 1984.
62. A. Aynsley-Green, T. E. Adrian, and S. R. Bloom, *Acta Paediatr. Scand.* **71,** 379 (1982).
63. P. M. Rahilly, *Arch. Dis. Child.* **55,** 265 (1980).
64. A. Lucas and A. Aynsley-Green, *Arch. Dis. Child.* **55,** 741 (1980).
65. S. A. Calvert, G. Soltesz, P. A. Jenkins, D. Harris, C. Newman, T. E. Adrian, S. R. Bloom, and A. Aynsley-Green, *Biol. Neonate* **47,** 189 (1985).
66. A. Lucas, A. M. Blackburn, A. Aynsley-Green, D. L. Sarson, T. E. Adrian, and S. R. Bloom, *Lancet* **i,** 1267 (1980).

15

Discussion: Part II. Birth from the Nutritional Point of View A. Nutrition in the Postpartum Period

W. Allan Walker
Harvard Medical School
Boston, Massachusetts, U.S.A.

In my view the primary purpose of the initiation of discussion is not to present new information but to focus general discussion on cogent points raised by the presenters which have both general and specific application to nutrition in the postpartum period. Accordingly, my remarks will principally address these issues.

This afternoon's session was very interesting in that it addressed important aspects of the newborn's response to the extrauterine environment at the specific organ level as well as with respect to the need for new functions outside of the intrauterine milieu. Each speaker stressed the importance of adoptive responses to the extrauterine environment and the importance of environmental factors per se, especially in the premature, to a successful adaptation.

From my perspective several key general questions were raised from the presentations. Many of these were underscored by specific explanations made by the speakers. For example, it became apparent that the link maintained between the infant/maternal contact in the intrauterine environment vis-à-vis the placenta should be continued by the ingestion of breast milk (colostrum) by the young infant in the postnatal environment. We know from recent studies (1,2) that breast milk is a dynamic fluid providing not only the appropriate nutrients for the premature or full-term newborn but additional factors (hormones, antibodies, and growth factors) which profoundly and positively affect newborn development. This phenomenon has been illustrated in several ways over the last few years. Studies that have examined the composition of breast milk in mothers of preterm infants compared to that of mothers delivering after 40 weeks of gestation suggest that the protein, electrolyte content, and fatty acid composition differ in the two groups and contain nutrients appropriate for the age of the infant (3). In addition, we now know that breast milk contains factors that facilitate the absorption of trace elements such as zinc (4,5), thus allowing for the efficient uptake of this nutrient at a time when the need is greatest. Furthermore, there is strong evidence (6,7) to suggest that "growth" factors in breast milk affect organ development, particularly of the small intestine. Dr. William Heird's group has suggested that intestinal disaccharidase activity is enhanced by the ingestion of natural milk (8). This observation supports and extends the report by Dr. Elsie Widdowson (7) on general gut changes after the initial ingestion of colostrum. In more basic studies in our laboratory, we have suggested that breast milk and hormonal growth factors in breast milk may affect the enterocyte's microvillus membrane composition and subsequentially the interaction of toxins, microorganisms, and food antigens (9,10). We need to consider other consequences of this extrauterine maternal–infant association as it pertains to bacterial colonization and active/passive intestinal host defenses.

Another important general principle from this session was the importance of nutrition in the newborn period in the successful adaptation of the infant to the external environment. In the 1960s, when I was training in pediatrics, the general practice was to delay feeding the premature for extended periods because of the possibility of developmental anomalies, etc. This practice contributed significantly to infant morbidity and mortality in this age group. Today we know that early nutritional support is essential for the newborn case. We must now begin to determine the appropriateness of specific substrates, that is, short-chain fatty acids versus long-chain fatty acids, proteins versus peptides, etc., and the optimal approach to delivery of calories, that is, intravenous versus enteric or a combination. For example, a number of studies (11,12) have suggested that the early introduction of enteric calories after intestinal insult in young infants affects a rapid response of the intestine to the damage. This approach is of utmost importance in the very young newborn infant.

In like manner, we must determine the effect of short-term starvation (24–72 hr) on neonatal gut function. This occurrence, which is common in the care of premature infants with distention or suspicion of necrotizing enterocolitis, may have a profound effect on the immature intestine of young infants and may produce the same viscious cycle seen in severe protein-calorie malnutrition, namely, malnutrition followed by decreased gut function and increased susceptibility to infections leading to diarrhea and ongoing malnutrition. Short-term depletion of calories must be studied and its effect as a stress factor on neonatal extrauterine adaptation determined.

In summary, the general issues regarding birth from the nutritional point of view need be considered with respect to gut, liver, and renal development and their impact on intestinal colonization, mucosal defense, and metabolic/endocrine interrelationships. This can be accomplished by further definition of normal developmental environmental factors on organ development and by determining additional needs (nutritional and otherwise) under conditions of altered function, that is, stress due to infections, malnutrition, delayed maturation, etc.

With respect to specific points raised by each of the session speakers, I have identified certain issues which appeared important. I'm sure each of you have your own specific concerns. I will raise these issues as a starting round for discussion. Dr. Stahlman presented very convincing evidence for the need of vitamin A in lung differentiation and repair. We must have more specific data on nutrient requirements in the newborn, particularly with the increasing number of more premature infants. We must carefully determine the effect of breast milk on bacterial colonization along the lines addressed by Dr. Nord. This pertains to factors in milk affecting bacterial adherence to the gut surface, a necessary step in colonization. Dr. Hanson reviewed the category of mucosal immune development. In my mind a critical issue is the possible role of breast milk factors in the *active* stimulus to neonatal mucosal immune defense. For example, do lymphokines in breast milk affect epithelial turnover or plasma cell maturation? We need to understand factors controlling development of liver (Dr. Strandvik) and renal (Dr. Aperia) functions and be assured that acceleration of maturation doesn't have an adverse effect on adaptation of the premature to the extrauterine environment. Finally, we need more well-controlled and designed *human* studies such as those reviewed by Dr. Aynsley-Green to answer questions in man on metabolic/endocrine interrelationships. This requires a need for better noninvasive technology to approach this problem.

REFERENCES

1. Pittard, W. B. Breast milk immunology: A frontier in infant nutrition. *Am. J. Dis. Child.* **133,** 83–87 (1979).
2. American Academy of Pediatrics Committee on Nutrition. Commentary: Breast feeding. *Pediatrics* **62,** 591–601 (1978).
3. Lepage, G., Goulet, S., Kien, L. C., and Roy, C. C. The composition of preterm milk in relation to the degree of immaturity. *Am. J. Clin. Nut.* **40,** 1042–1049 (1984).
4. Eckhert, C. D., Sloan, M. V., and Duncan, J. R. Zinc binding: A difference between human and bovine milk. *Science* **195,** 789–790 (1977).
5. Fransson, G.-B., and Lönnerdal, B. O. Zinc, copper, and magnesium in human milk. *J. Pediatr.* **101,** 504–508 (1982).
6. Steiner, K. S., Packard, R., and Hilder, D. The serum-free growth of cultured cells in bovine colostrum and in milk obtained later in the lactation period. *J. Cell. Physiol.* **109,** 223–234 (1981).
7. Hall, R. A., and Widdowson, E. M. Response of the organs of rabbits to feeding during the first days after birth. *Biol. Neonate* **35,** 131–139 (1979).
8. Heird, W., Schwarz, S., and Harzer, I. Colostrum-induced enteric mucosal growth in beagle puppies. *Pediatr. Res.* **18,** 512–515 (1984).
9. Stern, M., Harmatz, P. R., Kleinman, R. E., and Walker, W. A. Food proteins and gut mucosal barrier. III. The influence of lactation and prolactin on the *in vitro* binding and uptake of bovine serum albumin and ovalbumin in the rat jejunum. *Pediatr. REs.* **19,** 320–324 (1985).
10. Pang, K. Y., Newman, A. P., Udall, J. N., and Walker, W. A. Development of the gastrointestinal mucosal barrier. VII. *In utero* maturation of the microvillus surface by cortisone. *Am. J. Physiol.* **249,** G85–G91 (1985).
11. Christie, D. L., and Ament, M. E. Dilute elemental duct and continuous infusion technique for management of short bowel syndrome. *J. Pediatr.* **87,** 705–708 (1975).
12. Green, H. L., McCane, D. R., and Merenstein, G. B. Prenatal diarrhea and malnutrition in infancy: Changes in intestinal morphology and disaccharidase activities during treatment with total intravenous nutrition, or oral elemental ducts. *J. Pediatr.* **87,** 695–704 (1975).

16

Discussion: Part II. Birth from the Nutritional Point of View B. Birth and Longer Term Well-Being in the Third World

R. G. Whitehead

Dunn Nutrition Unit
Medical Research Council
Cambridge, England

I. BIRTH WEIGHT AND MATERNAL DIETARY STATUS

In considering birth from a Third World nutritional point of view, one should always take into account the complexities of maternal nutrition during pregnancy. All expert committees setting recommended daily dietary allowances have reasoned

TABLE I

Extra Daily Nutrient Allowances for Pregnancy[a]

Nutrient	Nonpregnant	Pregnant	Increase
Energy (kcal)	2100	2400	300
Protein (g)	44	74	30
Retinol (μg)	800	1000	200
Vitamin D (μg)	7.5	12.5	5
Vitamin E (mg)	8	10	2
Vitamin C (mg)	60	80	20
Riboflavin (mg)	1.3	1.6	0.3
Nicotinic acid (mg)	14	16	2
Vitamin B_6 (mg)	2.0	2.6	0.6
Folate (μg)	400	800	400
Thiamin (mg)	1.1	1.5	0.4
Calcium (mg)	800	1200	400
Iron (mg)	18	S[b]	S[b]
Zinc (mg)	15	20	5

[a]From NRC (1).

[b]S denotes that the increased requirement cannot be obtained from the diet and thus supplemental iron was recommended.

that pregnancy imposes a substantial extra dietary energy and nutrient load on the mother. The most complete set of increments is that compiled by the National Research Committee of the American Academy of Sciences (NRC) and Table I summarizes the published views of the most recent group of experts (1). While Americans do tend to be rather overprotective, when it comes to setting dietary allowances, especially where the vitamins are concerned, their deliberations do not differ too dramatically from those of other national and international bodies. With one or two exceptions, the recommendations are relatively greater for the micronutrients than for energy, but even the latter is raised by some 15% in order to cover the *total* extra energy cost of pregnancy estimated to be around 80,000 kcal (2). The net result is that during pregnancy some 2500 kcal/day has been deemed to be desirable for the average American woman.

II. THIRD WORLD ENERGY INTAKES DURING PREGNANCY

Table II shows the contrasting measured intakes of pregnant Third World women (3). The energy gap between theory and practice is so great that it is not surprising that the basic accuracy of the intake data

TABLE II

Reported Energy Intakes of Poorly Nourished Child-Bearing Women during Pregnancy[a]

Source	Country	Energy intake (kcal/day)
Prentice (wet season)	The Gambia	1350–1450
Oomen and Malcolm	New Guinea	1360
Gopalan	India	1400
Venkatachalam	India	1410
Lechtig *et al.*	Guatemala	1500
Gebre-Medhin and Gobezie	Ethiopia	1540
Rajalakshmi	India	1570
Mora *et al.*	Colombia	1620
Prentice (dry season)	The Gambia	1600–1700
Arroyave	Guatemala	1720
Maletnlema and Bavu	Tanzania	1850
Demarchi *et al.*	Iraq	1880
Bagchi and Bose	India	1920
Thanangkul and Amatyakul	Thailand	1980
Mata, Urrutia, and Garcia	Guatemala	2060

[a]From Ref. (3).

has been challenged. It must be accepted that the measurement of food intake of "free-living" people is difficult but the consistently low values obtained by all investigators from a wide range of countries make it highly unlikely that the average Third World mother is protected from nutritional stress during pregnancy in accordance with national and international recommendations. Table II deals only with energy; the discrepancies with many of the micronutrients is even greater.

III. MATERNAL PHYSIOLOGICAL RESPONSE TO PREGNANCY

How do mothers cope with such dietary regimes? There has understandably been much speculation about the presence of physiological adaptive mechanisms which enable the mother to protect fetal development but it is only recently that actual mechanisms have come to be investigated and even these studies have been limited to considerations of dietary energy.

Studies carried out by the research group of the Dunn Nutrition Unit, resident in the village of Keneba in The Gambia, West Africa, have shown that both major components making up the bulk of the theoretically cal-

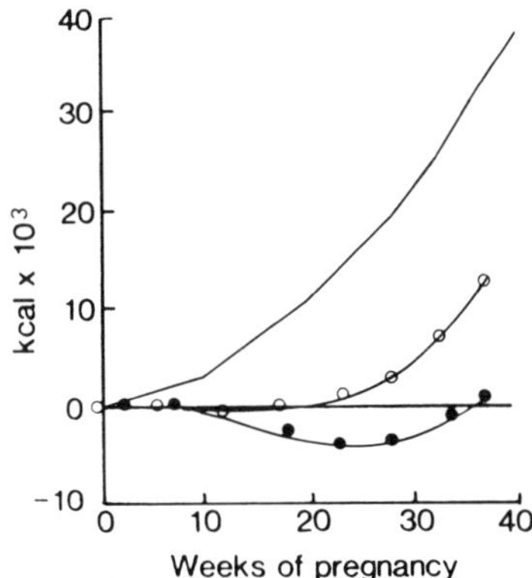

Fig. 1. Cumulative increments or decrements in basal metabolic rates (4) in supplemented (○) and unsupplemented (●) rural Gambian women during pregnancy in comparison with the theoretically derived change (upper line).

culated extra energy need during pregnancy, a raised basal metabolism (36,000 kcal) and the building up of maternal adipose tissue stores (36,000 kcal), appear to respond to imposed dietary stress.

As Fig. 1 shows, in the absence of maternal dietary supplementation in Keneba, changes in basal metabolic rate (BMR) result in a net increase of only 1000 kcal (4) over the whole of pregnancy, only 3% of the theoretical amount. The mechanism by which this dramatic BMR energy saving appears to have been achieved has still to be elucidated, but we have observed a highly significant reduction in body temperature (5) in the latter half of pregnancy and during the whole of the first year of lactation, which could indicate some slowing of metabolism at a cellular level. The influence of dietary intake as a determinant of the extent to which BMR energy-saving mechanisms may operate has been further implicated by studies on a group of comparable women who received extra dietary supplements during pregnancy, also shown in Fig. 1. The supplemented women increased their BMR during pregnancy more than the unsupplemented group, by an amount totaling 13,000 kcal by term, but still by only 30% of the theoretically estimated amount.

IV. FAT DEPOSITION AND MATERNAL ENERGY ECONOMIES

Likewise reductions in fat deposition can be a major source of energy saving. In Western countries, extra deposition by the end of pregnancy totals 3–4 kg. In unsupplemented Gambian women only an estimated 1 kg of fat was deposited early in pregnancy, when most of the fat is

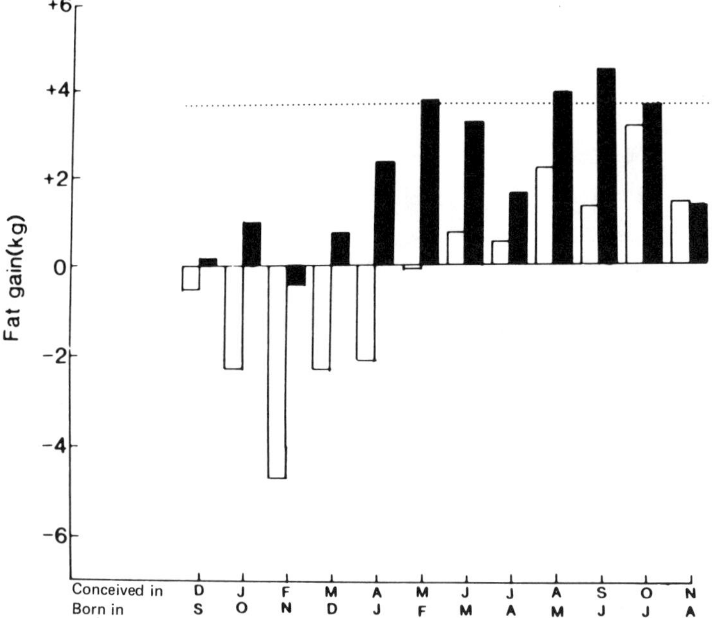

Fig. 2. Net changes in body fat (6) in rural Gambian women during pregnancy depending on the month of conception and the coincidence of the latter part of pregnancy with the annual hungry season. Data for supplemented (solid) and unsupplemented (open) women are contrasted with European mean increments (dotted line).

normally laid down, and even this was subsequently mobilized in the last trimester, leading overall to a net loss of body fat amounting to 300 g (2800 kcal) at term (6). Supplementation again improved the situation, with supplemented women gaining about 1.7 kg fat overall but still considerably less than their Western counterparts. Of importance were the major seasonal variations in the amount of fat deposited. In unsupplemented women delivering at the end of the preharvest "hungry season," for example, losses of fat were greatly magnified, astonishingly to more than 4 kg at term. Figure 2 shows these seasonal swings as well as the alleviating effect of supplementation.

V. MATERNAL ACTIVITY PATTERNS AND ENERGY ECONOMIES

Further energy savings were also possible from alterations in patterns of physical activity, although this effect is highly seasonal in nature in The Gambia owing to the demands of traditional agricultural practices.

Nonetheless, after statistical adjustment for the influence of season, a gradual reduction in the amount of physical activity was still discernible during pregnancy even in Keneba, equivalent to an ultimate significant saving of between 150 and 250 kcal/day at term (7).

VI. FETAL PROTECTION IN UNDERNOURISHED MOTHERS

The presence of these apparent mechanisms to accommodate dietary energy shortcomings has definite limits, however. Below a certain threshold, perhaps a mean intake of around 1800 kcal/day, fetal growth can no longer be completely protected. To what extent dietary deficiency does give rise to low birth weight babies in the Third World is not easy to say with complete quantitative confidence. It is necessary to take into account the influence of maternal height on mean predicted birth size as well as the influence of factors other than diet which may be adversely affecting fetal development, such as infections. In tropical African countries malaria, for example, is known to have a profound effect on placental function. There are grounds for believing that in practice the influence of malaria and undernutrition on fetal size may be of the same order of magnitude, around 300 g each. Thus if both adverse factors have been operative, average birth size may be 600 g less than the maternal height-adjusted target weights would suggest as desirable.

VII. LOW BIRTH WEIGHT, NEONATAL, AND POSTNEONATAL MORTALITY

Ashworth and Feachem (8) have recently reviewed the significance of low birth weight to survival. They analyzed data from both the Western World as well as the Third World and their combined calculations for the standardized relative risks of neonatal mortality and postneonatal mortality by birth weight are shown in Table III. Both types of mortality are clearly influenced: the risk of neonatal and postneonatal mortality is 3–6 times greater in children weighing 2000–2500 g at birth, a value frequently encountered in Third World countries, than in children weighing 3000–3500 g, a range which would encompass most children in the industrialized world. Importantly, the same standardized mortality relationships with birth weight exist for industrialized and Third World countries, indicating a basic pathophysiological connection. When coupled with the total neonatal and postnatal mortality rates, the major influence of birth weight on survival becomes even more dramatic. Ash-

TABLE III

Relative Mortality Rates According to Birth Weight[a]

Country	Neonatal			Postneonatal		
	2000–2500	3000–3500	Mortality rate	2000–2500	3000–3500	Mortality rate
U.S.A. (1974–1975)	3.8	0.5	8.2	1.9	0.6	4.3
India (1969–1975)	1.4	0.8	34.8	2.3	0.6	51.6
Brazil (1968–1970)	4.0	0.5	28.2	—	—	—
Guatemala (1964–1972)	3.4	—	39.0	0.8	0.5	60.0

[a]2500–3000 g = 1. From Ashworth and Feachem (8).

worth and Feachem (8) also reviewed a number of studies which indicated a link between low birth weight and a subsequent impaired gastrointestinal physiology, including immunological function and increased diarrhea rates, but it was quite apparent that more information was desirable on this important topic.

VIII. MATERNAL DIETARY SUPPLEMENTATION DURING PREGNANCY

If maternal diet is a limiting factor in birth weight in the Third World one would expect that maternal dietary supplementation during pregnancy should have a beneficial effect. This hypothesis has been tested in a number of small-scale trials in different parts of the world but the results have been variable. Furthermore, although in some countries a statistically significant effect was achieved, quantitatively the gain has been relatively small, between 100 and 300 g. There have been, however, a number of shortcomings in these trials. The energy increment has been extremely variable, often bearing little relationship to the habitual food intake of the mothers, and rarely has an attempt been made either to quantify or to control for the substitution effect of the supplement on habitual food intake.

There is one further factor which has not always been considered: whether or not the mother's habitual food energy intake is below the threshold of physiological accommodation. In the Gambian study, for example, in spite of *relatively* low energy intakes throughout the year, it was only during the annual hungry/wet season, when food availability in the village is particularly low, that dramatic improvements in birth weight were observed (9). Likewise in studies reviewed by Ashworth

TABLE IV

Food Supplementation, Birth Weight, and Prevalence of LBW in the Third World (<2.5 kg)[a]

	Increase in BW (%)	Reduction in LBW (%)
The Gambia	120	68
Guatemala	117	41
Mexico	213	80
Colombia	51	21
Taiwan	16	48

[a]From Ashworth and Feachem (8).

and Feachem (8) and carried out in four developing countries (Table IV) where the prevalence of low birth weight babies is greater than 15%, The Gambia, Guatemala, Mexico, and India, supplementation did result in a satisfactory and statistically significant drop in the incidence of low birth weight babies. However, in countries where the situation was not so extreme, albeit undesirable by Western standards, it was more difficult to demonstrate a convincing improvement.

On a public health level, one needs to be careful not to judge the value of a maternal dietary supplementation scheme on just one parameter, birth weight. The physiological studies from The Gambia indicate substantial changes in maternal metabolism and life-style in order to protect the well-being of the fetus. Some of these could definitely be considered pathophysiological and the confining life-style undesirable from a social point of view. Alleviating these stresses to the mother is just as desirable as ensuring a healthy birth weight.

IX. LONG-TERM BENEFITS FROM MATERNAL DIETARY SUPPLEMENTATION

Assuming a successfully improved birth weight, what is the evidence that this leads to better long-term health and generally improved well-being for the infant and young child? Unfortunately there is a dearth of really solid information on this crucially important issue. This reflects a universal problem in the organization and funding of long-term investigations. Under the stop-and-go constraints under which most of us have to operate, a failure to provide answers to such questions is only too likely. At the same time one has to admit that planning the perfect investigation would not be easy, particularly in view of the ethical constraints that would correctly be imposed on the researchers. Ideally a randomized controlled trial would have to be initiated in which not only birth weight but subsequent exposure to unhygienic circumstances, infection, as well as infant food intake would all have to be statistically controlled for. Although in the follow-up to the Gambian study these scientific precautions were impossible to impose, a sustained improvement, particularly of the wet-season birth cohort, has been observed. Figure 3 summarizes one such set of data for boys born in 1981 and 1982 and compared with data for similar children from the same village born prior to the maternal supplementation program. The improved growth was *not* due to an increased maternal milk output nor to improved weaning practices but it did correlate with a reduction in the incidence of diarrheal disease. An attractive hypothesis would be that the increased birth weight led to a fitter child, better able to mount an effective immune reaction to infection, especially the diarrheal diseases.

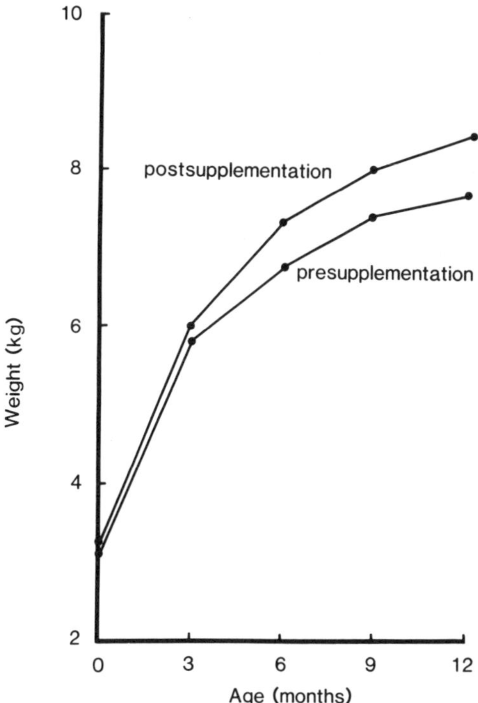

Fig. 3. The sustained effect of an improved birth weight among boys achieved by maternal dietary supplementation during pregnancy and subsequent infant growth rates.

X. CONCLUSION

Although the available data contain many shortcomings, the bias of the evidence is that low birth weight is an important determinant of infant mortality in the Third World and that where this is a consequence of poor maternal dietary status, well-organized dietary supplementation programs to improve the nutritional well-being of the mother during pregnancy can be very effective. There is also respectable, even if circumstantial, evidence that the subsequent growth of babies from supplemented mothers is significantly improved too.

REFERENCES

1. "NRC Recommended Dietary Allowances," 9th Ed. Natl. Acad. Sci., Natl. Res. Counc., Washington, D.C., 1980.
2. F. E. Hytten and I. Leitch, "The Physiology of Human Pregnancy," 2nd Ed. Blackwell, Oxford, 1971.
3. A. M. Prentice, *in* "Maternal Nutrition during Pregnancy and Lactation" (H. Aebi and R. G. Whitehead, eds.), pp. 167–183. Huber, Berne, 1980.
4. M. Lawrence, F. Lawrence, W. H. Lamb, and R. G. Whitehead, *Lancet* **ii,** 363–365 (1984).
5. R. G. Whitehead, M. Lawrence, and A. M. Prentice, *Hum. Nutr. Appl. Nutr.* **40A,** Suppl. 1, 1–10 (1986).
6. M. Lawrence, W. A. Coward, F. Lawrence, T. J. Cole, and R. G. Whitehead, *Proc. Int. Cong. Nutr., 13th Brighton, Engl.* Abstr. p. 154, (1985).
7. M. Lawrence, J. Singh, F. Lawrence, and R. G. Whitehead, *Am. J. Clin. Nutr.* **42,** 753–763 (1985).
8. A. Ashworth and R. G. Feachem, *Bull. W. H. O.* **63,** 165–184 (1985).
9. A. M. Prentice, R. G. Whitehead, M. Watkinson, W. H. Lamb, and T. J. Cole, *Lancet* **i,** 489–492 (1983).

Part III

The First Feed

17

Intestinal Transport of D-Glucose, Bile Salts, Phosphate, and Calcium during Maturation

Fayez K. Ghishan
Department of Pediatric Gastroenterology
Vanderbilt University School of Medicine
Nashville, Tennessee, U.S.A.

I. INTRODUCTION

It is generally recognized that most organ systems of various mammalian species exhibit characteristic developmental patterns. The gastrointestinal tract undergoes morphological, biochemical, and functional changes. These changes occur secondary to multiple factors, many of which include genetic, hormonal, and dietary factors. The intestinal transport system of the infant rat demonstrates the phenomena of developmental changes with evidence suggesting increased permeability when compared with the older rat (Ghishan *et al.*, 1980, 1981, 1984). These studies employed *in vivo* techniques which describe the overall picture of transport across the intestine. To define the characteristics and mechanisms underlying the changes in intestinal function of nutrients, we have developed methods for isolating brush border membrane vesicles from rats at different ages (suckling, weanling, and adolescent). This methodology offers the advantage of setting the experimental conditions on both faces of the membrane in the absence of cell metabolism (Murer and Kinne, 1980). To validate the transport system in brush border membrane vesicles, we have used D-glucose and taurocholate as models for transport in the jejunum and ileum, respectively. The developmental maturation of intestinal transport of calcium and phosphate was then determined.

II. MATERIAL AND METHODS

A. Preparation of Brush Border Membrane Vesicles

Sprague–Dawley rats of varying ages (suckling, 2 weeks; weanling, 3 weeks; adolescent, 6 weeks) were fed standard food for 2 weeks until their sacrifice by cervical dislocation. After sacrifice, the jejunum and ileum were removed, washed with ice-cold 0.9% NaCl, and everted over a glass rod. Brush border membrane vesicles were prepared by sequential precipitation with 0.01 *M* $MgCl_2$ and differential centrifugation (Ghishan and Wilson, 1985). The purity of the vesicle preparation for rats of varying ages was assessed by morphological, biochemical, and functional criteria (Ghishan and Wilson, 1985; Barnard *et al.*, 1985).

B. Transport Assays

Uptake of radiolabeled substrates by brush border membrane vesicles was measured by the rapid filtration technique (Berner *et al.*, 1976). Typically membrane vesicles were brought up in 300 m*M* mannitol and 20 m*M* HEPES–Tris buffer (pH 7.4) at 0°C. Transport was initiated by adding 20 μl of membrane suspension to 100 μl incubation media and kept in a water bath at 37°C. The composition of the incubation is given in the figure legends. At the desired time interval, a 20-μl aliquot was removed from the incubation suspension and diluted in 1 ml of ice-cold stop solution. The composition of the stop solution varied according to the substrate studied. The stop solution containing the vesicle was immediately pipetted onto the middle of a prewetted filter (cellulose nitrate, 0.45-μm pore size) and kept under suction. The filter was then removed and dissolved in Bray's solution and radioactivity counted.

III. RESULTS

A. Ontogenesis of D-Glucose Transport

Figure 1 depicts D-glucose uptake in rats at different ages. In the presence of inwardly directed Na^+ gradient, D-glucose uptake at all ages showed a typical transient accumulation "overshoot" at 20 sec compared to equilibrium uptake at 20 min. When vesicles were preincubated in K^+ media and studied with inwardly directed Na^+ gradient (Na^+ outside, K^+ inside) and in the presence of nigericin, an ionophore which allows the electroneutral exchange of K^+ for Na^+, no "overshoot" was seen. In the presence of valinomycin, an ionophore which mediates the electrogenic movement of K^+ down its concentration gradient, there was a marked increase in the "overshoot" at all ages, suggesting that D-glucose was driven by a Na^+-dependent electrogenic process. The magnitude of the "overshoot" was significantly decreased in suckling rat jejunal vesicles as compared to adolescent rat vesicles.

To examine whether differences in the magnitude of the overshoot are secondary to changes in the Na^+ solute cotransporter activity (putative carrier), counter transport experiments were performed under conditions of D-glucose and Na^+ equilibrium. Table I shows the effect of age on tracer exchange of D-glucose uptake. The activity of the transporter was similar, indicating that other mechanisms must account for the differences in the overshoot. To test whether the driving force for D-glucose is different with age, $^{22}Na^+$ uptake experiments were performed. Table II depicts the effect of age on time course of ^{22}Na. The ^{22}Na uptake was significantly greater at 20 sec, 1 min, and 2 min in brush border membranes of suckling rats compared to adolescent rats. Therefore, it appears that faster dissipation of the Na^+ gradient in suckling rats results in a decrease in the magnitude of the "overshoot" (Ghishan and Wilson, 1985).

B. Ontogenesis of Taurocholate Transport

[^{3}H]Taurocholate transport was studied in ileal brush border membrane vesicles prepared from suckling, weanling, and adolescent rats. Figure 2 depicts taurocholate uptake as a function of time and Na^+ or K^+ gra-

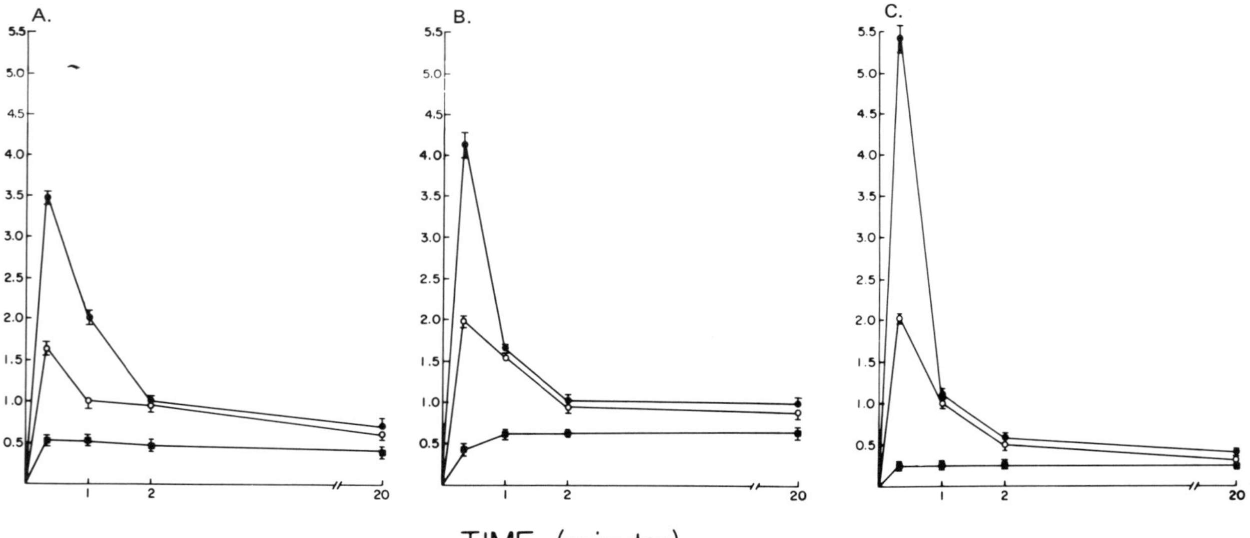

Fig. 1. Uptake of D-glucose in brush border membrane vesicles from 2-week-old suckling (A), 3-week-old weanling (B), and 6-week-old adolescent (C) rats preincubated in 100 m*M* KCl, 100 m*M* mannitol, and 20 m*M* HEPES–Tris buffer (pH 7.4) for 1 hr at room temperature. Preincubated vesicles were then incubated in media containing 100 m*M* NaCl and 20 m*M* HEPES–Tris buffer (pH 7.4), with (●) or without (○) 10 μg valinomycin/mg protein and with 10 μg/mg N protein nigericin (■). As seen in presence of valinomycin and Na^+ gradient, there was a severalfold increase in magnitude of the "overshoot" at 20 sec at all age groups over that seen in presence of Na^+ gradient alone. The magnitude of overshoot in presence and absence of valinomycin was significantly greater in adolescent rat (C) than that seen in suckling rat (A). Reproduced by permission of *American Physiological Society*, Vol. 248, p. G90. Copyright 1985.

TABLE I

Effect of Age on Trans Stimulation of D-Glucose Uptake[a]

Time (min)	Glucose uptake (pmol/mg protein)	
	Suckling (2 weeks)	Adolescent (6 weeks)
0.33	264 ± 10	275 ± 28
1	252 ± 5	264 ± 6
2	240 ± 25	335 ± 30
60	262 ± 20	243 ± 49

[a]Values are means ± SE. Jejunal brush border membrane vesicles of suckling and adolescent rats were preincubated for 60 min with 100 m*M* mannitol, 100 m*M* NaCl, 0.1 m*M* D-glucose, 20 m*M* HEPES–Tris buffer (pH 7.4), and 6 μg/mg protein gramicidin. The reaction was started by the addition of 20 μl of preincubated vesicles to 100 μl of incubation media containing 100 m*M* mannitol, 100 m*M* NaCl, 0.1 m*M* D-glucose, and 50 μCi radiolabeled D-glucose. Samples were taken at 0.33, 1, 2, and 60 min. Reproduced by permission of *American Journal of Physiology*, Vol. 248, p. G90. Copyright 1985.

dient. Taurocholate uptake in suckling rat brush border membrane vesicles was similar under Na^+ and K^+ gradient conditions. By contrast, uptake in weanling and adolescent rats was significantly enhanced at 20 sec and at 1, 2, and 5 min of incubation in the presence of a Na^+ gradient when compared to under K^+ gradient conditions ($p < .05$). Figure 3 depicts isotope exchange conditions of taurocholate uptake in suckling, weanling, and adolescent rats. A plot of active uptake velocity versus taurocholate concentration (0.1–1.0 m*M*) in suckling rat vesicles

TABLE II

Effect of Age on Time Course of Na^+ Uptake[a]

Time (min)	Na^+ uptake (nmol/mg protein)	
	Suckling (2 weeks)	Adolescent (6 weeks)
0.33	112 ± 9[b]	63 ± 3
1	175 ± 4[b]	100 ± 5
2	227 ± 7.5[b]	131 ± 14
60	180 ± 7	140 ± 20

[a]Values are means ± SE. Jejunal brush border membrane vesicles of suckling and adolescent rats were brought up in 300 m*M* mannitol and 20 m*M* HEPES–Tris buffer (pH 7.4). The reaction was started by the addition of 20 μl of vesicles to 100 μl of incubation media containing 100 m*M* mannitol, 100 m*M* NaCl, 20 m*M* HEPES–Tris buffer (pH 7.4), and tracer ^{22}Na. Samples were taken at 20 sec and 1, 2, and 60 min. Reproduced by permission of *American Journal of Physiology*, Vol. 248, p. G91. Copyright 1985.

[b]Mean values of suckling (2-week-old) rats are significantly higher than corresponding mean values of adolescent (6-week-old) rats.

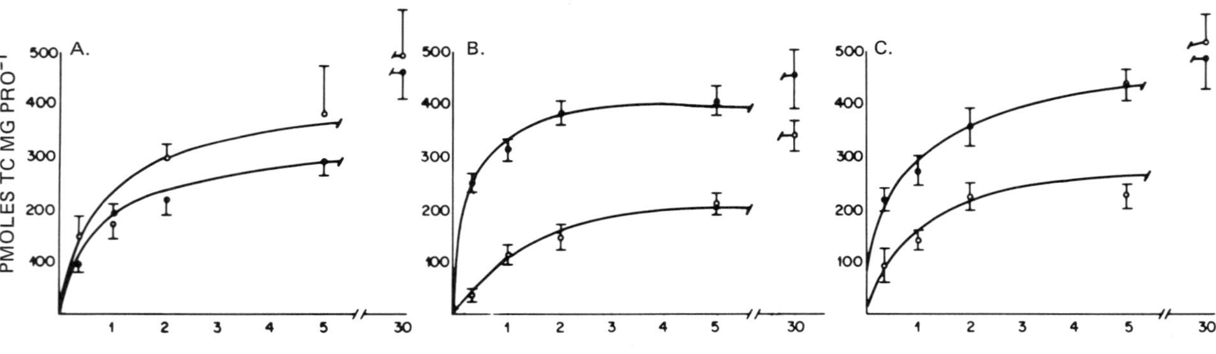

Fig. 2. Uptake of taurocholate as a function of time and Na^+ (●) or K^+ (○) gradient in 2-week suckling (A), 3-week weanling (B), and 6-week adolescent (C) vesicle preparations. In each instance, vesicles were preloaded with 280 m*M* mannitol and 20 m*M* HEPES–Tris (pH 7.4) and then incubated at 37°C in (●) 100 m*M* NaCl, 20 m*M* HEPES–Tris (pH 7.4), 100 m*M* mannitol, and 0.1 m*M* [^{3}H]taurocholate or (○) 100 m*M* KCl, 20 m*M* HEPES–Tris (pH 7.4), 100 m*M* mannitol, and 0.1 m*M* [^{3}H]taurocholate. Each point represents the mean ± SE from eight or more determinations. Pro, protein; TC, taurocholate. Reproduced by permission of *Journal of Clinical Investigation,* Vol., 75, p. 870. Copyright 1985.

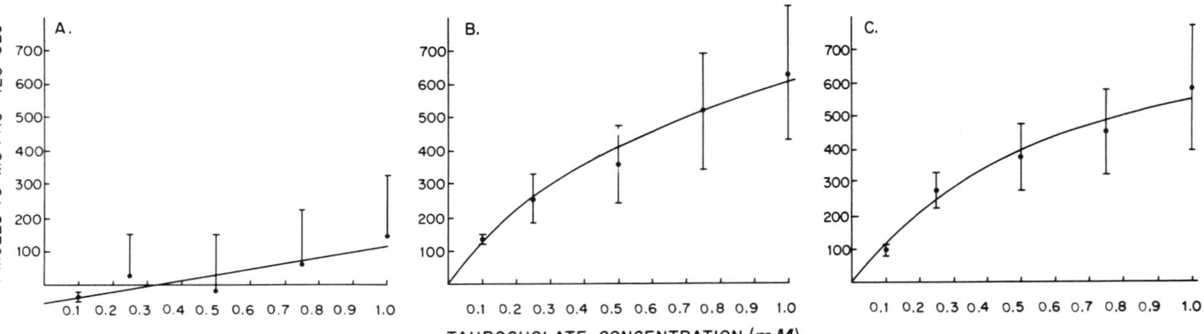

Fig. 3. Kinetics of taurocholate transport in 2-week suckling (A), 3-week weanling (B), and 6-week adolescent (C) vesicle preparations. Ileal membrane vesicles were preloaded with 100 m*M* mannitol, 100 m*M* choline chloride or Na^+ chloride, 20 m*M* HEPES–Tris (pH 7.4), and unlabeled taurocholate at the indicated concentrations. Incubations (37°C, 120 sec) were initiated in an identical solution excepting the presence of tracer amounts of [^{3}H]taurocholate and 6 μg gramicidin/mg protein. Each data point represents the arithmetic difference ± the standard error of the difference between tracer uptake in presence of Na^+-preequilibrated and choline-preequilibrated conditions (n = 8). TC, taurocholate; pro, protein. Reproduced by permission of *Journal of Clinical Investigation*, Vol. 75, p. 871. Copyright 1985.

was linear and approached the horizontal axis, suggesting the absence of active transport. However, similar plots in weanling and adolescent rats described a rectangular hyperbola, indicating a Na^+-dependent, saturable cotransport system. Woolf–Augustinsson–Hofstee plots of the uptake velocity versus concentration data from weanling and adolescent rats yielded V_{max} values that were not significantly different; 844 and 884 pmol uptake/mg protein/120 sec respectively. The respective K_m values were 0.59 and 0.66 m*M* taurocholate. The induction of an electrochemical diffusion potential by valinomycin did not significantly enhance taurocholate uptake in all rats. Corticosteroid therapy in 11-, 12-, and 13-day-old rats resulted in the appearance of a carrier-mediated, Na^+-dependent transport process in the 2-week-old suckling rat ileal vesicles. The data indicate that the taurocholate transport into rat ileal brush border membrane vesicles is mediated by an electroneutral, sodium-coupled, cotransport system that is incompletely developed in the 2-week-old suckling rats but fully developed by the time of weaning (Barnard *et al.*, 1985). This system, however, can be induced by the administration of glucocorticoids (Barnard and Ghishan, 1986).

C. Ontogenesis of Phosphate Transport

^{32}P uptake was determined in jejunal brush border membrane vesicles isolated from rats at different ages. Figure 4 depicts phosphate uptake

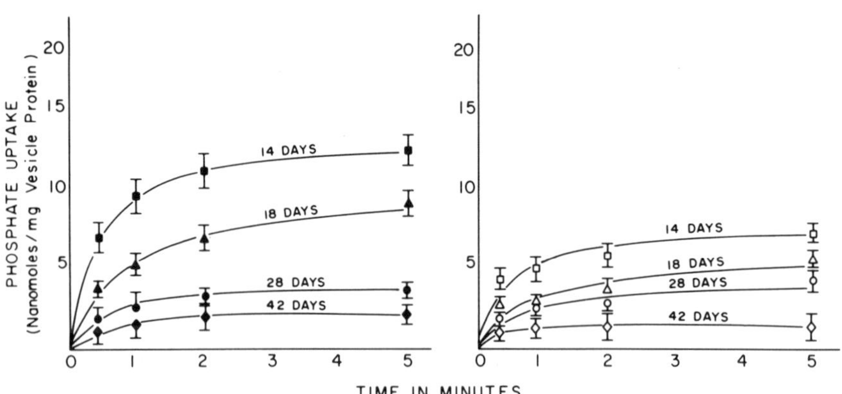

Fig. 4. Phosphate uptake into jejunal brush border membrane vesicles and the effects of increasing age. Vesicles were loaded with a buffer containing 100 m*M* mannitol, 100 m*M* choline, and 20 m*M* HEPES–Tris buffer (pH 7.4). On the left, vesicles were incubated in a medium containing 100 m*M* mannitol, 20 m*M* HEPES–Tris (pH 7.4), and 100 m*M* NaCL. On the right, vesicles were incubated in a medium containing 100 m*M* mannitol, 20 m*M* HEPES–Tris pH 7.4), and 100 m*M* KCl. Reproduced by permission of *Pediatric Research,* Vol. 19(12), p. 1310. Copyright 1985.

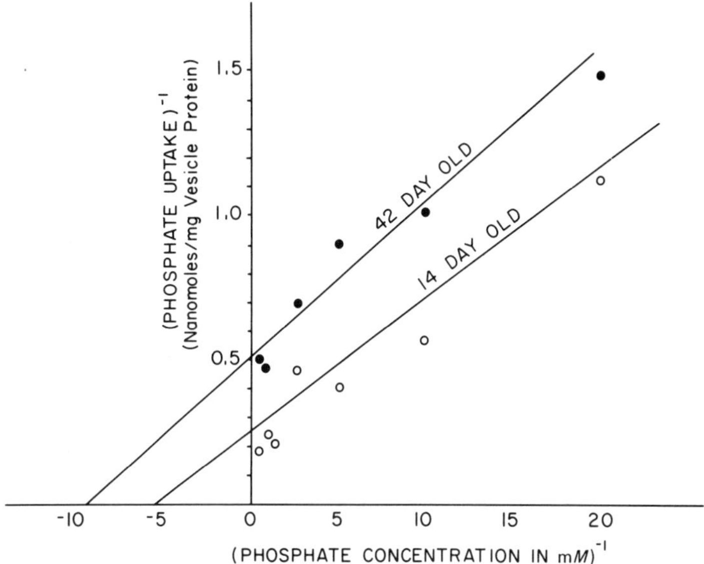

Fig. 5. Lineweaver–Burk plots of active phosphate transport. Lineweaver–Burk double reciprocal plots were constructed for the active component of phosphate uptake (sodium-dependent minus sodium-independent uptakes) from 42-day-old animals (●) and 14-day-old animals (○). For the 42-day-old animals the line $y = 0.39x + 5.66$ has a correlation coefficient of 0.96. $K_m$is 0.07 mM and V_{max} is 1.766 nmol/mg protein/10 sec. For the 14-day-old animals, the line $y = 0.45x + 2.14$ has correlation coefficient of 0.97. K_m is 0.210 mM and V_{max} is 4.673 nmol/mg protein/10 sec. Reproduced by permission of *Pediatric Research*, Vol. 19(12), p. 1311. Copyright 1985.

into jejunal vesicles in the presence of Na^+ and K^+ gradients. Na^+ gradient stimulated phosphate uptake as compared to K^+ gradient at all ages studied. Both sodium-dependent and sodium-independent transport demonstrated a progressive decline with increasing postnatal ages. Valinomycin experiments indicated that phosphate transport was by an electroneutral process. Figure 5 depicts V_{max} and K_m of the sodium-dependent uptake. As seen, V_{max} of the phosphate uptake was 1.7 and 4.7 nmol/mg protein/10 sec in adolescent and suckling rats, respectively. K_m was 0.069 and 0.2 mM for adolescent and suckling rats, respectively. These data indicate that the Na^+–phosphate transporter activity is significantly greater in suckling rats as compared to adolescent rats. To further investigate the activity of the Na^+–phosphate transport, tracer exchange experiments were done. Figure 6 depicts tracer exchange uptake of phosphate in suckling and adolescent jejunal vesicles. Uptake was significantly greater in suckling rats as compared to adolescent rats. Therefore, our findings demonstrate that there are maturational changes in phosphate uptake into jejunal brush border membrane. The increased

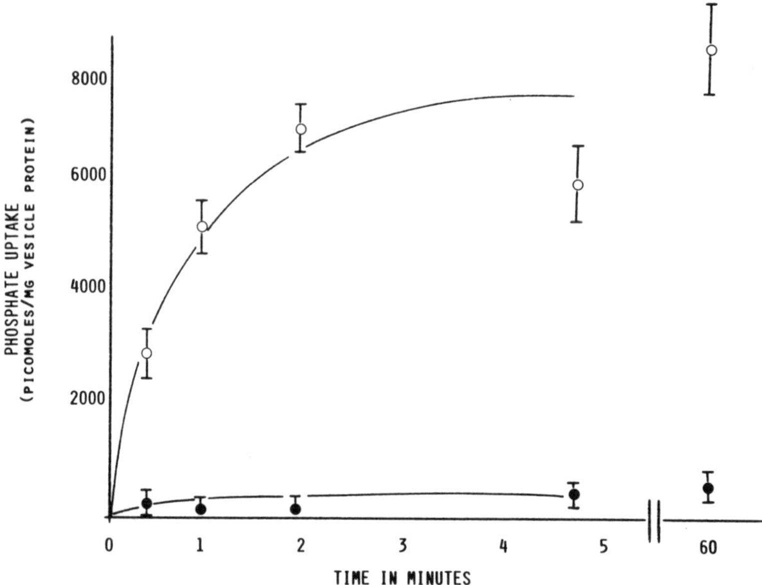

Fig. 6. Isotope exchange uptake of phosphate into jejunal brush border membrane vesicles. Jejunal brush border membrane vesicles from 42-day-old (●) or 14-day-old (○) rats were loaded with 100 m*M* mannitol, 100 m*M* NaCl, 0.8 m*M* KH_2PO_4, 20 m*M* HEPES–Tris (pH 7.4), and gramicidin (6 μg/ml). The vesicles were incubated in a medium containing 100 m*M* mannitol, 100 m*M* NaCl, 0.8 m*M* KH_2PO_4, and 20 m*M* HEPES–Tris (pH 7.4). Reproduced by permission of *Pediatric Research,* Vol. 19(12), p. 1311. Copyright 1985.

uptake in the younger animals is related to an increase in the active uptake of phosphate and an increase in the passive permeability to phosphate (Borowitz and Ghishan, 1985).

D. Ontogenesis of Calcium Transport

Calcium transport was investigated in our laboratory using the *in vivo* perfusion technique and *in vitro* everted gut sacs and plasma membranes (brush border and basolateral membranes). We have shown that calcium absorption occurs mainly by a passive process during the suckling period. However, a change to a predominately carrier-mediated process occurs by the time of weaning (Ghishan *et al.* 1980). To determine the kinetics of calcium uptake, the unidirectional flux was determined in the duodenal and jejunal sacs of suckling, weanling, adolescent, and adult rats. Figure 7 depicts calcium uptake into the duodenal gut sacs at 3 min in rats at different ages. The active component of transport became more pronounced with increasing age. Table III depicts apparent K_m and V_{max} of

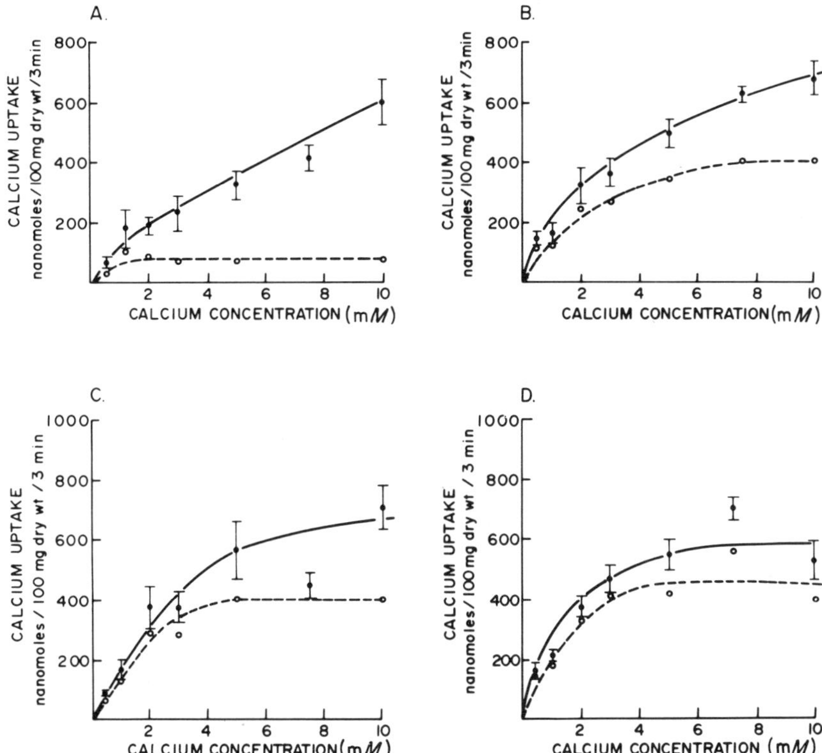

Fig. 7. Duodenal tissue uptake of calcium at 3 min in suckling (n = 6) (A), weanling (n = 4) (B), adolescent (n = 5) (C), and adult (n = 6) (D) rats in relation to calcium concentrations in the medium. With increasing age, a more saturable process is noted. Each point represents mean ± SD. The curves were analyzed using Michaelis–Menton kinetics in the double reciprocal plot. The solid lines represent total uptake (active and passive) and the dashed lines represent the active component. K_m and V_{max} values of each group are shown in Table III. Reproduced by permission of *Pediatric Research,* Vol. 18, p. 237. Copyright 1984.

duodenal and jejunal calcium uptake in rats at different ages. In adult rats, K_m and V_{max} of ^{45}Ca duodenal and jejunal uptake were severalfold greater than corresponding mean values for suckling rats. Moreover, the permeability to calcium decreased with age (Ghishan *et al.* 1984).

Because calcium transport represents uptake at the brush border level and exit at the basolateral membranes, we have further defined these processes in suckling and adolescent rats. Calcium uptake by brush border membrane vesicles represented binding and uptake into the intravesicular space. This binding is influenced by ionic strength, pH, and surface charge. This process does not appear to be the active step in

TABLE III

Apparent K_m and V_{max} of Duodenum and Jejunal Calcium Uptake in Rats during Maturation[a]

	Suckling		Weanling		Adolescent		Adult	
	K_m	V_{max}	K_m	V_{max}	K_m	V_{max}	K_m	V_{max}
Duodenum	0.58	79	0.65	409	2.0	465	1.6	550
Jejunum	0.5	104	1.3	153	3.8	554	4.8	606

[a] K_m values are expressed in m*M* and V_{max} values in nmol/100 mg dry weight/3 min. Reproduced by permission of *Pediatric Research,* Vol. 18, p. 238. Copyright 1984.

Ca^{++} transport across the cell, but rather the exit step at the basolateral membrane appears to be the active step. Calcium uptake by basolateral membrane occurs by two processes, an ATP-dependent process and a Ca^{++}/Na^{+} exchange mechanism. Both processes are present in the suckling rat, however, the ATP-dependent process appears to be more pronounced in adult rats.

These studies indicate that ontogenic trends occur in intestinal transport processes and that these trends are not similar for all transport mechanisms, but occur differentially as influenced by hormonal changes or demands for growth.

ACKNOWLEDGMENT

This work was supported in part by National Institute of Health Grant ROI AM 33209-01.

REFERENCES

Barnard, J. A., and Ghishan, F. K. (1986). *J. Lab. Clin. Med.* **108,** 549–555.
Barnard, J. A., Ghishan, F. K., and Wilson, F. A. (1985). *J. Clin. Invest.* **75,** 869–873.
Berner, W., Kinne, R., and Murer, H. (1976). *Biochem. J.* **160,** 467–474.
Borowitz, S. M., and Ghishan, F. K. (1985). *Pediatr. Res.* **19,** 1308–1312.
Ghishan, F. K., and Wilson, F. A. (1985). *Am. J. Physiol.* **248,** G87–G92.
Ghishan, F. K., Jenkins, J. T., and Younoszai, M. K. (1980). *J. Nutr.* **110,** 1622–1628.
Ghishan, F. K., Parker, P. H., and Helinek, G. L. (1981). *Pediatr. Res.* **15,** 985–990.
Ghishan, F. K., Parker, P., Nichols, S., and Hoyumpa, A. (1984). *Pediatr. Res.* **18,** 235–339.
Murer, H., and Kinne, R. (1980). *J. Membr. Biol.* **55,** 81–95.

18

Stable Isotope Probes: Potential for Application in Studies of Amino Acid Utilization in the Neonate

Vernon R. Young, Naomi K. Fukagawa, Kenneth J. Storch, Robert Hoerr, and Thomas Jaksic

Laboratory of Human Nutrition
Department of Applied Biological Sciences, and Clinical Research Center
Massachusetts Institute of Technology
Cambridge, Massachusetts, U.S.A.

Dennis M. Bier

Departments of Medicine and Pediatrics
Washington University School of Medicine
St. Louis, Missouri, U.S.A.

I. INTRODUCTION

The nutritional needs of the neonate, as well as those of older individuals, might be met with oral feeds or ingestion of usual foods and/or via the administration of nutrients by vein, to either supplement or totally replace the provision of an oral intake. Questions that arise, therefore, are the appropriate composition of nutritional formulations, especially the amino acid component, for either enteral or parenteral administration, and whether the formulation should differ according to its intended route of delivery to the patient. Precise answers to these questions cannot be given at present and so we will consider briefly some issues that still need to be explored. Particularly, we would like to give attention to the application of stable isotope tracer approaches for offering new insights into the assessment of amino acid metabolism and requirements in man under different physiological and pathological conditions.

Because relatively few studies along these lines have been attempted in the neonate we will refer to our own studies, conducted in the adult human model, to further justify and explain our points of view. We will begin with a short, and somewhat speculative, discussion of the metabolic basis of the requirements for nitrogen and indispensable (essential) amino acids. This will lead us to a consideration of the effect of route of administration of amino acids for meeting the physiological needs of the newborn. On the basis of this brief assessment, we will then describe some of our own approaches and studies, conducted recently at MIT, that might aid in the design of optimal mixtures of amino acids for use with enteral and parenteral regimens in the feeding of the newborn. Our purpose is not to present an exhaustive review but rather to focus attention on a few specific issues that the reader might find interesting, relevant, and challenging.

II. THE MAJOR FATE OF THE AMINO ACIDS, WITH REFERENCE TO PROTEIN SYNTHESIS AND AMINO ACID OXIDATION

Following the release of amino acids from ingested proteins, or from amino acid mixtures, and absorption from the gastrointestinal tract, or their direct entry into the blood stream via intravenous feeding, the amino acids follow one of three major metabolic fates (Fig. 1): (i) they act as a substrate for the maintenance or net synthesis of proteins; (ii) they serve as precursors for many metabolically significant nonprotein nitrogen-containing compounds, such as epinephrine, serotonin, and the poly-

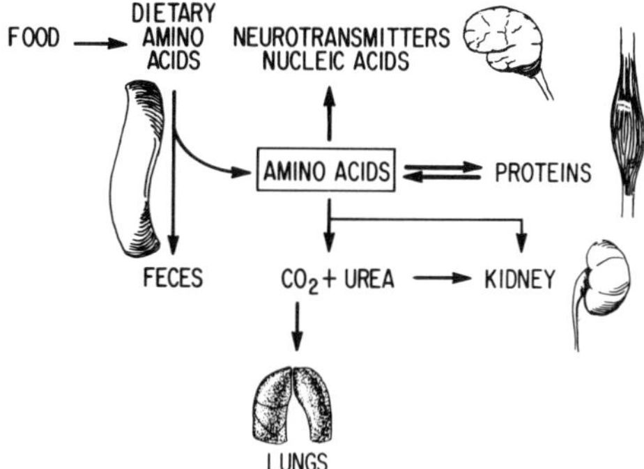

Fig. 1. A schematic outline of the major fates of exogenous (dietary) amino acids.

amines, as well as provide nitrogen and carbon skeletons for the dispensable amino acids; or (iii) they may enter catabolic pathways leading to the elimination of the nitrogen moiety, principally in the form of urea and ammonia, with incorporation of the carbon skeleton into pathways of metabolism common to carbohydrates and lipids.

In the context of our specific purpose here it is worth examining briefly the possible relationship between the intake of amino acids (or protein)

TABLE I

A Partial Survey of Estimated Rates of Whole-Body Protein Synthesis in Human Infants

Group	Tracer	Sample[a]	Protein synthesis (g kg^{-1} day^{-1})	Reference
4 term (AGA)	[1-^{13}C]Leu	P Leu	5 ± 1	Frazer and Bier (2)
4 term (AGA)	[^{15}N]Lys	P Lys	6 ± 1	
5 prem (AGA)	[^{15}N]Gly	U total N	8 ± 3	Heine *et al.* (3)
5 prem (AGA)	[^{15}N]Gly	U total N	8 ± 2	
24 prem (AGA)	[^{15}N]Gly	U urea	8 ± 1	Duffy *et al.* (4)
3 prem (SGA)	[^{15}N]Gly	U NH_3	11 ± 3	Jackson *et al.* (5)
7 prem (AGA)	[1-^{13}C]Leu	U Leu	11 ± 1	De Benoist *et al.* (6)
10 prem (AGA)	[^{15}N]Gly	U urea	11 ± 4	Catzeflis *et al.* (7)
		U NH_3	6 ± 2	
3 prem	[^{15}N]Gly	U urea	13 ± 2	Nicholson (8)
3 prem	[^{15}N]Gly	Urinary NH_3	15 ± 2	
20 prem (AGA)	[^{15}N]Gly	U urea	14 ± 4	Pencharz *et al.* (9)
20 prem (SGA)	[^{15}N]Gly	U urea	18 ± 5	
6 prem (AGA)	^{15}N]Gly	U urea	26 ± 7	Pencharz *et al.* (10)

[a]Plasma (P) or urine (U).

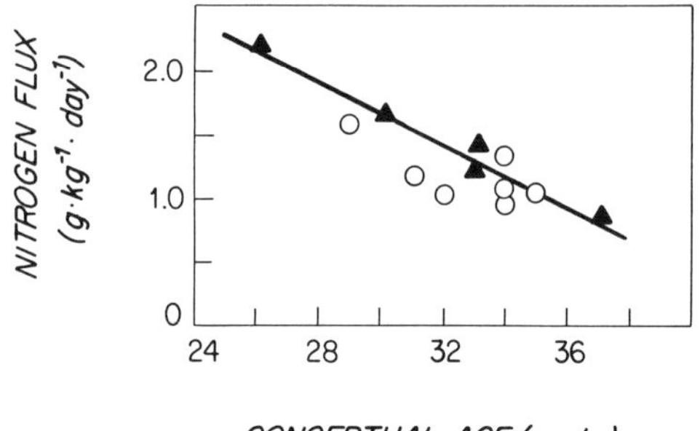

Fig. 2. Relationship between whole-body nitrogen flux and conceptual age in infants. Taken from Nissim *et al.* (11).

and their fate with respect to the synthesis of body proteins in order to develop an assessment of the metabolic basis for the nutritional requirement.

As reviewed earlier (1), rates of protein synthesis in the newborn are generally high, with values ranging from about 5–6 g kg^{-1}/day^{-1} (a value not markedly greater than that for the adult) to 18–26 g kg^{-1}/day^{-1} (Table I). The variation in the estimated rates of protein synthesis for this younger age group is undoubtedly due to methodological, as well as clinical, variables (1). However, there does appear to be a sound basis for concluding that rates of synthesis in the newborn are high relative to those occurring in older children and adults. Also using the same method, Nissim *et al.* (11) found a fall in protein synthesis (or nitrogen turnover) with increase in conceptual age (Fig. 2). Furthermore, with progressive growth and development, protein synthesis rates continue to fall and, from the summary presented in Table II, it may be concluded

TABLE II

Some Estimates of Total-Body Protein Synthesis in Humans at Different Stages in the Life Cycle[a]

Subjects	Body weight (kg)	Total protein synthesis		
		g/kg/day	$g/kg^{0.75}$	g/kcal BMR
Prematures	1.9 ± 0.6	17.4	20.6	0.15
Infants (1 year)	9 ± 0.5	6.9	11.9	0.13
Adults	71	3.0	8.9	0.11
Elderly	56	2.0	5.3	0.11

[a]Data from Young *et al.* (12), based on use of [^{15}N]glycine, except for infants, from Picou and Taylor-Roberts (13).

that during early growth and development the rate of whole-body protein turnover (synthesis and breakdown) is high and falls before adulthood is reached. Beyond this stage the rate continues to decline, although more slowly than during early life.

From a nutritional standpoint, these data for whole-body protein turnover reveal that protein synthesis (expressed as grams per unit body weight) proceeds at a rate that is considerably higher than the estimated dietary requirement for protein at each stage in life (see Ref. 14). This means that most of the protein that is synthesized occurs through the recycling of amino acids that are liberated during endogenous protein breakdown. In addition, even in the very young, net body protein gain may only account for about 10–20% of the total rate of protein synthesis (9), implying that in this age group the maintenance of existing tissue and organ protein is a major component of the economy of protein and amino acid metabolism. These observations have a number of additional nutritional implications.

First, the high rates of protein turnover in the young are, of course, associated with relatively high requirements for protein and for indispensable amino acids (e.g., Ref. 14). Indeed, as suggested in Table III, there is a relatively constant relationship between the rate of body protein synthesis within each age group and the proposed dietary allowances for that age group. In considering these relationships it should be pointed out that numerous values also have been reported for whole-body protein synthesis rates in healthy adults, and many are lower than the estimate given in this table (see, e.g., Ref. 16). In spite of this, and in agreement with a suggestion that we made earlier (12), the major differences in protein needs, when expressed per unit of body weight, between the various age groups are minimized when these needs are related to rates

TABLE III

Rates of Whole-Body Protein Synthesis Compared with Dietary Protein Allowances at Various Ages in Man[a]

Group	Protein synthesis (A)[b]	Protein allowance (B)[b]	Ratio A/B
Infant (premature)	11.3; 14	~3.0	4.5
Child (15 months)	6.3	~1.3	5
Child (2–8 years)	3.9	~1.1	4
Adolescent (~13 years)	~5	~1.0	5
Young adult (20 years)	~4.6	~0.75	6

[a]Taken from summary prepared by Young *et al.* (15).
[b]Values are g protein kg^{-1} day^{-1}.

of body protein synthesis. From the comparisons shown here, approximately 1 g of dietary protein appears to be required to support 5 g of total-body protein synthesis.

More importantly, however, before concluding that the total protein and amino acid requirement is directly determined by the protein synthesis rate per se, there may be other aspects of amino acid metabolism that have a more causal relationship to the quantitative dietary needs for nitrogen and for the indispensable amino acids. In this context, we have found (15) that the rate of irreversible oxidation of the indispensable amino acids, leucine and lysine, is significantly and positively correlated with the plasma concentration of the amino acid. This is of significance because correlations have been established between the plasma amino acid level, the intake of the amino acid, its oxidation rate, and, especially in growing animals, the physiological requirement for the amino acid (see Ref. 15 for review). Hence, we are inclined to the view that, at least in the human adult, it is the status of the oxidative catabolism of amino acids that is directly responsible for determining the level of amino acid intake necessary to maintain a given state of body protein and amino acid nutriture. Of course, in the growing organism, where there is net protein synthesis, the deposition of amino acids in tissue proteins will also account for a portion of the absolute daily need for amino acids and nitrogen. However, this is probably a relatively small percentage of the total requirement, as suggested from the calculations shown in Table IV; about 50% of the leucine and lysine requirement in the premature

TABLE IV

The "Requirement" for Leucine and Lysine in Premature and Older Infants and Children Compared with the Amount of These Amino Acids Deposited in Protein Gain[a]

Parameter	Infant		Child
	Premature	6 months	(10 years)
"Requirement" (A) for			
Leucine	279 (300)[b]	161	45
Lysine	198 (427)	103	60
Amount (B) deposited			
Leucine	137	21	3
Lysine	119	18	3
Ratio B/A (%)			
Leucine	60 (44)	13	7
Lysine	49 (28)	18	5

[a]All values are mg kg^{-1} day^{-1}.

[b]Values in parentheses suggested by Rigo and Senterre (17).

newborn, and even less in young infants, can be attributed directly to net protein deposition.

We have introduced this view of the metabolic relationships between the intake and plasma levels of indispensable amino acids, on the one hand, and their utilization for protein synthesis or loss via irreversible oxidation, on the other hand, because it appears to us that this might provide a useful basis for further exploring the metabolic and nutritional significance of observations on the responses of different groups of newborn infants to various intakes of amino acids and of nitrogen.

III. BLOOD AMINO ACID LEVELS AND INTAKE IN THE NEWBORN

Following from the preceding discussion, and because plasma amino acid levels have been monitored as a basis for assessing the amount and composition of amino acid mixtures required to minimize distortions in blood levels and to maximize nitrogen retention (e.g., Refs. 18–22), it would be desirable to explore further the relationships between blood amino acid levels and the kinetics of amino acid metabolism in the newborn. Thus, various investigators have demonstrated that blood amino acid levels reflect the composition and amount of the amino acid solutions given to babies (18,19) and, as shown by the studies of Anderson *et al.* (23), the change in blood amino acid concentration varies with the specific amino acid under study as well as the total amount fed. From the relationship depicted in Fig. 3 it may be seen that at low levels of amino acid intake, achieved in this case be feeding a milk formula, blood amino

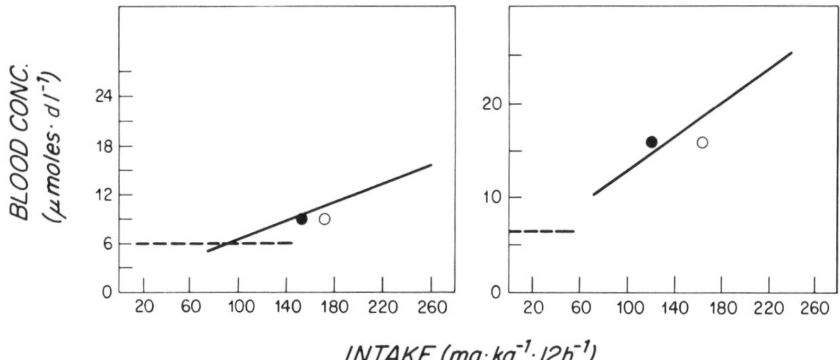

Fig. 3. Relationship between leucine and lysine intake and blood amino acid concentrations in infants receiving an amino acid mixture intravenously in varying amounts (——), in a milk formula (- - -), and intake of free case in hydrolysate (●) and total casein hydrolysate (○). Taken from part of Fig. 3 of Anderson *et al.* (23).

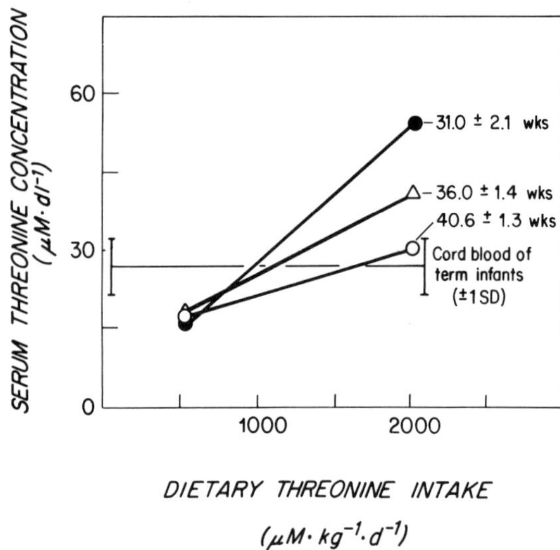

Fig. 4. Relationship between threonine intake and blood threonine levels in infants of varying gestational age. Taken from Rigo and Senterre (17).

acid levels were unchanged but with higher amino acid intakes, by intravenous feedings of a crystalline amino acid mixture or a single level of casein hydrolysate, blood levels increased at rates characteristic for each amino acid. It would be worthwhile to know the dynamic status of the metabolism of the specific amino acids at these varying levels of blood amino acids so that the metabolic and nutritional significance of a given blood amino acid concentration could be judged more precisely. Furthermore, the intake-blood level–oxidation relationship might differ in the very young, as compared to that in the adult described above (15), as suggested by the observations of Rigo and Senterre (17), who report, for equivalent threonine intakes, that preterm infants show a higher plasma threonine level than term infants (Fig. 4). Indeed, the effects of the immaturity and early development on pathways of amino acid metabolism, including the aromatic and sulfur amino acids in the preterm infant, are now well recognized (24) and for these reasons it is now important to introduce tracer amino acid kinetic approaches into the study of neonatal and perinatal aspects of protein and amino acid nutrition.

Whether the route of administration of the amino acids has an important effect on the level and pattern of amino acids achieved in blood plasma with a given intake level and whether this has important implications for amino acid utilization and requirements are not entirely clear. It might be expected, however, that differences in the fate and in the efficiency of utilization of at least some of the amino acids might arise as a consequence of giving amino acids by vein as contrasted to the oral route. Rigo and Senterre (17) state that the relationships between serum amino acid concentration and intake were similar regardless of the route of administration, except for the phenylalanine concentration, which was significantly higher during parenteral nutrition. Nevertheless, the organism has evolved a complex series of interorgan relationships in amino acid metabolism (25) and the splanchnic region is responsible for a major proportion of the metabolism of amino acids obtained from dietary sources. In reference to this point, for example, and using amino acid solutions free of cysteine, Stegink and den Besten (26) found in adults that the parenteral route of administration resulted in lower plasma cysteine levels than those achieved with oral administration of the same amino acid solution. Also the gut plays an important role in the processing of amino acids and in nitrogen metabolism, especially of glutamine and alanine (25), and so the precise fate of an exogenous supply of amino acids could be influenced, on this basis alone, by the route by which they were administered.

In addition to the question of the specific metabolic fate of amino acids, the impact of route of administration on the status of tissue and whole-body protein metabolism is also relevant. Thus, Duffy and Pencharz (27) examined the effect of route of feeding in neonates using [^{15}N]glycine to estimate whole-body nitrogen turnover. They found that the rates of body protein synthesis and nitrogen turnover were 40% higher during enteral as compared to the intravenous feeding of an amino acid–glucose–lipid regimen. These investigators interpret their observations to suggest a more extensive synthesis and turnover of gut proteins in the enterally fed infant.

From these various findings it seems to us that the further improvement in the design of the amino acid component of nutritional formulations might be aided by a better understanding of the dynamic and quantitative aspects of amino acid metabolism and utilization under various conditions of feeding in the neonate. To gain this knowledge a noninvasive approach is required and we consider that an expanded application of current stable isotope tracer methods might offer a valuable opportunity for meeting this purpose. Hence, we discuss briefly three major examples, based on our research in adults, to suggest the possible benefit to be derived with this approach.

IV. STABLE ISOTOPE TRACER APPROACHES

A. Methionine–Cysteine Relationships

The first example to be presented concerns the metabolism of methionine and the interaction between methionine and cysteine. This is of possible interest to the neonatologist because of the low hepatic trans-

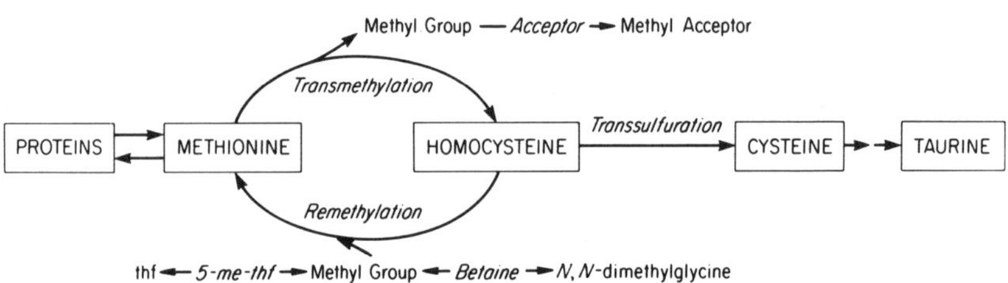

Fig. 5. A schematic depiction of the methionine cycle, with major components being transmethylation, remethylation, transsulfuration, and methionine entry into and release from tissue and organ proteins.

sulfuration enzyme activity in the neonate (28,29), which has led to the suggestion that cysteine may be an essential dietary constituent for the preterm and newly born infant. Although direct metabolic studies (30,31) have failed to show that addition of cysteine to parenteral amino acid solutions improves nitrogen retention and weight gain in the newborn, and particularly in the preterm infant, the question of the essentiality of cysteine is perhaps still unresolved. Stegink (32) considers that the evidence, based in part on considerations of plasma amino acid data, suggests that cysteine should be present in parenteral solutions. Thus, we have begun to develop a tracer approach with the intent of exploring various aspects of methionine metabolism, especially the quantitative components of the methionine cycle (depicted in Fig. 5) in man at different phases of life. By use of a dual tracer model (Fig. 6), and exploiting the framework of Waterlow *et al.* (16) and our previous experience with constant isotope infusion studies (33), methionine labeled in the methyl group (with ^{2}H) and the carboxyl moiety (with ^{13}C) has made it possible to determine the *in vivo* rates of transmethylation and remethylation of methionine under various metabolic and nutritional states. The specifics

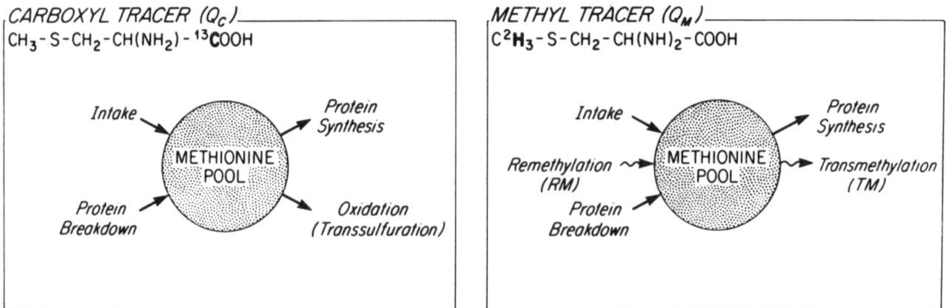

Fig. 6. A schematic portrayal of the dual tracer methionine model. With the IIA [^{13}C] carboxyl- labeled methionine, transsulfuration can be determined, and from the [$^{2}H_3$]-methyl-labeled tracer, in combination with the ^{13}C tracer, rates of transmethylation and remethylation can be estimated. $Q_M - Q_C$ = RM; TM = RM + oxidation.

of our approach, involving administration of the dual isotope tracer by vein or by the oral route in healthy young men, will be described in detail elsewhere (K. Storch, D. A. Wagner, J. Burke, and V. R. Young, in preparation). However, for purposes of example, the results of two recent studies will be summarized here.

In the first we attempted to assess the extent to which dietary methionine was metabolized during its initial entry into the splanchnic bed. As summarized in Table V, we estimated that about 20% of dietary methionine was removed during its first pass through this region, with about half of this amount being oxidized and the remainder disappearing into tissue proteins. Hence, the major fraction of absorbed methionine appeared in the peripheral circulation, at least for the conditions studied where the subjects received an adequate methionine intake. It appears possible, then, from these data that the transsulfuration of methionine and so its conversion to cysteine might be enhanced by giving methionine orally as contrasted to an intravenous route. However, a direct test of this hypothesis remains to be undertaken.

In a second experiment, as another example of the potential value of a noninvasive stable isotope approach for unraveling aspects of amino acid utilization in the neonate, we examined the effects of the methionine-sparing effects of dietary cystine in subjects receiving a methionine-free diet. The results are depicted in Fig. 7 and show that cystine reduced methionine oxidation from a rate of 1.15 μmol kg^{-1} hr^{-1} without cystine to 0.65 μmol kg^{-1} hr^{-1} when cystine was added to the sulfur amino acid-free diet. This sparing of methionine was due, as shown in Table

TABLE V

Estimate of First Pass Fate within the Splanchnic Region of Dietary Methionine in Young Adults[a]

Parameter	Rate
Intake	16.5
Removed during first pass	3.2
% removed	19.4
Fate of removed	
Oxidation	1.8
% oxidized	56
Protein synthesis	1.4
% for protein synthesis	44

[a]Values are μmol kg^{-1} hr^{-1} except where noted. Means for four subjects. Unpublished MIT data of K. Storch.

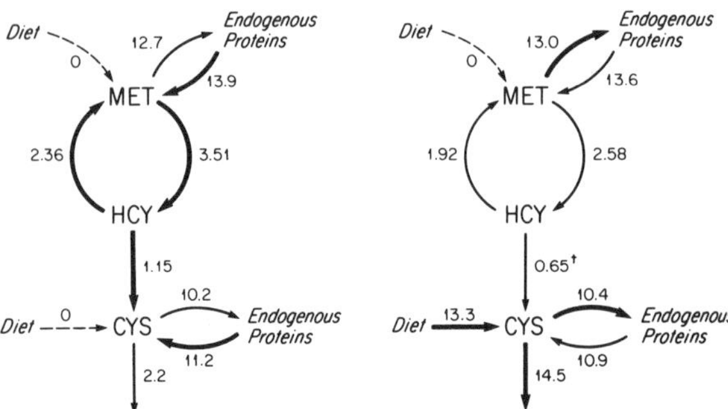

Fig. 7. Effect of dietary cystine on the methionine cycle in healthy young adult men. Subjects received either a sulfur amino acid-free (left) or cystine-supplemented diet (right) for 5 days prior to estimating the various components of the methionine cycle, with the aid of a continuous intravenous infusion of [^{2}H]methyl[1-^{13}C] Methionine. The values in the figure are μmol kg^{-1} hr^{-1} for the various metabolic processes measured. † Indicates p = .05. (Unpublished MIT data of K. Storch.)

VI, to a reduction in the rate of entry of methionine into the transsulfuration pathway (TM) and to a more efficient remethylation of homocysteine (RM/C in Table VI). These *in vivo* findings in man are consistent with the demonstration by Womack and Rose (34) that cystine could replace the methionine requirement in the rat by about 70%. Furthermore, they extend the conclusions of Finkelstein and co-workers (35,36) that the homocystein locus is a key point of regulation of methionine homeostasis by cysteine. This effect of cysteine is apparently due to an inhibition of the activity of cystathionine synthase. Our studies also reveal that, in addition to the homocysteine locus, the methionine locus is an important point of control, because transmethylation was reduced to a greater extent than was methionine oxidation. Whether these types of interrelationships and mechanisms would be observed and operative in the neonate where cystathionase is, perhaps, at lower levels (28,29) would be an exciting problem to investigate. Indeed studies along these lines may well help to clarify the metabolic and nutritional associations between methionine and cysteine in this age group. Further, by including in future investigations a direct estimate of cyst(e)ine flux, the quantitative interrelationships between methionine and cysteine under different conditions of amino acid feeding could be defined more precisely than from measures of nitrogen retention, growth, and plasma amino acid levels, as has been monitored in the previous studies (30,31). It is apparent that stable isotope probes offer a valuable opportunity to better understand the physiology and nutritional aspects of sulfur amino acids in the neonate.

TABLE VI

Dynamic State of the Components of the Methionine Cycle When Cystine is Added to a Diet Devoid of Methionine[a]

Parameter	Without cystine	With cystine	Net change[b]
Methionine flux (methyl group)	16.3	15.5	
Methionine oxidation (C)	1.15	0.65[c]	0.5
Transmethylation (TM)	3.5	2.6	0.9
Remethylation (RM)	2.4	1.9	−0.44
RM/C	2	3	

[a]Values are μmol kg^{-1} hr^{-1}. Mean values for four young adult subjects. Unpublished MIT data of K. Storch.
[b]With cystine − without cystine.
[c]Significantly different ($p<.05$) from without cystine.

B. Dietary Utilization of Leucine

Leucine and the other branched-chain amino acids (BCAA), valine and isoleucine, are commonly thought to escape extensive metabolism by the gut and liver following their release from dietary proteins and transport into the epithelial cells of the intestinal mucosa (37,38). However, there is significant activity of branched-chain amino acid transaminase in the human gut (39) and the liver possesses relatively high activity of the branched-chain keto acid dehydrogenase (40). To optimize the level and balance of branched-chain amino acids intended for oral or parenteral administration to the neonate we require a more complete picture of the relative roles played by the splanchnic region versus peripheral tissues in the uptake and metabolism of these amino acids. Again, this problem remains to be studied in the neonate, but based on the results described below that we have obtained in the young adult, it is also likely that stable isotope techniques offer a new approach to help explore this area of amino acid metabolism.

For example, by giving equivalent leucine tracers (i.e., [^{13}C]leucine and [$^{2}H_3$]leucine) we have found that the estimates of leucine flux, and therefore of derived values for body protein synthesis rates, in young men differ according to the route of isotope administration (Table VII). This finding suggests, at least, an important removal and metabolism of dietary leucine within the splanchnic region. On the basis of our observations we estimate (Table VIII) that about 25% of the leucine absorbed from a meal is removed on a first pass. Our studies do not permit an estimate of the specific metabolic fate of the leucine removed but we

TABLE VII

Estimates of Leucine Flux as Derived from Use of Different Routes of Isotope Tracer Administration and from Measurement of the Labeling in Different Plasma Products (Leucine or KIC)[a]

Plasma product	Route and tracer given	Metabolic state	
		Postabsorptive	Fed
[^{13}C]Leu	[^{13}C]Leu (ig)[b]	118 ± 12	184 ± 13
[^{13}C]KIC	[^{13}C]Leu (ig)	118 ± 6	202 ± 25
[^{2}H]Leu	[^{2}H]Leu (iv)	93 ± 3	137 ± 5
[^{2}H]KIC	[^{2}H]Leu (iv)	131 ± 7	137 ± 7

[a]Means ± SEM for five subjects (values are μmol kg^{-1} hr^{-1}). Unpublished MIT data of R. Hoerr.

[b]ig and iv refer to intragastric and intravenous routes, respectively.

conclude, tentatively, that the first pass removal is due to incorporation of leucine into proteins and, in part, conversion to α-ketoisocaproate. Preliminary results suggest that orally administered leucine is oxidized to a similar extent as that entering the circulation via protein breakdown and, thus, the route of administration may not be an important determinant of the efficiency of leucine retention. However, this is speculation and further work will be necessary to establish whether this is true. Nevertheless, we hope that these observations suggest a possible approach that might also be used to explore the quantitative aspects of branched-chain amino acid metabolism and utilization in infants receiving these amino acids in different amounts and proportions and by different routes. Measurement of plasma amino acid responses or of nitrogen balance would not seem to be sufficient to assess the comparative utilization

TABLE VIII

An Isotopically Derived Estimate of the Immediate Fate of Dietary Leucine[a]

Parameter	Value
Leucine intake	81 ± 1
First pass removal (f)	0.24 ± 0.05
Amount removed	18.1 ± 5
First pass (% of iv flux)	14 ± 3.5
Entered peripheral circulation	63

[a]Values are μmol kg^{-1} hr^{-1}. Means ± SEM for five subjects. Unpublished MIT data of R. Hoerr.

of leucine, or other indispensable amino acids, when given by gut as compared to a venous route of administration.

C. Dispensable Amino Acid Metabolism

A final example, again from a series of our experiments, that is worth mentioning concerns the dispensable amino component of the total nitrogen requirement in the neonate. This aspect of amino acid nutrition is important because of the quantitative importance of the nonessential (dispensable) amino acids in total-body nitrogen metabolism (e.g., Table IX). Furthermore, these amino acids are synthesized via various metabolic routes that might be affected by nutritional and developmental factors.

First, we have explored the effects of changes in the total dietary nitrogen intake and in the ratio of indispensable to dispensable amino acids on the whole-body alanine and glycine kinetics in healthy young adults (41). Combined intravenous infusions of indispensable and dispensable amino acids labeled with stable isotopes (e.g., Refs. 42,44) were given to estimate the rates of whole-body *de novo* synthesis of glycine and alanine. We chose to examine these two amino acids in view of their different responses to changes in dietary protein intake and to meal feeding (42–44). As summarized in Fig. 8, our results show that glycine synthesis rates changed in response to an alteration in the intake of indispensable amino acids; this response contrasted with that found for alanine (41), since the rate of *de novo* alanine nitrogen synthesis was unaffected by the changes in level of dietary nitrogen and amino acid

TABLE IX

An Approximation of the Contribution of Indispensable (IDAA) and Dispensable (DAA) Amino Acids in the Nitrogen Economy of Adult Man[a]

	Amino acids per 70 kg body wt.		
Source of amino acid	Total (g)	IDAA (g)	DAA (g)
Diet			
"Minimum" needs	56	6	50
Usual diet	90	45	45
Absorbed (and secreted gut proteins)	150	75	75
Free amino acid pools			
Plasma	0.7	0.2	0.5
Tissues	70	10	60
Daily body protein turnover	300	150	150

[a]Kindly provided by Professor H. N. Munro.

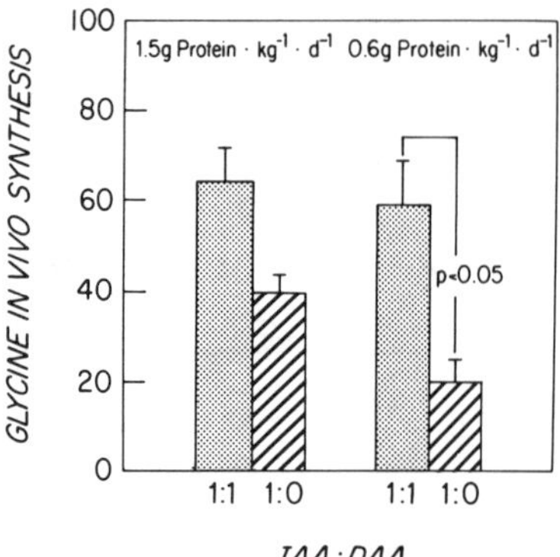

Fig. 8. Estimates of *de novo* rate of whole-body glycine synthesis in young adults receiving one of two levels of "protein" intake with the dietary ratio of indispensable (IAA) to dispensable (DAA) amino acids being 1 : 1 or 1 : 0. Drawn from Yu *et al.* (41).

composition examined in this study. Thus, the metabolism of glycine nitrogen appears to be responsive to the amino acid component of the diet; the rate of glycine synthesis is reduced when a low level of total amino acid intake is combined with the replacement of dispensable amino acids by a mixture of indispensable amino acids.

The physiological or functional significance of the decline in whole-body glycine synthesis, especially at the lower intake level of total amino acid intake, cannot be judged adequately at this time. From simultaneous measures of leucine flux in our study (41) it is apparent that an absence of dietary dispensable amino acids for the brief dietary periods examined (7 days) in our adult subjects did not result in any major change in the rate of whole-body protein breakdown. Because we did not measure the rate of leucine oxidation in this study we were not able to determine whether restriction of the dietary supply of dispensable amino acids affected the rate of incorporation of amino acids into body proteins. However, in relation to the nutritional support of the neonate, it has been observed that there is improved growth of infants receiving diets supplying relatively low intakes of high-quality protein when supplemented with so-called "nonspecific" nitrogen (45). Furthermore, from results of studies with [^{15}N]glycine, Jackson *et al.* (5) have speculated that supplementation of diets with glycine may be necessary to assure a satisfactory rate of lean tissue growth in preterm infants. Thus, it would be highly worthwhile to explore the consequences of changes in the intake and route of administration of glycine, and its precursors and other dispensable amino acids, on the metabolic economy of nitrogen metabolism in the neonate.

Finally, by way of emphasizing the significance of dispensable amino acids in the responses of whole-body protein and amino acid metabolism to nutritional factors, we have begun to explore the regulation of proline metabolism and proline synthesis in human subjects. These studies were initiated because it has been shown that there is feedback regulation of proline synthesis in cultured cells (46) and it was important to establish whether this applies to the intact human. Using a dual amino acid tracer model (42) to estimate the *in vivo* rate of proline synthesis we (T. Jaksic *et al.*, unpublished data) have observed that when proline is given intravenously at a rate approximating a usual rate of proline ingestion in the adult, there is a significant reduction in the *de novo* rate of proline synthesis (see Fig. 9). Again, this observation points to the regulation of dispensable amino acid metabolism and the impact of nutritional factors on the rate of synthesis of these amino acids. Indeed, these various studies indicate that more critical attention should be given to the so-called nonspecific nitrogen, or dispensable amino acid, component of the total protein or amino acid need in the newborn. The recent recommendation by Schroder and Paust (47) that the proline concentration of the amino acid solution they administered to preterm infants should be reduced, coupled with the observation (48), based on isotopic procedures, that for the growing pig a dietary source of proline is essential, further underscores the need to explore these aspects of "dispensable" amino acid metabolism and nutrition in the neonate.

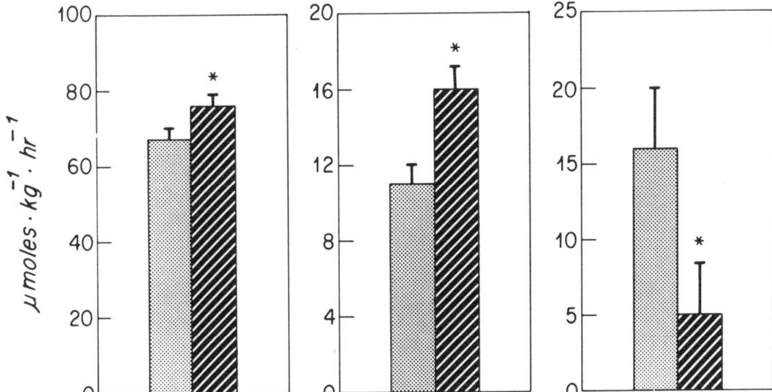

Fig. 9. Effects of an intravenous infusion of proline (hatched) (20 μmol kg^{-1} hr^{-1}) on the flux (left graph), oxidation (middle graph), and rate of *de novo* proline synthesis (right graph) in healthy young men compared to basal values (shaded). Asterisk indicates $p < .01$. (Unpublished MIT data of T. Jaksic *et al.*)

V. SUMMARY AND CONCLUSION

Meeting the physiological needs of the neonate for indispensable (essential) amino acids and for nitrogen (or dispensable amino acids), especially with respect to the design of nutritional formulations intended for either enteral or parenteral administration, is still based largely on empirical approaches. With increased use and availability of stable isotope technology the potential now exists to quantify more precisely the various aspects of amino acid metabolism in the neonate and to explore the consequences of route of administration, as well as other nutritional factors, on the fate of exogenously derived amino acids and their possible nutritional implications. Hence, in this chapter we have considered the importance of the oxidative fate of amino acid oxidation as a major and primary determinant of the amino acid requirement. Because of the existence of predictable relationships between amino acid intake and plasma amino acid levels and between the latter and amino acid oxidation, we are led to the proposition that it is timely to consider a vigorous application of stable isotope tracer methodology for quantifying the metabolic fate of parenterally and orally administered amino acids in the newborn. It is anticipated that results of such studies would enhance our ability to optimize the design of amino acid solutions to support the nutritional needs of the young patient. Examples were presented of the use of this technology for purposes of unraveling various aspects of the physiology and dietary utilization of sulfur amino acids and of leucine. These examples were drawn from our studies in the adult since comparable investigations have yet to be carried out in the neonate. Some consideration was also given to dispensable amino acid metabolism in view of its importance in the overall nitrogen economy of the host. We consider that with an expanded effort to try to unravel the complexity of the quantitative aspects of amino acid metabolism *in vivo*, in part based on application of noninvasive stable isotope tracer approaches, the efficiency of the nutritional management of various groups of newborn infants should be improved significantly beyond that possible at present.

ACKNOWLEDGMENTS

The unpublished studies from the authors' laboratories were supported by grants from the U.S. National Institutes of Health and the U.S. Department of Agriculture.

REFERENCES

1. Bier, D. M., and Young, V. R. (1986). Assessment of whole-body protein-nitrogen kinetics in the human infant. *In* "Energy and Protein Needs during Infancy" (S. J. Fomon and W. C. Heird, eds.), pp. 107–125. Academic Press, New York.

2. Frazer, T. E., and Bier, D. M. (1980). Essential amino acid turnover in the human newborn. *Pediatr. Res.* **14,** 571.
3. Heine, W., Plath, C., Richter, I., Wutzke, K., and Towe, J. (1983). ^{15}N-tracer investigations into the nitrogen metabolism of preterm infants fed mother's milk and a formula diet. *J. Pediatr. Gastroenterol. Nutr.* **2,** 606.
4. Duffy, B., Gunn, T., Collinge, J., and Pencharz, P. (1981). The effect of varying protein quality and energy intake on the nitrogen metabolism of parenterally fed very low birthweight (<1600 g) infants. *Pediatr. Res.* **15,** 1040.
5. Jackson, A. A., Shaw, J. C. L., Barber, A., and Golden, M. H. N. (1981). Nitrogen metabolism in preterm infants fed human donor breast milk: The possible essentiality of glycine. *Pediatr. Res.* **15,** 1454.
6. De Benoist, B., Abdulrazzak, Y., Brooke, O. G., Halliday, D., and Millward, D. J. (1984). The measurement of whole body protein turnover in the preterm infant with intragastric infusion of L-[1-^{13}C]leucine and sampling of the urinary leucine pool. *Clin. Sci.* **66,** 155.
7. Catzeflis, C., Schutz, Y., Micheli, J. L., Welsch, C., Arnaud, M. J., and Jequier, E. (1985). Whole body protein synthesis and energy expenditure in very low birth weight infants. *Pediatr. Res.* **19,** 679.
8. Nicholson, J. F. (1970). Rate of protein synthesis in premature infants. *Pediatr. Res.* **4,** 389.
9. Pencharz, P. B., Masson, M., Desgranges, F., and Papageorgiou, A. (1981). Total-body protein turnover in human premature neonates: Effects of birth weight, intra-uterine nutritional status and diet. *Clin. Sci.* **61,** 207.
10. Pencharz, P. B., Steffee, W. P., Cochran, W., Scrimshaw, N. S., Rand, W. M., and Young, V. R. (1977). Protein metabolism in human neonates: Nitrogen-balance studies, estimated obligatory losses of nitrogen and whole-body turnover of nitrogen. *Clin. Sci. Mol. Med.* **52,** 485.
11. Nissim, I., Yudkoff, M., Pereira, G., and Segal, S. (1983). Effects of conceptual age and dietary intake on protein metabolism in premature infants. *J. Pediatr. Gastroenterol. Nutr.* **2,** 507.
12. Young, V. R., Steffee, W. P., Pencharz, P. B., Winterer, J. C., and Scrimshaw, N. S. (1975). Total human body protein synthesis in relation to protein requirements at various ages. *Nature (London)* **253,** 192.
13. Picou, D., and Taylor-Roberts, T. (1969). The measurement of total body protein synthesis and catabolism and nitrogen turnover in infants in different nutritional states and receiving different amounts of dietary protein. *Clin. Sci.* **36,** 283.
14. FAO/WHO/UNU (1985). Energy and protein requirements. *W. H. O. Tech. Rep.* Ser. No. 724.
15. Young, V. R., Meredith, C., Hoerr, R., Bier, D. M., and Matthews, D. E. (1985). Amino acid kinetics in relation to protein and amino acid requirements: The primary importance of amino acid oxidation. *In* "Substrate and Energy Metabolism in Man" (J. S. Garrow and D. Halliday, eds.), p. 119. Libbey, London.
16. Waterlow, J. C., Garlick, P. J., and Millward, D. J. (1978). "Protein Turnover in Mammalian Tissues and in the Whole Body" p. 804. North-Holland Pub., Amsterdam.
17. Rigo, J., and Senterre, J. (1982). Amino acid requirements in preterm infants on oral or parenteral nutrition. *In* "Clinical Nutrition '81" R. I. C. Wesdorp and P. B. Soeters, eds.), p. 71. Churchill-Livingstone, Edinburgh.
18. Stegink, L. D., and Baker, G. L. (1971). Infusion of protein hydrolysates in the newborn infant. Plasma amino acid concentrations. *J. Pediatr.* **78,** 595.
19. Abitol, C. L., Feldman, D. B., Ahmann, P., and Rudman, D. (1975). Plasma amino acid patterns during supplemental intravenous nutrition of low-birth-weight infants. *J. Pediatr.* **86,** 766.
20. Winters, R. W., Hierd, W. C., Dell, R. B., and Nicholson, J. F. (1977). Plasma amino acids in infants receiving parenteral nutrition. *In* "Clinical Nutrition Update–Amino

Acids" (H. L. Greene, M. A. Holliday, and H. N. Munro, eds.), p. 147. Am. Med. Assoc., Chicago, Illinois.
21. Lindblad, B. S., Settergren, G., Feychting, H., and Persson, B. (1977). Total parenteral nutrition in infants. Blood levels of glucose, lactate, pyruvate, free fatty acids, glycerol, D-β-hydroxybutyrate, triglycerides, free amino acids and insulin. *Acta Paediatr. Scand.* **66,** 409.
22. Lindblad, B. S. Alfven, G., and Zetterstöm, R. (1978). Plasma free amino acid concentrations of breast-fed infants. *Acta Paediatr. Scand.* **67,** 659.
23. Anderson, G. H., Bryan, H., Jeejeebhoy, K. N., and Corey, P. (1977). Dose–response relationship between amino acid intake and blood levels in newborn infants. *Am. J. Clin. Nutr.* **30,** 1110.
24. Räihä, N. C. R. (1974). Biochemical basis for nutritional management of preterm infants. *Pediatrics* **53,** 147.
25. Christensen, H. N. (1982). Interorgan amino acid nutrition. *Physiol. Rev.* **62,** 1193.
26. Stegink, L. d., and den Besten, L. (1972). Synthesis of cysteine from methionine in normal adult subjects; effect of route alimentation. *Science* **178,** 514.
27. Duffy, B., and Pencharz, P. (1986). The effect of feeding route (IV or oral) on the protein metabolism of the neonate. *Am. J. Clin. Nutr.* **43,** 108.
28. Sturman, J. A., Gaull, G., and Räihä, N. C. R. (1970). Absence of cystathionase in human fetal liver: Is cystine essential? *Science* **169,** 74.
29. Gaull, G. Sturman, J. A., and Räihä, N. C. R. (1972). Development of mammalian suflur metabolism: Absence of cystathionase in human fetal tissue. *Pediatr. Res.* **6,** 538.
30. Zlotkin, S. H., Bryan, M. H., and Anderson, G. H. (1981). Cysteine supplementation to cysteine-free intravenous feeding regimens in newborn infants. *Am. J. Clin. Nutri.* **34,** 914.
31. Malloy, M. H., Rassin, D. K., and Richardson, C. J. (1984). Total parenteral nutrition in sick preterm infants: Effects of cysteine supplementation with nitrogen intakes of 240 and 400 mg/kg/day. *J. Pediatr., Gastroenterol. Nutri.* **3,** 239.
32. Stengik, L. D. (1986). Parenteral amino acid requirements: Special problems and possible solutions. *In* "Energy and Protein Needs during Infancy" S. J. Fomon and W. C. Hiered, (eds.), p. 183. Academic Press, New York.
33. Matthews, D. E., MOtil, K. J., Rohrbaugh, D. K., Burke, J. F., Young, V. R., and Bier, D. M. (1980). Measurements of leucine metabolism in man from a primed continuous infusion of L-[1-^{13}C]leucine. *Am. J. Physiol.* **238,** E473.
34. Womack, M., and Rose, W. C. (1941). Partial replacement of dietary methionine by cystine for purposes of growth. *J. Biol. Chem* **141,** 375.
35. Finkelstein, J. D., and Mudd, S. H. (1967). Transsulfuration in mammals. The methionine sparing effect of cysteine. *J. Biol Chem.* **242,** 873.
36. Finkelstein, J. D., Martin, J. J., and Harris, B. J. (1986). Effect of dietary cystine on methionine metabolism in rat liver. *J. Nutri.* **116,** 985.
37. Felig, P. (1973). The glucose–alanine cycle. *Metab., Clin. Exp.* **22,** 179.
38. Smith, R., and Elia, M. (1983). Branched-chain amino acids in catabolic states. *Proc. Nutr. Soc.* **42,** 473.
39. Goto, M., Shinno, H., and Ichihara, A. (1977). Isozyme patterns of branched-chain amino acid transaminase in human tissues and tumors. *Gann* **68,** 663.
40. Khatra, B. S., Chawla, R. K., Sewell, C. W., and Rudman, D. (1977). Distribution of branched-chain α-keto acid dehydrogenases in primate tissues. *J. Clin. Invest.* **59,** 558.
41. Yu, Y. M., Yang, R. D., Matthews, D. E., Burke, J. F., Bier, D. M., and Young, V. R. (1985). Quantitative aspects of glycine and alanine nitrogen metabolism in young men: Effect of level of nitrogen and dispensable amino acid intake. *J. Nutri.* **115,** 399.

42. Robert, J.-J., Bier, D. M., Zhao, X. H., Matthews, D. E., and Young, V. R. (1982). Glucose and insulin effects on *de novo* amino acid synthesis in young men: Studies with stable isotope labeled alanine, glycine, leucine and lysine. *Metab.* **31,** 1212.
43. Young, V. R., and Bier, D. M. (1981). Protein metabolism and nutritional state in man. *Proc. Nutri. Soc.* **40,** 343.
44. Yang, R. D., Matthews, D. E., Bier, D. M., Wen, A. M., and Young, V. R. (1986). Response of alanine metabolism in humans to manipulation of dietary protein and energy intakes. *Am. J. Physiol.* **250,** E39.
45. Synderman, S. E., Holt, L. E., Jr., Dancis, J., Roitman, E., Boyer, A., and Baylis, M. E. (1962). "Unessential" nitrogen: A limiting factor for human growth. *J. Nutr.* **78,** 57.
46. Ladato, R. F., Smith, R. J., Valle, D., Phang, J. M., and Aoki, T. T. (1981). The regulation of pyroline-5-carboxylate synthase activity by ornithine. *Metab. Clin. Exp.* **30,** 908.
47. Schroder, H., and Paust, H. (1986). Plasma amino acids in a supplementary parenteral nutrition of preterm infants. *Acta Pediatr. Scand.* **75,** 302.
48. Ball, R. O., Atkinson, J. L., and Bayley, H. S. (1986). Proline as an essential amino acid for the young pig. *Br. J. Nutri.* **55,** 659.

19

The Regulation of Human Milk Flow

Michael W. Woolridge and J. David Baum
Department of Child Health
University of Bristol
Royal Hospital for Sick Children
Bristol, England

I. INTRODUCTION

Is human milk flow regulated? If so how is this achieved, and by whom, the mother or her infant? To answer these questions we should perhaps first ask: Is there any functional necessity in or biological advantage from regulating milk flow?

Milk *flow* may be considered as its *integral*, the *net volume* of milk transferred from mother to infant. Undoubtedly there is an upper limit to the amount of milk a mother can produce. Such a limit will not be reached for some time after birth, during which time regulatory processes will presumably be in operation setting milk production at the appropriate level.

It would be energetically inefficient for a mother to produce (very much) more milk than is required to meet an infant's nutritional needs, and a small baby will require less than a large baby.

A simple mechanism by which such regulation might operate would be for the baby to determine his or her own specific needs, to let *demand regulate supply*. If so how does the baby communicate his demand for milk?

The net amount of the baby's sucking at the breast (frequency and duration) determines maternal prolactin release. Yet with increasing postnatal age milk production rises [up to 3–4 months, at least (1–3)] while both the number and duration of feeds generally decline (4,5). This may reflect the baby's increased efficiency in obtaining milk (or of the mother in releasing it). An increased intake obtained in a shorter time means that the rate of transfer of milk from mother to baby must have increased. So by what means is milk flow regulated?

II. CAN REGULATION OF MILK FLOW BE DEMONSTRATED?

We may start with the proposition that there is no apparent regulation of intake—the infant simply consumes all milk currently stored in the breast. But milk can be expressed from the breast at the termination of a feed. Such expression is, however, unphysiological and may remove milk which was unavailable to the infant. Nevertheless, in a study of Burmese mothers conducted throughout the first 12 months of lactation, an additional 25% volume of milk was expressed after feeds (6).

It is known that babies take on average between one-fourth to one-third less milk from the second compared with the first breast of a feed (7), suggesting that the second breast is not "emptied." However, mothers frequently offer both breasts at a feed, alternating the breast which is offered first at consecutive feeds. If the breasts can potentially supply equal amounts of milk but *less* is taken from the *second* breast, then at the next feed more will be available from the *first* breast. To demonstrate that the baby chooses to take less milk from the second breast, while overcoming this confounding influence, it is necessary to conduct an experiment that randomizes the breast from which the baby is first fed (Fig. 1).

In a group of 29 babies treated in this way (8), 5 babies refused the second breast and the remaining 24 babies took a significantly smaller volume from the second breast, demonstrating that babies do not take all the milk available. This result shows that the process of milk transfer

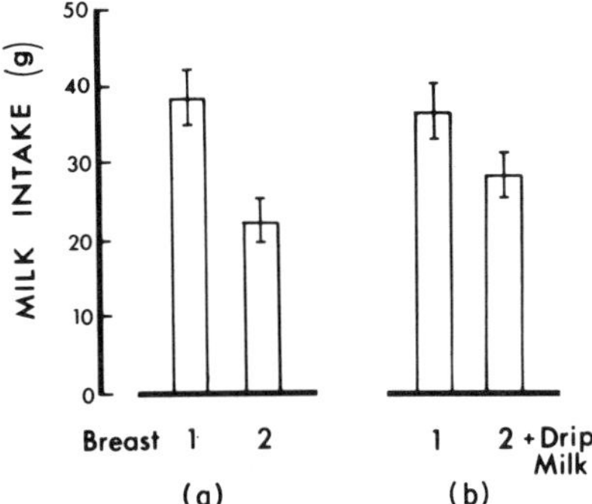

Fig. 1. Net milk intake (mean ±SE) from the first and second breast in 29 6-day-old babies, for whom the choice of first breast was determined at random ($P < .001$) (a). The significant difference in intake between sides is still present when 5 babies, who took no milk from the second side, were omitted and when intake from the second breast was adjusted to include 'leaked' milk from that side while the baby had been feeding on the first breast ($P < .01$) (b). [Reprinted with permission from *Physiol. Behav.* **26.** Milk taken by human babies from the first and second breast, by Drewett, R. F. and Woolridge, M. W., Copyright 1981, Pergamon Journals Ltd.]

from mother to infant can be *regulated,* so that milk which is not required is retained in the breast.

III. VARIABILITY IN THE RATE OF MILK TRANSFER

How much variation is there in the rate of milk transfer and what insight can this lend to the mechanisms regulating milk flow? From "fractional test weighing" studies, it is apparent that there is considerable interindividual variation in the rate of milk transfer (7). As illustrated in Fig. 2 there is at least a fivefold variation between the two extremes.[1] It is hard to imagine that such variability can be brought about solely by changes in the efficiency of babies' feeding or sucking patterns. A substantial proportion of the difference must reflect variability in the strength or efficiency of the mothers' milk ejection reflex.

Despite the variation in *rates* of intake, babies in this study took roughly comparable volumes of milk after feeding for different lengths of time.

[1]For these 20 infants studied at 6 days of age, mean intake was 68.7 g (range 30–111 g) taken in a mean of 15.2 min (range 4–31 min), resulting in a mean rate of transfer of 5.6 g/min (range 1.75–12 g/min, CV = 65%).

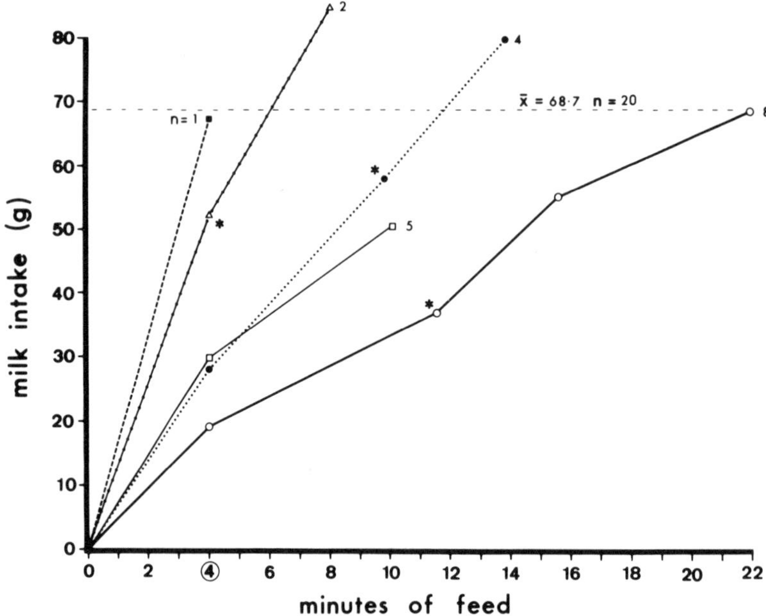

Fig. 2. Pattern of milk intake at a feed in 20 6-day-old babies grouped with respect to the length of the feed. A pre-feed weighing, intermediate (after 4 min feeding) and final weighing were collected for each breast. For babies who were switched between breasts at the 4 min weighing this constituted final intake from that breast. No restrictions were placed on the length of feeds, which were terminated either by the mother or baby. The number of babies in each group is shown at the upper end of each curve. The horizontal dashed line represents the mean final intake for all 20 babies. Asterisk indicates a change of breast [From Woolridge *et al.*, 1982 (7)].

In fact, rate of intake and feed duration were inversely correlated ($r = -0.68$, 18 df, $p = .001$), mothers or babies thus compensating for a slow rate of transfer by feeding for an extended period. Mothers do not appear to be "aware" of the rate at which their milk is transferred, yet one or the other partner appears to be an effective *transducer* of this rate, regulating net milk intake by changes in feed duration.

IV. WHO INFLUENCES THE RATE OF TRANSFER?

Does the mother or the baby exert the dominant influence over the rate of milk transfer? This question was addressed directly with the opportunity to study the infants of two sisters who had cross-nursed their baby sons and were prepared to do so while fractional test weighings were carried out (7) (Fig. 3). The two babies were of dissimilar sizes and

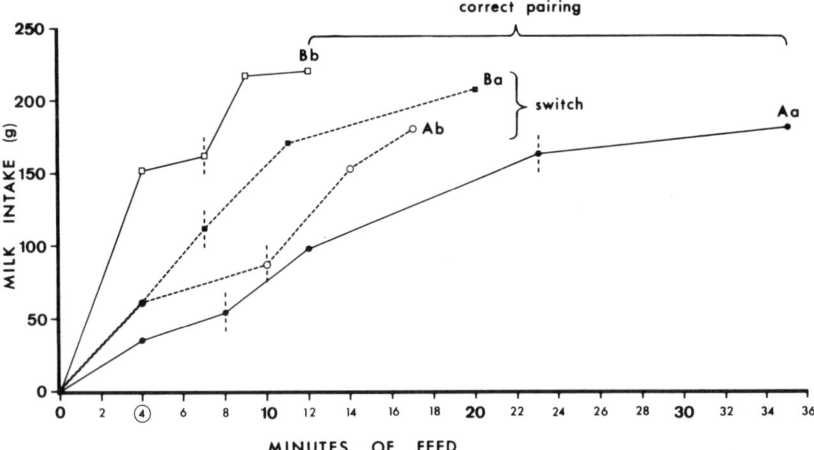

Fig. 3. Individual profiles of the time course for milk transfer in 2 infants (aged 15 and 22 weeks), when fed by their mothers (correct pairings—Aa and Bb), and when cross-nursed by their aunts (switched pairings—Ab and Ba). Dashed vertical line indicates a change of breast. [From Woolridge *et al.*, 1982 (7)].

had different rates of milk intake. When cross-nursed the larger, "faster" baby (b) accelerated the rate of milk transfer from the "slower" mother (A), but on this occasion did not increase the total amount of milk delivered, whereas the smaller, "slower" baby (a) retarded the rate of intake from the "faster" mother (B) and took an elevated volume. This simple study demonstrates that in the cross-nursing situation both the rate of intake and the feed duration were a compromise of those values for the infants when correctly paired with their natural mothers. This implies that the rate of milk transfer for a mother–infant pair is mutually determined by both the capacity for milk release by the mother and the rate of milk demand of her baby.

It seems likely then that both the mother and her baby influence the rate and pattern of milk flow. To identify the mechanisms involved some consideration must be given to their separate contributions.

A. Maternal Factors

The two most conspicuous maternal factors likely to influence milk flow are (i) milk synthesis, which is prolactin regulated; and (ii) milk release or ejection, an oxytocin-mediated reflex. However, the levels of these hormones are themselves influenced by the infant's sucking and are not therefore determined by the mother in isolation.

In our studies on milk production, we have assumed that only a small proportion of mothers are genetically incapable of secreting sufficient milk. It follows then that some cases of apparent milk insufficiency must reflect an inappropriate *demand* for milk by the infant (e.g., impaired appetite control), or an inadequate opportunity to express that demand (i.e., incorrect feed management).

Changes in feed management should not be undertaken without giving due consideration to underlying physiology. For example, the assumption that babies may extend feeds by sucking for "comfort" ignores other possible direct physiological outcomes such as elevation of prolactin levels. However, while prolactin release determines future milk production, oxytocin has a more immediate influence on milk flow at a feed, and so only this will be considered at length.

The milk ejection reflex may be viewed as a maternal mechanism facilitating the transfer of milk from mother to infant, and conditioning of the response to cues from the infant allows it to become *anticipatory*, thereby avoiding delays in the milk being made available. However, it has been suggested that the milk ejection reflex not only results in the active expulsion of milk into the baby's mouth at the onset of the feed but is necessary throughout the feed to maintain movement of the milk from the storage alveoli into the lacteal sinuses, where it can be stripped by the "milking" action of the baby's tongue and jaw (9).

Oxytocin then has two functions, the active expulsion of milk and the sustained positive pressure within the milk ducts facilitating milk removal by the infant.

A discrete milk ejection reflex is most clearly apparent in established lactation, a month or so after birth, for example. Feeds at this time are usually shorter than in early lactation, and the discrete release of oxytocin can be readily detected (10). But in the first week after delivery the discrete release of oxytocin is difficult to demonstrate, though serum levels *are* elevated (10,11). It seems likely that in the early postnatal period oxytocin release is either diffuse or disorganized, but may still be effective in creating sustained positive ductal pressure. With time, it becomes more organized into a discrete pattern of release, perhaps concurrent with its development as a conditioned reflex.

Conditioned reflexes develop in response to very specific sets of environmental stimuli, and they are easily disrupted by departures from this pattern. This is very important for ensuring that the conditioned response does not occur under inappropriate circumstances. Thus, whereas conditioned milk release may work for a mother at home, it may *not* work for her in a strange location.

The corollary to this, which is well recognized for most conditioned responses, is that the original *un*conditioned stimulus (in this case sucking) always retains its ability to evoke the response, irrespective of and uninhibited by extraneous stimuli. This means that even under adverse conditions, should the mother wish to feed, fixing her baby to the breast will produce the necessary infant stimulation leading to sucking-induced milk release.

However, this sucking-induced oxytocin response may remain diffuse, unlike perhaps the more discrete form of the conditioned reflex, so that milk release may be slowed and the infant may show overt signs of frustration under conditions which are adverse to the mother but not apparently so to her infant!

B. Infant Factors

There are a number of infant-related factors which are associated with a baby's milk intake and which are not open to manipulation: birth weight is an example. However, infants of differing birth weight may grow to the same size later in infancy and may still command differing intakes. There must then be differences in the efficiency, vigor, or appetite of infants which influence intake over and above simple physical attributes. A consideration of some of these factors follows.

1. *Oral Dynamics*

Intraoral dynamics during infant feeding are likely to have a substantial influence on the rate of breast milk flow. This may be of clinical importance in cases of impaired oral anatomy (e.g., babies with a cleft palate) and in infants with incoordination resulting from neurological abnormality.

We have examined the internal dynamics of the baby's mouth during feeding using ultrasonography (12) and it is clear that there is much variability both in the physical relationship of the baby's mouth to the breast tissue and in the relative coordination of sucking, swallowing, and breathing. To date, we have not quantified directly how these changes affect the rate of milk flow, although they clearly do so.

2. *Physiological Changes during Feed*

Considerable progress has been made in determining the relationships between milk flow and sucking patterns. During the course of a breast feed there are certain clear and quantifiable changes.[2] First, following an initial latency period, milk flow swiftly reaches a peak and thereafter declines as the feed progresses, although apparently it rarely falls to a level where milk flow has ceased altogether. The pattern of "nonnutritive" sucking, often seen prior to milk release, never reappears in its purest form at the end of a feed, which questions the legitimacy of im-

[2]All those changes described relate to infants at 6 days of age unless otherwise specified.

plying that infants may prolong feeds by sucking for comfort alone. Of relevance to this are the changes in milk composition over the course of a feed.

There are marked changes in the composition of the milk, most notably in the fat content, during feeds. There is a clear *inverse relationship* between the rate of milk flow and the fat content of that milk (Fig. 4). There appears to be a direct physical interaction between milk flow and fat content, of the sort proposed by Hytten (15) to account for changes in fat content during milk removal from the breast. As smaller volumes of milk are removed from the breast, so the fat and hence the caloric concentration increases. This means that the *profile* for the *caloric content* of a breast feed is very different from that for *volume* intake, and the point at which peak caloric intake is reached will be later in the feed than that for volume intake. Even the very small amounts of milk taken at the end of the feed may contribute significantly to the baby's net caloric intake.

In contrast to fat, the changes in protein and lactose concentration occur in proportion to the *reduction* in the aqueous fraction of the milk (i.e., reciprocal of increases in fat). A doubling of the fat concentration (say from 5% to 10% by volume) will cause a relatively small decrease in the aqueous component (from 95% down to 90%). So whereas changes in feed management (e.g., in the length of time for which a baby feeds on one breast) may affect the total fat intake dramatically, if the volume taken is only slightly affected then the influence on other constituents will be minor. It is worth reaffirming that changes in the baby's fat intake from breast milk will have a commensurate effect on caloric intake, on the intake of fat-soluble vitamins (A,D,E, and K), and on intake of drugs or other contaminants which are differentially fat soluble.

Can changes be demonstrated in patterns of sucking contingent upon alterations in flow and composition?

3. *Sucking Patterns*

Sucking shows a clear burst/pause pattern during a breast feed: a continuous, slow pattern with few if any pauses is typical of a high rate of milk flow, while a disjointed pattern of short, fast bursts interrupted by relatively short pauses indicates slow milk flow or its absence. Toward the end of a feed as milk flow subsides, the rate of sucking (within a burst) increases, and feeding is interrupted more frequently by pauses of increasing length.

Sucking rate shows a direct change with milk flow, as shown both by quantification of normal feeds (16) and by direct manipulation of flow rate on the breast (17). It would appear that sucking rate changes *in response to* changes in flow rate, becoming slower with increasing flow. Pauses become longer and more frequent as the feed progresses but are not statistically related to changes in rate. In contrast, they may be related

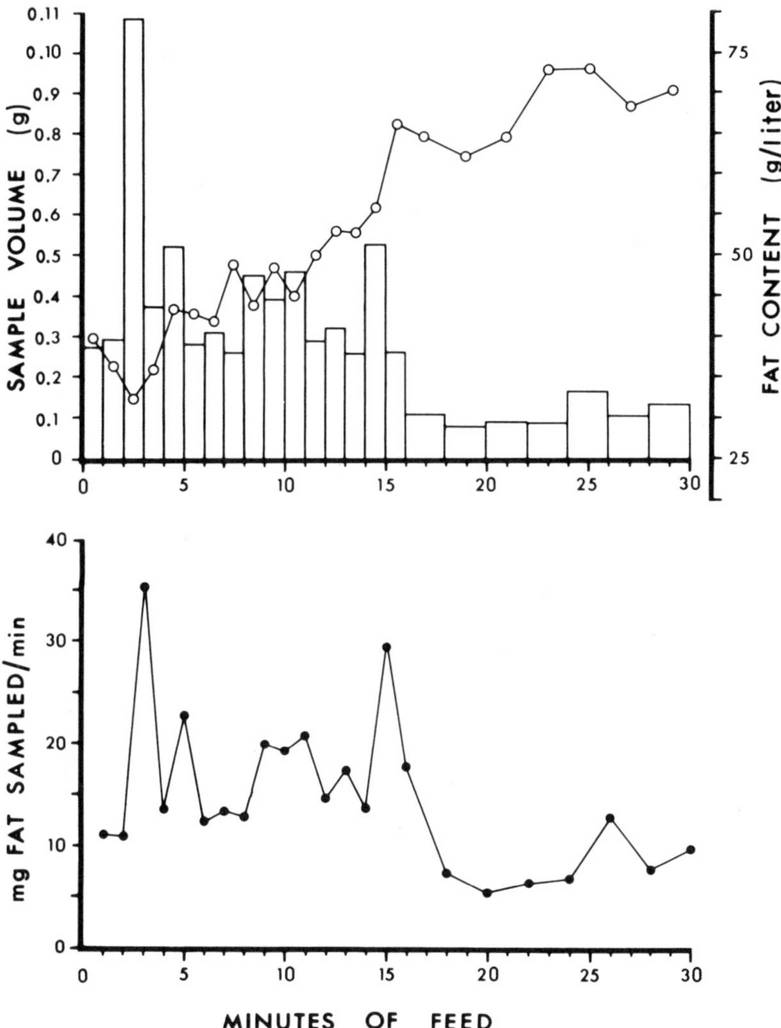

Fig. 4. (Upper graph) volume profile (columns) and fat concentration profile (○) for sequential samples of suckled breast milk, removed during a feed with an automatic sampling nipple shield (13,14). This mother typically fed for 30 min from one breast only. (Lower graph) product of upper two profiles showing rate at which fat is sampled. Sampling system removes milk roughly in proportion to the rate of milk transfer from mother to infant, so this profile may be equated with the baby's rate of fat intake (●).

to changes in composition, though in the studies carried out to date there is no clear statistical relationship (18,19).

An integrated view of these relationships is provided by use of a Doppler ultrasound flow transducer (mounted in a thin latex nipple shield) and by observations of sucking patterns made concurrently with use of

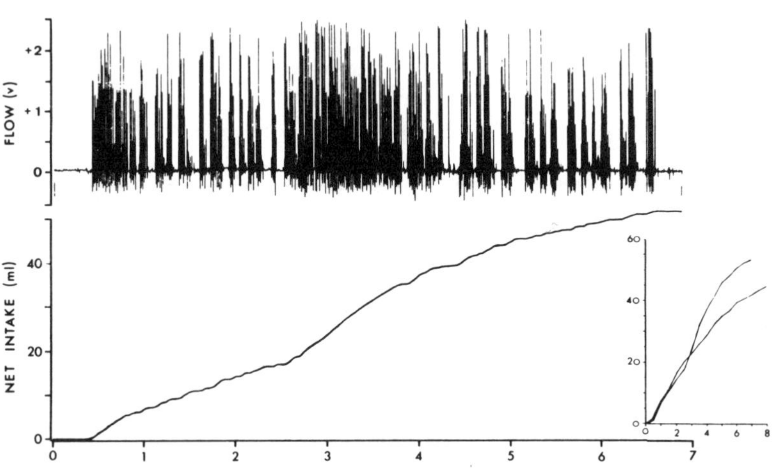

Second Breast

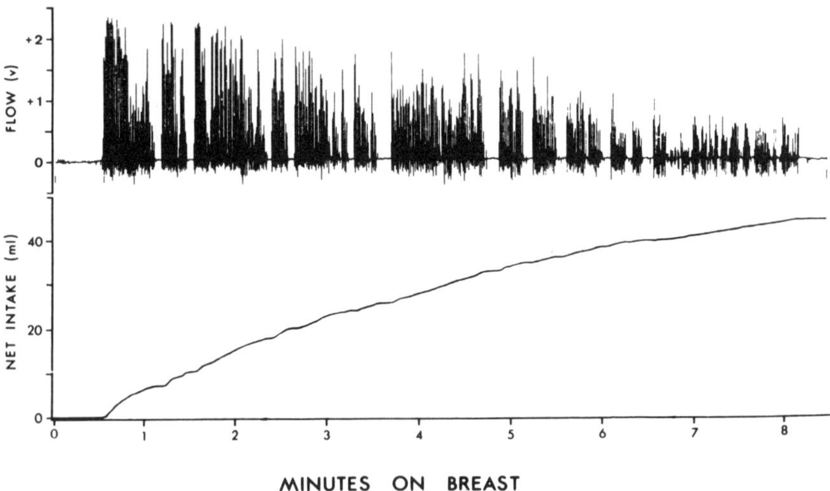

Fig. 5. Instantaneous (analogue) and cumulative milk flow profiles for a single feed from both breasts obtained with a miniature Doppler ultrasound flow transducer. Vertical excursions on the instantaneous profile correspond to peak flow velocity per suck, which are integrated over time to give cumulative volume intake. Absence of activity represents pauses between bursts of sucking. [From Woolridge *et al.*, 1982 (20)].

the automatic sampling shield. Figure 5 shows *analogue* data collected using the ultrasound flow transducer (20). The two sets of curves represent feeding on the first (upper two traces) and second breast (lower two traces) at the same feed. The upper profile in each case represents instantaneous flow with each vertical excursion corresponding to an individual suck. The curve below represents the electronic integration of instantaneous flow providing a cumulative flow or intake profile. Both integrated profiles show a roughly similar pattern with the intake falling off gradually toward the end of the feed. On the first breast the amplitude of individual sucks remains relatively constant (i.e., equal volume intake per suck), the curtailment of intake being achieved by a change in sucking pattern, with pauses becoming more frequent and of increased duration. On the second breast a different picture emerges: the pattern of sucking remains relatively static, but the amplitude of each suck, reflecting milk flow, falls off throughout the feed. This raises questions of the causes of the change in sucking pattern on the first breast and whether the reduction in intake on the second breast represented true depletion of the milk available or involuntary withholding of milk by the mother in response to cues of satiety by her infant.

Figure 6 shows a slightly different view obtained by digital processing of the flow signal. In this case flow information is digitized, summed over a 10-sec period, and stored in a single location in solid-state memory. These data are "downloaded" from a Doppler flow recorder to a microcomputer and plotted both as a continuous output of successive memory locations and as a cumulative flow plot by progressive summation of these values. The time resolution on the horizontal axis is 10 sec. Sucks and pauses are not distinct in these profiles as a result, with up to 10–15 sucks contributing to each point.

This plot gives a clearer overview of the feed, although with the burst/pause pattern of sucking obscured, but indicating more clearly when milk ejection is likely to have occurred. There is a moderate but distinct peak of flow early on the first breast, after an initial latency of nearly 5 min, with a more marked surge at the start of feeding on the second breast.

In a similar manner information on sucking patterns can be collected concurrently with use of the automatic sampling shield (13,14). We have already shown that giving due consideration to the fat concentration of the milk consumed shifts the peak for fat intake to later in the feed relative to peak flow. Does a similar outcome result when the reduction in the number of sucks per unit time during the feed is also taken into account?

Figure 7 shows the profiles for volume and fat intake per unit time for a single feed and their equivalents expressed as intake per suck, each

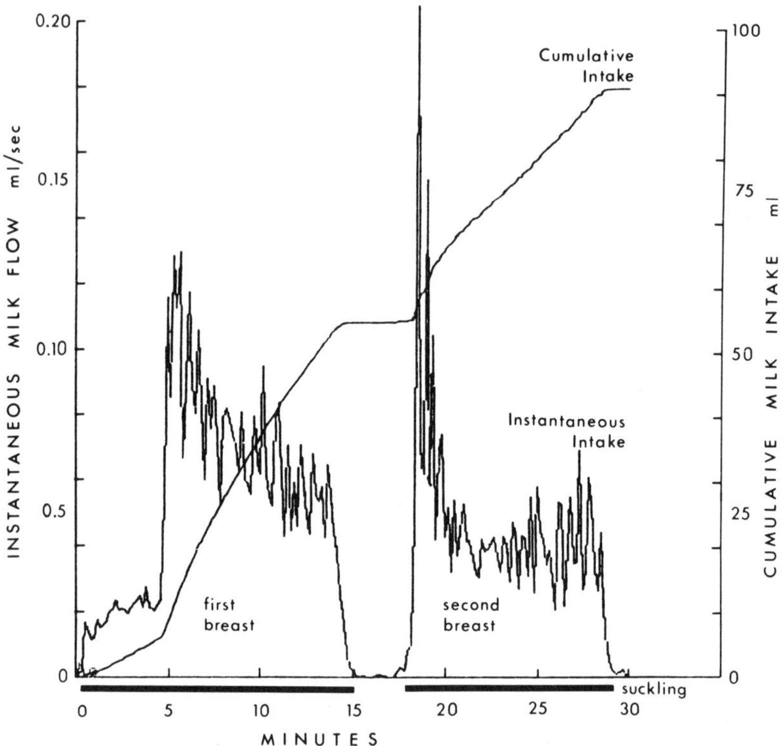

Fig. 6. Digital flow profile for a single feed from both breasts. Vertical excursions represent aggregated flow over successive 10 sec periods. Cumulative intake derived by summation of successive 10 sec totals. [From Woolridge *et al.*, 1985 (21)].

profile being adjusted so that the values are expressed as a percentage of the peak (=100%) rate of intake.

Why is this relevant to the regulation of flow? Principally, if the infant regulates flow as he approaches satiety, it is important to know the events antecedent to the termination of feeding for their potential involvement as causal mechanisms in the process. It is quite probable that a baby finishes feeding on a breast when a "point of diminishing returns" is reached, but if so what is the "currency" of this process—volume or calories, per unit time or per suck? It may be that a critical reduction in the volume available, that is, in flow rate, acts as the cue. However, though a direct effect of fat concentration on sucking patterns has not yet been demonstrated, caloric intake would appear to be important in determining satiety (23,24), so that fat intake per unit time may also be important. Furthermore, the infant may not in fact be an "analogue

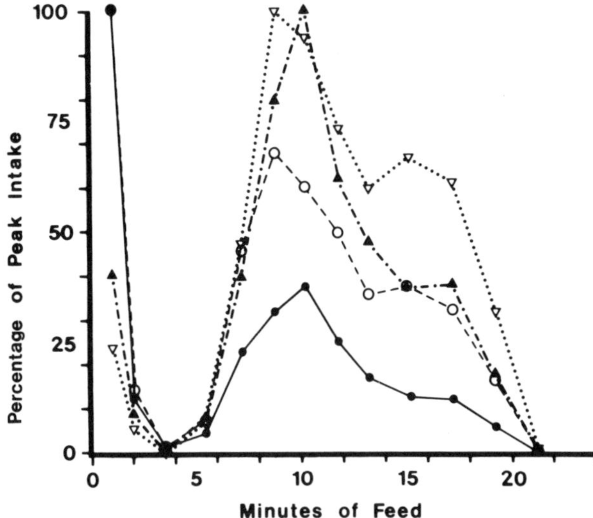

Fig. 7. Volume and fat intake profiles for a single feed derived from concurrent records of intake (by use of the automatic sampling shield) and sucking patterns [transcribed from video recordings (22)]. Volume and fat intake expressed both as intake per unit time, and intake per suck, as a percentage of peak intake (= 100%). Volume/min, ●——●; volume/suck, ○ - - - ○; fat/min, ▲-.-.▲; fat/suck, ▽····▽.

transducer" of rate (i.e., responsive to changes in intake per unit time) but rather more a "digital" one (e.g., monitors intake per unit suck).

The general conclusion from Fig. 7 is that on a *per suck* basis greater significance should be attached to the later stages of the feed than would be on the basis of intake *per unit time,* the greatest percentage drop at the end of the feed occurring in *fat intake per suck.* Rather than the infant ceasing to feed despite there still being moderate returns for continued effort, it would appear that the baby *is* capable of acting as a transducer of milk availability and stops sucking when insufficient returns are detected.

V. CONCLUSION

It is apparent that a variety of influences, originating from both the mother and her infant, as well as from the specific interaction between them, preside in the determination of milk flow at a feed. Some of these are summarized in Fig. 8.

Further proliferation of these influences occurs when milk intake is considered over the course of a day, or over 2–3 days, when the in-

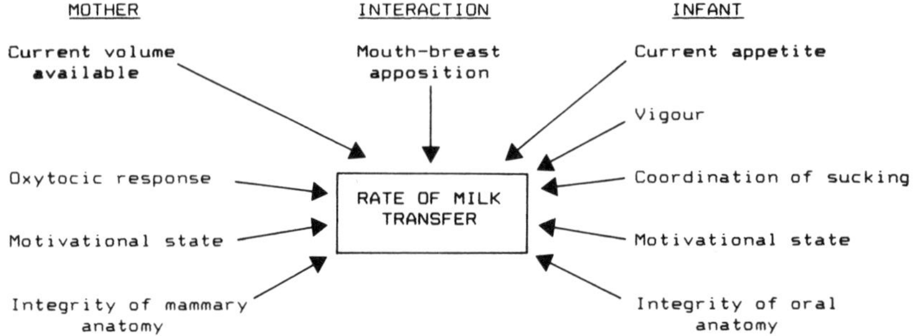

Fig. 8. Schematic representation of the factors specific to the mother, her infant, and the interaction between them during a breast feed, which influence the rate of milk transfer.

volvement of prolactin in the longer-term balance between "supply" and "demand" becomes an important factor. Nevertheless, the observations made in this paper indicate the need for detailed study of the way in which sucking patterns and reflex milk ejection interact in determining milk transfer and how they change with alterations in the oral dynamics of feeding and with infant appetite.

REFERENCES

1. Wallgren, A. (1944). Breast-milk consumption of healthy full-term infants. *Acta Paediatr. Scand.* **32,** 778–790.
2. Hofvander, Y., Hagman, U., Hillervik, C., and Sjölin, S. (1982). The amount of milk consumed by 1–3 month old breast- or bottle-fed infants. *Acta Paediatr. Scand.* **71,** 953–958.
3. Dewey, K. G., and Lönnerdal, B. (1983). Milk and nutrient intake of breast-fed infants from 1 to 6 months: Relation to growth and fatness. *J. Pediatr. Gastroenterol. Nutr.* **2,** 497–506.
4. Butte, N. F., Garza, C., Smith, E. O., and Nichols, B. L. (1984). Human milk intake and growth in exclusively breast-fed infants. *J. Pediatr.* **104,** 187–195.
5. Imong, S. M., Jackson, D. A., Yootabootr, Y., Woolridge, M. W., and Baum, J. D. (1985). The relationship between nursing patterns and breast milk intake in the first year of life. *Pediatr. Res.* **20,** 1051.
6. Khin-Maung-Naing, Tin-Tin-Oo, Kywe-Thein, and Nwe-New-Hlaing (1980). Study on lactation performance of Burmese mothers. *Am. J. Clin. Nutr.* **33,** 2665–2668.
7. Woolridge, M. W., Baum, J. D., and Drewett, R. F. (1982). Individual patterns of milk intake during breast-feeding. *Early Hum. Dev.* **7,** 265–272.
8. Drewett, R. F., and Woolridge, M. W. (1981). Milk taken by human babies from the first and second breast. *Physiol.Behav.* **26,** 327–329.
9. Woolridge, M. W. (1986). The "anatomy" of infant sucking. *Midwifery* **2,** 164–171.
10. McNeilly, A. S., Robinson, I. C. A., Houston, M. I., and Howie, P. W. (1983). Release of oxytocin and prolactin in response to sucking. *Br. Med. J. No. 286,* 257–259.

11. Lucas, A., Drewett, R. F., and Mitchell, M. D. (1980). Breast-feeding and plasma oxytocin concentrations. *Br. Med. J. No. 281,* 834–835.
12. Weber, F., Woolridge, M. W., and Baum, J. D. (1985). An ultrasonographic study of the organisation of sucking and swallowing by newborn infants. *Dev. Med. Child. Neurol.* **28,** 19–24.
13. Woolridge, M. W., McLeod, C. N., and Baum, J. D. (1983). A proportional sampling system for estimating the dietary content of a breast-feed. Presented at 55th Annu. meeting Brit. Paed. Assoc., York, 1983.
14. Jackson, D. A., Woolridge, M. W., Imong, S. M., McLeod, C. N., Yootabootr, Y., Amatayakul, K., and Baum, J. D. (1987). The automatic sampling shield: A device for obtaining suckled breast milk samples. *Early Hum. Dev.* **15** (5). (in press).
15. Hytten, F. E. (1954). Clinical and chemical studies in human lactation. II. Variation in major constituents during a feeding. *Br. Med. J.* **i,** 176–179.
16. Bowen-Jones, A., Thompson, C., and Drewett, R. F. (1982). Milk flow and sucking rates during breast-feeding. *Dev. Med. Child. Neurol.* **24,** 626–633.
17. Woolridge, M. W., and Drewett, R. F. (1983). Changing the rate of milk flow on the breast; its effect on sucking patterns. *Annu. Meet. Br. Paediatr. Assoc., 55th, York, Engl. 1983.*
18. Woolridge, M. W., Baum, J. D., and Drewett, R. F. (1980). Does a change in the composition of human milk affect sucking patterns and milk intake? *Lancet* **ii,** 1292–1294.
19. Nysenbaum, A. N., and Smart, J. L. (1982). Sucking behaviour and milk intake of neonates in relation to milk fat content. *Early Hum. Dev.* **6,** 205–213.
20. Woolridge, M. W., How, T. V., Drewett, R. F., Rolfe, P., and Baum, J. D. (1982). The continuous measurement of milk intake at a feed in breast-fed babies. *Early Hum. Dev.* **6,** 365–373.
21. Woolridge, M. W., Butte, N., Dewey, K. G., Ferris, A. M., Garza, C., and Keller, R. P. (1985). Methods for measurement of milk volume intake of the breast-fed infant. *In* "Human Lactation: Milk Components and Methodologies" (R. G. Jensen and M. C. Neville, eds.), pp. 5–22, Plenum Press, New York.
22. Woolridge, M. W., and Drewett, R. F. (1986). Sucking rates of human babies on the breast: A study using direct observation and intraoral pressure measurements. *J. Repro. Infant Psych.* **4,** 67–73.
23. Fomon, S. J., Filer, L. J., Thomas, L. N., Anderson, T. A., and Nelson, S. E. (1975). Influence or formula concentration on caloric intake and growth of normal infants. *Acta Paediatr. Scand.* **64,** 172–181.
24. Brooke, O. G., and Kinsey, J. M. (1985). High energy feeding in small for gestation infants. *Arch. Dis. Childhd.* **60,** 42–46.

20

Digestion and Absorption of Human Milk Lipids

Olle Hernell*, Lars Bläckberg†, and Stefan Bernbäck†

*Department of Pediatrics
†Department of Physiological Chemistry
University of Umeå
Umeå, Sweden

I. INTRODUCTION

From an energetic point of view lipids are the main nutrient of the newborn infant. More than 95% of the lipids are triglycerides (triacylglycerol). With a concentration of 3–5% the triglycerides constitute about half of the energy content of human milk. Assuming a milk consumption of 150–180 ml/kg per day it follows, calculated per kilogram body weight, that a newborn infant has at least a threefold higher daily intake of triglyceride than the average Western adult. Indeed, triglyceride digestion and absorption are generally relatively efficient processes even in preterm breast-fed infants. This, however, is contradictory to the situation in many formula-fed newborns. For a detailed understanding of the reasons behind this discrepancy it is essential first to explore the sequential steps of the digestion and absorption of human milk triglyceride. In this chapter we summarize our current view on this topic.

II. THE TWO-PHASE MODEL OF FAT DIGESTION

Based on the now classical studies of Hofmann and Borgström (1), lipid digestion in general, and triglyceride digestion in particular, has until recently been regarded as a two-phase process occurring in the upper part of the small intestine. In short, the triglycerides enter the duodenum as an emulsion of oil in water, that is, large water-insoluble lipid droplets (diameter 250–500 nm) dispersed in the aqueous phase of intestinal contents. At the oil/water interphase colipase-dependent pancreatic lipase hydrolyzes the triglycerides. Since this lipase cannot release the fatty acid esterified to the *sn*-2-position of the glycerol molecule, each triglyceride gives rise to one *sn*-2 monoglyceride and two free fatty acids (2). In the duodenal contents bile salts are also present. They distribute between the aqueous phase and the oil/water interphase, where they displace amphiphilic products, including lipolysis products, from the interphase into the water. However, at physiological concentration bile salts also displace the lipase from its substrate. Thus, bile salts are supposed to inhibit lipolysis. To prevent this, colipase is needed. This cofactor, also secreted from the pancreas, forms a complex with lipase and anchors the enzyme to its substrate in the presence of bile salts. According to this view the essential function of colipase is to prevent inhibition of pancreatic lipase caused by bile salts (3).

In the aqueous phase bile salts, above their critical micellar concentration (CMC), spontaneously form aggregates called micelles, which dramatically increase the solubility of the products of lipolysis in the aqueous phase. Mixed micelles, that is, bile salt micelles saturated with lipolytic products, are spherical particles with a hydrodynamic radius of up to 5 nm that carry the lipids from the interphase to the enterocytes for absorption (4).

According to the described view of fat digestion and absorption, low intraluminal concentrations of colipase-dependent pancreatic lipase and/ or of bile salts should be obvious reasons for fat malabsorption. Therefore, one would expect newborn infants with comparatively high triglyceride intake to have high intraluminal concentrations of lipase and bile salts. However, because the pancreatic and liver functions at birth are not fully developed, this is not the situation. Thus, intraluminal fasting levels of digestive enzymes secreted from the pancreas are considerably lower than in adults during the first 2–12 months, and the adult level of response to pancreozymin may not be seen until the end of the first year of life (5,6). Consistent with this we found that levels of colipase-dependent lipase in duodenal contents after a meal were on average only 4% in preterm infants when compared with that in adults (7). Similarly, others have reported a 5- to 10-fold lower postprandial intraluminal bile salt concentration in preterm infants than in adults (8,9). In fact, such low concentrations, that is 1–2 m*M*, are close to or even below the CMC. Hence they would not, according to theory, be compatible with efficient solubilization, transport, and ultimately absorption of lipolytic products. Nonetheless, digestion and absorption of triglyceride are often remarkably efficient even in preterm breast-fed infants.

III. HUMAN MILK TRIGLYCERIDE AS SUBSTRATE FOR COLIPASE-DEPENDENT PANCREATIC LIPASE

Until recently, very little interest was focused on the importance of the nature of the triglyceride substrate for hydrolysis by colipase-dependent lipase. In fact, much of the data from which the two-phase model gained support came from experiments *in vitro* with rather unphysiological lipid substrates. Therefore, it was of decisive interest to extend these studies to digestion of human milk triglyceride, the physiological dietary lipid of the newborn infant. Interestingly, under identical conditions in which purified colipase-dependent lipase readily hydrolyzed an artificial emulsion of long-chain triglyceride in gum arabic, it did not hydrolyze the triglyceride of isolated human milk fat globules (10) (Fig. 1). Since no bile salts were present in the incubations, bile salt inhibition was not the reason. An obvious cause, however, was the milk fat globule membrane, that is, the layer of protein and phospholipid that envelops the triglyceride core of the globule (11). To test this possibility we prepared model emulsions of long-chain triglyceride with the surface of the emulsion droplets covered either with various proteins or with phospholipid (12). All these emulsions were hydrolyzed more slowly by the lipase (in the absence of colipase and bile salts) than was the un-

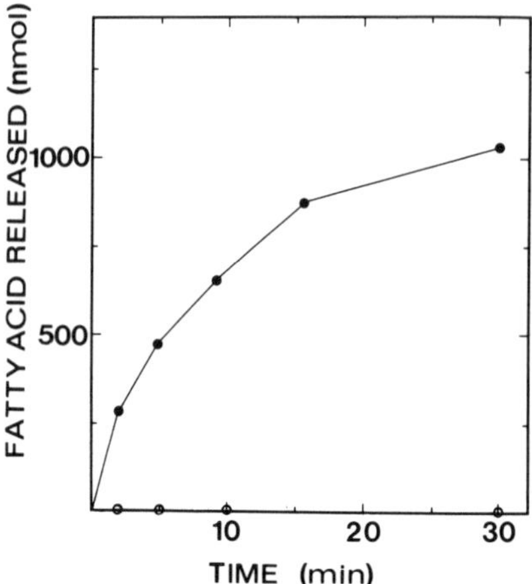

Fig. 1. Hydrolysis of milk fat globules (○) and of long-chain triglyceride (Trioleate) emulsified in gum arabic (●) by colipase-dependent pancreatic lipase. Purified porcine colipase-dependent pancreatic lipase (0.25 μg/ml) was added at start to either isolated human milk fat globules or an emulsion of trioleate in gum arabic. The triglyceride concentration was 4,500 nmol/ml, the pH 6.5, and the concentrations of $CaCl_2$ and NaCl were 20 m*M* and 0.15 *M*, respectively. Values of fatty acid released are expressed per milliliter of incubation mixture. [For details see Bläckberg *et al.* (10). Reproduced by copyright permission of the American Society for Clinical Investigation.]

covered control emulsion (Table I). Thus, both protein and phospholipid, the major constituents of the milk fat globule membrane (11), impeded the action of the lipase, probably by denying lipase access to the triglyceride core.

Thus, considering the low concentrations of bile salts and colipase-dependent pancreatic lipase in postprandial duodenal contents in newborn infants and the slow hydrolysis of milk fat globule triglyceride by this lipase, it is evident that the two-phase model must be an oversimplification, at least in the breast-fed infant.

IV. MILK TRIGLYCERIDE DIGESTION IN THE STOMACH

It is an old observation that hydrolysis of dietary triglyceride is already initiated in the stomach (13). Borgström *et al.*, for instance, noticed in adults that some 20% of dietary triglyceride had been hydrolyzed before a meal reached the proximal duodenum (14). Probably based on the fact that in healthy adults colipase-dependent pancreatic lipase is secreted in such high concentration that it theoretically can account for complete

TABLE I

Inhibition of Pancreatic Colipase-Dependent Lipase by Proteins or Phospholipid[a]

Addition	Fatty acid released (nmol)
None	1540
Lactoferrin[b]	660
Lysozyme[b]	110
Bovine serum albumin[b]	60
β-Lactoglobulin[b]	30
Phospholipid[c]	12

[a]0.1 *M* Tris–HC1 (pH 7.5), 4 m*M* Ca^{2+}, triglyceride–gum arabic emulsion corresponding to 4 mg/ml triglyceride, 37 °C, purified porcine colipase-dependent lipase (0.4 μg/ml). Data listed are the amounts of fatty acid released during the first 8 min of incubation per milliliter medium. [For further details see Bläckberg *et al.* (12). Reproduced by copyright permission of the American Society for Clinical Investigation.]

[b]The various proteins were added to final concentrations of 5 mg/ml 20 min before the lipase.

[c]Triglyceride-rich particles from Intralipid corresponding to 4 mg/ml triglyceride.

hydrolysis of the daily intake of triglyceride in minutes (15), the quantitative contribution of lipid digestion in the stomach has been considered unimportant and thus neglected. However, given that patients with isolated deficiency of colipase-dependent pancreatic lipase (16) and patients with deficiency due to cystic fibrosis (17) hydrolyze and absorb as much as 50% or more of dietary triglyceride, it seems that gastric lipolysis can be of quantitative importance, at least in pathological conditions. Since newborn infants, especially preterm infants, are in a state of phsyiolocial deficiency of pancreatic digestive enzymes, renewed interest in gastric lipolysis has focused mainly on its function during the neonatal period. In fact, it has been suggested that as much as 70% of triglyceride digestion may occur in the stomach of healthy preterm infants. Although this may be an overestimation, it indicates that the capacity to synthesize and secrete the responsible enzyme(s) is well developed before term (18).

A. Lipases Operating in the Stomach

The tissue origin of the lipase activity recoreded in stomach contents is controversial (19). Originally in man the name gastric lipase was used (13). More recently the main enzyme activity found in gastric aspirates

TABLE II

Characteristics of Lipases Operating in the Stomach of Different Species[a]

Characteristic	Calf	Man	Rat
Molecular weight	41,700	45,000[b]	42,600
Specific activity[c]	75	45	150
Optimum pH	4.5–6.0	4–6	4–6
N-terminus	H_3N–Phe–Leu–Gly–	n.d.[d]	H_3N–Leu–Phe–Gly–
Glycosylation	+	n.d.[d]	+

[a]Data from Bernbäck *et al.* (20) (calf), Field and Scow (21) and Docherty *et al.* (22) (rat), and Tiruppathi and Balasubramanian (23) (man).

[b]Carbohydrate included while values for calf and rat are based on the peptide chain.

[c]Long-chain triglyceride as substrate but not identical assay conditions. Values are micromoles fatty acid released per minute and milligram protein.

[d]Information not yet available.

was attributed to the von Ebner secretory glands located beneath the circumvallate papillae of the tongue, and therefore, by analogy with the rat, the name lingual lipase was adopted (18). In calves the enzyme is secreted from the tongue as well as from other oropharyngeal tissue and hence the name pregastric lipase is used (20). It is tempting to speculate that all these names denote one and the same principal enzyme which may be secreted from different tissues and may have slightly different molecular structures in different species. However, it has been suggested that there are in fact two lipases, one secreted from the tongue and another from the gastric mucosa, and that these may have different properties implicating different physiological functions (18). So far no conclusive evidence exists to ascertain such heterogeneity on the molecular level or in function of lipase operating in the stomach contents of man. On the contrary, the enzymes purified from rat tongue (21,22), calf espophageal tissue (20), and human gastric content (23) show many similarities (Table II), and we have found that there is also an immunochemical cross-reaction between the pregastric lipase purified from calf and the enzyme in human gastric content. In the following the name pregastric lipase is used because most studies were conducted with the enzyhme purified from calf.

B. The Unique Function of Pregastric Lipase

In contrast to colipase-dependent pancreatic lipase, pregastric lipase, without any cofactor, readily hydrolyzes human milk fat globule triglyceride. Thus, the milk fat globule membrane does not cause inhibition of its activity. The same difference is also seen with model emulsions in which the surface of the emulsion particles is covered with protein or phospholipid. In fact, triglyceride particles covered with dietary phospholipid and protein together with the slightly acidic pH of postprandial stomach contents are probably ideal conditions for pregastric lipase hydrolysis. At acidic pH (5–6) the released long-chain fatty acids are protonated and should remain associated to the oil phase, that is, the emulsion particle (24). This is supported by observations by light microscopy of lipolysis by rat lingual lipase (25). Hence, at least *in vitro* gastric lipolysis will soon slow down, probably due to product inhibition, that is, accumulation of protonated free fatty acids. At higher pH, as in the duodenal contents, the long-chain fatty acids progressively become ionized (pK 7.0) and form fatty acid soaps. These distribute between the aqueous and oil/water interphases of duodenal content (24). At the interphase the soaps compete with, and thus desorb, components of the milk fat globule membrane into the aqueous phase. Hence, inhibition of colipase-dependent pancreatic lipase is relieved. This view is supported from studies *in vitro*. When colipase-dependent pancreatic lipase, by itself devoid of activity against milk fat globule triglyceride, was added (as human pancreatic juice) after purified pregastric lipase had hydrolyzed a few percent of the milk triglyceride, the rate of activity became much higher than the sum of activities for each lipase alone (Table III). In other words, gastric lipolysis had transformed the milk fat globule to a substrate accessible for hydrolysis by the pancreatic enzyme.

TABLE III

Effect of Pregastric Lipase on Pancreatic Juice-Catalyzed Lipolysis[a]

Addition	Fatty acid released[b] (μmol)
Pancreatic juice[c]	0.1
Pregastric lipase[d]	0.5
Pregastric lipase + pancreatic juice	5.7

[a]Incubation mixtures contained 200 μl/ml pasteurized human milk, 0.2% bovine serum albumin (as fatty acid acceptor), 0.15 *M* NaCl, 5 m*M* Ca^{2+}, and 2 m*M* of a physiological mixture of bile salts (26). The pH was 6.0 during the first 30 min and then raised to 7.6.

[b]After 60 min of incubation 1 ml of assay mixtures was withdrawn and the free fatty acids extracted and titrated.

[c]Human pancreatic juice (20 μl/ml) was added after 30 min of incubation.

[d]Purified pregastric lipase (2 μg/ml) was added at start.

V. MILK TRIGLYCERIDE DIGESTION IN DUODENAL CONTENTS

Hydrolysis of milk fat globule triglyceride by colipase-dependent pancreatic lipase is further enhanced by colipase and bile salts. We found that the inhibition caused by the milk fat globule membrane can also be relieved by colipase (10). When colipase was added to an incubation of purified colipase-dependent lipase with milk fat globules there was a dramatic increase in activity. This was also true in the absence of any bile salt, although the effect was enhanced by bile salt (Fig. 2). Thus, the sole function of colipase cannot be to overcome an inhibition caused by bile salt as previously thought. Somehow it also improves the catalytical efficiency of the lipase at the substrate surface. This effect might be as important. This is consistent with a similar effect of colipase observed with model emulsions with a surface coat of protein or phospholipid (12). Note, however, that colipase, in concentration of the pancreatic juice, could not by itself relieve the inhibition of lipase (Table III).

A. Pancreatic Carboxylic Ester Hydrolase

Like colipase-dependent lipase, carboxylic ester hydrolase (CEH) is also secreted into duodenal contents during fat digestion. This enzyme was previously not thought to be a true lipase, that is, to have activity

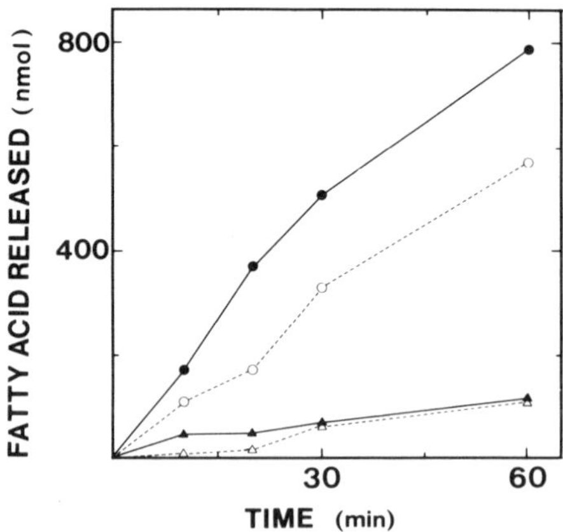

Fig. 2. Effect of colipase and/or bile salt on the hydrolysis of milk fat globules by colipase-dependent lipase. 0.15 μg/ml lipase was added at start. As indicated, 1.5 m*M* sodium taurocholate (NaTC) and/or colipase (40 μg/ml) was added 10 min before the lipase. Other conditions were as in Fig. 1. [△---△, No addition; ▲——▲, NaTC; ○---○, colipase; ●——●, colipase and NaTC.] [For details see Bläckberg *et al.* (10). Reproduced by copyright permission of the American Society for Clinical Investigation.]

against emulsified lipids. The name cholesteryl ester hydrolase denoted its function to hydrolyze cholesteryl- and fat-soluble vitamin esters (27). However, the enzyme is a nonspecific lipase which in fact at similar rates can hydrolyze a variety of milk lipids independent of physical state or chemical structure. Hence, its activity against emulsions of long-chain triglyceride is higher than that against cholesteryl ester (28). Therefore, its role in milk triglyceride digestion has probably not been fully recognized. This may be illustrated by the fact that in suckling rats the counterpart of CEH is the major lipolytic enzyme secreted from the pancreas; it is not until the rats are weaned that the colipase-dependent lipase becomes dominating (29). Thus, CEH may be of particular importance during the neonatal period or when milk is the main food and thus it may be one of the reasons for efficient fat digestion in spite of low activities of colipase-dependent lipase.

B. Human Milk Bile Salt-Stimulated Lipase

In man, contradictory to most other species, an immunochemically identical counterpart to CEH is secreted with the milk (28). This enzyme, the bile salt-stimulated lipase (BSSL), but for a slightly higher molecular weight, is in other respects identical to CEH (Table IV) and it is assumed that the two share a common physiological function (34). There is much evidence that BSSL is synthesized in the mammary gland and not in the pancreas (35). Hence, it is tempting to speculate that the same gene is coding for the two enzymes but that this gene, normally repressed in

TABLE IV

Comparison of Carboxylic Ester Hydrolase of Human Pancreatic Juice and Bile Salt-Stimulated Lipase of Human Milk[a]

Characteristic	Carboxylic ester hydrolase	Bile salt-stimulated lipase
Molecular weight	100,000	107,000
N-terminus	Alanine	Alanine
Percentage proline residues	13	11
Specific activity, long-chain triglyceride	84[b]	87
Specific activity, cholesteryl ester	0.8[b]	0.8
Cofactor	Primary bile salt	Primary bile salt
Inhibition by eserine and diisopropylfluorophosphate	Yes	Yes

[a]Data collected from Rudd and Brockman (27), Bläckberg *et al.* (28), Bläckberg and Hernell (30), Lombardo *et al.* (31), Wang and Lee (32), and Wang and Johnson (33).

[b]Micromoles fatty acid released per minute and milligram protein.

the mammary gland, has become derepressed in man and a few other species (36). BSSL constitutes about 1% of the milk protein (30); its concentration is also high in milk of mothers delivering preterm (37) and of unprivileged mothers in developing countries (38). In fact, from indirect measurements it can be deduced that the major part of this enzyme activity (at least two-thirds) in postprandial duodenal contents after a milk meal is due to BSSL, while the minor part is of endogenous origin, that is, due to CEH (39).

In spite of its high concentration in milk BSSL is not active in the milk itself. For activity against an emulsion of long-chain triglyceride it must first be activated. This activation exclusively occurs with certain bile salts, that is, BSSL is first activated when it reaches the duodenal contents, where it mixes with bile (40). The specificity in activation as well as a protective effect of bile salts against degradation by intestinal proteases is also shared between CEH and BSSL.

C. Bile Salt-Stimulated Lipase as Promotor of Milk Triglyceride Digestion

Interestingly, with human milk fat globule triglyceride as substrate, not even activation of BSSL by a proper bile salt is enough to cause hydrolysis *in vitro* (Fig. 3). It seems that the milk fat globule membrane impedes the action of BSSL, as it does for colipase-dependent lipase, illustrating that the native globule is not the physiological substrate. Again, however, if a few percent of the triglycerides are first hydrolyzed by pregastric lipase, the generated fatty acid soaps *in vivo*, probably together with other factors such as bile salts (11) and the shear forces that the globules are exposed to in the stomach and during passage through the pyloric canal (24), will cause disruption of the milk fat globule membrane. This allows binding of BSSL (and CEH) to the globule surface and thus hydrolysis of the triglycerides is promoted. The principal phenomenon is illustrated in Fig. 3. Note the difference in rate of hydrolysis (30–60 min) when BSSL is operating alone compared to when it acts together (after) with pregastric lipase. Obviously, pregastric lipase together with BSSL, with minor contribution of CEH, constitutes a route of milk triglyceride digestion even in the complete absence of colipase-dependent lipase. Thus, BSSL is the most obvious reason for the more efficient utilization of triglyceride from human milk than from cow's milk-based formula. This view gains support from balance studies of fat absorption in preterm infants. Pasteurization of milk that completely inactivates BSSL (40) reduced the coefficient of fat absorption by approximately one-third (41). Likewise, in another study the coefficient of fat absorption was about one-third lower from pasteurized banked milk as compared with fresh, raw milk delivered by the preterm infant's own

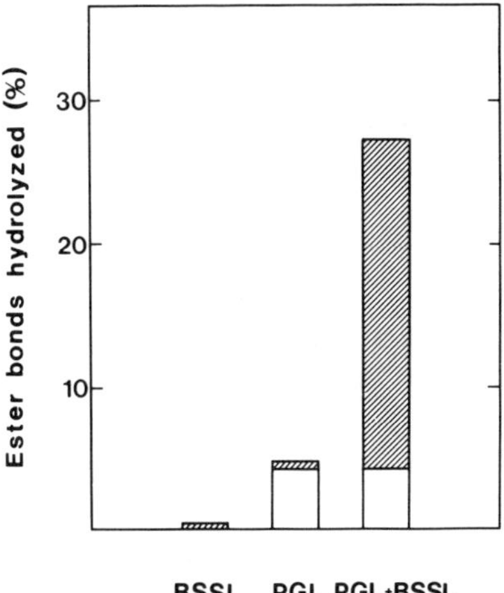

Fig. 3. Initiating effect of pregastric lipase on milk triglyceride digestion by BSSL. Incubations contained 200 μl/ml pasteurized human milk, 2% bovine serum albumin, and 0.15 *M* NaC1. The pH was 6.0 during the first 30 min, whereafter it was raised to 9.0. At the same time sodium taurocholate (5 m*M*) was added. Purified pregastric lipase (1 μg/ml) (PGL) and/or bile salt-stimulated lipase (20 μg/ml) (BSSL) were added at start as indicated. It should be noted that pasteurization inactivates BSSL in milk (40). Thus, the milk itself was devoid of activity. After 60 min aliquots of 1 ml were withdrawn and the released fatty acids extracted and titrated. Values are ester bonds hydrolyzed as a percentage of total ester bonds. □, 0–30 min; ▨, 30–60 min.

mother (42). Consistent with this we found that the retinyl ester-hydrolyzing capacity of postprandial duodenal contents in preterm infants was threefold higher 1 hr after a meal of raw as compared with pasteurized human milk (39). This also illustrates the importance of BSSL in the breast-fed infant's utilization of vitamin A in milk.

That BSSL and CEH are true nonspecific lipases is also illustrated by their lack of positional specificity, that is, contradictory to colipase-dependent lipase, all three fatty acids are released from a triglyceride molecule so that the end products of digestion are free glycerol and free fatty acid. This is particularly well illustrated when, in a model system, colipase-dependent lipase is acting with or without support from BSSL. The pancreatic enzyme hydrolyzes an emulsion of long-chain triglyceride to mainly *sn*-2 monoglyceride and free fatty acid. Since reesterification to triglyceride from mono- and diglyceride also occurs (43), the reaction reaches an equilibrium and net lipolysis stops unless the lipolytic products are effectively removed, that is, *in vivo* by absorption. Low intraduodenal bile salt concentrations in newborn infants (8,9) may make this a slow process. If BSSL is added to such a mixture at equilibrium the relative concentration of *sn*-2 monoglyceride rapidly decreases, while the relative concentration of free glycerol increases (44). Evidently, the sn-2 monoglyceride is an excellent substrate for BSSL, which thus confers a terminating step to triglyceride digestion. Since glycerol is completely water soluble it will be released from the interphase into the water, where it is no longer available for reesterification. Hence, lipolysis proceeds to completeness.

VI. ABSORPTION OF HUMAN MILK TRIGLYCERIDE

A shift of the end products of triglyceride digestion to glycerol, rather than *sn*-2 monoglyceride, and three, rather than two, free fatty acids for eaach triglyceride may also favor absorption. Indirect evidence supports the view that absorption of free fatty acid is less hampered than that of monoglyceride when intraluminal bile salt concentrations are low. This probably reflects a difference in distribution of these two lipolytic products between the oil and aqueous phases, that is, at low bile salt concentration the ratio of fatty acid to monoglyceride is higher in the aqueous phase, from which absorption occurs, than in the oil phase. Thus, absorption in newborn infants who are known to have low intraluminal bile salt concentration, and thus a reduced capacity to solubilize the end products of lipolysis as mixed micelles, should benefit from the BSSL hydrolysis of monoglyceride to fatty acid and glycerol (44). This could also explain why fat absorption does not seem to be dependent on the intraluminal bile salt concentration in breast-fed infants, while it certainly is in infants fed cow's milk-based formula (8).

Also of importance in this respect is the recent suggestion that in aqueous duodenal contents unilamellar vesicles coexist with mixed micelles. According to Carey *et al.* (24), the vesicular phase should be dominating at a low bile salt to lipid ratio, which is the situation of the newborn. It is tempting to speculate that fatty acid has a higher solubility in the vesicular phase than has monoglyceride. This, as well as the complete absorptive process, is an important area of future research, particularly in the breast-fed infant.

ACKNOWLEDGMENTS

We thank Ms. Mona Olsson for excellent secretarial assistance. Financial support from the Swedish Medical Research Council (19X-05708), the Medical Council of Swedish Life Insurance Companies, the Swedish Nutrition Foundation, the Swedish Society of Medical Sciences, and the Medical Faculty, University of Umeå, is gratefully acknowledged.

REFERENCES

1. A. F. Hofmann and B. Borgström, *J. Clin. Invest.* **43,** 247 (1964).
2. H. Brockerhoff, *Biochim. Biophys. Acta* **159,** 296 (1968).
3. B. Borgström, C. Erlanson-Albertsson, and T. Wieloch, *J. Lipid Res.* **20,** 805 (1979).
4. A. F. Hofmann and H. S. Mekhjian, *in* "The Bile Acids" (P. P. Nair and D. Kritchevsky, eds.), Vol. 2, p. 103. Plenum, New York, 1971.
5. G. Zoppi, G. Andreotti, F. Pajno-Ferrara, D. M. Njai, and D. Gaburro, *Pediatr. Res.* **6,** 880 (1972).
6. E. Lebenthal and P. C. Lee, *Pediatrics* **66,** 556 (1980).
7. B. Fredrikzon and T. Olivecrona, *Pediatr. Res.* **12,** 631 (1978).
8. E. Signer, G. M. Murphy, S. Edkins, and C. M. Anderson, *Arch. Dis. Child.* **49,** 174 (1974).
9. M. J. Brueton, H. M. Berger, G. A. Brown, L. Ablitt, N. Iyngkaran, and B. A. Wharton, *Gut* **19,** 95 (1978).
10. L. Bläckberg, O. Hernell, and T. Olivecrona, *J. Clin. Invest.* **67,** 1748 (1981).
11. S. Patton, B. Borgström, B. H. Stemberger, and U. Welsch, *J. Pediatr., Gastroenterol. Nutr.* **5,** 262 (1986).
12. L. Bläckberg, O. Hernell, G. Bengtsson, and T. Olivecrona, *J. Clin. Invest.* **64,** 1303 (1979).
13. F. Schoenheyder and K. Volqvartz, *Acta Physiol. Scand.* **11,** 349 (1946).
14. B. Borgström, G. Lundh, A. Dahlqvist, and J. Sjövall, *J. Clin. Invest.* **36,** 1521 (1957).
15. J. S. Patton, *in* "Physiology of the Gastrointestinal Tract" (L. R. Johnson, ed.), p. 1123. Raven, New York, 1981.
16. D. P. R. Muller, J. P. K. McCollum, R. S. Trompeter, and J. T. Harries, *Gut* **16,** 838 (1975).
17. B. Fredrikzon and L. Bläckberg, *Pediatr. Res.* **14,** 1387 (1980).
18. M. Hamosh, *in* "Lipases" (B. Borgström and H. L. Brockman, eds.), p. 49. Elsevier, Amsterdam, 1984.
19. L. Bläckberg, O. Hernell, B. Fredrikzon, and H. K. Åkerblom, *Acta Paediatr. Scand.* **66,** 473 (1977).
20. S. Bernbäck, O. Hernell, and L. Bläckberg, *Eur. J. Biochem.* **148,** 233 (1985).
21. R. B. Field and R. O. Scow, *J. Biol. Chem.* **258,** 14563 (1983).
22. A. J. P. Docherty, M. W. Bodmer, S. Angal, R. Verger, C. Riviere, P. A. Lowe, A. Lyons, J. S. Emtage, and T. J. R. Harris, *Nucleic Acids Res.* **13,** 1891 (1985).
23. C. Tiruppathi and K. A. Balasubramanian, *Biochim. Biophys. Acta* **712,** 692, (1982).
24. M. C. Carey, D. M. Small, and C. M. Bliss, *Annu. Rev. Physiol.* **45,** 651 (1983).
25. J. S. Patton, M. W. Rigler, T. H. Liao, P. Hamosh, and M. Hamosh, *Biochim. Biophys. Acta* **712,** 400 (1982).
26. A.-L. Järvenpää, D. K. Rassin, P. Kuitunen, G. E. Gaull, and N. C. R. Räihä, *Pediatrics* **72,** 677 (1983).
27. E. A. Rudd and H. L. Brockman, *in* "Lipases" (B. Borgström and H. L. Brockman, eds.), p. 185. Elsevier, Amsterdam, 1984.
28. L. Bläckberg, D. Lombardo, O. Hernell, O. Guy, and T. Olivecrona, *FEBS Lett.* **136,** 284 (1981).
29. W. S. Bradshaw and W. J. Rutter, *Biochmistry* **11,** 1517 (1972).
30. L. Bläckberg and O. Hernell, *Eur. J. Biochem.* **116,** 221 (1981).
31. D. Lombardo, O. Guy, and C. Figarella, *Biochim. Biophys. Acta* **527,** 142 (1978).
32. C.-S. Wang and D. M. Lee, *J. Lipid Res.* **26,** 824 (1985).
33. C.-S. Wang and K. Johnson, *Anal. Biochem.* **133,** 457 (1983).
34. O. Hernell and L. Bläckberg, *J. Pediatr., Gastroenterol. Nutr.* **2,** S242 (1983).

35. L. Bläckberg, P.-J. Blindh, B. Ljungberg, and O. Hernell, *J. Pediatr., Gastroenterol. Nutr.* **4,** 441 (1985).
36. O. Hernell, L. Bläckberg, and S. Bernbäck, *in* "Proteins and Non-Protein Nitrogen in Human Milk" (S. A. Atkinson and B. Lönnerdal, eds.). CRC Press, Boca Raton, Florida, in press.
37. N. R. Mehta, J. B. Jones, and M. Hamosh, *J. Pediatr., Gastroenterol Nutr.* **1,** 317 (1982).
38. O. Hernell, M. Gebre-Medhin, and T. Olivecrona, *Am. J. Clin. Nutr.* **30,** 508 (1977).
39. B. Fredrikzon, O. Hernell, L. Bläckberg, and T. Olivecrona, *Pediatr. Res.* **12,** 1048 (1978).
40. O. Hernell, *Eur. J. Clin. Invest.* **5,** 267 (1975).
41. S. Williamson, E. Finucane, H. Ellis, and H. R. Gamsu, *Arch. Dis. Child.* **53,** 555 (1978).
42. S. A. Atkinson, M. H. Bryan, and G. H. Anderson, *Pediatrics* **99,** 617 (1981).
43. B. Borgström, *Biochim. Biophys. Acta* **13,** 491 (1954).
44. O. Hernell and L. Bläckberg, *Pediatr. Res.* **16,** 882 (1982).

21

Polio and Typhoid Vaccinations of Lactating Women and the Antibody Response in the Milk

Barbro Carlsson[*,†], L. Å. Hanson[†], and Mirjana Hahn-Zoric[*,†]
*Department of Pediatrics
†Department of Clinical Immunology
University of Göteborg
Göteborg, Sweden

Fehmida Jalil
Department of Social and Preventive Pediatrics
King Edward Medical College
Lahore, Pakistan

I. INTRODUCTION

The dominating immunoglobulin in human milk is secretory IgA, sIgA, a molecule which is specially adapted to function on mucus membranes. The secretory IgA response in milk has been demonstrated to originate especially from antigenic stimulation in the gut. Lymphoid cells in the Peyer's patches home to various sites of local sIgA production after they have been in contact with antigen originating from the intestine. This homing of cells from the gut to the mammary gland is called the *enteromammaric pathway* and gives a possibility for the newborn breast-fed infant to receive passive mucosal protection against antigens which are exposing the gut. A similar transfer of sIgA antibody production is also produced by the bronchomammaric pathway, where inhaled antigens can stimulate transfer of committed lymphocytes to the mammary gland (Hanson and Brandtzaeg, 1987).

It is usually difficult to induce a long-lasting local sIgA response, since the immunologic memory is weak. The sIgA response, seems to remain only for a few weeks or months. Bacterial and viral infections often give an antibody response in both secretions and serum (Waldman and Ganguly, 1974). Local immune responses are mainly the result of antigen stimulation on the mucosa, but this is not applicable to the mammary gland.

A secretory response can be seen after vaccinations, depending on which route of vaccination is used and also on the type of vaccine, for example, live or inactivated. The best intestinal immunity was seen in an animal model for cholera toxoid with a subcutaneous priming and subsequent oral boosting (Pierce and Sack, 1977). In other studies the most efficient sIgA response has been obtained after mucosal priming followed by a parenteral booster. This was the case for Pakistani women naturally exposed to *Vibrio cholerae,* who showed increased sIgA levels in breast milk after parenteral vaccination. A similar increase was not seen in Swedish, nonexposed women (Svennerholm *et al.*, 1980).

II. VACCINATION OF LACTATING MOTHERS

A. Poliovirus Vaccine

Natural exposure to poliovirus or vaccination with live vaccine is known to give an antibody response in secretions as well as in serum (Ogra *et al.*, 1983). Inactivated poliovirus vaccine given parenterally to Pakistani mothers has been shown to give a boost of the milk sIgA antibodies (Svennerholm *et al.*, 1981; Hanson *et al.*, 1984). Swedish mothers who were not exposed to wild poliovirus and vaccinated with a parenteral inactivated vaccine gave a minor and short-lasting milk sIgA response (Svennerholm *et al.*, 1981).

We have studied lactating women in Pakistan after vaccination with either live trivalent Oral-Virelon (Behringwerke AG, Mahrburg-Lahn,

Marburg, FRG), Swedish killed trivalent poliovirus vaccine (Swedish National Bacteriological Laboratory, Solna, Sweden), or Dutch trivalent inactivated vaccine (kindly provided by Dr. Van Wezel, Rijks Instituut voor de Volksgesundheid, Bilthoven, The Netherlands). A fourth group of women was first given oral vaccine followed 2 weeks later by a parenteral booster. An unvaccinated control group was also followed during the same time period.

When live peroral polio vaccine was offered to Pakistani women the prevaccination sIgA milk antibody titers often decreased dramatically. If a booster was given after oral vaccination with inactivated Swedish vaccine, the antibody titers did increase.

The reason for the decrease of milk sIgA antibody titers after vaccination with live poliovirus vaccine is not clear. Already after 2 weeks it was possible to induce a booster response if a parenteral vaccine was used, which speaks against tolerance as an explanatory mechanism. A temporary suppressor effect would be a more likely explanation for this decrease. It is also possible that live vaccine virus propagates in the gut and causes the specific IgA-producing cells to redistribute to the gut from the mammary gland. There are other studies though which demonstrate similar antibody level decreases after food proteins were given perorally during early lactation (Cruz and Hanson, 1987).

The milk antibody levels were increasing when the inactivated poliovirus vaccines were administered to the Pakistani women, who were all showing prevaccination titers due to exposure to wild poliovirus. The Swedish vaccine did cause increases of milk sIgA titers, but the response was not very long-lasting and attained levels close to those of prevaccination within 6–8 weeks.

A more impressive rise in sIgA antibody titers was seen after vaccination with the inactivated Dutch vaccine. After a 50-fold increase during the first 2 weeks the titers again came down to prevaccination levels at about 8 weeks after the vaccine dose was given.

It is obvious that inactivated poliovirus vaccine can induce a sIgA response in milk, especially when given to mothers who have been primed in the gut by wild poliovirus. The Dutch vaccine seemed to give a more dramatic increase, which probably can be explained by the fact that it is very antigen rich compared to the Swedish vaccine.

B. Typhoid Vaccine

To study whether the decrease in milk sIgA levels to poliovirus antigen after vaccination with live poliovirus vaccine was unique to this vaccine, or could also be demonstrated with another peroral live vaccine, such as the new typhoid vaccine described by Wahdan *et al.* (1980), another study was designed. Groups of 10 Pakistani women were vaccinated with lyophilized live typhoid vaccine, Vivotif Bern (Swiss Serum and Vaccine Institute, Bern, Switzerland), given in capsules perorally. Two groups were given either live poliovirus vaccine (Behringwerke AG, Mahrburg-Lahn, Marburg, FRG) or a heat-inactivated whole-cell cholera vaccine (Swedish National Bacteriological Laboratory, Solna, Sweden) together with the typhoid vaccine. A typhoid vaccine in a more stable capsule was given to one group, and both poliovirus vaccine as well as cholera vaccine were also given alone. A control group of unvaccinated women was followed during the same period.

All the mothers had antibodies in serum, milk, and saliva directed against the lipopolysaccaride (LPS) antigen from the typhoid vaccine strain, Ty21a and Ty2 (equivalent to Ty21a), before vaccination. The typhoid vaccine gave a good serum IgG antibody response with 9 of 10 mothers showing increases. Only 4 of 10 mothers showed small sIgA increases in their breast milk and 3 of 10 had decreasing levels. The salivary sIgA levels were not affected by the vaccination. The group of mothers who were given the more efficiently coated vaccine capsules had a much higher IgG antibody response in serum but there was still little effect on the sIgA antibody levels in secretions.

The combination of either cholera or live poliovirus vaccine with the typhoid vaccination had no apparent effect on the typhoid antibody response. The number of responders was approximately the same in all groups. The typhoid vaccine had no striking effect on the antibody responses to either *V. cholera* LPS or poliovirus type I antigens in the two groups given the vaccines in combination. The parenteral cholera vaccine given alone showed a very striking serum IgG antibody increase as well as a sIgA milk response against *V. cholera* LPS antigen. The live poliovirus vaccine had only minor effects on either serum IgG antibody levels against poliovirus antigen or the mucosal sIgA response.

The typhoid vaccine thus gave a consistent serum IgG response and surprisingly only a very minor milk sIgA response. Combination of the typhoid, polio, and cholera vaccines did not influence either positively or negatively the serum or the sIgA response. The explanation for this limited sIgA response is not obvious but may be partly due to high prevaccination titers.

It has been suggested that milk sIgA antibodies originate not only from local production in the mammary gland but that dimers of IgA are also transported from serum to the milk via the secretory component on the epithelial cells. There is evidence for such a transfer in mice (Halsey *et al.*, 1983), but similar findings in man are not available. It is, however, of importance to determine the origin of milk antibodies, since it may have relevance in determining the most optimal mode of vaccination to induce a sIgA response. It is possible that the response may vary for different antigens. It has been demonstrated that when rats are immunized in the Peyer's patches with *Escherichia coli* O6 bacteria carrying type 1 pili, more of the IgA anti-O6 LPS antibodies could be found in bile than in milk in these animals. The reverse could be shown for the IgA antibodies against the pili antigen (Hanson *et al.*, (1986). The mechanism behind this difference between antigens is not known, but it may be necessary in the future to test various antigens before they are assumed to have effect on the milk antibody increase.

III. CONCLUSION

Milk antibodies can be influenced by parenteral and peroral vaccination of the mother. Parenteral vaccination of women living in areas where a natural exposure of virus or bacteria in the gut is very likely to have occurred quite consistently have an enhanced milk sIgA response after parenteral administration of a vaccine. Perorally given vaccines more often give rise to decreasing milk antibody levels. Breast milk antibodies against poliovirus antigen may be of special interest in developing countries since poliomyelitis is still common among young infants. The protective value of the milk sIgA antibodies has to be further investigated. Since the magnitude of the milk antibody response seems to be dependent on the antigen content of the vaccine, and also the route of vaccination, it will be of great importance to develop antigen-rich vaccines for parenteral use which can be a safe alternative for use in developing countries to protect both mothers and infants.

ACKNOWLEDGMENTS

The skillful technical assistance of Eeva Nisshagen, Eva Ågren, Ingela Carlsson, and Monica Sundbom is highly appreciated. The studies were supported by grants from the Swedish Medical Research Council (No. 215), the Swedish Agency for Research Cooperation with Developing Countries, the Ellen, Walter, and Lennart Hesselman Foundation for Research, and the Swedish National Bank Fund.

REFERENCES

Cruz, J. R., and Hanson, L. Å. (1987). *J. Pediatr., Gastroenterol. Nutr.* (in press).

Halsey, J. F., Craig, M., and McKenzie, S. J. (1983). *Ann. N.Y. Acad. Sci.* **409,** 452–460.

Hanson, L. Å., and Brandtzaeg, P. (1987). *In* "Immunological Diseases in Infants and Children," 3rd Ed., Saunders, Philadelphia, Pennsylvania (in press).

Hanson, L. Å., Carlsson, B., Jalil, F., Lindblad, B. S., Khan, S. R., and van Wezel, A. L. (1984). *Rev. Infect. Dis.* **6,** Suppl. 2, 356–360.

Hanson, L. Å., Ahlstedt, S., Carlsson, B., Dahlgren, U., Hahn-Zoric, M., Jalil, F., Khan, S. R., Mellander, L., Porras, O., and Wold, A. (1986). *In* Human Lactation 2. Maternal–Environmental Factors. (S. M. Hamosh and A. Goldman, eds.), pp. 541–545. Raven, New York.

Ogra, P. L., Losonsky, G. A., and Fishaut, M. (1983). *Ann. N.Y. Acad. Sci.* **409,** 82–95.

Pierce, N. F., and Sack, R. B. (1977). *J. Infect. Dis.* **136,** S113–S117.

Svennerholm, A. M., Hanson, L. Å., Holmgren, J., Lindblad, B. S., Nilsson, B., and Quereshi, F. (1980). *Infect. Immun.* **30,** 427–430.

Svennerholm, A. M., Hanson, L. Å., Holmgren, J., Jalil, F., Lindblad, B. S., Khan, S. R., Nilsson, B., and Svennerholm, B. (1981). *J. Infect. Dis.* **143,** 707–711.

Wahdan, M. H., Serie, Ch., Germanier, R., Lackany, A., Cerisier, Y., Guerin, N., Sallam, S., Geoffrey, P., Sadekel Tantawi, A., and Guesny, P. (1980). *Bu WHO* **58,** 469–474.

Waldman, R. H., and Ganguly, R. (1974). *J. Infect. Dis.* **130,** 419–440.

Discussion: Part III. The First Feed A. General Comments

Gyula Soltész
Department of Pediatrics
University Medical School of Pécs
Pécs, Hungary

Dr. Gishan has studied the developmental maturation of intestinal transport of D-glucose, taurocholate, calcium, and phosphate in suckling, weanling, and adolescent rats. Following the preparation of brush border membrane vesicles, he measured the uptake of radiolabeled substrates by the rapid filtration technique.

D-Glucose uptake was extremely fast during the first 20 sec of incubation at all ages, but this rapid glucose accumulation was of a lesser magnitude in young, suckling animals. Since glucose uptake is Na^+-dependent and the isolated uptake of Na^+ tracer was found to be faster in suckling rats, the decreased initial glucose "overshoot" was interpreted as a result of a faster dissipation of the Na^+ gradient.

Active taurocholate transport was found to be poorly developed in the suckling rat but fully active by the time of weaning and inducible by corticosteroids. It may be of some interest to note that premature infants have a decreased pool and biosynthesis of bile acids and possibly their rate of absorption is also decreased.

Calcium transport was investigated by the *in vivo* perfusion technique, by the *in vitro* everted sacs technique, and by using isolated brush border and basolateral membranes. It was also mainly a passive process during the suckling period as compared to the predominantly carrier-mediated process by the time of weaning.

In contrast to glucose, taurocholate, and calcium, phosphate transport was very rapid in the younger animals with a progressive decline with increasing postnatal age.

In summary, Dr. Gishan's studies demonstrated the postnatal developmental changes of intestinal transport processes, emphasizing that the trends are not similar for all transport mechanisms. The different ontogenic trends of the intestinal transport of calcium and phosphate are of particular significance in view of their complex interrelationships. It would be fascinating to know whether such transport systems are operational in the human. The rapid postnatal maturation of calcium and phosphate transport is especially relevant for the better understanding of the rickets of prematurity.

Dr. V. Young's paper has reminded us of the insufficiency of our information regarding both the overall protein synthesis rate as well as the kinetics of the individual amino acids in the newborn infant.

As his review table has shown, the variation in the estimated rates of protein synthesis published by the various groups is more than fivefold. In my opinion, this must be due mainly to methodological variables since such enormous differences in the growth rate of the human newborns studied are unlikely. In fact, some of the published values are almost as high as those we have measured in the newborn lamb, which grows at a rate several times faster than the human infant (1). The study of methionine–cysteine relationships might solve the controversy over the essentiality of cystine in view of the conflicting enzymatic and direct metabolic studies.

Leucine and alanine are also good examples for future kinetic studies in the neonate. In fact, preliminary data of neonatal leucine utilization using [1-^{13}C]-leucine have just been published by a German group (2). Threonine can be another important candidate for stable isotope studies in view of the very high threonine levels reported in formula-fed premature infants.

The current renaissance in the popularity of breast-feeding has stimulated renewed interest in the regulation of milk synthesis, composition, and flow. In taking advantage of the precision provided by averaging electronic balances, Dr. Baum used the "fractional test weighing" technique to study the regulation of milk flow. In the first part of their paper, simple and elegant studies (the cross-nursing experiment was particularly impressive) demonstrated that both the mother and her baby influence the rate and pattern of milk flow. Then some special aspects of these maternal and infant factors were separately considered. Since the most relevant maternal factor that has an immediate effect on milk flow at a feed is the oxytocin-mediated milk ejection reflex, this was discussed in more detail by reviewing some published data.

The major part of the paper, however, dealt with some of the infant factors studied by using two novel methods. (1) They visualized the developmental changes of intraoral dynamics during feeding using ultrasound, although it has yet to be quantified how these changes affect the rate of milk flow. (2) With the use of a flow transducer mounted in a nipple shield they succeeded in making uninterrupted measurements of milk intake. Used in conjunction with sequential milk sampling, the flow as well as the composition of suckled breast milk could be obtained.

The demonstrated data gave a true insight into the physiological changes during a feed by describing the relationship between milk flow and sucking patterns as well as between milk flow and milk composition. Perhaps one of the most interesting observations was the inverse relationship between the rate of milk flow and the fat content of that milk. This observation provides a firm physiological basis for the old maternal wisdom that even small amounts of milk taken at the end of the feed on the second breast are important for the baby, because they may contribute significantly to the infant's net caloric intake.

Although the presence of a potent lipase in human milk (Frauenmilchlipase) was described more than 30 years ago, the biological significance of this enzyme has become known only during the last decade.

Dr. Hernell's work helped us to understand that the secretion of the "bile salt-stimulated lipase" (BSSL) with the human milk is an adaptation to the special conditions in the gastrointestinal tract of the newborn, which is characterized by low intraduodenal concentrations of pancreatic lipase and bile salts. This lipase supplements the low pancreatic lipase activities and also hydrolyzes the monoacylglycerols produced by pancreatic lipase.

Another important aspect of neonatal fat digestion is the function of lingual (pregastric) lipase, which renders the surface of the milk fat globule more accessible to both pancreatic and milk lipase.

Thus, the BSSL together with pregastric lipase ensures efficient milk triglyceride digestion. It is of interest, particularly in light of Dr. Stahlman's presentation yesterday, that 80% of vitamin A in the human milk is esterified, so it also needs to be hydrolyzed. One would also like to know the postnatal dynamics of these enzymes and how this is affected by the type of feeding, for example, intermittent and continuous gastric feeding and transpyloric feeding.

Dr. Carlson's work on the antibody response in the milk of polio- and typhoid-vaccinated lactating women began to explore new and promising possibilities for the protection of the newborn exposed to dangerous viral and bacterial organisms.

REFERENCES

1. G. Soltész, J. Joyce, and M. Young, *Biol. Neonate* **23,** 139 (1973).
2. W. Park, *Clin. Nutr.* **5,** Spec. Suppl., p. 38, Abstr. (1986).

23

Discussion: Part III. The First Feed B. The View from the Third World Countries

Oscar Brunser
Institute of Nutrition and Food Technology (INTA)
University of Chile
Santiago, Chile

Children born in the less developed countries, especially those who belong to the lower strata of society, are subject to risks that are intimately related to their high mortality and morbidity rates and that modulate the expression of their potential for growth and development. In this context, two of the main risk factors are (1) the loss of breast-feeding and the unavailability of weaning foods adequate in quantity and quality, resulting in malnutrition and its consequences (Mönckeberg, 1983), and (2) the presence of heavy environmental microbiological contamination, which causes abnormal colonization of the gut (Mata, 1978). This leads to asymptomatic infection and environmental enteropathy and to episodes of acute diarrhea favored by the fact that formula bottles and other foodstuffs are vehicles for enteropathogens and promote the ocurrence of acute diarrhea. Diarrhea and malnutrition act synergistically and worsen the clinical condition of patients (Scrimshaw, 1983).

Malnutrition appears in two main clinical forms: marasmus, the nonedematous form of protein-energy malnutrition, and kwashiorkor, characterized by edema and signs of deficiency of vitamins and other nutrients. Pure forms of marasmus and kwashiorkor are relatively infrequent, with most patients exhibiting a mixed symptomatology (Wellcome Trust Working Party, 1970). In some countries, such as Chile, marasmus predominates, while in other areas, such as Africa, the Caribbean, and some parts of Asia, kwashiorkor and mixed forms are more frequent.

Because the gastrointestinal tract is lined by a highly differentiated epithelium with intense metabolic activity, complex transport mechanisms, and rapid cell turnover, it is logical to expect that nutrient deprivation will damage it, and this may be detected in morphological and functional studies. Many years ago we demonstrated (Brunser *et al.*, 1968) that in young infants with pure, severe marasmus due to lack of adequate food intake secondary to unfavorable socioeconomic conditions, the intestinal mucosa was thin and its architecture was preserved. The cytology of the mucosa was also normal. However, the mitotic index in the crypts of Lieberkhün was reduced. Because the total thickness of the mucosa was somewhat decreased, it is difficult to ascertain whether this lowered mitotic index truly represents a slower turnover rate or the normal replacement of a smaller cell population. Experiments in rats using tritiated thymidine confirmed a decreased cell renewal (Brown *et al.*, 1963; Wiebecke *et al.*, 1969).

By contrast, the morphology of the small intestinal mucosa in most children with kwashiorkor was severely altered, with flattening of the surface, disappearance of the villi, elongation of the crypts, damage to the surface epithelium, and increased cellularity of the lamina propria. The mitotic index was only slightly decreased. An occasional patient had a normal histology (Brunser *et al.*, 1968). Studies of the fine structure of the intestinal epithelium in marasmus disclosed alterations in many organelles: the microvilli of the brush border were short, sparse, and bi- or trifurcated in many cells. Large autophagosomes were observed in the supranuclear cytoplasm and their transition to residual bodies could be visualized in many instances. Underlying the epithelial cells, there were deposits of fibrillar and finely granular, dense material in the lamina propria. Fat droplets were sometimes embedded in these deposits. Nutritional rehabilitation was associated with improvement of this epithelial damage except for the fact that alterations in mitochondrial morphology in the cytoplasm at the base of the cells became apparent (Brunser *et al.*, 1976). This latter change could be explained by subclinical nutrient deficiencies when growth resumes. These findings have been confirmed by investigations in Brazil and in England (Martins Campos *et al.*, 1979).

In kwashiorkor, fine structural changes have been reported to vary between cases in which absorptive cells appear normal except for the accumulation of lipids in the area of the Golgi apparatus and others in which the surface epithelium is severely altered, with damage to all organelles and cytoplasmic differentiations (Shiner *et al.*, 1973; Theron *et al.*, 1971). From a functional point of view, absorption was found to be almost normal in marasmus: some cases evinced minimal disturbances of D-xylose and vitamin B_{12} absorption, while in kwashiorkor nutrient malabsorption, sometimes quite severe, was the rule (Castillo and Brunser, 1974). Histological lesions and functional disturbances of the stomach and the pancreas probably contribute to the deranged absorption of nutrients observed in these patients (Gracey *et al.*, 1977; Pitchumoni, 1973). In cases of marasmus, decreased volumes of pancreatic secretion and enzymatic activity have been reported (Danus *et al.*, 1970). Although in most publications it is mentioned that patients were free of enteral infections at the time of the study, it is not known what effects previous infections may have played in the genesis of the mucosal damage described.

Infants born in the less developed countries acquire enteropathogens and their intestinal flora very early in life. In a study carried out in 225 newborns (Araya *et al.*, 1986) during their first week of life, rotavirus was detected in 4.4% of cases. Enteropathogenic bacteria were isolated in the feces of 14% of a subsample of these infants and enteroparasites in one case (2.6%); commensals were found in 7.7% of cases. It is of interest that no differences could be established for the presence of enteropathogens in relation to the socioeconomic stratum of the children's families. In the case of rotavirus, cases were concentrated in one phototherapy ward of a hospital that provided obstetric and neonatology care to families of the low socioeconomic stratum. On the other hand, the only cases in which *Salmonella paratyphi* and *Giardia lamblia* were excreted belonged to the high socioeconomic stratum. Fecal excretion of enteropathogens always began after the third day of life, lasted for a short period of time (1 to 3 days), stopped spontaneously, and was not associated with any clinical symptoms. The absence of symptoms could be explained by two facts. One may be related to immaturity of the host's intestinal epithelium, to which enteropathogens could not adhere. This idea is supported by the fact that the electrophoresis of the viral RNA detected revealed a single electropherotype which was contemporaneously identified in older children who were admitted to hospitals in Santiago for acute diarrhea and dehydration. The other possibility refers to the protective effect of maternal milk.

We have demonstrated that asymptomatic infection in Chilean children is as frequent in breast-fed as in bottle-fed infants (Figueroa *et al.*, 1983). However, the former did not develop diarrhea. This has also been observed for *Vibrio cholera* infections in Bangladesh (Glass *et al.*, 1983). Later in life, the incidence of bacterial and parasitic carriage decreases from the 20% observed in infants to 6–8% in preschool and school-age children, to 1% in adults. As for asymptomatic infection, episodes of acute diarrhea are also more frequent among younger children. This is probably related to their immunological immaturity during the first months of life. In a longitudinal, long-term survey of children under 7 years of age living in a periurban slum in Santiago, the highest incidence of diarrhea was observed in infants (Araya *et al.*, 1985). When breast-feeding was encouraged, this was associated with a drop in the incidence of this condition in infants under 6 months of age.

Little is known about the effects of the repeated passage of enteropathogens along the gastrointestinal tract. From studies in adults it is evident that this induces asymptomatic but detectable alterations of the mucosal morphology and function, which conforms to the condition that has been called "chronic environmental enteropathy" (Scrimshaw *et al.*, 1983). It is unclear at what age these changes become established, because systematic studies have not been carried out in children. However, indirect evidence suggests that it probably begins at an early age. This is of more than academic importance, as it has been shown that it induces increased fecal losses of nutrients, which may be of significance when the diet is of borderline quality and/or quantity (Espinoza *et al.*, 1984).

REFERENCES

Araya, M., Figueroa, G., Espinoza, J., Montesinos, N., Spencer, E., and Brunser, O. (1985). *J. Hyg.* **95,** 457–467.

Araya, M., Sandino, A. M., Figueroa, G., Espinoza, J., Brunser, O., and Spencer, E. (1986). *Proc. Annu. Meet. Lat. Am. Soc. Pediatr. Res., 24th, Rio de Janeiro* **1,** 34–35.

Brown, H. O., Levine, M. L., and Lipkin, M. (1963). *Am. J. Pysiol.* **205,** 868–872.

Brunser, O., Reid, A., Mönckeberg, F., Maccioni, A., and Contreras, I. (1968). *Am. J. Clin. Nutr.* **21,** 976–980.

Brunser, O., Castillo, C., and Araya, M. (1976). *Gastroenterology* **70,** 495–507.

Castillo, C., and Brunser, O. (1974). *Rev. Chil. Pediatr.* **45,** 585–586.

Danus, O., Urbina, A. M., Valenzuela, I., and Solimano, G. (1970). *J. Pediatr.* **77,** 334–337.

Espinoza, J., Brunser, O., Araya, M., Egaña, J. I., Pacheco, I., and Krause, S. (1984). *In* "Protein Energy Requirement Studies in Developing Countries: Results of International Research" (W. M. Rand, R. Uauy, and N. S. Scrimshaw, eds.), Food Nutrition Bulletin, Suppl. 10, pp. 294–305. UNU Press, Tokyo.

Figueroa, G., Troncoso, M., Araya, M., Espinoza, J., and Brunser, O. (1983). *J. Hyg.* **91,** 499–507.

Glass, R. I., Svennerholm, A. M., Stoll, B. J., Khan, M. R., Hossain, K. M. B., Huq, M. I., and Holmgren, J. (1983). *N. Engl. J. Med.* **308,** 1389–1392.

Gracey, M., Cullity, G. J., Suharjono, Sunoto (1977). *Arch. Dis. Child.* **52,** 325–328.

Martins Campos, J. B., Neto, U. F., Patricio, F. R. S., Wehba, J., and Carvallo, A. A. (1979). *Am. J. Clin. Nutr.* **32,** 1575–1591.
Mata, L. J. (1978). "The Children of Santa Maria Cauque: A Prospective Field Study of Health and Growth," pp. 228–253. MIT Press, Cambridge, Massachusetts.
Mönckeberg, F. (1983). *In* "Nutrition Intervention Strategies in National Development" (B. A. Underwood, ed.), pp. 13–20. Academic Press, New York.
Pitchumoni, C. S. (1973). *Am. J. Clin. Nutr.* **26,** 374–379.
Scrimshaw, N. S. (1983). *In* "Nutrition Intervention Strategies in National Development" (B. A. Underwood, ed.), pp. 209–226.. Academic Press, New York.
Scrimshaw, N. S., Brunser, O., Keusch, G., Molla, A., Ozalp, I., and Torun, B. (1983). *In* "Diarrhea and Malnutrition: Interactions, Mechanisms and Intervention" (L. C. Chen and N. Scrimshaw, eds.), pp. 269–286. Plenum, New York.
Shiner, M., Redmond, A. O. B., and Hansen, J. D. L. (1973). *Exp. Mol. Pathol.* **19,** 61–78.
Theron, J. J., Wittman, W., and Prinsloo, J. G. (1971). *Exp. Mol. Pathol.* **14,** 184–199.
Wellcome Trust Working Party (1970). *Lancet* **ii,** 302–303.
Wiebecke, B., Heybowitz, R., Löhrs, U., and Eder, M. (1969). *Virchows Arch. B* **4,** 164–175.

Part IV

Special Problems Relating to the Preterm and Surgical Newborn Infant

24

Impact of Maternal Blood Glucose Control on Neonatal Morbidity in Diabetic Pregnancies

Bengt Persson and Ulf Hanson

Department of Pediatrics and
Department of Obstetrics and Gynecology
Karolinska Institutet
St. Göran's Children's Hospital and
Karolinska Hospital
Stockholm, Sweden

I. INTRODUCTION

The outlook for the offspring of a mother with diabetes melitus has continued to improve worldwide. The marked decline in both neonatal mortality and morbidity in diabetic pregnancy, seen in most specialized units throughout the world, is usually attributed to improved blood glucose control during pregnancy. Although controlled clinical trials are lacking, this explanation is supported by circumstantial evidence.

However desirable it may be to maintain maternal blood glucose close to or within the physiological range throughout pregnancy—a matter that in recent years sometimes seems to have received an almost obsessional attention—it is still uncertain how stringent the achieved degree of blood glucose control should be in order not to compromise perinatal outcome. It should also be recalled that the impact on perinatal outcome of other interventions, such as various new techniques for fetal surveillance as well as for management of neonatal complications, in particular respiratory distress, has not been assessed. Furthermore, it must be recognized that infants of diabetic mothers constitute a heterogeneous group. Thus, factors such as maternal age, weight, parity, acute complications during pregnancy, duration of diabetes, and degree of diabetic angiopathy may have pronounced effects on fetal health and development.

Before discussing in detail the relationship between maternal blood glucose control during pregnancy and neonatal morbidity, it may first be useful to consider briefly some of the pathogenic mechanisms that have been proposed to explain clinical problems in the newborn.

II. PATHOGENESIS

According to the classical hypothesis described by Pedersen, episodic maternal hyperglycemia leads to fetal hyperglycemia, which in turn stimulates the fetal pancreas to increased insulin production. The maternal hyperglycemia–fetal hyperinsulinism theory has been expanded to include the stimulatory effect of free amino acids on beta-cell replication and insulin production (1,2). This concept, which is based on animal and *in vitro* studies of isolated pancreas, is also supported by the recent observation of significant correlations not only between maternal blood glucose and amniotic fluid C-peptide as an index of fetal insulin secretion but also between maternal branched-chain amino acid and C-peptide in amniotic fluid (3). Both clinical and experimental data indicate that fetal hyperinsulinemia is accompanied by enhanced somatic growth resulting in selective organomegaly, mainly affecting adipose tissue, heart, liver, and adrenals. Fetal growth acceleration is frequently seen in association with poor metabolic control, particularly in mothers with short duration of diabetes. If, on the other hand, the fetal supply line is compromised by uterine spiral artery lesions, as is not unusual in mothers with long-standing diabetes (White's classes D–F) or mothers who develop hypertensive disorders during pregnancy, fetal growth may be severely retarded.

Maternal insulin does not cross the placenta unless there are insulin-binding antibodies present, in which case the insulin–antibody complex may be transferred to the fetus (4). It has been proposed that placental tissue could represent an additional source of insulin or insulinlike growth factors for the fetus. Thus, insulin-related genes are expressed in the human placenta and to a greater extent in the placenta of a diabetic mother; this latter finding is perhaps related to enhanced supply of nutrients (5). An excess of insulin and insulinlike growth factors has been suggested to be responsible for enlargement of the placenta with increased branching of chorionic villi (6,7). This may lead to reduction of the intervillous space and thereby to a decreased maternal placental blood flow (8) and, as a consequence, impaired fetal oxygenation. Hyperinsulinemia may further contribute to the development of fetal hypoxia. Experiments in fetal lambs have demonstrated that sustained hyperinsulinemia leads to increased peripheral oxygen consumption by approximately 25% without compensatory increase of placental blood flow (9,10). Poorly regulated maternal diabetes with elevated hemoglobin A_{1c} (HbA_{1c}) may further threaten fetal oxygen supply by decreasing red cell oxygen release (11). In addition, a significant delay in the onset of the switchover from fetal to adult hemoglobin synthesis, as was recently described in offspring of diabetic mothers, possibly as a consequence of fetal hyperinsulinemia, may also adversely influence fetal oxygen delivery (12). Elevated concentrations of erythropoietin in fetal blood and increased extramedullary erythropoiesis and polycythemia may well represent the physiological responses to acute and/or chronic episodes of fetal hypoxia (13,14).

Metabolic deviations in the newborn, such as decreased hepatic glucose production rate, hypoglycemia, increased removal rate of intravenously administered glucose, as well as suppressed lipid mobilization, can most likely be attributed to neonatal hyperinsulinism.

III. DIABETIC CONTROL AND PERINATAL OUTCOME

For obvious reasons, it is impossible to perform randomized prospective studies to compare the effects of different levels of maternal blood glucose on neonatal outcome. The impact of the intensity of care on neonatal mortality and morbidity can, however, be illustrated by results of two series of diabetic pregnancies in different hospitals in Sweden during approximately the same time period. Series I ($n = 157$), collected during 1967 to 1971 from a region without specialized care of diabetic pregnancies, showed a perinatal mortality rate of 22.3% (stillbirth rate 7.2%). Macrosomia occurred in 43.4% and idiopathic respiratory distress

(IRDS) in 9.8% of patients, respectively. Series II ($n = 107$), from 1966 to 1973, supervised at a specialized care unit, had a perinatal mortality rate of 5.6% (stillbirth rate 1.9%), a frequency of macrosomia of 16%, and of IRDS 1.9% (15,16). This marked difference in outcome between the two series could not be attributed to differences in socioeconomic factors, or access to appropriate obstetric or pediatric care, but was most likely due to a less satisfactory quality of maternal metabolic control in series I. This view is supported by a positive relationship between maximum blood glucose level during the last week of pregnancy and perinatal mortality rate. In series II there was no such relationship but mothers in this series maintained average blood glucose levels during the last trimester of pregnancy that were close to the physiological range.

A significant association between maternal blood glucose control during the last trimester of pregnancy and neonatal morbidity has been recorded by some authors (17–19) but not by others (19–21). One of the most frequently cited studies in this regard, that by Karlsson and Kjellmer (17), reports a positive association between the third trimester mean blood glucose level and the occurrence of neonatal complications such as IRDS and hyperbilirubinemia. Unfortunately, the data in this study do not allow these conclusions since gestational age at delivery is not given in the different subgroups according to blood glucose levels. Thus, the increased frequency of neonatal complications in infants born to mothers with an average blood glucose above 5.5 mmol/liter could equally well be explained by a higher frequency of prematurity in this group. The same objection could be raised against the study by Artal *et al.* (18), who found an association between the variability of the third trimester blood glucose values and neonatal morbidity. Furthermore, the frequencies of neonatal complications were equal in White classes A, B, and C, whereas they were twice as high in White class D. Glucose variability, on the other hand, was of the same magnitude in White classes C and D, suggesting that neonatal complications had to be attributed to factors other than blood glucose control alone. Excellent results with a minimal perinatal morbidity rate have recently been reported by Jovanovic and Peterson (22). This series included 53 insulin-dependent diabetic women subjected to a program of daily home monitoring of blood glucose concentration with a goal of euglycemia. The patients seemed to be highly motivated and well selected and although the degree of blood glucose control was documented only by blood glucose profiles at the start of pregnancy and just before the delivery, most patients were probably normoglycemic throughout pregnancy.

To minimize problems with selection of patients and to obtain a sufficient number of patients over a reasonable period of time, we conducted a multicenter study in the Stockholm area between 1979 and 1982 (21).

This prospective study included all diabetic pregnancies with a duration of more than 28 weeks. Two twin pregnancies, the second infants of three mothers with two pregnancies during the study period, and three cases of congenital malformations were excluded from the analyses in order to obtain statistically independent samples. The remaining 92 mothers (according to White's classification: 35 B, 22 C, 26 D, and 9 F) and their infants were divided into three groups according to the occurrence and severity of neonatal morbidity. Infants with morbidity were arbitrarily divided into two groups: minor or severe morbidity. Minor morbidity was defined as asymptomatic hypoglycemia (blood glucose below 1.7 mmol/liter), hyperbilirubinemia requiring only phototherapy, feeding problems lasting for less than 3 days, and need of observation in the neonatal intensive care unit for 4–6 days. Severe morbidity was defined as respiratory distress (IRDS or transient tachypnea), symptomatic hypoglycemia, hyperbilirubinemia requiring exchange transfusion, feeding problems for more than 3 days, and need of observation in the neonatal intensive care unit for 7 days or more.

Diabetic control was based on four daily determinations of blood glucose from the 32nd week of gestation until delivery and hemoglobin HbA_{1C} determined in early pregnancy (weeks 8 to 16), twice during the last trimester (weeks 32 and 36), and at the time of delivery. The average of the individual mean pregnancy glucose values was 5.9 mmol/liter, which is approximately 1 mmol/liter higher than values from a reference group of nondiabetic pregnant patients. Infants exhibiting severe morbidity ($n = 28$) had the following characteristic features: longer duration of maternal diabetes, higher frequency of hypertension in pregnancy, shorter gestational age at delivery, and higher frequency of premature delivery and cesarean section compared to the groups with no ($n = 35$) or minor ($n = 27$) morbidity. Somewhat unexpectedly, however, there were no significant group differences regarding hemoblobin HbA_{1C} values determined at any time during pregnancy or blood glucose control (mean or variability) during the third trimester.

Since several of the factors studied are interrelated, discriminant analysis was used to determine which factor had the greatest impact on severe morbidity. This analysis clearly demonstrated that *gestational age at delivery* had the most significant influence on the occurrence of severe morbidity. After correction had been made for gestational age, other factors such as maternal duration of diabetes, measures of third-trimester blood glucose control, HbA_{1c} values, occurrence of hypertension, and mode of delivery made no further significant contribution to the classification of severe infant morbidity. It must be noted, however, that this conclusion is only valid for the degree of blood glucose control achieved, that is, an average of 5.9 mmol/liter (range 3.9–8.5 mmol/liter).

Of course, the argument could be raised that blood glucose control early in pregnancy, during the first and second trimesters, may influence neonatal morbidity. A more recent study including 34 consecutive type-1 diabetic pregnancies from 1983 to 1984 (White classes: 12 B, 8 C, 11 D, and 3 F) confirmed an association between gestational age and the occurrence of severe neonatal morbidity. In this study, no significant differences in maternal blood glucose values during the first, second, and third trimesters were disclosed between mothers of the infants with severe morbidity compared to those with minor or no morbidity (23). This observation should not be interpreted to suggest that maternal blood glucose control during pregnancy is unimportant. This point is convincingly illustrated by the observations of Ylinen *et al.*, who related maternal HbA_{1c} to neonatal outcome (24). Mothers of infants with neonatal hypoglycemia or hyperbilirubinemia had significantly higher hemoglobin HbA_{1C} values during the second and/or third trimester of pregnancy than mothers whose infants had no such neonatal complications but were of comparable gestational age. The seemingly contradictory findings in comparing our study and that by Ylinen *et al.* can most likely be explained by differences in quality of diabetic control. The average hemoglobin HbA_{1C} in our group of patients was below +1 SD of the mean of a reference group without diabetes, whereas the average value in the study by Ylinen *et al.* exceeded their control mean HbA_{1C} by about +4 SD.

Altogether these data suggest that there is a glucose threshold for morbidity, that is, that maternal hyperglycemia becomes an important factor contributing to the development of neonatal complications when glucose values exceed a certain critical level. Particularly interesting in this context are results of a careful multiple logistic analysis of maternal factors significantly associated with macrosomia in IDMs which clearly indicated that the glucose threshold for development of macrosomia was 7.2 mmol/liter and above (25).

In view of the close association between severe morbidity and short gestational age, it is also important to consider factors contributing to preterm delivery. One such factor is the liberal use of various techniques for fetal surveillance, which may increase the risk of false positive tests and hence unnecessary preterm delivery. Apart from premature deliveries that are unavoidable because of acute severe complications during pregnancy, such as hypertension, there is also an increased frequency of spontaneous preterm labor (26–28). A spontaneous premature delivery rate as high as 26% has been reported in patients with insulin-dependent diabetes (27). It is possible that the precipitating event leading to premature labor in some patients is polyhydramnios, known to occur frequently in pregnancies complicated by diabetes. There is surprisingly little information available regarding the possible influence of blood glucose control on the occurrence of spontaneous preterm delivery. In our two series of diabetic pregnancies, the spontaneous premature delivery rates were only 10 and 6%, respectively (21,23), which corresponds to the Swedish national figure. This finding is also in exact agreement with that of 6.1% reported by Roversi *et al.* in a larger series of diabetic patients who were treated with maximal tolerated doses of insulin (28). These results suggest that the quality of diabetic control could influence the frequency of spontaneous preterm labor and thus neonatal outcome.

IV. CONCLUSION

Available data suggest that if the maternal blood glucose concentration is kept close to the physiological range, prematurity is the most important single factor predisposing to severe neonatal complications. Therefore, in addition to striving for strict diabetic control, much effort should be directed to avoiding unnecessary premature delivery.

ACKNOWLEDGMENTS

Supported by grants from the Swedish Medical Research council (project No. 3787) and Tielman's Fund for Pediatric Research.

REFERENCES

1. N. Freinkel and B. E. Metzger, *In* "Pregnancy, Metabolism, Diabetes and the Fetus" (K. Elliott, M. O'Conner, eds.), Ciba Foundation Symposium, Vol. 63, pp. 2–23. Excerpta Med. Found., Amsterdam, 1979.
2. R. D. G. Milner, *in* "The Diabetic Pregnancy. A Perinatal Perspective" (I. R. Merkatz and P. A. J. Adam, eds.), pp. 145–153. Grune & Stratton, New York, 1979.
3. B. Persson, H. Pschera, N.-O. Lunell, J. Barley, and K. A. Gumaa, *Am. J. Perinatol.* **3,** 100 (1986).
4. W. A. Bauman and R. S. Yalow, *Proc. Natl. Acad. U.S.A.* **78,** 4588 (1981).
5. K.-S. Liu, C.-Y. Wang, N. Mills, M. Gyves, and J. Ilan, *Proc. Natl. Acad. U.S.A.* **82,** 3868 (1985).
6. O. Björk and B. Persson, *Placenta* **3,** 367 (1982).
7. O. Björk and B. Persson, *Acta Obstet. Gynecol. Scand.* **63,** 37 (1984).
8. L. Nylund, N. O. Lunell, R. Lewander, B. Persson, and B. Sarby, *Am. J. Obstet. Gynecol.* **144,** 298 (1982).
9. B. S. Carson, A. F. Philipps, M. A. Simmons, F. C. Battaglia, and G. Meschia, *Pediatr. Res.* **14,** 147 (1980).
10. J. R. Milley, A. A. Rosenberg, A. F. Philipps, R. A. Molteni, M. D. Jones, and M. A. Simmons, *Am. J. Obstet. Gynecol.* **149,** 673 (1984).

11. J. Ditzel, *Fed. Proc., Fed. Am. Soc. Exp. Biol.* **38,** 2484 (1979).
12. S. P. Perrine, M. F. Greene, and D. V. Faller, *N. Engl. J. Med.* **312,** 334 (1985).
13. J. A. Widness, J. B. Susa, J. F. Garcia, D. B. Singer, P. Seghal, W. Oh, R. Schwartz, and H. C. Schwartz, *J. Clin. Invest.* **67,** 637 (1981).
14. K. Shannon, J. C. Davis, J. L. Kitzmiller, S. A. Fulcher, and H. M. Koenig, *Pediatr. Res.* **20,** 161 (1986).
15. Y. Larsson and J. Ludvigsson, *Laekartidningen* **71,** 155 (1974).
16. B. Persson, *In* "Size at Birth," Ciba Foundation Symposium, Vol. 27, p. 247. Elsevier Excerpta Med. Found., 1974.
17. K. Karlsson and I. Kjellmer, *Am. J. Obstet. Bynecol.* **112,** 213 (1972).
18. R. Artal, S. M. Golde, F. Borey, S. N. McClellan, J. Gratacos, T. Lirette, M. Montoro, P. Y. Wu, B. Anderson, and Y. Mestman, *Am. J. Obstet. Gynecol.* **147,** 537 (1983).
19. K. Leveno, J. C. Houth, L. C. Gilstrop *et al., Am. J. Obstet. Gynecol.* **135,** 853 (1979).
20. J. P. Lovin, B. R. Lovelace, M. Miodovnik, H. C. Knowles, T. P. Barden, *Am. J. Obstet. Gynecol.* **137,** 742 (1983).
21. U. Hanson, B. Persson, and M. Stangenberg, *Diabetes Res.* **3,** 71 (1986).
22. L. Jovanovic and C. M. Peterson, *Diabetes Care* **5,** Suppl. 1, p. 24 (1982).
23. U. Hanson, unpublished observations, 1986.
24. K. Ylinen, K. Raivio, and K. Teramo, *Br. J. Obstet. Gynaecol.* **88,** 961 (1981).
25. S. P. William, K. J. Leveno, D. S. Guzick, M. L. Williams, and P. J. Whalley, *Am. J. Obstet. Gynecol.* **154,** 470 (1986).
26. R. W. Beard and C. Lowy, *Br. J. Obstet. Gynaecol.* **89,** 783 (1982).
27. L. Molsted-Pedersen, *In* "Carbohydrate Metabolism in Pregnancy and the Newborn" (H. W. Sutherland and J. M. Stowers, eds.), pp. 391–406. Springer-Verlag, Berlin and New York, 1978.
28. G. D. Roversi, E. Pedretti, M. Garigiulo, and G. Tronconi, *J. Perinat. Med.* **10,** 249 (1982).

25

Trace Elements in the Perinatal Period

Bo Lönnerdal
Department of Nutrition
University of California at Davis
Davis, California, U.S.A.

I. INTRODUCTION

During pregnancy, the trace elements zinc, copper, and manganese are efficiently accumulated by the fetus from the maternal circulation. These elements are accrued not only by the expanding mass of fetal tissue but also on a per gram basis. Although the consequences of a diminished supply of trace elements on fetal outcome are known, our knowledge regarding the mechanisms for trace element accrual and how they can be affected by trace element deficiency is very limited. First, the placenta has to translocate the elements from the maternal blood flow into the fetal circulation. Second, fetal tissues have to incorporate the elements into rapidly proliferating tissues. In early life, trace elements need to be transported through the intestinal mucosa and delivered to the liver for further transport into extrahepatic tissues. Again, our knowledge about the efficacy of these processes and how they can be affected by maturity and trace element deficiency or excess is limited. In this paper, I will discuss the crucial role of biological membranes in trace element transport and accumulation in light of our work on trace element metabolism in the perinatal period. Although our experience is mainly in the area of zinc metabolism, I will also discuss recent findings in the areas of copper and manganese metabolism.

II. TRACE ELEMENTS IN THE FETUS

Zinc accumulation by the human fetus increases dramatically during the latter part of the third trimester (Widdowson *et al.*, 1974). Of a total zinc content of 60 mg, as much as 30% (18 mg) is in the liver. In comparison, adult liver contains only 2% of total body zinc. The remainder of the zinc in the body of the fetus is likely to be found primarily in muscle and bone. Within the liver, it has been shown that zinc is bound to high molecular weight proteins, a protein with intermediate molecular weight (about 30,000) believed to be copper,zinc-superoxide dismutase (Cu,Zn-SOD), and the low molecular weight protein metallothionein (Keen *et al.*, 1984a). The latter protein, metallothionein (MT), is believed to represent a store of zinc to be utilized in early fetal life. It has been shown that the concentration of MT-bound zinc decreases precipitously after birth in the rat (Mason *et al.*, 1980). The concentration of zinc bound to other zinc pools in the liver, however, remained constant, supporting a role for MT-bound zinc as a store of zinc to be depleted first in situation of need (e.g., rapid growth).

During the final stage of the third trimester, accumulation of copper by the fetus is even more pronounced than for zinc (Widdowson *et al.*, 1974). While the total amount of copper at term is only one-third that of zinc, or 18 mg, the amount of copper in the liver, 9 mg, corresponds to 50% of the whole-body copper. As with zinc, this high proportion of hepatic copper is significantly higher than in the adult. Copper in the liver is bound to high molecular weight proteins, an intermediate molecular weight protein (most likely Cu,Zn-SOD), and MT. The high molecular weight proteins have not yet been characterized but are likely to contain ceruloplasmin (ferroxidase I) and other copper-containing enzymes. Metallothionein binds both copper and zinc, but the various forms appear to have different turnover rates and sensitivity to pH changes and consequently the utilization of these two trace elements from metallothionein is likely to differ. In contrast to liver copper, fetal serum copper concentration (0.5 μg/ml) is much lower than in later life (0.9–1.1 μg/ml). This is consistent with the finding that levels of ceruloplasmin, the major copper-binding protein in serum, are low in neonatal blood. It is interesting to note that serum from fetuses obtained at earlier stages of gestation has a higher copper concentration than that of term fetuses (Widdowson *et al.*, 1974). It therefore appears that some accrual mechanism(s) are activated in late gestation that remove copper from fetal serum into the liver. After birth, there is an initial increase in MT-Cu but thereafter liver MT-Cu decreases (Mason *et al.*, 1980). Serum copper as well as ceruloplasmin levels increase after birth, indicating that MT may represent a store of copper which can be utilized for ceruloplasmin synthesis. The increase in Cu,Zn-SOD that occurs after birth (Zidenberg-Cherr *et al.*, 1985) would also require a supply of copper and zinc. It is not yet known whether newly synthesized apoproteins can acquire these elements directly from MT as suggested by some researchers (Udom and Brady, 1980) or if they are first released from MT by degradation.

Manganese in the fetus has received far less attention than zinc and copper. This has been due in part to analytical problems of measuring manganese at low levels and, possibly, because of a lack of concern about manganese nutrition of the human fetus. The concentration of manganese in fetal liver appears to be constant throughout gestation (Widdowson *et al.*, 1972). Manganese is found in bone and liver, but no stores are believed to exist for manganese (Widdowson *et al.*, 1974). The distribution of manganese within the liver is not known, but manganese–superoxide dismutase (Mn-SOD) and arginase are examples of manganese-dependent enzymes in liver (Keen *et al.*, 1984b). Manganese concentration in serum is very low (1–2 ng/ml) and there are few data on serum or blood manganese levels in the fetus.

III. MECHANISMS OF PLACENTAL TRACE ELEMENT UPTAKE

Zinc in serum is bound primarily to serum albumin (about 60%), α_2-macroglobulin (about 35%), and low molecular weight ligands such as free amino acids (Giroux, 1975). During pregnancy, there is a decrease in maternal serum zinc levels which is most pronounced during the third trimester (Zimmerman *et al.*, 1984). Hemodilution appears to be only partially responsible for this decrease (Swanson and King, 1983). It therefore appears likely that the need for zinc by the fetus is causing maternal serum levels to fall. Zimmerman *et al.* (1984) found that zinc levels in serum decreased to a significantly greater extent than serum protein or serum albumin. These investigators also observed that, in early pregnancy, the maternal zinc to α_2-macroglobulin ratio fell but not thereafter, while the zinc to serum albumin ratio decreased later in pregnancy. In the study of Swanson and King (1983), serum albumin levels of pregnant women were found to be about 25% lower than in nonpregnant controls. The proportion of zinc bound to serum albumin and α_2-macroglobulin, however, was similar in the pregnant and the nonpregnant women. A concomitant decrease in serum albumin and zinc was reported earlier by Giroux *et al.* (1976) and Butte *et al.* (1981). As pointed out by Swanson and King (1983), however, it is important to recognize that the total amount of circulating albumin-bound serum zinc is higher in women during late pregnancy than in nonpregnant women (1900 vs. 1660 μg zinc). In this study zinc intake was quite good (>25 mg/day), and it is likely that fetal requirements for zinc were met. The minimum serum zinc level needed for adequate fetal zinc supply is still unknown.

Terry *et al.* (1960) showed that when pregnant rabbits were injected intravenously with ^{65}Zn, recovery of the radioisotope in fetal tissues rose sharply near term. The major part of radio-zinc incorporated into the fetus was found in the liver, suggesting maturation of acceptor mechanisms in the fetal liver. However, since zinc placental transfer of ^{65}Zn was similar when fetuses were removed, it appears that the transfer is not dependent on fetal mechanisms. Metallothionein has also been found in rat placenta (Waalkes *et al.*, 1984). The amount of zinc bound to the placenta, calculated stoichiometrically from the amount of MT present, would not be more than about 0.2 μg/g tissue. This is considerably lower than the amount of zinc in fetal rat liver at term, 92 μg/g (Mason *et al.*, 1980), and of total placental zinc, 11 μg/g (Herman *et al.*, 1985). It is therefore unlikely that placental MT would be involved in a major control mechanism for placental zinc transfer.

We have postulated that placental zinc uptake occurs via receptor-mediated processes and that these may be up-regulated during late pregnancy (Flynn *et al.*, 1986). We prepared syncytiotrophoblast microvillous plasma membrane vesicles from human placenta and found a high rate of zinc uptake from serum albumin and an even higher rate when zinc was bound to α_2-macroglobulin. Both mechanisms were very slow at 4°C compared to 37°C, indicating the possibility of receptor-mediated mechanisms. Receptors for α_2-macroglobulin have been described in hepatocytes, macrophages, and fibroblasts (Gliemann and

Davidsen, 1986). Johnson *et al.* (1985) reported binding of α_2-macroglobulin to the trophoblast membrane of human placenta, possibly to a surface-exposed protease. We found that the uptake of zinc from α_2-macroglobulin was significantly higher in the presence of excess zinc than at low zinc concentration. It is conceivable that the binding of zinc to α_2-macroglobulin may induce a conformation more favorable to binding to a putative receptor in the placenta. It is also possible that there is a minimum requirement for proper binding of α_2-macroglobulin to its membrane receptor. Consequently, in light of the findings of a changed ligand to zinc ratio in serum during pregnancy (Zimmerman *et al.*, 1984), it is possible that a low ratio of zinc to α_2-macroglobulin can reduce zinc delivery via placental receptors and/or that suboptimal placental zinc supply may reduce efficiency of receptor-mediated processes. In both cases, fetal supply of zinc would be reduced, potentially precipitating a zinc deficiency.

Information gained so far implicates serum zinc as a primary regulator of fetal zinc supply. Although it has been suggested that low levels of amniotic fluid zinc can be correlated to low birth weight (Favier *et al.*, 1972) and hypotrophic newborns (Kynast *et al.*, 1979), recent studies failed to confirm a correlation between amniotic fluid zinc and high-risk pregnancies (Rösick *et al.*, 1983). Consequently, this source of zinc may not be reflective of fetal zinc status. Although erythrocyte zinc concentration is almost 10 times higher than the zinc level of serum, this pool of zinc primarily consists of carbonic anhydrase-bound zinc. This latter pool does not appear to be an available pool of zinc; carbonic anhydrase is only metabolized in the bone marrow.

The process of copper delivery to the placenta is still largely unknown. Copper in serum is largely (90–95%) bound to ceruloplasmin and only to a small extent to albumin (about 5%) and low molecular weight ligands (1–2%). During pregnancy, maternal serum copper concentration increases dramatically, concomitant with an increase in serum ceruloplasmin level (Kiilholma *et al.*, 1984a). It is believed that this increase is induced by the higher levels of circulating estrogen in pregnant women (Kiilholma *et al.*, 1984b). This is supported by the observation that nonpregnant women using estrogen-containing oral contraceptive agents also have higher serum copper and ceruloplasmin levels (Halsted *et al.*, 1968). It appears likely that receptors on the placenta would bind ceruloplasmin and that copper would be translocated into fetal circulation. Fetal serum copper and ceruloplasmin levels are low (Widdowson *et al.*, 1974) and it is possible that circulating non-ceruloplasmin-bound copper in the fetus could be efficiently incorporated into fetal tissues. Ceruloplasmin receptors have been described in aorta and erythrocytes (Stevens *et al.*, 1984; Barnes and Frieden, 1984). Weiss and Linder (1985) have shown that ceruloplasmin is the preferred plasma ligand for incorporation of copper into cells. While it has been suggested that serum albumin-bound copper would be the form of copper that should be delivered into intracellular pools through mediation by amino acids, Laurie and Pratt (1986) argue against this mechanism because of the slow reaction rate of albumin-copper.

Our knowledge regarding manganese uptake by the placenta is very limited. Recently, Scheuhammer and Cherian (1985) reported that transferrin is the major (about 50%) manganese-binding protein in human and rat plasma, while only a small fraction of manganese is bound to albumin (about 5%). Thus, transferrin may play a significant role not only in iron but also in manganese transport. Since placental receptors for transferrin have been described and iron uptake is facilitated by these receptors (McArdle *et al.*, 1985), it is feasible that manganese may be translocated to the fetus by the same mechanism(s).

IV. EFFECTS OF MATERNAL TRACE ELEMENT DEFICIENCY DURING PREGNANCY

A. Zinc

The severe teratological effects caused by dietary zinc deficiency during gestation have been described in the rat (Hurley *et al.*, 1971). In pronounced zinc deficiency, prenatal death was common and malformations such as cleft lip and palate, herniations, and brain and eye abnormalities are found in surviving offspring (Hurley, 1981). The mechanisms behind these effects are still not completely known, but the role of zinc in enzymes involved in protein and nucleic acid synthesis is believed to be a causative factor. Several zinc-dependent enzymes have decreased activity in zinc-deficient animals or humans, and chromosomal aberrations have been described. More recently, maternal zinc deficiency has been shown to impair prenatal development of the pancreas, lungs, and immune function (Hurley, 1983). It is interesting to note that even short-term (2–4 days) zinc deficiency during pregnancy can lead to congenital malformations (Hurley and Mutch, 1973). The reason for this rapid precipitation of effects is that plasma zinc will fall very shortly after introduction of a diet deficient in zinc (Hurley *et al.*, 1982). Since it is believed that the pregnant dam does not have any significant stores available from which to draw zinc, fetal supply of zinc is more or less immediately reduced. If this occurs during a critical period of organogenesis, the outcome of pregnancy can be severely impaired.

Observations from experimental animals led Jameson (1976) to investigate the potential effects of low maternal serum zinc during pregnancy on complications of pregnancy and infant outcome. The results indicated that lower than normal serum zinc levels in early pregnancy could be associated with prolonged labor, increased blood loss, and incidence of malformations. Serum zinc concentrations fall significantly early in the first trimester in control subjects (Breskin *et al.*, 1983), but Jameson postulated that a larger than normal decrease in serum zinc could be indicative of zinc deficiency. Women consuming diets low in zinc and in forms of low bioavailability could be at risk for zinc deficiency during pregnancy. We have investigated the effect of zinc deficiency in animals on zinc accumulation of the fetus (Masters *et al.*, 1983a). It was found that dams fed a zinc-deficient diet deposited about 240% of the amount of zinc provided by diet into products of conception (fetuses, uterus, and placentas). Size and number of live fetuses were considerably lower than normal in zinc-deficient dams and fetal zinc content was 78% of that of controls. It is therefore evident that the accumulation of zinc in fetuses of zinc-deficient rats is dependent in part on catabolism of maternal tissues. In fact, we could show that if maternal catabolism was increased by fasting during late pregnancy, fetal outcome was improved as compared to feeding a zinc-deficient diet (Masters *et al.*, 1983b). We have subsequently shown by radioisotope labeling that the major part of the fetal zinc derived from zinc-deficient dams during the last 3 days of pregnancy comes from maternal muscle catabolism (Masters *et al.*, 1986). We were also able to show that when calcium deficiency was induced concomitant to zinc deficiency, teratological effects were reduced. This reduction was shown to be due to release of zinc from bone during early pregnancy when organogenesis is occurring. While this "store" of zinc normally would be unavailable, bone catabolism induced by the calcium deficiency also releases zinc. It is consequently possible that both inanition due to zinc deficiency and calcium deficiency could aid in releasing zinc from muscle and bone, thereby protecting the fetus.

The interrelationship between zinc and iron metabolism deserves special attention. On one hand, we have shown that when zinc-deficient diets are fed during pregnancy, fetal liver iron is significantly increased compared to that of controls (Reinstein *et al.*, 1984). The consequences of this high level of fetal liver iron are not known, but one effect could be increased oxidative stress potentially leading to tissue damage. On the other hand, the potential effects of high iron levels taken in during pregnancy on zinc absorption and metabolism must be considered. Iron and zinc at high levels can compete for plasma uptake processes (Solomons and Jacob, 1981), which led to the suggestion that zinc status may be impaired when iron supplements are given. However, Fairweather-Tait *et al.* (1984) showed in the pregnant rat that iron supplements at different levels did not impair maternal or fetal zinc status. Similarly, we have shown that iron supplements given to children for 3 months did not affect plasma zinc levels (Yip *et al.*, 1985). It is possible that the effects on plasma zinc noted by Solomons and Jacob (1981) occur only at nonphysiological levels or that the effect is only transitory and on plasma zinc flux and does not necessarily reflect retention. The technique of measuring plasma zinc uptake has been shown to not correlate well with whole-body retention data (Valberg *et al.*, 1985). We have shown that a high iron to zinc ratio, when both minerals are given in a meal at physiological levels, does not affect zinc retention in human adults (Sandström *et al.*, 1985). Some effect could be observed at the highest ratio given when the minerals were given alone in water, possibly explaining the effects of Solomons and Jacob. This latter situation, however, is less likely to be common in humans during pregnancy.

B. Copper

Although the consequences of dietary copper deficiency during fetal life may appear to be less drastic than those of zinc deficiency, the postnatal consequences can be both permanent and sometimes fatal (Hurley *et al.*, 1980). Copper deficiency primarily affects enzymes involved in connective tissue and bone metabolism as well as in iron metabolism and impairment in these enzymes does not have a strong teratological effect. However, when the copper deficiency is exacerbated by the use of chelating drugs, fetal survival is reduced (Keen *et al.*, 1983b). Offspring born to copper-deficient dams have skeletal lesions caused by a reduction in the activity of lysyl oxidase, a copper-dependent enzyme (Rucker and Tinker, 1977). Connective tissue abnormalities induced by impaired elastin and collagen synthesis are the cause of the sudden death observed in copper deficiency. Reduced lysyl oxidase activity impairs the crosslinking of amino acids in elastin and collagen, leading to a more soluble matrix. The high mortality rate of copper-deficient animals is the result of internal hemorrhage caused by rupture of the heart, aorta, or other vessels in the cardiovascular system (O'Dell, 1976).

Another factor contributing to the cardiovascular problems of copper deficiency has been suggested by Klevay (1975). It has been shown that copper deficiency leads to an increase in serum cholesterol concentration and since dietary copper intake of adults in the United States can be low, this could potentially be a risk factor involved in coronary heart disease. Neurological disorders, such as ataxia, observed in copper-deficient animals are believed to be caused by a reduction in the enzyme cytochrome oxidase, which is involved in one of the terminal steps in the respiratory chain. A low level of cytochrome oxidase could be the reason for the impairment of brain myelination in copper-deficient animals.

The anemia of copper deficiency which has been described in human infants (Cordano *et al.*, 1964) as well as in experimental animals is due to a reduction in the enzyme ferroxidase I (or ceruloplasmin). This enzyme catalyzes the oxidation of ferrous iron to ferric from the cell. Consequently, iron supplementation will not alleviate anemia due to copper deficiency.

It appears unlikely that dietary copper deficiency during pregnancy in humans would precipitate immediate signs of copper deficiency in the early neonatal period. Although the diet consumed during pregnancy may contain less copper than currently recommended (2 mg/day), it is unlikely that it would be seriously devoid of copper. Furthermore, it appears that copper stores accumulated by the fetus, even if lower than normal, would provide a resource to draw from in the immediate postnatal period. Dauncey *et al.* (1977) have described net copper losses by premature infants who would have lower than normal copper stores. Cordano (1978) reviewed the literature on copper deficiency in infants and found that the majority of the cases reported were later in the neonatal period and associated with either prematurity combined with low copper diets, malnutrition combined with low copper diets, or malnutrition combined with increased intestinal losses (diarrhea, enteropathies). In these cases, low serum copper levels, anemia, neutropenia, and bone lesions were found. Hillman *et al.* (1981) found no difference in ceruloplasmin or serum copper levels of infants fed formulas with different levels of copper supplementation. Recently, Tyrala (1986) found negative copper balances in several premature infants regardless of copper level in the formulas used. It therefore may be some functional immaturity in the prematurely born infants that prevents proper copper accumulation by the body. Another possibility, suggested by Hillman *et al.*, is that liver copper stores may be increased but that ceruloplasmin synthesis, and thus copper efflux from the liver, is immature.

We have studied fetal accumulation of copper in pregnant rats fed copper-deficient diets (Masters *et al.*, 1983a). In contrast to zinc, only 15% of the dietary copper consumed during pregnancy was deposited into products of conception. Thus, although the copper concentration of the diet was very low (0.7 μg copper/g diet), the percentage of copper in the diet incorporated into the fetus was low. If this situation is similar in the human, this could explain the lack of reports of prenatal copper deficiency.

C. Manganese

Manganese deficiency during pregnancy in experimental animals leads to high perinatal mortality and poor survival of the offspring (Hurley, 1981). The exact reason for the high mortality rate is not yet known. Manganese is part of the metalloenzyme manganese–superoxide dismutase, which is primarily present in mitochondria (Keen *et al.*, 1984b). Reduced levels of this enzyme can lead to increased lipid peroxidation and ultrastructural derangement of christae in mitochondria. It is possible that these pathologies are involved in the high mortality. Among the surviving offspring, ataxia is a common sign. By supplementing manganese-deficient rats during different periods of pregnancy, Hurley and Everson (1963) were able to reduce the incidence of ataxia and to define the critical period for developing the lesion. They found that the formation of otoliths in the inner ear was impaired. These structures, which are important for normal righting reflexes, contain glycosaminoglycans. The enzyme galactosyltransferase, which is responsible for glycosaminoglycan synthesis, is decreased in manganese deficiency. Low levels of this enzyme could also explain the skeletal malformations observed in manganese-deficient animals (Hurley *et al.*, 1961), since proper matrix formation is dependent on galactosyltransferase activity. Leach *et al.* (1969) showed that cartilage formation was impaired in manganese-deficient chicks and that chondroitin sulfate synthesis was severely affected.

The likelihood of manganese deficiency occurring during pregnancy in the human is unknown. First, the average diet contains ample amounts of manganese and, second, the signs of deficiency in humans remain to be defined. Although a dietary insufficiency of manganese may appear unlikely, there is a possibility that excessive intakes of iron during pregnancy may interfere with manganese uptake (see Section V, C). Use of prenatal iron supplements is common and the levels used can be quite high. Consequently, analysis of whole-blood manganese, which is believed to be a good indicator of manganese status (Keen *et al.*, 1983c), during pregnancy may be of diagnostic value.

V. TRACE ELEMENT ABSORPTION IN EARLY POSTNATAL LIFE

The newborn infant has few diets to choose from. The healthy term infant is likely to be fed either breast milk or a formula based on cow's milk. It should be recognized that, although not recommended, evaporated cow's milk and soy formula will be given to some infants in early life. Assessment of trace element absorption from different infant foods in *infants* has been very limited. Balance studies have been used but are limited in value as endogenous losses cannot be quantitated and true absorption (or rather retention) cannot be determined. Various approaches to overcome this difficulty include the use of human adults or experimental animals. Naturally, a critical question is the validity of these models to assess absorption in the neonate. Gastric acid secretion, activity of pancreatic function, bile flow, and intestinal maturation are all different in the newborn than in adulthood. Several of these functions can be even less developed in the premature infant. Our attempts to assess trace element uptake in infants have therefore included adult humans, suckling rats, and infant primates.

A. Zinc

Absorption of zinc from human milk is considerably higher than from other infant diets in human adults (Sandström *et al.*, 1983a), suckling rat pups (Sandström *et al.*, 1983b), and infant rhesus monkeys (Lönnerdal *et al.*, 1986b). The lowest zinc absorption in humans was found for soy formula (14%), as compared to cow's milk (28%), cow's milk formula (31%), and human milk (41%). Human milk produced during early lactation has a higher concentration of zinc than that produced later in lactation, and we have used this as a norm to which other diets can be compared (Lönnerdal *et al.*, 1984). Using absorption values from human adults, it is evident that zinc-supplemented formula would provide amounts equal or higher than that provided by early human milk, while cow's milk would not. Soy formula would provide significantly lower amounts of zinc than human milk, even when supplemented to a level of 8 mg/liter. It could be argued that these differences in the adult may not be the same in the newborn. In fact, we have shown that zinc retention in human adults and in infant rhesus monkeys is clearly correlated to each other, the only difference being that the relative differences in absorption values are larger in the infant than in the adult. Therefore, it is likely that relative differences in zinc bioavailability in adults are amplified in the human infant. We have suggested that the high bioavailability of zinc from human milk is due to its relatively large proportion of zinc bound to casein (Lönnerdal *et al.*, 1980). We have subsequently shown a high bioavailability of zinc from all major fractions of human milk: fat, casein, whey, and low molecular weight ligands (Lönnerdal *et al.*, 1985c). In contrast, zinc absorption from bovine casein was found to be low. As a consequence, milk containing a high ratio of casein to whey (80 : 20) resulted in lower zinc absorption than that from milk with a low ratio (40 : 60) of casein/whey (Lönnerdal *et al.*, 1984).

Roth and Kirchgessner (1985) have also demonstrated a lower zinc bioavailability from bovine casein than from bovine whey. While we have found that addition of citrate did not enhance zinc absorption from human milk, cow's milk, or cow's milk formula, it should be recognized that these diets already contain citrate in significant quantities (>200-fold molar excess of citrate to zinc). It is likely that citrate-bound zinc represents an easily accessible pool of zinc and that, when present, inhibitors of zinc absorption, such as bovine casein and phytate, are stronger determinants of zinc bioavailability. We have shown a significant inhibitory effect of phytate in soy formula. When phytate was added to cow's milk formula at a level similar to that in soy formula, zinc absorption fell from 31 to 14% (Lönnerdal *et al.*, 1984). This latter value is similar to what was found for soy formula. We have recently shown in infant rhesus monkeys that removal of phytate in soy formula by an industrial process based on isoelectric precipitation increases zinc absorption from this formula to a level similar to that of cow's milk formula (Lönnerdal *et al.*, 1986b). Thus, it may be possible to produce a soy formula with improved zinc bioavailability.

It seems reasonable to assume that regulation of zinc uptake by the brush border membrane in the small intestine is more regulated by intraluminal factors than direct regulation of uptake processes. In order to be absorbed, zinc must be in a soluble form from which it can be absorbed. Incomplete digestion of bovine casein, resulting in insoluble or inaccessible casein–zinc complexes, could explain the low bioavailability of zinc from bovine casein, while formation of unavailable zinc–phytate complexes yields poor zinc absorption from soy. It is not known whether there are homeostatic mechanisms for zinc absorption, similar to what has been found for iron. Cousins (1985) has described mucosal uptake of zinc as partly active, courier-mediated transport and partly passive uptake. We have assessed zinc absorption in infant rhesus monkeys born to either zinc-deficient or control mothers (Lönnerdal *et al.*, 1986a). Using plasma zinc as an index of zinc status, we found no correlation between status and zinc absorption. It should be recognized, however, that plasma zinc may not be a good indicator of zinc status. It is evident that further studies are needed on zinc absorption in individuals with impaired zinc status.

Premature infants pose a significant challenge with regard to delivery of trace elements. Dauncey *et al.* (1977) and Widdowson *et al.* (1972) have shown that premature infants can be in negative zinc balance for prolonged periods of time. It is likely that this is due to increased body loss of zinc, as Ehrenkranz *et al.* (1984) have shown high zinc absorption (about 60–70%) in premature infants when using a stable zinc isotope. Recently developed infant formulas specifically designed for premature infants have taken this into account and include significantly increased levels of zinc (Friel, *et al.*, 1985). Tyrala (1986) demonstrated that when the zinc concentration of formula was 12.5 mg/liter (as compared to 6 mg/liter in conventional formula), premature infants exhibited positive zinc balance. No negative effect on copper balance was found with this high level of zinc, although copper balance was negative in some infants regardless of copper level fed.

B. Copper

Studies on copper absorption using radioisotopes pose an additional problem, as the available isotope (^{64}Cu) has a very short half-life. We have therefore assessed copper absorption by measuring liver uptake in suckling rat pups 6 hr after intubation (Lönnerdal *et al.*, 1985b). This technique is similar to the one we previously used for our zinc absorption studies in the rat and which was shown to correlate well to absorption in the adult human. The results obtained were also similar to those obtained for zinc; copper uptake into liver from human milk was 25%, from cow's milk formula 23%, from cow's milk 18%, and from soy formula 10%. We find it reasonable to assume that the factors previously shown to inhibit zinc absorption are also those inhibiting copper absorption, since these two elements have similar coordination chemistry. It is interesting to note that while copper absorption from cow's milk formula was not different from that of human milk, that from cow's milk was. In virtually all cases of copper deficiency described in human infants, cow's milk was fed (Cordano, 1980). While it has been correctly argued that cow's milk is low in copper, a low bioavailability of that copper could also have been a precipitating factor. Copper absorption from formula for premature infants was lower than from human milk, but this product is supplemented with copper to a level considerably higher than that in human milk. The adequacy of the level of copper chosen is uncertain, especially in light of Tyrala's (1986) finding of negative copper balance in several premature infants. Fischer and L'Abbe (1985) have reported that copper absorption by the brush border membrane of the small intestine is passive and thus would lack regulation. However, feeding high levels of zinc can induce intestinal MT synthesis and thus inhibit copper absorption (Fischer *et al.*, 1981).

C. Manganese

The concentration of manganese in infant diets can vary considerably (Stastny *et al.*, 1984). While the manganese concentration of human milk is very low, 4–10 μg/liter (Vuori, 1979), cow's milk, cow's milk formula, and soy formula contain considerably higher concentrations, 50–1300 μg/liter (Lönnerdal *et al.*, 1983). Manganese in human milk is predominantly bound to lactoferrin, the iron-binding protein of human milk, while manganese in cow's milk is bound to casein and low molecular weight ligands (Lönnerdal *et al.*, 1985a). Our knowledge of manganese uptake and excretion in the early neonatal period is still very limited. We have investigated the absorption and retention of manganese in suckling rat pups of different ages (Keen *et al.*, 1986). During the early suckling period, manganese retention was very high (70–90%) from all diets investigated (human milk, cow's milk, cow's milk formula, and soy formula). The reasons for this high retention may be twofold: (1) there appears to be little regulation of uptake by the brush border of the mucosal cell (Bell *et al.*, 1986) and (2) manganese excretion may be limited because the major excretory pathway for manganese via bile is immature at this age. Since the concentration of manganese in these diets varies and retention is high, the body load of manganese can be highly variable.

High levels of manganese can exert toxic effects such as neurological disorders (Keen *et al.*, 1984b) and abnormal glucose homeostasis (Baly *et al.*, 1985). Based on observations in experimental animals, it has been suggested that high manganese intake can be correlated to learning disabilities (Pihl and Parkes, 1977; Collipp *et al.*, 1983). While these studies in children implicated manganese status as only one factor involved in learning disabilities, the potential consequences of intake of high manganese levels in the neonatal period should be evaluated further. In our studies, it was evident that the manganese retained in the body of suckling rat pups was redistributed from liver to brain in the early suckling period. Later on, manganese in liver left the body and manganese retention by the brain was lower (Keen *et al.*, 1986). Another factor to consider is that manganese absorption in early life is closely correlated to iron absorption (Lönnerdal *et al.*, 1985a). When an infant is iron deficient, absorption of iron is increased as a result of homeostatic mechanisms and consequently manganese absorption would be further increased.

The possibility of manganese deficiency in early life cannot be completely ruled out. Since manganese stores are not thought to be present at birth, human milk would provide only a minimum supply. Whether this supply is adequate for proper manganese nutrition is unknown, primarily because the signs of manganese deficiency in humans remain to be characterized (Keen *et al.*, 1984). There is a possibility of increased oxygen stress due to reduced levels of manganese–superoxide dismutase. Manganese deficiency in young rats has been shown to lead to increased lipid peroxidation in liver (Zidenberg-Cherr *et al.*, 1985). Such consequences on tissue internal organs would be difficult to evaluate in clinical practice.

D. Trace Element Interactions

Trace elements having similar coordination chemistry and/or transport mechanisms are known to interact with each other (Lönnerdal and Keen, 1983). Examples of such interactions include zinc–copper, iron–manganese, and iron–zinc. Since the ratios of these elements in infant diets can be highly variable (Lönnerdal *et al.*, 1983), the potential effects of very low or high ratios should be investigated. As an example, Craig *et al.* (1984) reported lower plasma zinc levels in infants fed iron-supplemented formula as compared to those fed formula without iron supplements.

REFERENCES

Baly, D. L., Lönnerdal, B., and Keen, C. L. (1985). *Toxicol. Lett.* **25,** 95.

Barnes, G., and Frieden, E. (1984). *Biochem. Biophys. Res. Commun.* **125,** 157.

Bell, J. G., Keen, C. L., and Lönnerdal, B. (1986). *Fed. Proc., Fed. Am. Soc. Exp. Biol.* **45,** 368.

Breskin, M. W., Worthington-Roberts, B. S., Knopp, R. H., Brown, Z., Plovie, B., Mottet, N. K., and Mills, J. L. (1983). *Am. J. Clin. Nutr.* **38,** 943.

Butte, N., Calloway, D. H., and van Duzen, J. L. (1981). *Am. J. Clin. Nutr.* **34,** 2216.

Collipp, P. G., Chen, S. Y., and Maitinsky, S. (1983). *Ann. Nutr. Metab.* **27,** 488.

Cordano, A. (1978). *In* "Zinc and Copper in Clinical Medicine" (K. M. Hambidge and B. L. Nichols, eds.), pp. 119–126. Spectrum Publ., New York.

Cordano, A., Baertl, J. M., and Graham, G. G. (1964). *Pediatrics* **38,** 596.

Cousins, R. J. (1985). *Physiol. Rev.* **65,** 238.

Craig, W. J., Balback, L., Harris, S., and Vyhmeister, N. (1984). *J. Am. Coll. Nutr.* **3,** 183.

Dauncey, M. J., Shaw, J. C. L., and Urman, J. (1977). *Pediatr. Res.* **11,** 991.

Ehrenkranz, R. A., Ackerman, B. A., Nelli, C. M., and Janghorbani, M. (1984). *Am. J. Clin. Nutr.* **40,** 72.

Fairweather-Tait, S. J., Wright, A. J. A., and Williams, C. M. (1984). *Br. J. Nutr.* **52,** 205.

Favier, M., Yacoub, M., Racinet, C., Marka, C., Chabert, P., and Benbassa, A. (1972). *Rev. Fr. Gynecol.* **67,** 707.

Fischer, P. W. F., and L'Abbe, M. R. (1985). *Nutr. Res.* **5,** 759.

Fischer, P. W. F., Giroux, A., and L'Abbe, M. R. (1981). *Am. J. Clin. Nutr.* **34,** 1670.

Flynn, A., Glazier, C., and Lönnerdal, B. (1986). *Am. J. Clin. Nutr.* **43,** 675.

Friel, J. K., Gibson, R. S., Kawash, G. F., and Watts, J. (1985). *J. Pediatr., Gastroenterol. Nutr.* **4,** 746.

Giroux, E. (1975). *Biochem. Med.* **12** 258.

Giroux, E., Schechter, P. J., and Schoun, J. (1976). *Clin. Sci. Mol. Med.* **51,** 545.

Gliemann, J., and Davidsen, O. (1986). *Biochim. Biophys. Acta* **885,** 49.

Halsted, J. A., Hackley, B. M., and Smith, J. C. (1968). *Lancett* **ii,** 278.

Herman, Z., Greeley, S., and King, J. C. (1985). *Nutr. Res.* **5,** 211.

Hillman, L. S., Martin, L., and Fiore, B. (1981). *J. Pediatr.* **98,** 311.

Hurley, L. S. (1981). *Physiol. Rev.* **61,** 249.

Hurley, L. S. (1983). *In* "Biological Aspects of Metals and Metal-Related Diseases" (B. Sarkar, ed.), pp. 199–208. Raven Press, New York.

Hurley, L. S., and Everson, G. J. (1963). *J. Nutr.* **79,** 23.

Hurley, L. S., and Mutch, P. B. (1973). *J. Nutr.* **103,** 649.

Hurley, L. S., Everson, G. J., Wooten, E., and Asling, C. W. (1961). *J. Nutr.* **74,** 274.
Hurley, L. S., Gowan, J., and Swenerton, H. (1971). *Teratology* **4,** 199.
Hurley, L. S., Keen, C. L., and Lönnerdal, B. (1980). *In* "Biological Roles of Copper," Ciba Foundation Symposium, Vol. 79, pp. 227–245. Excerpta Med. Found., Amsterdam.
Hurley, L. S., Gordon, P., Keen, C. L., and Merkhofer, L. (1982). *Proc. Soc. Exp. Biol. Med.* **170,** 48.
Jameson, S. (1976). *Acta Med. Scand., Suppl.* 593, p. 3.
Johnson, P. M., Arnand, P., Weiner, P., and Galbraith, R. M. (1985). *Placenta* **6,** 323.
Keen, C. L., Cohen, N. L., Lönnerdal, B., and Hurley, L. S. (1983a). *Proc. Soc. Exp. Biol. Med.* **173,** 298.
Keen, C. L., Mark-Savage, P., Lönnerdal, B., and Hurley, L. S. (1983b). *Drug–Nutr. Interact.* **2,** 17.
Keen, C. L., Clegg, M. S., Lönnerdal, B., and Hurley, L. S. (1983c). *New Engl. J. Med.* **308,** 1230.
Keen, C. L., Cohen, N. L., Hurley, L. S., and Lönnerdal, B. (1984a). *Biochem. Biophys. Res. Commun.* **118,** 697.
Keen, C. L., Lönnerdal, B., and Hurley, L. S. (1984b). *In* "Biochemistry of the Essential Ultratrace Elements" (E. Frieden, ed.), pp. 89–132. Plenum, New York.
Keen, C. L., Bell, J. G., and Lönnerdal, B. (1986). *J. Nutr.* **116,** 395.
Kiilholma, P., Grönroos, M., Liukko, P., Pakarien, P., Hyörä, H., and Erkkola, R. (1984a). *Gynecol. Obstet. Invest.* **18,** 212.
Kiilholma, P., Erkkola, R., Pakarinen, P., and Grönroos, M. (1984b). *Gynecol. Obstet. Invest.* **18,** 45.
Klevay, L. M. (1975). *Am. J. Clin. Nutr.* **28,** 764.
Kynast, G., Saling, E., and Wagner, N. (1979). *J. Perinat. Med.* **7,** 69.
Laurie, S. H., and Pratt, D. E. (1986). *Biochem. Biophys. Res. Commun.* **135,** 1064.
Leach, R. M., Muenster, A. M., and Wein, E. M. (1969). *Arch. Biochem. Biophys.* **133,** 22.
Lönnerdal, B., and Keen, C. L. (1983). *In* "Reproductive and Developmental Toxicity of Metals" (T. W. Clarkson, G. F. Nordberg, and P. R. Sager, eds.), pp. 759–776. Plenum, New York.
Lönnerdal, B., Stanislowski, A. G., and Hurley, L. S. (1980). *J. Inorg. Biochem.* **12,** 71.
Lönnerdal, B., Keen, C. L., Ohtake, M., and Tamura, T. (1983). *Am. J. Dis. Child.* **137,** 433.
Lönnerdal, B., Cederblad, A., Davidsson, L., and Sandström, B. (1984). *Am. J. Clin. Nutr.* **40,** 1064.
Lönnerdal, B., Keen, C. L., and Hurley, L. S. (1985a). *Am. J. Clin. Nutr.* **41,** 550.
Lönnerdal, B., Bell, J. G., and Keen, C. L. (1985b). *Am. J. Clin. Nutr.* **42,** 836.
Lönnerdal, B., Keen, C. L., Bell, J. G., and Hurley, L. S. (1985c). *In* "Trace Elements in Man and Animals—TEMA 5" (C. F. Mills, I. Bremner, and J. K. Chesters, eds.), pp. 427–430. Commonw. Agric. Bur., Farnham Royal, England.
Lönnerdal, B., Keen, C. L., Bell, J. G., Golub, M., Gershwin, M. E., Hurley, L. S., and Hendrickx, A. G. (1986a). *Fed. Proc., Fed. Am. Soc. Exp. Biol.* **45,** 588.
Lönnerdal, B., Bell, J. G., Hendrickx, A. G., and Keen, C. L. (1986b). *Am. J. Clin. Nutr.* **43,** 674.
McArdle, H. J., Douglas, A. J., Bowen, B. J., and Morgan, E. H. (1985). *J. Cell. Physiol.* **124,** 446.
Mason, R., Bakka, A., Samarawickrama, G. P., and Webb, M. (1980). *Br. J. Nutr.* **45,** 375.
Masters, D. G., Keen, C. L., Lönnerdal, B., and Hurley, L. S. (1983a). *J. Nutr.* **113,** 1148.
Masters, D. G., Keen, C. L., Lönnerdal, B., and Hurley, L. S. (1983b). *J. Nutr.* **113,** 905.
Masters, D. G., Keen, C. L., Lönnerdal, B., and Hurley, L. S. (1986). *J. Nutr.* **116,** 2148.
O'Dell, B. (1976). *Med. Clin. N. Am.* **60,** 687.

Pihl, R. O., and Parkes, M. (1977). *Science* **198,** 204.
Reinstein, N. H., Lönnerdal, B., Keen, C. L., and Hurley, L. S. (1984). *J. Nutr.* **114,** 1266.
Rösick, U., Rösick, E., Brätter, P., and Kynast, G. (1983). *J. Clin. Chem. Clin. Biochem.* **21,** 363.
Roth, H. P., and Kirchgessner, M. (1985). *J. Nutr.* **115,** 1641.
Rucker, R. B., and Tinker, D. (1977). *Int. Rev. Exp. Pathol.* **17,** 1.
Sandström, B., Cederblad, A., and Lönnerdal, B. (1983a). *Am. J. Dis. Child.* **137,** 726.
Sandström, B., Cederblad, A., and Lönnerdal, B. (1983b). *Am. J. Clin. Nutr.* **38,** 420.
Sandström, B., Davidsson, L., Cederblad, A., and Lönnerdal, B. (1985). *J. Nutr.* **115,** 411.
Scheuhammer, A. M., and Cherian, M. G. (1985). *Biochim. Biophys. Acta* **840,** 163.
Solomons, N. W., and Jacob, R. A. (1981). *Am. J. Clin. Nutr.* **34,** 475.
Stastny, D., Vogel, R. S., and Picciano, M. F. (1984) *Am. J. Clin. Nutr.* **39,** 872.
Stevens, M. D., DiSilvestro, R. A., and Harris, E. D. (1984). *Biochemistry* **23,** 261.
Swanson, C. A., and King, J. C. (1983). *Obstet. Gynecol. (N.Y.)* **62,** 313.
Terry, C. W., Terry, B. E., and Davies, J. (1960). *Am. J. Physiol.* **198,** 303.
Tyrala, E. E. (1986). *Pediatrics* **77,** 513.
Udom, A. O., and Brady, F. O. (1980). *Biochem. J.* **187,** 329.
Valberg, L. S., Flanagan, P. R., Brennan, J., and Chamberlain, M. J. (1985). *Am. J. Clin. Nutr.* **41,** 37.
Vuori, E. (1979). *Acta Paediatr. Scand.* **68,** 571.
Waalkes, M. P., Poisner, A. M., Wood, G. W., and Klaassen, C. D. (1984). *Toxicol. Appl. Pharmacol.* **74,** 179.
Weiss, K. C., and Linder, M. C. (1985). *Am. J. Physiol.* **249,** E77.
Widdowson, E. M., Chan, H., Harrison, G. E., and Milner, R. D. G. (1972). *Biol. Neonate* **20,** 360.
Widdowson, E. M., Dauncey, J., and Shaw, J. C. L. (1974). *Proc. Nutr. Soc.* **33,** 275.
Yip, R., Reeves, J. D., Lonnerdal, B., Keen, C. L., and Dallman, P. R. (1985). *Am. J. Clin. Nutr.* **42,** 683.
Zidenberg-Cherr, S., Hurley, L. S., Lönnerdal, B., and Keen, C. L. (1985). *J. Nutr.* **115,** 460.
Zimmerman, A. W., Dunham, B. S., Nockinson, D. J., Kaplan, B. M., Clive, J. M., and Kunkel, S. L. (1984). *Am. J. Obstet. Gynecol.* **149,** 523.

26

Parenteral Nutrition and Amino Acid Metabolism in Neonatal Intensive Care

B. S. Lindblad, Stefan Hagelberg, Kenneth Palmér, and Anders Lundsjö

The Department of Paediatrics
Karolinska Institutet
St. Göran's Children's Hospital
Stockholm, Sweden

I. INTRODUCTION

It has been stated that the optimal amino acid supply to newborn infants should be sought in studies of infants receiving parenteral nutrition rather than from blind extrapolations from studies of the enterally fed (Winters *et al.*, 1984). We shall review studies of infants on parenteral nutrition with the intention of deciding first the intravenous nitrogen requirements of newborn infants and second the optimal amino acid balance of the solution for intravenous use.

II. REQUIREMENTS OF NITROGEN, OR REFERENCE PROTEIN QUANTITY

A. Full-Term Infants

Intravenously fed infants require only about 75% of the energy needed by enterally fed neonates to achieve the same growth rate. The iv requirements of amino acids are more debatable. Duffy and Pencharz (1986) have studied whole-body protein metabolism by the use of continuous infusion of [^{15}N]glycine in enterally and iv fed neonates. The turnover rates were 40% higher during peroral feeding on similar protein intakes in the same individuals. This could be interpreted as caused by the rapid growth and development of the gut in the enterally fed. However, the iv feeding was done 1–4 days after surgery and an underestimation is possible. Zlotkin (1984) has recently reported that the nitrogen intake required by parenterally fed infants to duplicate the accretion rate of

TABLE I

Experimental Design and Diagnoses for Newborn Infants Given Vamin and Vaminolac

Experimental design	Vamin	Vaminolac
Number of cases	8	10
Weight (g)	2920 ± 685	2460 ± 802
Treatment days	12 ± 4.3	14 ± 5.9
Glucose 15%	95 ml	
Intralipid 20%	20 ml = 97 kcal and 2.0 g protein	
Vamin/Vaminolac	31 ml per kg/day	
Diagnoses	**Vamin**	**Vaminolac**
Atresias	5	7
Gastroschisis	2	—
IRDS	1	—
NEC	—	1
Perforation	—	1
Volvulus	—	1

their milk-fed counterparts is 280 mg/kg/day. This estimated intravenous intake comes close to the result of the factorial approach of adding accretion in a reference infant, efficiency of utilization, and obligatory losses, namely, 130 + 56 + 120 = 306 mg/kg/day for a full-term newborn infant. Assuming a coefficient of variation of 15%, recommended intake would be 320 mg/kg/day, providing that adequate amounts of energy are infused (Table I). This is equivalent to 2.7 g of amino acids in the use of Vamin solution containing 134 mg N/g amino acids.

Eight newborn infants with surgical malformations were given Vamin, an amino acid solution based on the composition of whole egg, and 10 were given Vaminolac, based on the composition of human milk hydrolysate (Table I). Two grams of amino acids per kilogram per day gave low levels of all amino acids except alanine, taurine, and phenylalanine. (See Fig. 1.) One case with later confirmed phenylketonuria showed during this rather low supply of amino acids only a doubling of what

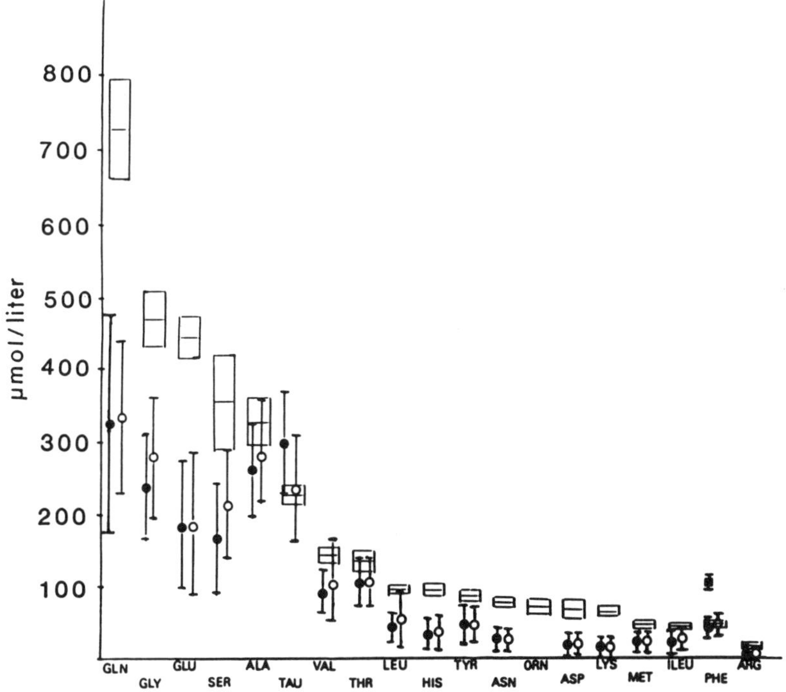

Fig. 1. The peripheral blood concentrations of free amino acids in newborn surgical infants on two different parenteral amino acid sulutions (see Table I). Boxes indicate mean values ± 2 SE in breast-fed infants. (●) Vamin, 2.0 g protein/kg/day. (○) Vaminolac, 2.0 g protein/kg/day.

was seen in the other cases (Fig. 1). This is an additional indication that the supply was not in excess of the requirement for protein synthesis. There were no differences in the amino acid concentrations of peripheral whole blood between the groups.

In one of these cases growth was severely retarded, probably caused by the stress of infection and reoperations. (See Fig. 2.) When the supply of all nutrients, by increasing the infusion rates, was equal to the supply consistent with the expected weight for age (compare the old German expression of "sollgewicht") (see star in Fig. 2), their weight rapidly increased while the blood levels remained normal (see Fig. 3). In Figs. 1 and 3 the normal background is provided by the levels found by us in whole blood by HPLC analysis in normal newborn, breast-fed, full-term

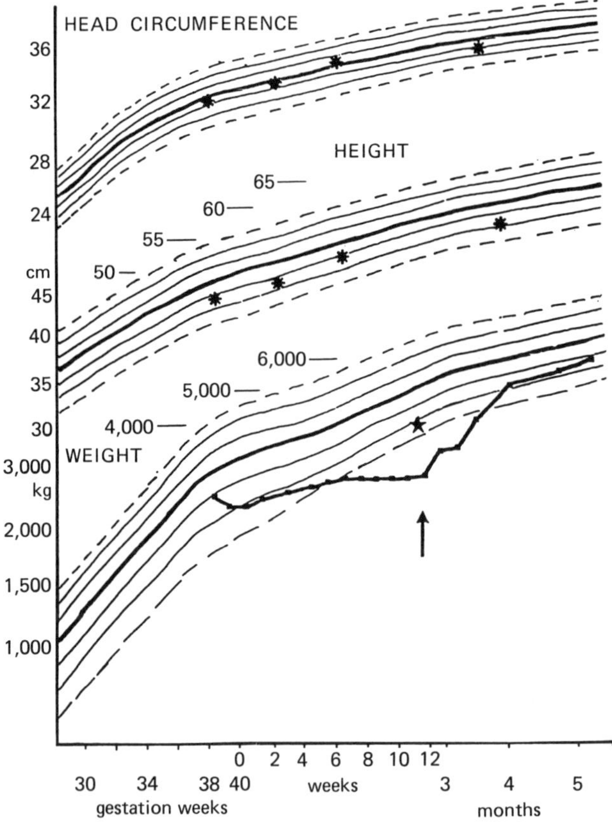

Fig. 2. Growth of a child on total parenteral nutrition before the after providing requirements according to expected weight for age. Mean ± SD after P. Karlberg.

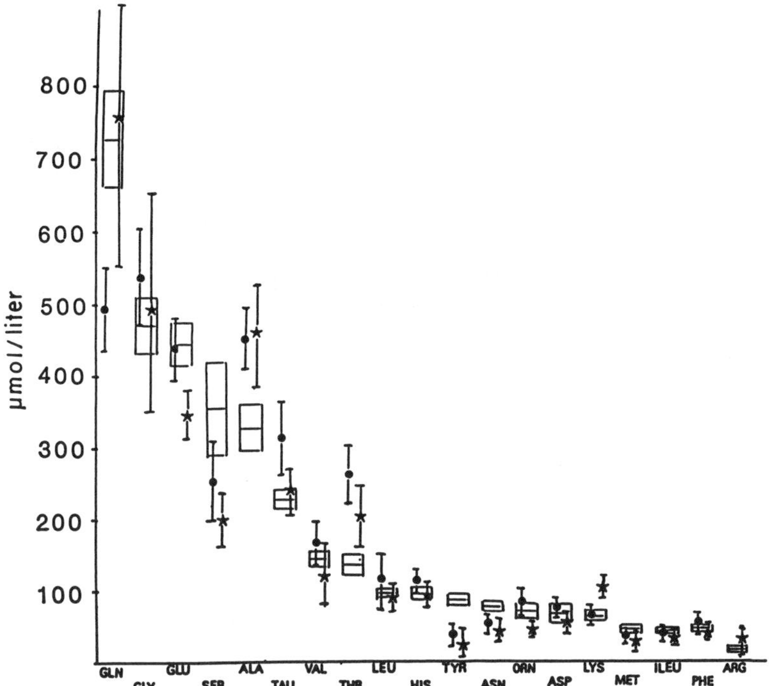

Fig. 3. The peripheral blood concentrations of free amino acids in a newborn infant on total parenteral nutrition with dosage according to actual weight (●) or according to expected weight for age (★) (see Fig. 2). The normal background represents the levels seen in normal newborn breast-fed infants during the first weight increase.

babies during the first postnatal weight increase. However, it should be realized that normality here is a questionable condition and is dependent on the mode of feeding (Lindblad, 1970; Lindblad *et al.*, 1978, 1984). In the case of the premature newborn infants no normality exists, since at that stage of development they would still be in the womb. *In utero*, the fetus is provided with amino acids actively transported against a gradient that varies substantially between the different amino acids (Lindblad and Baldesten, 1967) (Fig. 4). All amino acids have higher fetal than maternal levels, with, during normal delivery, especially high cord/maternal ratios for the dibasic amino acids (over 3/1) and taurine (over 4/1). Recent studies of samples collected during fetoscopies (Calvert *et al.*, 1985; see also Chapter 14) at 16–20 weeks show an overall higher fetal/maternal ratio (2.4 against 1.9) and a spectrum different from that of these earlier studies with sampling at birth.

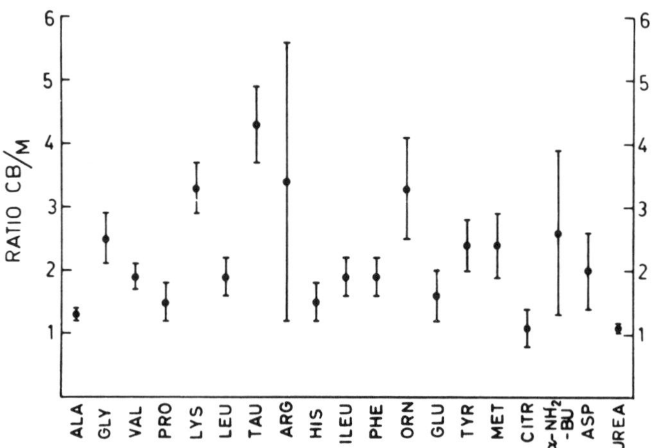

Fig. 4. The cord plasma/maternal venous plasma free amino acid levels during normal deliveries at term (Lindblad and Baldesten, 1967).

B. Preterm Infants

These figures for the full term should be compared to an accretion rate of around 350 mg/kg/day of nitrogen at the 28th week of gestation. But the newborn very low birth weight (VLBW) infant is not an extragestational fetus and no firm conclusions may be drawn from fetal accretion rates.

In studies with stable isotope probes de Benoist and co-workers (1984) have found whole-body protein synthesis and degradation in preterm infants of 11.3 and 9.5 g/kg/day on an intake of 465 mg N/kg/day. Nitrogen retention, measured by nitrogen balance, was similar to that calculated from the leucine retention (intake minus oxidation), namely, 310 and 301 mg of nitrogen per kg/day. Other kinetic tracer studies have shown a net protein synthesis of 2.2 g/kg/day in very small preterm infants, 1.9 g in moderately preterm, and 1.8 g in full term during peroral human milk feeding (Plath *et al.*, 1985). However, estimations of whole-body protein synthesis from distribution and excretion of stable isotopes are dependent on several assumptions which are difficult to validate and are considered to underestimate absolute rates by 10–20%. Considering the fact that preterm infants contain around 20% muscle tissue as compared to 40% found in adults, urinary excretion of 3-methylhistidine indicates a muscle protein turnover around three times that of adults in preterm newborn infants (Sander *et al.*, 1986).

Studies by Chessex and co-workers (1985) indicate that with intakes of 80 kcal/kg/day and 450 mg N/kg/day provided by chrystalline amino

TABLE II

Recommended Supply of Amino Acid Nitrogen Using Vamin (134 mg N/g)

Full term (40 weeks)	320 mg N/kg/day = 2.7 g/kg/day
Preterm (28 weeks)	450 mg N/kg/day = 3.4 g/kg/day

acid solutions, the parenterally fed preterm infant sustains a growth rate and a nitrogen retention similar to those of a third-trimester fetus. The rapid increase in weight, length, and head circumference points to the accretion of new tissue. This would mean a maximum of 3.4 g amino acids/kg/day in the use of Vamin solution. See Table II.

III. THE AMINO ACID BALANCE OF THE SOLUTION, OR REFERENCE PROTEIN QUALITY

A. Peroral Milk Protein Load and Amino Acid Metabolism

What is the tolerance to a nitrogen load in the form of an ideal protein, like that of human milk protein, given orally to the VLBW infant? In our experience a doubling of the human milk protein content of the mother's own milk (Hagelberg *et al.*, 1982) causes no derangement of the homeostasis of free amino acids, azotemia, or acid–base disturbance (Fig. 5). VLBW infants with genetically normal enzymes seem to be at minimal risk of developing hyperphenylalaninemia while receiving this increased supply of human milk protein (Rönnholm *et al.*, 1984). The low initial content of methionine and tyrosine in preterm milk might be an advantage (Britton, 1986) in view of the decreased capacity of the oxidative pathways encountered in VLBW infants for these amino acids. The high level of serine in preterm milk might be a result of the high amounts of immunoglobulin A in preterm milk; the availability of secretory IgA is not clear, however. The high content of arginine in preterm milk might be advantageous by protecting against hyperammonemia (Heird *et al.*, 1972).

B. Parenteral Amino Acid Load and Amino Acid Metabolism

No amino acid solution currently available results in a completely normal plasma amino acid pattern. Concerns over this are based on the long-established relationship between mental retardation and abnormal

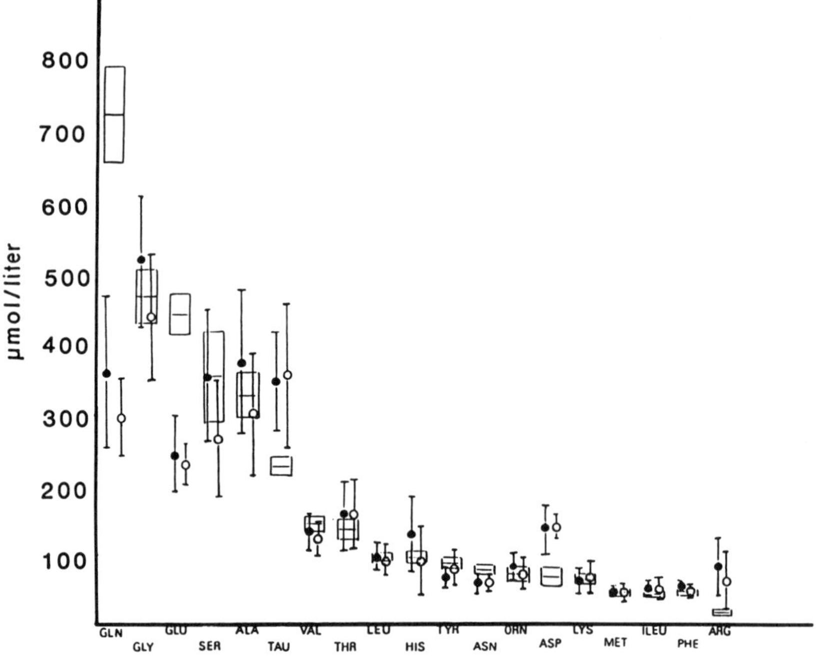

Fig. 5. The free amino acid levels of peripheral venous whole blood during feeding of VLBW newborn infants with (●) the mother's own milk enriched to double protein concentrations with human milk protein powder (Hagelberg *et al.*, 1982) or (○) cow's milk protein. Boxes indicate mean values ± 2 SE in breast-fed infants.

plasma amino acid concentrations in patients with various inborn errors of metabolism. It is conceivable that *in vivo* excesses or imbalances of certain amino acids in plasma could, through an effect on membrane transport, result in relative intracellular substrate excesses or limitations of other amino acids. Several amino acids are potentially neurotoxic when an imbalanced homeostasis is the result of an imbalanced supply or a defect metabolism.

C. Conditionally Indispensable Amino Acids

To the newly born immature individual all amino acids found in proteins are probably "conditionally indispensable" during fast growth, and there is general agreement that amino acid solutions should contain all these amino acids. The question of essentiality or not is probably irrelevant in this context. The VLBW newborn infant is perhaps best compared to an organ culture; in addition to the eight amino acids essential to man, organ cultures require cysteine, tyrosine, histidine, arginine, and glutamine. There are indications that all these amino acids are "conditionally indispensable" to the newborn premature infant. Gaull *et al.* (1972) observed that hepatic cystathionase, the rate-limiting enzyme in the production of cysteine from methionine, was virtually absent in second-trimester human fetuses. As preterm and term newborn infants increase in postnatal age, hepatic cystathionase rapidly increases. Snyderman (1971) documented an impaired nitrogen retention and weight gain in infants in the absence of an enteral source of cysteine. Zlotkin *et al.* (1982) and Malloy *et al.* (1984) have recently cast doubt on the essential nature of cysteine, observing that infants receiving cysteine-supplemented total parenteral nutrition (TPN) failed to retain nitrogen and gain weight better than infants who received unsupplemented TPN. However, over a short period of time it seems likely that, in the absence of an exogenous source of cysteine, glutathione may be an adequate source of cysteine for growth (Malloy *et al.*, 1984) so that the nitrogen balance may not be affected.

The essentiality of certain constituents present in human milk, but with unclear biological significance, has been discussed. Taurine, although not a constituent of proteins, is present in human milk and in very high concentrations in liver, brain, and muscle. It may have the important biological function of protecting cell membranes against oxidants and reduced oxygen molecules. Prolonged treatment with TPN without taurine to LBW infants may lead to a mild reversible electroretinographic abnormality, which is reversed by taurine (Geggel *et al.*, 1985). However, the addition of taurine to amino acid solutions for *short-term* general use does not seem to be supported by available data, nor can its role in the prevention of cholestasis be determined at present (Cooke *et al.*, 1984).

D. Biochemical Monitoring

The ideal protein for the newborn infant during *peroral* feeding is supposed to be represented by the composition of human milk. We know that glutamic acid, which dominates milk composition, is transaminated to alanine during gut absorption. Alanine is the leading gluconeogenetic amino acid and probably an ideal source of nonspecific nitrogen. A solution has therefore been suggested that is based on the composition of hydrolyzed human milk proteins with a decrease of glutamic acid concentration and an increase of alanine (Lindblad *et al.*, 1979); it is now produced by Vitrum Company, Stockholm, and is called Vaminolac. An evaluation has to be based on clinical experience with biochemical monitoring. Of special interest are the blood levels of the sulfur-containing amino acid methionine, the aromatic amino acids phenylalanine and tyrosine, threonine, and possibly glycine, for which the intermediate metabolism seems to be defective until term. Monitoring is now possible through HPLC analysis of very small amounts of whole blood (Watanabe and Imai, 1984).

E. Cholestasis

Biochemical monitoring should take into account the earliest signs of cholestasis, a complication of parenteral nutrition of LBW newborn babies that has been attributed to both amino acid toxicity and the lack of *enteral* nutrition. Methionine may obliterate bile salt-independent bile flow in perfused rat liver and alanine inhibits uptake of taurocholate by isolated rat hepatocytes (Whitington, 1985). Hypermethioninemia is seen in different hepatic disorders and is also a common disturbance seen during monitoring of TPN in premature infants (Cooper *et al.* 1984; Chessex *et al.*, 1985; Schröder and Paust, 1986). The severity of TPN-induced cholestasis depends on the duration of TPN and the quantity of protein infused. In an investigation of 75 preterm infants by Sankaran *et al.* (1985), all who received more than 2.5 g/kg/day of protein base for more than 4 weeks uniformly developed cholestatic jaundice, which was completely resolved after several weeks of oral feeding. In comparing two solutions with chrystalline amino acids, Aminosyn from Abbot and Vamin from Vitrum, there was a significantly decreased cholestasis in the Vamin group. The differences between these two solutions are that Aminosyn contains proportionately more methionine and threonine and Vamin more phenylalanine. Vamin also contains aspartic acid, glutamic acid, and cysteine/cystine, which are lacking in Aminosyn. There might also be differences in the preparation of the two solutions. With prolonged fasting the bile salt pool becomes sequestered in the liver or gallbladder and bile flow is presumably diminished. This phenomenon may potentially lead to cholestasis, or make the organism more susceptible to cholestatic factors (Merritt, 1986). Feeding infants and stopping TPN as early as possible are important in preventing liver disease and are the only effective means of reversing TPN cholestasis at present.

F. The Amino Acid Balance of the Solution

Greater nitrogen retention has been demonstrated for Vamin, which is based on the composition of whole egg, than for Travasol in newborn VLBW infants. Travasol contains a disproportionate amount of glycine and alanine as nitrogen sources, which leads to very high plasma levels of glycine, as high as those seen in nonketotic hyperglycinemia, and a high urinary glycine excretion. Few side reactions have been reported from the infusion of solutions with high glycine concentration, provided that the arginine content is sufficient to avoid hyperammonemia. Methionine levels more than four times higher than those present during human milk feeding were found when using Travasol. Higher plasma tyrosine concentrations and urinary excretion of para-hydroxy-phenylpyruvic acid (PHPPA) were found during the Vamin phase of these crossover studies.

It has been proposed that those amino acids which accumulate in peripheral blood should be lowered in the solution, and those which decrease should be raised. As Vernon Young *et al.* pointed out in Chapter 18, the relationship of plasma amino acid patterns to protein synthesis and to intracellular amino acid pools is largely unexplored. However, studies using a cell model, the granulocyte (Johnson and Metcoff, 1986), have indicated that protein synthesis is higher in smaller neonates. This is consistent with data from animal work (Nissim *et al.*, 1983) and ^{15}N studies of total-body nitrogen flux in preterm and smaller for date infants (Pencharz *et al.*, 1981). Furthermore, the protein synthesis rate seems to be predicted from the levels of a few intracellular amino acids (leucine, methionine, tyrosine, glycine, alanine, taurine), whose concentrations in turn can be predicted from specific sets of plasma amino acids (Johnson and Metcoff, 1986).

Trophamine is a solution for parenteral nutrition of newborn infants worked out by Dr. W. C. Heird and co-workers by computer analysis of available plasma amino acid data. One recent study from Japan claims a high nitrogen retention in the use of such a solution (Kanaya *et al.*, 1984). However, important problems remain. Let us take tyrosine as an example. (See Table III.) Fetal accretion during the last trimester is 265 μmol/kg/day. Because of the insolubility of tyrosine in water, the amount given with Vamin is 120 μmol/kg/day. In spite of the relatively low amounts, Vamin leads to increased amounts of aromatic amino acids and high PHPPA excretion in some low birth weight babies. Travasol provides 40 μmol/kg/day and leads to normal levels of tyrosine in all cases of VLBW on parenteral nutrition with adequate caloric supply. Does this imply that Travasol is "better"? Could it not mean that the

TABLE III

Tyrosine

Fetal accretion rate	265 μmol/kg/day
Vamin provides	120 μmol/kg/day
Travasol provides	40 μmol/kg/day

placenta provides amino acids in such a balanced composition that the efficient protein synthesis takes care of all tyrosine supplied without stress to the oxidizing system of the fetus? The obvious question would be: Is it rational to use a solution in which one essential amino acid is clearly far below the requirement for an optimal protein synthesis? In view of the metabolic immaturity seen, it could be just as logical to lower the total supply of amino acids. The clinical significance of the functional

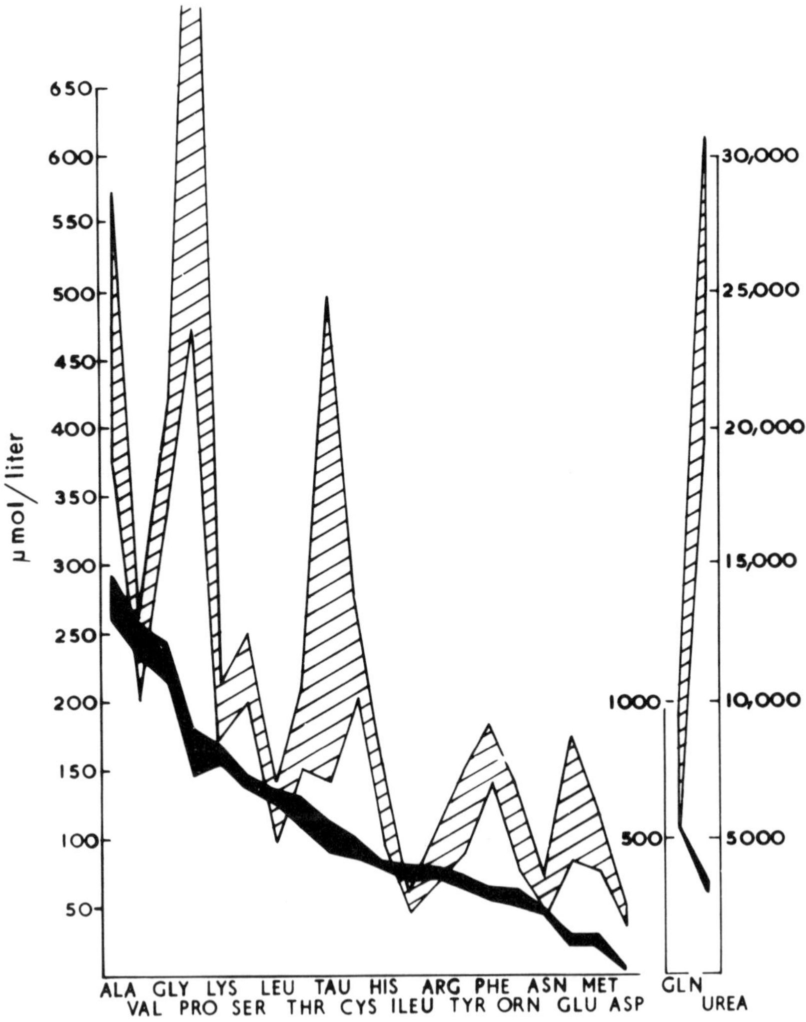

Fig. 6. Free amino acid levels in peripheral blood plasma of young infants during TPN and septic shock (Lindblad *et al.*, 1977).

overload of the tyrosine-oxidizing system is questionable. Impaired mental development has been associated with neonatal hypertyrosinemia, but other studies have failed to show any signs of central nervous system dysfunction after short-term hypertyrosinemia. However, the present-day experiments with more soluble dipeptides containing tyrosine must be thoroughly evaluated in view of the low tolerance found in the LBW newborn babies.

Higher threonine levels are seen in preterm infants given an excess of whey proteins, which means a higher threonine intake. The findings indicate a metabolic immaturity in the handling of threonine and caution the use of amounts of whey proteins greater than 60% of a total of 3 g/kg/day (Scott *et al.*, 1985; Calvert *et al.*, 1985). We found (Lindblad *et al.*, 1977) during monitoring of TPN in newborn infants that in the case of sepsis with shock, the levels of free amino acids in peripheral blood plasma could exceed what is tolerated in inborn errors of metabolism. The proline levels shown in Fig. 6 are higher than what we have seen in any conditions. Careful monitoring is mandatory during parenteral nutrition after a birth trauma, an operation, or an infection that decreases the protein synthesis rate and thereby renders the VLBW infant susceptible to accumulation of potentially toxic amino acids. A study of organ extraction of amino acids *in vivo* may provide additional information about the ideal composition of amino acid solutions. Studies in adults on muscle uptake are not as relevant to the problems of VLBW newborn infants, who have much less muscle tissue and proportionately more liver and brain tissue. However, even with the most modern, sensitive methods the A–V difference across organs, as in the brain, rarely are statistically significant (Settergren *et al.*, 1976).

IV. CONCLUSION

We believe that a thorough study of the relative speed of the amino acid release from the protein hydrolysis in the gastrointestinal canal, of gut mucosal metabolism of amino acids, and of the splanchnic extraction of amino acids under normal conditions would provide a basis for the composition of different intravenous solutions for clinical evaluation. Studies of amino acid metabolism under different pathological conditions are necessary to further modify the composition of special-purpose solutions.

TPN provides an ideal experimental situation for studying developmental aspects of the metabolism of individual amino acids by stable isotope technique. This will provide us with necessary data for the further development of an optimal amino acid solution for newborn infants.

Clinical evaluation of new solutions should include the study of nitrogen retention, protein synthesis rate, hormonal response, and growth.

REFERENCES

Britton, J. R. (1986). Milk protein quality in mothers delivering prematurely: Implications for infants in the intensive care unit nursery setting. *J. Pediatr., Gastroenterol. Nutr.* **5,** 116–121.

Calvert, S. A., Soltesz, G., Jenkins, P. A., Harris, D., Newman, C., Adrian, T. E., Bloom, S. R., and Aynsley-Green, A. (1985). Feeding premature infants with human milk or preterm milk formula. *Biol. Neonate* **47,** 189–198.

Chessex, P., Zebiche, H., Pineault, M., Lapage, D., and Dallaire, L. (1985). Effect of amino acid composition of parenteral solutions on nitrogen retention and metabolic response in very-low-birth weight infants. *J. Pediatr.* **106,** 111–117.

Cooke, R. J., Whitington, P. F., and Kelts, D. (1984). Effect of taurine supplementation on hepatic function during short term parenteral nutrition in the premature infant. *J. Pediatr., Gastroenterol. Nutr.* **3,** 234–238.

Cooper, A., Betts, J. M., Pereira, G. R., and Ziegler, M. M. (1984). Taurine deficiency in the severe hepatic dysfunction complicationg total parenteral nutrition. *J. Pediatr. Surg.* **19,** 462–466.

de Benoist, B., Abdulrazzac, Y., Brooke, O. G., Halliday, D., and Millward, D. J. (1984). The measurement of whole body protein turnover in the preterm infant with intragastric infusion of L-/[1-^{13}c]leucine and sampling of the urinary leucine pool. *Clin. Sci.* **66,** 155–164.

Duffy, B., and Pencharz, P. (1986). The effect of feeding route (IV or oral) on the protein metabolism of the neonate. *Am. J. Clin. Nutr.* **43,** 108–111.

Gaull, G. E., Sturman, J. A., and Räihä, N. C. R. (1972). Development of mammalian sulfur metabolism. Absence of cystathionase in human fetal tissues. *Pediatr. Res.* **6,** 538–547.

Geggel, H. S., Ament, M. E., Heckenlively, J. R., Martin, D. A., and Kopple, J. D. (1985). Nutritional requirement for taurine in patients receiving long-term parenteral nutrition. *N. Engl. J. Med.* **312,** 142–146.

Hagelberg, S., Lindblad, B. S., Lundsjö, A., Carlsson, B., Fonden, R., Fujita, H., Lassfolk, G., and Lindquist, B. (1982). The protein tolerance of very low birth weight infants fed human milk protein enriched mother's milk. *Acta Paediatr. Scand.* **71,** 597–601.

Heird, W. C., Nicholson, J. F., Driscoll, J. M., Jr., Schullinger, J. N., and Winters, R. W. (1972). Hyperammonemia resulting from intravenous alimentation using a mixture of synthetic L-amino acids: A preliminary report. *J. Pediatr.* **81,** 162–167.

Johnson, C., and Metcoff, J. (1986). Relation of protein synthesis to plasma and cell amino acids in neonates. *Pediatr. Res.* **20,** 140–146.

Kanaya, S., Nose, O., Harada, T., Kai, H., Ogawa, M., Maki, I., Tajiri, H., Kimura, S., Yabuuchi, H., Imura, K., Kamata, S., Itakura, T., Tagaki, Y., and Okada, A. (1984). Total parenteral nutrition with a new amino acid solution for infants. *J. Pediatr. Gastroenterol. Nutr.* **3,** 440–445.

Lindblad, B. S., (1970). The venous plasma free amino acid levels during the first hours of life. I. After normal and short gestation and gestation complicated by hypertension. With special reference to the "small for dates" syndrome. *Acta Paediatr. Scand.* **59,** 13–20.

Lindblad, B. S., and Baldesten, A. (1967). The normal venous plasma free amino acid levels of non-pregnant women and of mother and child during delivery. *Acta Paediatr. Scand.* **56,** 37–48.

Lindblad, B. S., Settergren, G., Feychting, H., and Persson, B. (1977). Total parenteral nutrition in infants. Blood levels of glucose, lactate, pyruvate, free fatty acids, glycerol, D-beta-/hydroxybutyrate, triglycerides, free amino acids and insulin. *Acta Paediatr. Scand.* **66,** 409–419.

Lindblad, B. S., Alfvén, G., and Zetterström, R. (1978). Plasma free amino acid concentrations of breast-fed infants. *Acta Paediatr. Scand.* **67,** 659–663.

Lindblad, B. S., Alfvén, G., and Ginsburg, B. E. (1979). The intravenous and peroral requirements of amino acids during early infancy. *In* "Nutrition and Metabolism of the Fetus and Infant" (H. K. A. Visser, ed.), pp. 325–339. Stenfert Kroese, Leiden.

Lindblad, B. S., Ginsburg, B. E., Lundsjö, A., Persson, B., and Zetterström, R. (1984). Plasma valine and urinary C-peptide in breast-fed and artificially fed infants up to 6 months of age. *Acta Paediatr. Scand.* **73,** 213–217.

Malloy, M. H., Rassin, D. K., and Richardson, C. J. (1984). Total parenteral nutrition in sick preterm infants: Effects of cysteine supplementation with nitrogen intakes of 240 and 400 mg/kg/day. *J. Pediatr., Gastroenterol. Nutr.* **3,** 239–244.

Merritt, R. J. (1986). Cholestasis associated with total parenteral nutrition. *J. Pediatr., Gastroenterol. Nutr.* **5,** 9–22.

Nissim, I., Yudkoff, M., Pereira, G., and Segal, S. (1983). Effects of conceptual age and dietary intake on protein metabolism in premature infants. *J. Pediatr., Gastroent. Nutr.* **2,** 507–516.

Pencharz, P. B., Masson, M., Desgranges, F., and Papageorgiou, A. (1981). Total body protein turnover in the human premature neonate: Effects of birthweight, intrauterine nutritional status and diet. *Clin. Sci.* **61,** 207–215.

Plath, C., Heine, W., Krienke, L., Richter, I., Wutzke, K. D., Töwe, J., and Krawielitzki, K. (1985). ^{15}N-tracer-kinetic studies on the nitrogen metabolism of very small preterm infants on a diet of mother's milk. *Hum. Nutr.: Clin. Nutr.* **39C,** 399–409.

Rönnholm, K. A. R., Simell, O., and Siimes, M. A. (1984). Human milk protein and medium-chain triglyceride oil supplementation of human milk: Plasma amino acids in very low birth weight infants. *Pediatrics* **74,** 792–799.

Sander, G., Hulsemann, J., Topp, H., Heller-Schöch, G., and Schöch, G. 91986). Protein and RNA turnover in preterm infants and adults: A comparison based on urinary excretion of 3-/methylhistidine and of modified one-way RNA catabolites. *Ann. Nutr. Metab.* **30,** 137–142.

Sankaran, K., Berscheid, B., Verma, V., Zakhary, G., and Tan, L. (1985). An evaluation of total parenteral nutrition using Vamin and Aminosyn as protein base in critically ill preterm infants. *JPEN, J. Parenter. Enteral Nutr.* **9,** 439–442.

Schröder, H., and Paust, H. (1986). Plasma amino acids in supplementary parenteral nutrition of preterm infants. *Acta Paediatr. Scand.* **75,** 302–307.

Scott, P. H., Berger, H. M., and Wharton, B. A. (1985). Growth velocity and plasma amino acids in the newborn. *Pediatr. Res.* **19,** 446–450.

Settergren, G., Lindblad, B. S., and Persson, B. (1976). Cerebral blood flow and exchange of oxygen, glucose, ketone bodies, lactate, pyruvate and amino acids in infants. *Acta Paediatr. Scand.* **65,** 343–353.

Snyderman, S. E. (1971). The protein anmd amino acid requirements of the premature infant. *In* "Metabolic Processes in the Fetus and Newborn Infant" (J. H. P. Jonxis, H. K. A. Visser, and J. A. Troelstra, eds.), pp. 128–141. Stenfert Kroese, Leiden.

Watanabe, Y., and Imai, K. (1984). Sensitive detection of amino acids in human serum and dried blood disc of 3 mm diameter for diagnosis of inborn errors of metabolism. *J. Chromatogr.* **309,** 279–286.

Whitington, P. F. (1985). Cholestasis associated with total parenteral nutrition in infants. *Hepatology* **5,** 693–696.

Winters, R. W., Heird, W. C., and Dell, R. B. (1984). History of parenteral nutrition in pediatrics with emphasis on amino acids. *Fed. Proc., Fed. Am. Soc. Exp. Biol.* **43,** 1407–1411.

Zlotkin, S. H. (1984). Intravenous nitrogen intake requirements in full-term newborns undergoing surgery. *Pediatrics* **73,** 493–496.

Zlotkin, S. H., Anderson, G. H., and Bryan, M. H. (1982). Cysteine supplementation to cysteine-free intravenous feeding regimens in newborn infants. *Am. J. Clin. Nutr.* **36,** 862–867.

27

Evaluation of a Pediatric Multiple-Vitamin Preparation for Total Parenteral Nutrition: Blood Levels of Vitamins A, D, and E

Harry L. Greene
and Mary E. Courtney Moore
Department of Pediatric Gastroenterology and Nutrition
Vanderbilt University School of Medicine
Nashville, Tennessee, U.S.A.

Barry Phillips and Linda Franck
Department of Pediatric Gastroenterology
Oakland Children's Hospital
Oakland, California, U.S.A.

I. INTRODUCTION

Total parenteral nutrition (TPN) is being used as the major source of nutrition in large numbers of infants throughout North America and Europe. Although vitamins are essential components of TPN, no studies that systematically evaluate blood levels of vitamins A, D, and E in infants receiving either short- or long-term total parenteral nutrition have been published. Reports of lipid-soluble vitamin deficiencies (Callenbach *et al.*, 1981; Shike *et al.*, 1981; Howard *et al.*, 1980), as well as toxicities (Di Palma and Ritchie, 1977; Lorch *et al.*, 1985), illustrate the need for more information on the vitamin needs of the typical infant requiring total parenteral nutrition. In addition, the putative roles of vitamins A and D in normal cell differentiation (Wolf, 1984; Mangelsdorf *et al.*, 1984) and vitamin E in the prevention of retinopathy and intraventricular hemorrhage associated with prematurity (Hittner *et al.*, 1984; Chiswick *et al.*, 1983) emphasize the need for information on these specific vitamins in the premature infants. The need for guidelines for use of vitamins in total parenteral nutrition was recognized by the American Medical Association (AMA) Nutrition Advisory Group (NAG) (Nutrition Advisory Group, 1975), which published recommendations for intravenous use based on Recommended Dietary Allowances (RDA) (National Research Council, 1980). Recently, a commercial preparation containing the amount of vitamins suggested by the AMA was made available for use in pediatric patients in the United States (MVI Pediatric, Armour Pharmaceutical, N.Y.).

This paper documents blood levels of vitamins A, D, and E in premature infants receiving total parenteral nutrition (primarily those weighing less than 1500 g). Because infants less than 1000 g may have different requirements than the larger premature, two doses of vitamin E were used in this group of patients.

II. METHODS

A. Vitamins in Total Parenteral Nutrition

The vitamin mixture used for the study was MVI Pediatric, manufactured and marketed by Revlon Health Care (Armour Pharmaceutical). Vitamins were added to the total parenteral nutrition mixture of glucose (10 to 27.5%), amino acids (2 to 3%), macrominerals, and trace minerals (including zinc and iron). MVI is a mixture of all water-soluble and fat-soluble vitamins which is provided as a lyophilized preparation. Each vial contains the daily amount of vitamins suggested by the AMA NAG recommendations for term infants and children. Premature infants re-

TABLE I

Comparison of Recommended Intakes and Dose Given

	Recommended Daily Allowance or safe and adequate intake for children				Daily dose given	
Vitamin	0.05 year	0.5–3 years	4–6 years	7–12 years	Preterm infants	Infants and children[a]
A (μg)[b]	420	400	500	700	455	700
D (IU)[c]	400	400	400	400	260	400
E (mg)[d]	3	4–5	6	7	4.6	7

[a]American Medical Association National Advisory Group recommendation.
[b]Retinol equivalents: 1 retinol equivalent = 1 μg of retinol or 6 μg of β-carotene.
[c]As cholecalciferol: 10 μg of cholecalciferol = 400 IU of vitamin D.
[d]Alpha-tocopherol equivalents: 1 α-tocopherol equivalent = 1 mg of D-α-tocopherol.

ceived 65% of the vial in the TPN mixture, which was delivered continuously over a 24-hr period each day. Daily doses are listed in Table I and are compared with the most current RDA or "safe and adequate intake". Intralipid 10%, made by Kabi : Vitrum, Stockholm, was used as a source of calories and essential fatty acids in the majority of infants. This solution contains minimal amounts of α-tocopherol but substantial amounts of γ-tocopherol, which has little antioxidant activity. Measurement of tocopherol by HPLC discriminates the various tocopherols and results given in this paper describe only the α-tocopherol levels.

B. Patients

Patients were all of appropriate weight for gestational age. Group 1 consisted of 18 infants with weights between 740 and 1830 g; eight patients weighed less than 1000 g and received TPN as the sole source of calories for at least 3 weeks (mean 28 days). The remainder received TPN for a mean duration of 16 days. This group of infants received 65% of the MVI vial (dose listed in Table I) and blood levels of all vitamins were assayed. Results of the water-soluble vitamins are published elsewhere (Moore *et al.*, 1986).

Twelve of the infants received oral α-tocopherol supplements (Aquasol E, 80 to 150 mg/day). These supplements were standard practice in the nursery and were prescribed primarily for those patients of lowest birth weight; consequently, the number of unsupplemented infants weighing less than 1000 g was insufficient to allow comparison between supplemented and unsupplemented infants in this weight category. It was necessary to compare supplemented and unsupplemented infants for Group 1 as a whole.

Group 2 consisted of 49 infants who received no oral vitamin supplements and were evaluated for two doses of the vitamin (MVI) preparation. In this study, only the blood levels of α-tocopherol were evaluated. These infants were further divided into two groups: (2a) those less than 1000 g who received 65% (4.7 mg α-tocopherol) of the MVI vial and (2b) those less than 1000 g who received 30% of the MVI vial (2.2 mg α-tocopherol) daily.

C. Laboratory Analyses and Reference Values

All vitamin determinations for this study were done in the Clinical Nutrition Research Unit Laboratory at Vanderbilt University. Quality control measures used in the laboratory meet the requirements of the Joint Commission of American Hospitals and the College of American Pathologists.

Measurement of retinol and α-tocopherol were made by high-pressure liquid chromatography using retinyl acetate and D-α-tocopherol acetate as internal standards (Bieri *et al.*, 1979). The intrassay coefficient of variability was 2.78% for retinol and 3.43% for α-tocopherol.

Assays for 25-OH vitamin D were performed using competitive protein binding (Haddad and Ghyu, 1971). Samples were compared with standards (known concentrations) using a spectrophotometric extinction coefficient. The infused vitamin was D_2, but the assay determines both 25-OH D_2 and D_3. Therefore, levels reflected both exogenous administration and endogenous synthesis. Retinol-binding protein was measured by a binding assay using commercially available radial diffusion plates (Behring Diagnostics, Somerville, NJ).

D. Data Analysis

The limitations in blood volume made it impossible to perform each analysis for each patient at each time point. Because of the missing data, changes in vitamin levels between baseline and other time points were analyzed by paired *t* test rather than analysis of variance or by repeated measures analysis using a randomized block design. Differences between different groups (e.g., infants <1000 g and those >1000 g) were evaluated by unpaired *t* test.

III. RESULTS

No patients showed substantial changes in laboratory values for hematologic or hepatic function as determined by serum transaminase or direct bilirubin levels during the period of vitamin infusion.

A. Vitamin A (Retinol)

Group 1.

Although there was little intraindividual variation, the large interindividual variation caused a large standard error when infants were grouped as a whole. Mean plasma concentration was low initially (13.9 ± 1.3 μg/dl) and decreased to 12.3 ± 2.7 μg/dl by the third week (change not significant) (Table II). Because of the wide interindividual variation in the samples, the patients were grouped according to birth weight. These data are depicted in Fig. 1 and demonstrate that, after 4 days, infants with birth weights less than 1000 g had significantly lower plasma retinol levels than the larger infants.

Hepatic retinol was measured in one infant of 30 to 31 weeks gestational age who died of lung disease after 3 weeks of therapy. The level was 8 μg/g of liver, which was at the lower end of the range of values found in fetuses of similar gestational age (Montreewasuwat and Olson, 1979).

Retinol-binding protein levels are listed in Table II and showed somewhat less interpatient variability than vitamin A. The coefficient of correlation between retinol-binding protein and retinol levels was 0.564. Although there were no significant differences between retinol-binding protein levels in infants weighing less than 1000 g and those greater than 1000 g initially, infants weighing greater than 1000 g had significantly higher levels on days 14 and 21 ($p < .05$).

B. Vitamin E

Group 1.

The mean levels of vitamin E up to 28 days of treatment are shown in Table III. Although the mean initial level of α-tocopherol (0.31 ± 0.03

TABLE II

Retinol and 25-OH Vitamin D Levels in Very Low Birth Weight Infants (Group 1)[a]

Day	Retinol (μg/dl)	RBP (mg/dl)	25-OH D (ng/dl)
0	13.9 ± 1.3	2.1 ± 0.14	12.25 ± 1.27
4	14.6 ± 1.1	2.0 ± 0.17	17.17 ± 2.56
7	10.4 ± 1.5	1.8 ± 0.17	23.95 ± 3.3
14	13.0 ± 2.8	2.3 ± 0.25	27.8 ± 2.7
21	12.3 ± 2.7	1.9 ± 0.30	—
28	13.5 ± 2.5	2.0 ± 0.50	—

[a]Reference values from term infant cord blood: retinol = 15.7 ± 1.2 μg/dl, retinol-binding protein (RBP) = 3.14 ± 0.17 mg/dl, 25-OH vitamin D (25-OH D) = 17.4 ± 1.4 ng/dl. No retinol or RBP values were different from the baseline; 25-OH D levels were different from the baseline on days 7 and 14.

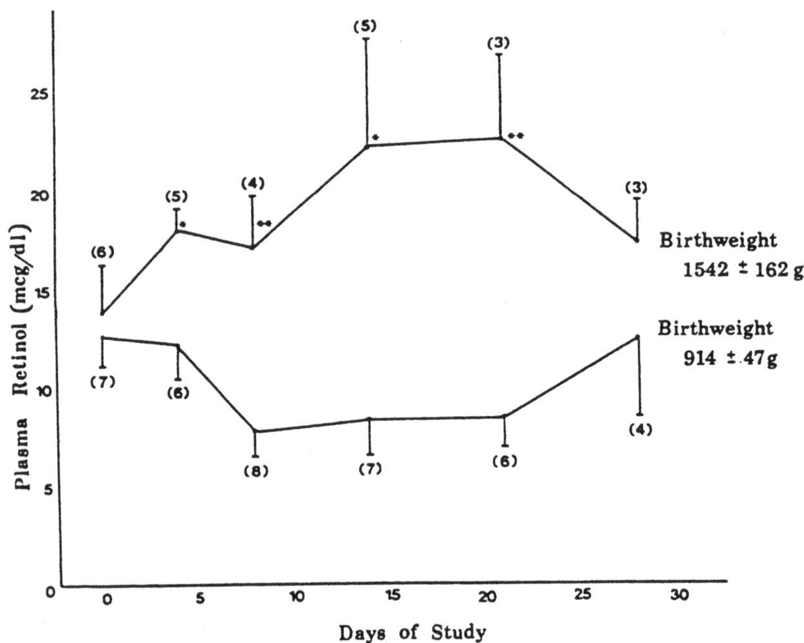

Fig. 1. Vitamin A levels in infants with birth weights greater than and less than 1000 g. Numbers of infants are shown in parentheses. Differences between the two groups are significant $*P < .05$; $**P < .01$. Bars are means + SEM. Reproduced by permission of *Pediatrics*, Vol. 77, pp. 542 and 544. Copyright 1986.

mg/dl) was within the reference range for term infants, seven infants had levels below 0.22 mg/dl, a level generally associated with increased RBC peroxide hemolysis. Figure 2 illustrates the rapid increase in vitamin E levels with total parenteral nutrition and a comparison of the infants receiving oral vitamin E with those not given oral vitamin E. Those without oral supplements showed an increase to a peak mean of 1.47 ± 0.20 mg/dl (different from the initial value, $p < .01$). In the orally supplemented group, there was a progressive increase in vitamin E levels to 3.49 ± 0.57 mg/dl by the third week. Three of these infants reached levels of 5.6, 5.6, and 5.4 mg/dl. Only one of the unsupplemented infants received TPN for as long as 4 weeks. This infant had a blood level of 1.9 mg/dl at the end of 4 weeks, compared with a mean plasma level of 3.4 ± 0.58 mg/dl in the seven supplemented infants who received TPN for 4 weeks. Blood cholesterol levels were only performed sporadically because of the small volume of blood available for assay. There was little difference in the comparative results, in that the unsupplemented group showed a mean level of 10.4 ± 0.8 mg/g of cholesterol. The supplemented

TABLE III

Alpha-Tocopherol Levels in Very Low Birth Weight Infants[a]

Group	Baseline	Day of study							
		1	2	3	4	7	14	21	28
Group 1	0.31 ± 0.03	—	—	—	165 ± 0.17	1.91 ± 0.17	2.11 ± 0.24	3.08 ± 0.45	3.00 ± 0.52
Group 2a	0.25 ± 0.02	—	1.46 ± 0.18	1.78 ± 0.31	—	1.88 ± 0.21	1.76 ± 0.37	1.65 ± 0.32	—
Group 2b	0.26 ± 0.03	0.75 ± 0.21	1.16 ± 0.17	1.21 ± 0.20	—	1.18 ± 0.18	1.00 ± 0.21	—	—

[a]Results given in mg/dl. Reference normals from term infant cord blood = 0.29 ± 0.04 mg/dl. All values are different from the baseline at $p < .001$.

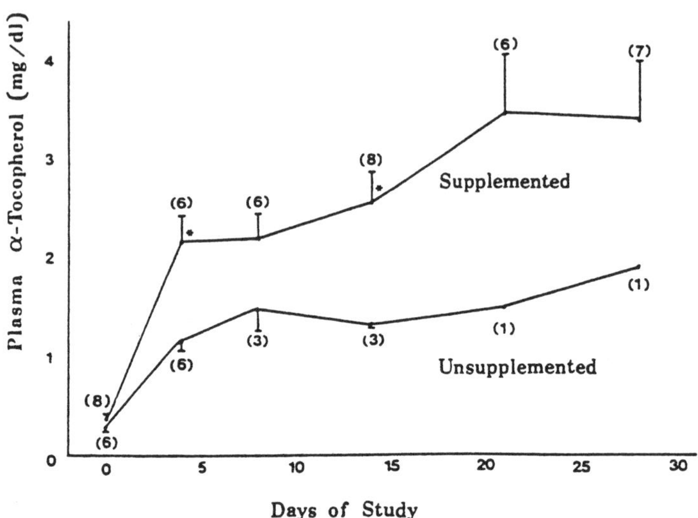

Fig. 2. Vitamin E levels in infants supplemented with oral vitamin E and those not supplemented. Numbers of infants are shown in parentheses. They do not equal the numbers for the total group because four infants supplemented for only a short time were excluded. Differences are significant: $^{*}P < .01$. Bars are means + SEM. Reproduced by permission of *Pediatrics,* Vol. 77, pp. 542 and 544. Copyright 1986.

group had a mean level of 19 ± 0.8 mg/g of cholesterol after 3 weeks of treatment. All except three infants received Intralipid during the study. Intralipid contains 0.77 mg of α-tocopherol per deciliter and has a total vitamin E activity of approximately 1.83 mg/dl (Gutcher *et al.,* 1984a). Thus, these infants received 0.13 ± 0.16 mg (range 0.04 to 0.31 mg) of α-tocopherol per day from Intralipid. Blood α-tocopherol levels in infants receiving Intralipid were no different from those in the infants who did not receive lipid infusions.

Group 2.

Results of vitamin E measurements in infants receiving different doses of the vitamin mixture are shown in Table III. Infants in both Groups 2a and 2b showed a significant increase in α-tocopherol within 48 hr of beginning the intravenous vitamin, although those in Group 2a, receiving the higher dose (4.7 mg/day), had substantially higher levels than those receiving the lower dose. None of the infants in Group 2a showed levels of less than 1 mg/dl, although one-third had levels greater than 3.5 mg/dl during the treatment period. On the other hand, one-third of the smaller infants (Group 2b) who received the smaller dose (2.3 mg/day) had blood levels below 1 mg/dl; none had levels in excess of 3 mg/dl.

IV. DISCUSSION

Because the lipid-soluble vitamins can be stored in the liver or body fat for long periods, it is difficult to estimate the potential for deficiency of the lipid-soluble vitamins in children or adults who receive total parenteral nutrition for only 3 weeks. On the other hand, premature infants have little storage of lipid-soluble vitamins and low circulating levels of the vitamins. Thus, short-term studies may provide more meaningful information concerning their intravenous vitamin needs. Although it is clear that blood vitamin levels may not necessarily reflect body content at this age, it is presently the most acceptable method of monitoring vitamin nutriture. Recent findings indicating an association between bronchopulmonary dysplasia and low circulating levels of vitamin A (Hustead *et al.*, 1984) and very low hepatic retinol levels in premature infants receiving total parenteral nutrition indicate the emergent need for adequate provision of vitamin A during this critical period of development. The need for exogenous vitamins E and D is equally important in the premature infants.

Infants in this study were receiving no enteral vitamins. Thus, we believe that the blood levels are a reflection of the intravenous intake alone, except in the Group 1 infants who received oral doses of vitamin E as indicated.

A. Vitamin A

Vitamin A circulates bound to retinol-binding protein. The retinol-binding protein is synthesized in the liver and bound to retinol in the hepatocyte before secretion. Thus, the level of circulating vitamin A may be affected by synthesis of retinol-binding protein from available energy and amino acids, as well as the presence of a stimulus, such as vitamin A, to promote synthesis of retinol-binding protein. Because little is known about the ontogeny of retinol-binding protein, there is some concern that persistently low circulating levels of vitamin A in premature infants simply reflect inadequate synthesis of retinol-binding protein as a result of hepatic immaturity. Therefore, the low circulating levels do not necessarily reflect the absence of hepatic stores of vitamin A and a higher dose could conceivably result in excessive hepatic accumulation of vitamin A. Only two premature infants showed a substantial increase in retinol-binding protein (above 3.5 mg/dl). Both infants were also the only ones who showed an increase in vitamin A above 30 μg/dl. Because one of the patients weighed 970 g, it seems likely that the capacity for the liver to synthesize retinol-binding protein is present at an early period of life in at least some infants. Further evidence for inadequate vitamin

A supplementation was the low hepatic retinol level in one patient on TPN for 3 weeks previously. In healthy children and adults, plasma retinol-binding protein and retinol exist in a 1:1 molar ratio and demonstrate a high correlation over all concentration ranges (Ingenbleek *et al.*, 1975). However, other investigators have found low molar ratios of vitamin A to retinol-binding protein, as well as a lack of correlation between vitamin A and retinol-binding protein, in premature infants (Shenai *et al.*, 1981a; Woodruff *et al.*, 1983). Our findings further support the lack of correlation between RBP and vitamin A levels in very low birth weight infants.

Our findings regarding vitamin A coincide with other reports that indicate that premature infants given total parenteral nutrition receive insufficient vitamin A (Shenai *et al.*, 1981a; Woodruff *et al.*, 1983). The dose required to raise blood levels and establish hepatic stores of vitamin A to levels present at term gestation infants has not been determined.

Another difficulty with interpretation of the dose–response of vitamin A relates to substantial losses of the vitamin that may occur in the delivery system. As much as 70 to 80% of retinol can be lost by absorbance to the plastics in the delivery system (Gillis *et al.*, 1983; Shenai *et al.*, 1981b; Gutcher *et al.*, 1984b). In addition, retinol may be further degraded by exposure to lights commonly used in neonatal intensive care units (Greene *et al.*, 1985). Recent findings showed that losses of retinol are greatest during initial exposure to plastic (Shenai *et al.*, 1981b). This suggests that patients receiving small volumes of total parenteral nutrition are the ones most likely to have the greatest losses of retinol in the delivery systems (Greene *et al.*, 1985). Because the dose of retinol received cannot be determined as a result of unknown losses in the tubing, it is not possible from our data to speculate on the actual intravenous retinol needs for the premature infant.

Lipid-soluble vitamins would be expected to be incorporated into the micellar phase of lipid emulsions and, therefore, to be protected from exposure to the plastic or light. *In vitro* studies have suggested that Intralipid (Cutter) may prevent the losses of vitamin A commonly encountered in the delivery system (Greene *et al.*, 1987). Alternatively, recent findings (Gutcher *et al.*, 1984b) demonstrate that the palmitate ester of retinol is associated with little loss onto plastic during total parenteral nutrition.

It seems clear from our data on Group 1 that the expected increase in blood vitamin A levels did not occur with total parenteral nutrition. The studies relating to vitamin A losses onto plastic and deterioration from light indicate that improvements in the method of delivery are necessary before any dose of vitamin A can be adequately evaluated for retinol delivery, and the use of retinol palmitate in the glucose–amino acid mixture or retinol mixed with intravenous lipids appears to be a fruitful area of investigation.

B. 25-OH Vitamin D

Appropriate bone mineralization is dependent on an adequate intake of calcium and phosphorus as well as optimal vitamin D metabolism. Osteopenia and rickets of prematurity are particularly problematic. Although infants with rickets of prematurity have occasionally needed oral intakes of vitamin D in excess of 260 IU for adequate treatment (Lewin *et al.*, 1971; Cifuentes *et al.*, 1980), it appears that the major contributor to poor bone mineralization is inadequate absorption of calcium and phosphorus (Tsang *et al.*, 1981), a particular problem in very low birth weight infants requiring total parenteral nutrition. The poor solubility of calcium and phosphorus in total parenteral nutrition solutions has been largely overcome with a recently released pediatric amino acid solution (Trophamine, added with cysteine HCl, McGraw Laboratories). Presently, the suggested oral intake of vitamin D in premature infants is 400 IU. However, with the tendency for lipid malabsorption in very low birth weight infants, it is likely that less than 400 IU given orally would be adequate. For this reason, a dose of 260 IU was used for this study. This dose was associated with an increase in blood 25-OH vitamin D levels in each of the six infants in whom a sufficient sample was available for assay. The lowest value of 12.8 ng/ml was only slightly below the reference values and twice the pretreatment level. Given these findings we believe that the dose of 260 IU should be evaluated in the context of higher doses of intravenous calcium and phosphorus before adjusting the dosage.

C. Vitamin E

Because of the reported benefit from vitamin E in prevention of retinopathy (Hittner *et al.*, 1984) or intraventricular hemorrhage associated with prematurity (Chiswick *et al.*, 1983), the routine use of oral vitamin E supplements has become widespread. Oral daily doses have ranged between 25 and 100 mg and in some instances parenteral doses of this order have been used.

Recently, 38 deaths have been attributed to the use of intravenous tocopherol acetate at daily doses of 25 to 50 mg/kg. The preterm infants in this study received 4.7 mg of α-tocopherol per day from MVI Pediatric, plus a mean of 0.13 mg/day from Intralipid. Thus, Intralipid contributed only 2.8% of the α-tocopherol intake. The results suggest that a daily intravenous dose of 4.6 mg is sufficient to maintain blood α-tocopherol within a range of 1.1 to 1.9 mg/dl. These levels are congruent with those recommended for preterm infants (Gutcher *et al.*, 1984c), although an even smaller intravenous dose (2.2 mg/day) was sufficient to increase blood α-tocopherol from 0.33 ± 0.05 to 1.28 ± 0.12 mg/dl in infants weighing less than 1000 g (Franck *et al.*, 1986).

It appears from these measurements that the prescribed dosage of vitamin E is sufficient to maintain blood levels of vitamin E within the reference ranges for all the study patients, but with oral supplements of vitamin E or intravenous lipid containing substantial amounts of α-tocopherol, higher levels may be achieved.

In summary, the findings in this study support the dosage recommendations for vitamins D and E for premature infants larger than 1000 g who are receiving total parenteral nutrition in that blood levels of the vitamins appear to be adequate. However, several infants smaller than 1000 g tended to have blood tocopherol levels above 3 mg/dl with dosage levels of 4.7 mg/day and an equal number had levels less than 1 mg/dl with the lower dose of 2.2 mg/day. At present, the optimal blood level of tocopherol which would be expected to lower the incidence of ventricular hemorrhage or retinopathy of prematurity is not established. Blood levels greater than 1 mg/day have been suggested and because of unestablished levels of toxicity, levels greater than 3 mg/dl, appear to be unwarranted. Because of some individual variation and apparent toxicity of vitamin E, we feel that levels above 5 mg/dl should be avoided, and levels between 1 and 3 mg/dl would appear to be safe. If future studies support the need to achieve blood levels between 1 and 3 mg/dl, a daily dose between 2.2 and 4.7 mg/day would appear most appropriate for infants weighing less than 1000 g.

ACKNOWLEDGMENTS

This work was supported in part by the National Institute of Arthritis, Diabetes, Digestive, and Kidney Diseases Grant AM 26657, Contract N01 AI02645, and a grant from the Revlon Health Care Group. We thank Tom Back for biostatistical assistance and Peter Wright, M.D., Juliette Thompson, M.S.N., and the Labor and Delivery staffs of Vanderbilt Hospital and Baptist Hospital for obtaining the reference samples.

REFERENCES

Bieri, J. G., Tolliver, T. J., and Catignani, G. L. (1979). *Am. J. Clin. Nutr.* **32,** 2143–2149.

Callenbach, J. C., Sheehan, M. B., Abramson, S. J., and Hall, R. T. (1981). *J. Pediatr.* **98,** 800–805.

Chiswick, M. L., Johnson, M., Woodhall, C., Gowland, M., Davies, J., Toner, N., and Sims, D. G. (1983). *Br. Med. J.* No. 287, 81–84.

Cifuentes, R. F., Kooh, S. W., and Radde, I. C. (1980). *J. Pediatr.* **96,** 252–255.

Di Palma, J. R., and Ritchie, M. D. (1977). *Annu. Rev. Pharmacol. Toxicol.* **17,** 133–148.

Franck, L. S., Greene, H. L., and Phillips, B. L. (1986). *Clin. Res.* **34,** 115A.

Gillis, J., Jones, G., and Pencharz, P. (1983). *JPEN, J. Parenter. Enteral Nutr.* **7,** 11–14.

Greene, H. L., Moore, M. C., Phillips, B., Shulman, R., Ament, M., Murrell, J. E., and Said, H. M. (1986). *Pediatrics* **77,** 539–547.

Green, H. L., Phillips, B. L., Franck, L., Fillmore, C. M., Said, H. M., and Moore, M. E. (1987). *Pediatrics* **79,** 952–956.

Gutcher, G. R., Lax, A. A., and Farrell, P. M. (1984a). *JPEN, J. Parenter. Enteral Nutr.* **8,** 269–273.

Gutcher, G. R., Lax, A. A., and Farrell, P. M. (1984b). *Am. J. Clin. Nutr.* **40,** 8–13.

Gutcher, G. R., Raynor, W. J., and Farrell, P. M. (1984c). *Am. J. Clin. Nutr.* **40,** 1078–1089.

Haddad, J. G., and Ghyu, K. J. (1971). *J. Clin. Endocrinol.* **33,** 922–995.

Hittner, H. M., Speer, M. E., Rudolph, A. J., Blifeld, C., Chadda, P., Blair Holbein, M. E., Godio, L. B., and Kretzer, F. L. (1984). *Pediatrics* **73,** 238–249.

Howard, L., Chu, R., Feman, S., Mintz, H., Ovesen, L., and Wolf, B. (1980). *Ann. Intern. Med.* **93,** 576–577.

Hustead, V. A., Gutcher, G. R., Anderson, S. A., and Zachman, R. D. (1984). *J. Pediatr.* **105,** 610–615.

Ingenbleek, Y., Van Den Schriek, H. G., De Nayer, P., and De Visscher, M. (1975). *Metab., Clin. Exp.* **24,** 633–641.

Lewin, P. K., Reid M., Reilly, B. J., Swyer, P. R., and Fraser, D. (1971). *J. Pediatr.* **78,** 207–210.

Lorch, V., Murphy, M. D., Hoèrsten, L. R. (1985). *Pediatrics* **75,** 598–602.

Mangelsdorf, D. J., Koeffler, H. P., Donaldson, C. A., Pike, J. W., and Hausler, M. R. (1984). *J. Cell Biol.* **98,** 391–398.

Montreewasuwat, N., and Olson, J. A. (1979). *Am. J. Clin. Nutr.* **32,** 601–606.

Moore, M. C., Greene, H. L., Phillips, B., Franck, L., Shulman, R. J., Murrell, J. E., and Ament, M. E. (1986). *Pediatrics* (in press).

National Research Council (1980). "Recommended Dietary Allowances," 9th Ed. Nat. Acad. Sci., Washington, D.C.

Nutrition Advisory Group (1975). "Guidelines for Multivitamin Preparation for Parenteral Use." Am. Med. Assoc., Chicago, Illinois.

Shenai, J. P., Chytil, F., Jhaveri, A., and Stahlman, M. T. (1981a). *J. Pediatr.* **99,** 302–305.

Shenai, J. P., Stahlman, enai, J. P., Stahlman, M. T., and Chytil, F. 91981b). *J. Pediatr.* **99,** 661–663.

Shike, M., Sturtridge, W. C., Tam, S. C., Harrison, J. E., Jones, G., Murray, T. M., Husdan, H., Whitwell, J., Wilson, D. R., and Jeejeebhoy, K. N. (1981). *Ann. Intern. Med.* **95,** 560–568.

Tsang, R. C., Greer, F., and Steichen, J. J. (1981). *Clin. Perinatol.* **8,** 287–305.

Wolf, G. (1984). *Phys. Rev.* **64,** 873–937.

Woodruff, C., Latham, C., and Hewett, J. (1983). *J. Am. Coll. Nutr.* **2,** 318A.

Fortified Human Milk Feeding in the Premature Infant

C. Garza and R. J. Schanler

USDA/ARS Children's Nutrition Research Center
and Department of Pediatrics
Baylor College of Medicine
and
Texas Children's Hospital
Houston, Texas, U.S.A.

R. Goldblum and A. S. Goldman

Department of Pediatrics
The University of Texas Medical Branch
Galveston, Texas, U.S.A.

I. INTRODUCTION

Feeding human milk to premature infants is of interest because of its presumed nutritional superiority and potential ability to aid digestion (Mehta *et al.*, 1982; Williamson *et al.*, 1978), the maturation of the gastrointestinal tract (Morriss, 1985), and host defense (Goldman and Smith, 1973). These expectations are based largely on studies in neonates of morbidity (Narayanan *et al.*, 1984) and the conventionally accepted food value of human milk (Barness *et al.*, 1957) and studies conducted *in vitro* of human milk components with digestive (Hernell, 1975), growth-promoting (Klagsburn, 1978; Nichols *et al.*, 1985), and protective properties (Hanson and Söderström, 1981). More recent studies (Atkinson *et al.*, 1981, 1983; Gross, 1983) are difficult to interpret, in which outcomes of premature infants fed human milk are compared with those of premature infants fed commercial cow milk formula. Unequal levels of nitrogen and energy often have been provided to the feeding groups and the analyses of the feeding experiments commonly do not adjust for differences in intakes, which may affect biochemical or other indices of functional maturation.

Major conceptual difficulties encountered in these studies center on the identification of optimal growth rates, biochemical indices of nutritional well-being, and other outcome measures that assess the efficacy of key components in human milk with presumed functional roles. To address these issues we have developed a total human milk preparation (Garza *et al.*, 1984) that maintains intrauterine growth rates without stressing the infant metabolically (Schanler *et al.*, 1985). The premise underlying our efforts is that a total human milk preparation should maximize potential benefits of human milk.

II. STUDY DESIGN

Our study subjects were very low birth weight (VLBW) infants who were fed either fortified human milk or a cow milk-based formula. Infant selection was based on the following criteria: 28 to 30 weeks gestation, appropriate birth weight for gestational age, absence of major congenital anomalies, no sustained cardiopulmonary disease, tolerance of complete enteral feedings by 15 days of life, and informed consent of their parents. Subject characteristics are summarized in Table I. Infants were fed either their mothers' fresh, unfrozen milk fortified with human milk fractions or commercial cow milk-based formula designed specifically for premature infants. Feeding group assignment was based on the parental desire to breast- or bottle-feed.

TABLE I

Characteristics of Study Infants[a]

Characteristics	Study I		Study II	
	FHM (n = 17)	CF (n = 14)	FHM (n = 8)	CF (n = 7)
Birth weight (g)	1178 ± 150	1194 ± 113	1177 ± 112	1057 ± 131
Gestational age (weeks)	29 ± 0.7	29 ± 0.5	29 ± 0.8	29 ± 0.5
Apgar (5 min)	8 ± 0.8	8 ± 1	8 ± 1	8 ± 1
Age at balance (days)				
First period	17 ± 3	16 ± 2	24 ± 5	20 ± 3
Second period	34 ± 4	36 ± 6	36 ± 7	37 ± 7

[a]FHM, fortified human milk; CF, commercial formula. Values expressed as mean ± SD.

Two principal studies have been conducted, I and II. Their major differences were the levels of Ca and P supplementation. Study II is in progress. Infants were enrolled during the first week of postnatal life and were studied until a body weight of 1800 g was achieved. Infants were nourished by continuous nasogastric feeding for approximately the first 3 weeks of life and by intermittent 3-hr nasogastric bolus feedings for the remainder of the study. Two 96-hr metabolic balances were performed at approximately 2.5 and 6.0 weeks of age. Energy, nitrogen, fat, sodium, potassium, calcium, phosphorus, magnesium, lysozyme, lactoferrin, secretory IgA (sIgA), and sIgA antibodies to a pool of *Escherichia coli* somatic O antigens were measured in the milks fed and in the infants' urine and feces. Milk proteins were hydrolyzed for the determination of total and individual amino acid levels. Total protein, albumin, prealbumin, amino acids, urea nitrogen, electrolytes, calcium, and phosphorus were determined in serum or plasma, and anthropometric measurements were obtained at periodic intervals. Details of the chemical and balance methods used in these studies have been described previously (Schanler *et al.*, 1985a,b).

III. HUMAN MILK PREPARATION

Skim and cream fractions of human milk are prepared as outlined in Fig. 1. Milk from individual mothers of premature infants is analyzed at weekly intervals for its nitrogen and gross energy contents and variable amounts of skim and cream fractions are added to each mother's milk to achieve an isocaloric, isonitrogenous comparison between feeding groups. The preparation of the skim fraction includes procedures for

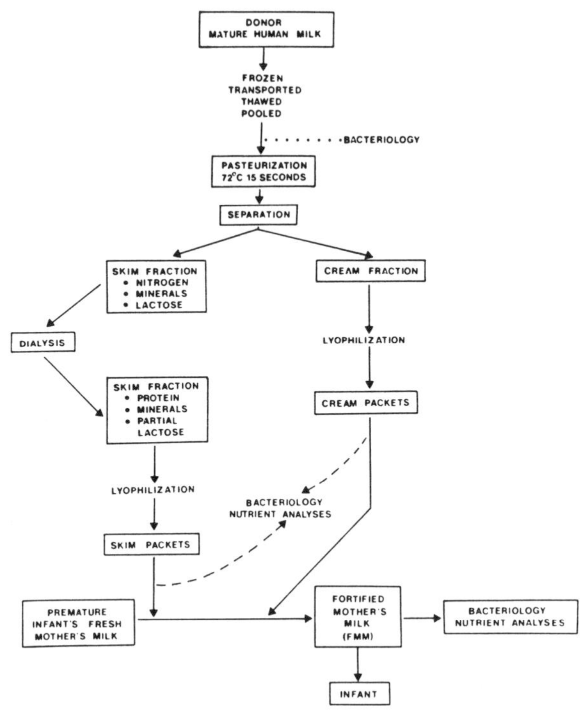

Fig. 1. Schematic outline of procedures used to fractionate donor milk.

maintaining the nitrogen to mineral ratio in the milk and significantly reducing the milk's lactose content. Whereas the rapid, high-temperature heating method used to increase the milk's bacteriological safety does not reduce significantly the immunoloical reactivity of lactoferrin, lysozyme, sIgA, and specific sIgA antibodies to a pool of *E. coli* somatic O antigens, it destroys the infectivity of added cytomegalovirus (Goldblum *et al.*, 1984). The composition of milks used in studies performed by our laboratory is outlined in Table II.

Data discussed in subsequent sections support the view that the processing protocol outlined in Fig. 1 does not alter the digestibility and absorption of human milk nitrogen. Disruption of the physical compartmentation of milk, however, occurs (Goldblum *et al.*, 1984) and is evidenced by a 400% increase in the immunological reactivity of lysozyme following the processing of human milk (Fig. 2). The significance of this disruption is not clear. The paucity of data that evaluate, *in vivo*, the role of lysozyme (Bolshakova *et al.*, 1984; Haneberg and Finne, 1974) and its innate compartmentation in milk impedes assessments of the disruption of the apparent physical compartmentation in human milk. A teleological

TABLE II

Comparison of Composition of Study Milks and Unfortified Human Milk[a]

	Study I				Study II		
	Balance period I		Balance period II				
Milk components	FHM (n = 17)	CF (n = 14)	FHM (n = 14)	CF (n = 10)	FHM (n = 8)	CF (n = 7)	Human milk[b]
Energy (kcal)	101 ± 8	100 ± 8	81 ± 8	78 ± 8	81 ± 4	83 ± 2	61–71
Nitrogen (mg)	342 ± 41	347 ± 37	269 ± 66	295 ± 54	313 ± 21	300 ± 7	200–290
Fat (mg)	5.3 ± 0.8	5.1 ± 0.4	4.0 ± 0.8	4.2 ± 0.4	4.5 ± 0.6	4.5 ± 0.3	2.8–5.3
Sodium (mg)	25 ± 4	22 ± 4	23 ± 8	28 ± 4	36 ± 8	36 ± 2	17–30
Potassium (mg)	71 ± 16	86 ± 12	65 ± 21	96 ± 12	84 ± 12	83 ± 4	55–65
Calcium (mg)	39 ± 4	52 ± 4	41 ± 12	61 ± 8	82 ± 7	93 ± 5	20–29
Phosphorus (mg)	24 ± 4	32 ± 1	19 ± 4	49 ± 8	45 ± 5	42 ± 1	9–15
Magnesium (mg)	5.4 ± 0.8	8.6 ± 2	5.0 ± 1.6	8.1 ± 3.7	4.8 ± 0.9	7.9 ± 0.5	1.5–3.6

[a]FHM, fortified human milk; CF, commercial formula. Values expressed as mean ± SD, per deciliter.
[b]Range in milk composition during fourth week of lactation from mothers delivering preterm infants.

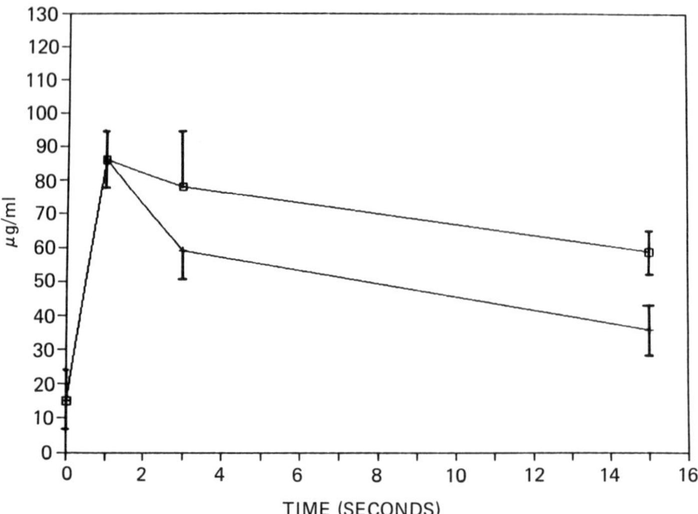

Fig. 2. Changes in immunoreactive lysozyme in donor milk heated to 72°C (□) or 87°C (+) for variable times (in seconds).

approach would suggest that such compartmentation is of functional significance and that its functional expression may be dependent on the infant's maturity. The possibility of interactive relationships among a normally mature, term gastrointestinal tract, the compartmentation of human milk components, and the expression of functional roles of compartmentalized components complicates assessments of compartmentation. The complexity of such issues is exaggerated when the immature VLBW infant is the focus of discussion.

IV. GROWTH

Figures 3A and 3B illustrate the weight gain and linear growth of both Study I feeding groups. Recovery of birth weight and a body weight of 1800 g were achieved at similar ages in both groups, 18 and 43 days, respectively. Postnatal gains in weight and length, after an initial period of weight loss, were similar to intrauterine growth rates.

Attainment of an intrauterine growth rate may be considered necessary but is not an adequate criterion by which to identify optimal intakes. The use of intrauterine growth rates as standards for assessing the nutritional management of VLBW infants has been controversial because of (1) concern that postnatal achievement of this rate imposes significant metabolic stress on the infant and (2) an inadequate description and un-

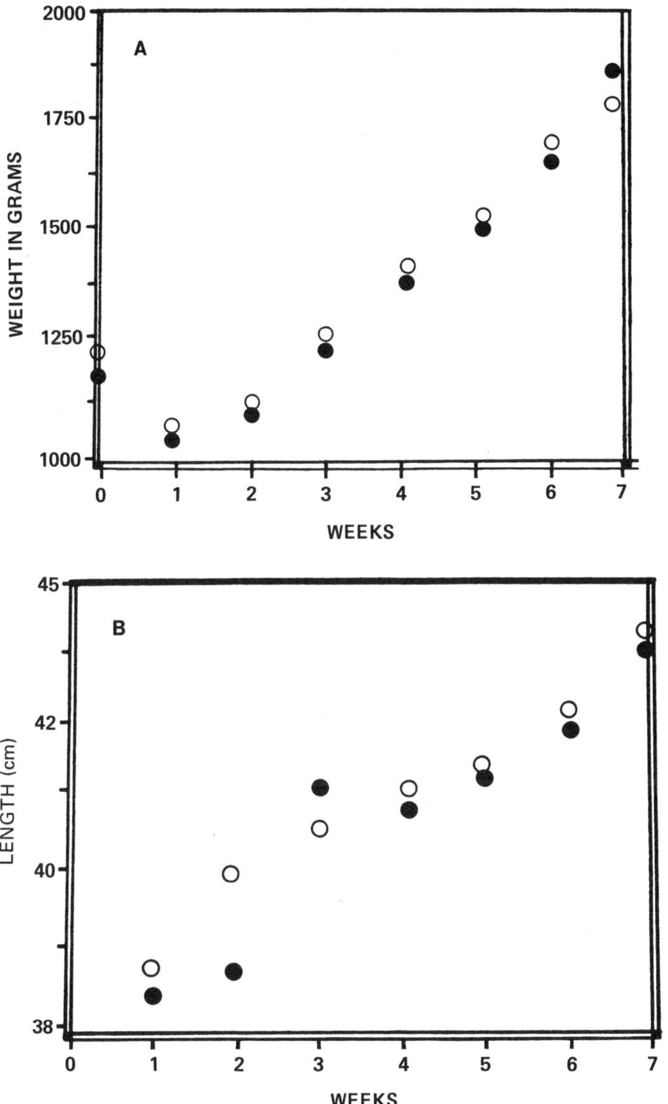

Fig. 3. (A) Growth (weight) of infants fed fortified mother's milk (●) or commercial formula (○). (B) Growth (length) of infants fed fortified mother's milk (●) or commercial formula (○).

derstanding of the significance of diverse tissue compositions of postnatal weight gains. Current experience supports the view that intrauterine rates of growth can be achieved postnatally without overt metabolic stress in "healthy" VLBW infants (Schanler *et al.*, 1985a; Järvenpää *et al.*, (1983). Attention then may be shifted to more rigorous indicators of metabolic well-being (Scott *et al.*, 1985; Pencharz *et al.*, 1983; Hagelberg *et al.*, 1982), functional maturity (Schanler *et al.*, 1986; Norin *et al.*, 1985), and body composition (Chessex *et al.*, 1983; Whyte *et al.*, 1983).

V. NUTRIENT UTILIZATION

This discussion is limited to the utilization of protein and total nitrogen. In addition to the usual considerations of nitrogen utilization, that is, nitrogen absorption and retention, the utilization of selected functional proteins is also assessed. Considerations of energy and macromineral utilization are not included because of space constraints. The choice of nitrogen as a focus for this discussion should not imply any ranking of issues central to the nutritional management of the very low birth weight infant.

A. Nitrogen: Absorption, Retention, and Excretion

Nitrogen absorption, retention, and excretion, when adjusted for intake by analysis of variance for repeated measures, using nitrogen intake as the single covariate, were similar between groups and balance studies in Study I (Table III). Adjusting for intake was necessary because formula-fed infants had a greater nitrogen intake during the second balance period of Study I. The higher intake resulted from our difficulties in the removal of sufficient lactose from the human skim milk fraction. Had nitrogen been matched in both groups, energy concentrations higher than desirable would have resulted. In Study II, the dialysis procedure was modified to reduce the lactose content. Nitrogen intakes were similar between groups throughout Study II. Apparent nitrogen retnetion in both groups and in both studies was similar to estimates of intrauterine nitrogen accretion at the corresponding ages studied.

Nitrogen absorption was similar in both groups, approximately 83% at 2.5 weeks of age and 86% at 6 weeks. These values substantiate similar nitrogen availability from both food sources. This type of balance data, however, does not allow a determination of the proportion of endogenous fecal nitrogen and food nitrogen, which comprised total fecal nitrogen in each group. Therefore the possibility that infants fed human milk excrete a greater or lesser amount of endogenous nitrogen in feces than do infants fed a cow milk-based formula could not be evaluated. The influence of the processing protocol outlined in Fig. 1 on the digestibility of human milk protein also was of interest. No differences were noted in the absorption of nitrogen from unfrozen expressed human milk obtained daily from each infant's mother and the donor processed

TABLE III

Nitrogen Utilization[a]

	Study I				Study II			
	Balance period I		Balance period II		Balance period I		Balance period II	
	FHM (n = 17)	CF (n = 14)	FHM (n = 14)	CF (n = 10)	FHM (n = 8)	CF (n = 7)	FHM (n = 8)	CF (n = 7)
Intake (mg/kg/day)	459 ± 45	451 ± 34	460 ± 41	543 ± 66	482 ± 37	469 ± 13	490 ± 40	481 ± 13
Fecal N (mg/kg/day)	81 ± 25	71 ± 15	71 ± 22	68 ± 19	81 ± 25	106 ± 24	73 ± 8	74 ± 16
Urinary N (mg/kg/day)	74 ± 16	68 ± 15	68 ± 19	80 ± 13	80 ± 20	77 ± 19	81 ± 8	68 ± 13
Absorption (%)	82 ± 4	84 ± 4	84 ± 4	87 ± 3	83 ± 6	77 ± 5	85 ± 3	85 ± 3
Retention (%)	66 ± 8	69 ± 4	70 ± 7	72 ± 3	67 ± 6	61 ± 7	68 ± 6	71 ± 7
N retained[b] / N absorbed[c]	80	82	83	83	80	79	81	83

[a]FHM, fortified human milk; CF, commercial formula. Values expressed as mean ± SD.

[b]N retained = intake − fecal N − urinary N.

[c]N absorbed = intake − fecal N.

milk used to fortify each mother's milk. This possibility was evaluated by regressing nitrogen absorption against the intakes of nitrogen from each source of milk, unfrozen maternal milk and processed donor milk.

The similarity in nitrogen absorption between the groups fed fortified human milk and the cow milk-based formula is of particular interest because of the resistance to digestion of key functional components in human milk which make up substantial proportions of total human milk protein (Hambraeus *et al.*, 1978). The quantities of lactoferrin, sIgA, and lysozyme measured in the stool were approximately 3, 9, and 0.1% of the respective amounts of each component that was fed (Schanler *et al.*, 1986). Figure 4 illustrates the proportion of fecal nitrogen that may be ascribed to these components. Measurements made after the chronic administration of the same food for approximately 6 weeks suggest that the usual intake and output of these components is reflected. These observations do not support the view that these proteins are nutritionally unavailable to the VLBW infant (Hambraeus *et al.*, 1984).

Measurements of urinary nitrogen support the conclusion that the biological value of absorbed nitrogen is similar for fortified human milk and the commercial formulas studied. Seventeen to 20% of absorbed nitrogen was excreted in urine (Schanler *et al.*, 1985a). This conclusion assumes that obligatory urinary nitrogen is similar in both feeding

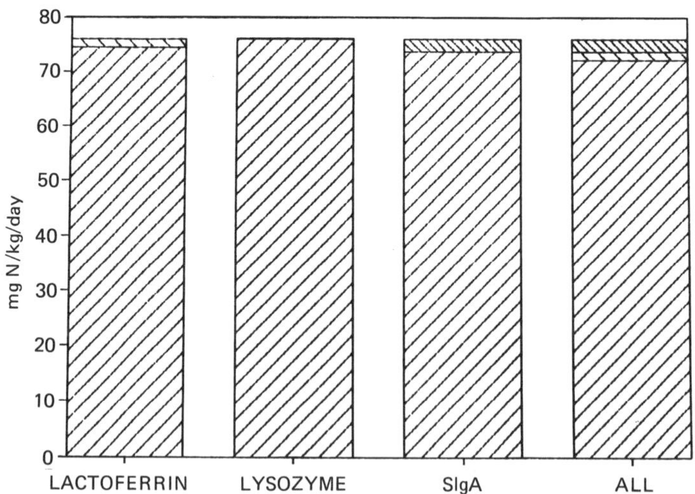

Fig. 4. Amounts of the immune factors of fecal lactoferrin (▭), lysozyme (▭), sIgA (▭) (expressed as mg N/kg/day), and all other fecal N (▭) excreted by VLBW infants fed fortified human milk. Measurements of lactoferrin, lysozyme, and sIgA are converted to N by dividing protein measurements to protein by 6.25.

groups. Balance data, however, do not allow an evaluation of this assumption. Recent evaluations of protein turnover in infants fed human milk or commercial formula do not suggest any differences in whole-body nitrogen turnover between feeding groups (Pencharz *et al.*, 1983). An evaluation of the effects of processing human milk as outlined in Fig. 1 on the biological value of absorbed protein also was of interest. This question was examined indirectly by regressing the amount of each infant's urinary nitrogen against the amount of nitrogen supplied by each mother's unfrozen milk and the amounts of nitrogen supplied by the donor processed milk. No differences were noted in the relative amounts of nitrogen retained from either source.

B. Utilization of Specific Nitrogen-Containing Functional Components

Evaluation of data that assess the use of specific functional components in human milk, such as lactoferrin, sIgA, and lysozyme, requires consideration of several possibilities. The underlying premise has been that functional components normally found in human milk and in feces of infants fed human milk originate primarily from the milk source (Hambraeus *et al.*, 1984). The alternative consideration is that such fecal constituents are synthesized by the infant. Although the former possibility has been considered the more likely of the two, no conclusive supporting data have been published. Recent results from our laboratory have led us to question this predominant veiw (Schanler *et al.*, 1986).

The amounts of lactoferrin, lysozyme, total IgA, sIgA, and specific antibodies to a pool of *E. coli* O somatic antigens were measured in four consecutive 24-hr urine collections and one concomitant 96-hr collection of feces in infants enrolled in Study I (Schanler *et al.*, 1986). The feces obtained from infants fed human milk had markedly greater quantities of lactoferrin, lysozyme, and IgA than those fed the cow milk-based formula (Table IV). Specific sIgA antibodies to *E. coli* were detected in the feces of 90% of the human milk-fed infants, but in none of the infants fed the cow milk-based formula. Other than a significant correlation between the fecal concentrations of specific sIgA antibodies to *E. coli* O somatic antigens and the concentration of these antibodies in the fortified human milk, no other significant relationships were detected between the milk concentrations or the infants' intakes of the other selected immune factors and the excretion of these factors in their feces. Significant relationships, however, were noted among the immune factors in the feces, but not among the concentrations of these factors in the fortified human milk (Table V). The increased quantity of selected immune factors in the feces of VLBW infants fed human milk may have resulted, there-

TABLE IV

Intake and Fecal Excretion of Selected Immune Factors Contrasted with Total Fecal Nitrogen of Infants Fed Fortified Human Milk[a]

Component	FHM (n = 33)	CF (n = 20)
Lactoferrin (mg/kg/day)		
Milk	308 (198; 376)	—
Feces	9 (3; 15)	0.05 (0.02; 0.1)
Lysozyme (mg/kg/day)		
Milk	25 (12; 35)	—
Feces	0.02 (0.00; 0.04)	0.00 (0.00; 0.01)
Total IgA (mg/kg/day)		
Milk	164 (118; 230)	—
Feces	14 (4; 22)	0.5 (0.2; 1.2)
Fecal nitrogen (mg/kg/day)	76 ± 7	70 ± 2

[a]FHM, fortified human milk; CF, commercial formula. Mean for balance periods 1 and 2, Study I; values in parentheses correspond to the 25th and 75th percentiles.

fore, from the passive ingestion and persistence of these factors throughout the gastrointestinal tract and/or from endogenous synthesis induced by unidentified factors in the milk.

Furthermore, the fecal output of these immune factors may have been underestimated. Lag times between the collection of fecal samples, preparation of the samples, and the analyses may have resulted in losses of the index components. We currently are evaluating the potential significance of these delays in our laboratories. A second possibility is that the immune factors adhere to the gastrointestinal epithelium. These infants were fed only fortified human milk for approximately 6 weeks. The continuous adherence of these constituents is unlikely and their eventual detachment is a certainty. Detachment may increase their digestibility and thereby render them nutritionally available to the infant. If the immune factors had retained their immunological identity after their detachment, they should have remained assayable. A related possbility is that these components are attached to sloughed epithelial cells or to other constituents of feces and are "invisible" to immunological assays. This possibility was not evaluated.

Finally, it is also possible that immunological assays which rely on polyclonal antibodies may lead to an overestimation of immune factors. Immunological assays used in these studies may detect fragments as well as intact proteins. The amounts of certain immunological factors in the feces may have been overestimated if passage through the gastrointestinal tract enhances epitope exposure in an undetermined manner.

TABLE V

Associations among Selected Immune Factors Excreted in Feces of VLBW Infants Fed Fortified Human Milk

Immune factors	r	p
Total IgA and lactoferrin	0.57	<.001
Total IgA and lysozyme	0.58	<.001
Lactoferrin and lysozyme	0.65	<.001

Preliminary fecal analyses using electrophoretic techniques and polyclonal antibodies to human lactoferrin indicate that in addition to the intact lactoferrin protein, a number of lactoferrin fragments ranging in weight from 20,000 to less than 80,000 are found commonly in feces.

Two recent reports (Stephens, 1986; Goldblum *et al.*, 1985) support the hypothesis that human milk may induce the infant's production of selected immune factors. Higher levels of salivary sIgA have been reported in early infancy when human milk was fed (Stephens, 1986). The mechanism underlying this observation is not understood despite several reports investigating the ontogeny of secretory immunity in various body secretions (Burgio *et al.*, 1980; Mellander *et al.*, 1984).

Supportive data have been obtained from preliminary analysis of urine of the VLBW infants fed fortified human milk in Study I. These infants excreted significantly greater amounts of urinary sIgA and lactoferrin than did the group fed the cow milk-based formula. Preliminary analysis of the molecular weight of urinary components with sIgA and lactoferrin immunoreactivity indicates the presence of both complete proteins and protein fragments. The urinary concentration and output of these materials were 100- to 200-fold greater in the human milk-fed group. The protein fragments were larger than peptides commonly found in urine. If these fragments and complete proteins were transported from the gastrointestinal tract to the kidney, differences may have been anticipated between the lactoferrin and sIgA serum concentrations of the two groups. However, none were detected.

C. Biochemical Indicators of Nitrogen or Protein Status

Serum total protein, albumin, and prealbumin, blood urea nitrogen, and hemoglobin values are summarized in Table VI. Most values fell with increases in postnatal age. No differences, however, were noted between the groups. The decline in serum protein concentrations has

TABLE VI

Biochemical Indicators[a]

	Study I				Study II			
	Balance period I		Balance period II		Balance period I		Balance period II	
	FHM (n = 17)	CF (n = 14)	FHM (n = 14)	CF (n = 10)	FHM (n = 8)	CF (n = 7)	FHM (n = 8)	CF (n = 7)
Total protein (g/dl)	4.9 ± 0.4	4.8 ± 0.4	4.4 ± 0.7	4.4 ± 0.3	4.7 ± 0.1	4.5 ± 0.1	4.3 ± 0.2	3.9 ± 0.1
Albumin (g/dl)	3.4 ± 0.4	3.4 ± 0.4	3.1 ± 0.7	3.1 ± 0.3	2.9 ± 0.1	2.9 ± 0.2	2.6 ± 0.1	2.3 ± 0.1
Prealbumin (mg/dl)	12.6 ± 3.7	12.7 ± 3.3	9.7 ± 2.6	10.6 ± 3.0	—	—	—	—
BUN (mg/dl)	6.1 ± 3.3	3.4 ± 1.1	3.9 ± 1.1	4.0 ± 1.5	3.6 ± 0.5	4.6 ± 1.8	3.1 ± 0.5	2.0 ± 0.1
Hemoglobin (g/dl)	14.2 ± 2.9	12.6 ± 2.2	11.2 ± 2.2	9.2 ± 2.6	12.0 ± 2.3	11.7 ± 3.0	9.6 ± 1.9	8.6 ± 0.4

[a]FHM, fortified human milk; CF, commercial formula. Values expressed as mean ± SD.

been observed previously and usually ascribed to the rapid growth of VLBW infants and to the immaturity of their livers (Hillman and Haddad, 1983). Other investigators have suggested that these changes are normal under extrauterine conditions (Fomon and Zeigler, 1977; Gaull *et al.*, 1977). These explanations are not satisfactory in view of the ability of the fetus to increase the concentration of serum proteins *in utero* when it has a greater relative rate of growth, a more expanded extracellular space, and a less mature liver than the extrauterine infant of similar post-conceptional age. Alternatively, falling levels of serum proteins may signal stress, unrecognized redistribution of serum proteins within extracellular compartments, or unmet nutritional needs.

We also have assessed the protein status of the infants (Schanler *et al.*, 1984) by comparing amino acid intakes and plasma levels and relationships of amino acid plasma levels to growth, nitrogen utilization, and selected biochemical markers of nutritional status in VLBW infants fed fortified human milk or a whey-predominant formula during the first 3 weeks of postnatal life (Study I). Heparinized arterial or arterialized capillary blood samples were obtained between 0800 and 1200 hr on the third or fourth day of the first balance period. This metabolic balance was performed while infants were fed continuously by intragastric infusions.

Although growth and nitrogen retentions were similar between groups, plasma amino acid levels differed. The differences could be accounted for by the dissimilar amino acid compositions of the milks and therefore the different intakes between the groups. Distinct associations were noted within each feeding group between specific plasma amino acid levels and indices of nitrogen utilization and other markers of protein status. We found that the group fed the fortified human milk had lysine levels which correlated positively with total serum proteins, suggesting that lysine levels were not adequate for the needs of this group. In contrast to this single association between plasma amino acid levels and other indices of protein status in the human milk group, seven amino acid levels were correlated to one or more indices of protein status in the group fed commercial formula. Indices of nitrogen retention were related positively to the plasma concentrations of five amino acids and five plasma amino acid concentrations were related negatively to whole blood hemoglobin levels. The absolute value of correlation coefficients relating these variables was 0.7 or higher ($p < .01$). The positive associations between these amino acids and indices of nitrogen utilization suggest that increases in the intakes of the amino acids would result in increased retentions of nitrogen or higher plasma protein levels; the negative associations between specific plasma amino acid levels and hemoglobin suggest that the pattern of amino acids fed was either inappropriate or that the amount provided was excessive. We have speculated that if amino acid or protein intakes were optimal, positive or negative relationships would be unlikely between plasma amino acid levels and other measures of protein status. We anticipate that amino acid plasma levels should be stable relative to other functional indices when protein or amino acid intakes are neither excessive nor deficient.

D. Comparison of Weight Gain and Results of Nitrogen Balance

A comparison of the total weight gained with the proportion of weight accounted for by nitrogen retention also suggests qualitative differences between groups in the composition of their respective weight gains. Three assumptions are required by the calculations which follow: (1) N balance results are a valid approximation of nitrogen retained, (2) the amount of nitrogen retained is a reflection of protein deposition, and (3) approximately 3 g of water is deposited with each gram of protein. Nitrogen retention, therefore, accounts for approximately 7.6 and 7.8 g/kg/day weight gain in infants fed fortified human milk or the cow milk-based commercial formula at approximately 2.5 weeks of age, respectively. Total weight gain during this period was approximately 16.5 g/kg/day.

At approximately 6 weeks of age, net apparent N retention accounted for approximately 8.0 and 9.8 g/kg/day, respectively, in the two groups. The results of analysis of covariance indicate that significant quantitative differences in N retention observed in this period were due to differences in N intake alone, that is, feeding group had no influence on N retention once N intake differences were taken into account. Weight gain of both groups, however, was not different during this period. Non-protein-associated weight gain of infants fed human milk, therefore, was 14 g/kg/day and that in infants fed commercial formula was 11 g/kg/day. These differences could be due to unequal hydration of body protein, more efficient utilization of the energy contents of human milk, or errors inherent to the balance method. Of the three, the latter two appear to be the more likely explanations. Although not statistically significant, the sum of triceps and subcapular skinfold measurements was greater in the human milk-fed group and evidence from term infants suggests more efficient utilization of energy in breast-fed than in bottle-fed infants (Butte *et al.*, 1984).

The relationship between the intake of protein and energy to the composition of tissue gained during growth is understood poorly. Although it is clear that energy storage occurs only when the intake of metabolizable energy exceeds that required for maintenance, the composition of weight gained is difficult to predict from measurements of protein and metabolizable energy intake. This issue poses a problem because increases (beyond maintenance levels) in metabolizable energy are associated with increases in (1) energy expenditure, (2) losses of energy substrates in urine and feces, and (3) energy storage (Whyte *et al.*, 1983). Determining the proportions of lean and adipose tissue gained when energy and protein exceed maintenance needs requires an approach similar to the energy balance technique of Sinclair and his co-workers (Whyte *et al.*, 1983) and an independent method that measures body composition by more direct measurements of body compartments (Deskins *et al.*, 1985; Sheng *et al.*, 1984).

VI. SUMMARY

Our evaluation of protein utilization by VLBW infants fed fortified human milk or cow milk-based formula indicates that intrauterine rates of growth can be achieved in both feeding groups for at least 2 months; however, several differences were observed between feeding groups. Although apparent N absorption and retention of absorbed N were similar between groups, relationships between plasma amino acid levels and selected indices of protein and total N utilization suggest that the amino acid pattern of neither milk was optimal. The amino acid pattern of fortified human milk, however, was closer in meeting our criteria of adequacy. More detailed studies of synthesis and breakdown of specific proteins are needed in infants fed either human milk or cow milk-based formula. When N intakes were not matched, as occurred in the second portion of the first study, differences in N retention were detected. These differences, coupled with similarities in weight gain between groups, underscored the need to pursue better methods for measuring body composition in this population. Perhaps most interesting of all was the possibility that an unidentified human milk constituent may induce the synthesis of lactoferrin, lysozyme, and sIgA by the gastrointestinal tract and other epithelial surfaces. The combination of active and passive protection which would result may help explain apparent differences in infection rates and nitrogen metabolism between bottle- and breast-fed infants.

ACKNOWLEDGMENTS

This work is a publication of the USDA/ARS Children's Nutrition Research Center, Department of Pediatrics, Baylor College of Medicine and Texas Children's Hospital,

Houston, Texas. This project has been funded in part with federal funds from the U.S. Department of Agriculture, Agricultural Research Service, under Cooperative Agreement No. 58-7MNI-6-100, and a contract (N01-HD-2-2814) from the National Institutes of Health. The contents of this publication do not necessarily reflect the views or policies of the U.S. Department of Agriculture, nor does mention of trade names, commercial products, or organizations imply endorsement by the U.S. Government. The authors wish to thank E. Roseland Klein for editorial assistance and N. Hayley for manuscript preparation.

REFERENCES

Atkinson, S. A., Bryon, M. H., and Anderson, G. H. (1981). Human milk feeding in premature infants: Protein, fat, and carbohydrate balances in the first two weeks of life. *J. Pediatr.* **99,** 617–624.

Atkinson, S. A., Raddle, I. C., and Anderson, G. H. (1983). Macromineral balances in premature infants fed their own mothers' milk or formula. *J. Pediatr.* **102,** 99–106.

Barness, L. A., Baker, D., Guilbert, P., Torres, F. E., and Gyorgy, P. (1957). Nitrogen metabolism of infants fed human and cow's milk. *J. Pediatr.* **51,** 29–39.

Bolshakova, A. M., Shcherbakova, E. G., Ivanova, S. D., Medvedeva, M. M., and Zhuravleva, T. P. (1984). Lysozyme in the feeding of premature infants with mixed pathology. *Antibiotiki (Moscow)* **29,** 784–790.

Burgio, G. R., Lanzauecchia, A., Plebani, A., Jayakar, S., and Ugazio, A. G. (1980). Otogeny of secretory immunity: Levels of secretory IgA and natural antibodies in saliva. *Pediatr Res.* **14,** 1111–1114.

Butte, N. F., Garza, C., Smith, E. O., and Nichols, B. L. (1984). Human milk intake and growth performance of exclusively breast-fed infants. *J. Pediatr.* **104,** 187–195.

Chessex, P., Reichman, B., Verellen, G., Putet, G., Smith, J. M., Heim, T., and Swyer, P. R. (1983). Quality of growth in premature infants fed their own mother's milk. *J. Pediatr.* **102,** 107–112.

Deskins, W. G., Winter, D. L., Sheng, H. -P., and Garza, C. (1985). Use of a resonating cavity to measure body volume. *J. Acoust. Soc. Am.* **77,** 756–758.

Fomon, S. J., and Zeigler, E. E. (1977). Protein intake of premature infants. *J. Pediatr.* **90,** 504–506.

Garza, C., Schanler, R. J., Goldman, A. S., Dill, C., and Nichols, B. L. (1984). Preparation and evaluation of fortified human milk for very low birthweight infants. *In* "Human Milk Banking." (A. F. Williams and J. O. Baum, eds.), Nestle' Nutrition Workshop Series, Vol. 5, pp. 101–106. Raven, New York.

Gaull, G. E., Rassin, D. K., and Räihä, N. C. R. (1977). Protein intake of premature infants: A reply. *J. Pediatr.* **90,** 507–510.

Goldblum, R. M., Dill, C. W., Albrecht, T. B., Alford, E. S., Garza, C., and Goldman, A. S. (1984). Rapid high temperature treatment of human milk. *J. Pediatr.* **104,** 380–385.

Goldblum, R. M., Schanler, R. J., Garza, C., and Goldman, A. S. (1985). Enhanced urinary lactoferrin excretion in premature infants fed human milk. *Pediatr. Res.* **19,** 342A.

Goldman, A. S., and Smith, C. W. (1973). Host resistance factors in human milk. *J. Pediatr.* **82,** 1082–1090.

Gross, S. J. (1983). Growth and biochemical response of preterm infants fed human milk or modified infant formula. *N. Engl. J. Med.* **308,** 237–241.

Hagelberg, S., Lindblad, B. S., Lundsjö, A., Carlsson, B., Fondén, R., Fugita, H., Lassfolk, G., and Lindquist, B. (1982). The protein tolerance of very low birthweight infants fed human milk protein enriched mothers milk. *Acta Paediatr. Scand.* **71,** 597–601.

Hambraeus, L., Lönnerdal, B., Forsum, E., and Gebre-Medhin, M. (1978). Nitrogen and protein components of human milk. *Acta Paediatr. Scand.* **67,** 561–565.

Hambraeus, L., Fransson, G. B., Lönnerdal, B. (1984). Nutritional availability of breast milk protein. *Lancet* **ii,** 167–168.

Haneberg, B., and Finne, P. (1974). Lysozymes in feces from infants and children. *Acta Paediatr. Scand.* **63,** 588–594.

Hanson, L. A., and Söderström, L. A. (1981). Human milk: Defense against infection. *In* "Nutrition and Child Health," pp. 147–159. Reiss, New York.

Hernell, O. (1975). Human milk lipases III. Physiologic implications of the bile-sale stimulated lipase. *Eur. J. Clin. Invest.* **5,** 267–272.

Hillman, L. S., and Haddad, J. G. (1983). Serial analyses of serum vitamin D-binding protein in preterm infants from birth to post conceptual maturity. *J. Clin. Endocrinol. Metab.* **56,** 189–191.

Järvenpää, A. L., Räihä, N. C. R., Rassin, D. K., and Gaull, G. E. (1983). Preterm infants fed human milk attain intrauterine weight gain. *Acta Paediatr. Scand.* **72,** 239–243.

Klagsburn, M. (1978). Human milk stimulates DNA synthesis and cellular proliferation in cultured fibroblasts. *Proc. Natl. Acad. Sci.* **75,** 5057–5061.

Mehta, N. R., Jones, J. B., and Hamosh, M. (1982). Lipases in preterm human milk: Ontogeny and physiologic significance. *J. Pediatr., Gastroenterol. Nutr.* **1,** 317–326.

Mellander, L., Carlsson, B., and Hanson, L. A. (1984). Appearance of secretory IgM and IgA antibodies to *Escherichia coli* in saliva during early infancy and childhood. *J. Pediatr.* **104,** 564–568.

Morriss, F. H., Jr. (1985). Methods for investigating the presence and physiologic role of growth factors in milk. *In* "Human Lactation" (R. E. Jensen and M. C. Neville, eds.), pp. 193–200. Plenum, New York.

Narayanan, I., Prakash, K., Murthy, N. S., and Gujral, V. V. (1984). Randomized controlled trial of effect of raw and holder pasteurized human milk and of formula supplements on incidence of neonatal infection. *Lanct* **ii,** 1111–1113.

Nichols, B. L., McKee, K., Putman, M., and Garza, C. (1985). Heavy molecular weight human colostral fraction stimulates intestinal crypt mitosis. *J. Am. Coll. Nutr.* **4,** 371A.

Norin, K. E., Gustafsson, B. E., Lindblad, B. S., and Midtvedt, T. (1985). The establishment of some microflora associated biochemical characteristics in feces from children during the first years of life. *Acta Paediatr. Scand.* **734,** 207–212.

Pencharz, P. B., Farri, L., and Papageorgiou, A. (1983). The effects of human milk and low-protein formulae on the rates of total protein turnover and urinary 3-methyl histidine excretion of preterm infants. *Clin. Sci.* **64,** 611–616.

Schanler, R. J., Garza, C., and Nichols, B. L. (1984). Plasma amino acids in preterm infants fed fortified mothers' milk. *Pediatr. Res.* **18,** 211A.

Schanler, R. J., Garza, C., and Nichols, B. L. (1985a). Fortified mother's milk for very low birthweight infants: Results of growth and nutrient balance studies. *J. Pediatr.* **107,** 437–445.

Schanler, R. J., Garza, C., and Smith, E. O. (1985b). Fortified mothers' milk for very low birthweight infants: Results of macromineral balance studies. *J. Pediatr.* **107,** 767–774.

Schanler, R., Goldblum, R., Garza, C., and Goldman, A. S. (1986). Enhanced fecal excretion of selected immune factors in very low birthweight infants fed fortified human milk. *Pediatr. Res.* **20,** 711–715.

Scott, P. H., Berger, H. M., and Wharton, B. A. (1985). Growth velocity and plasma amino acids in the newborn. *Pediatr. Res.* **19,** 446–450.

Sheng, H. P., Deskins, W. G., Winter, D., and Garza, C. (1984). Estimation of total body fat and protein by densitometry. *Pediatr. Res.* **18,** 212A.

Stephens, S. (1986). Development of secretory immunity in breast-fed and bottle-fed infants. *Arch. Dis. Child.* **61,** 263–269.

Whyte, R. K., Haslam, R., Vlainic, C., Shanon, S., Samulski, K., Campbell, D., Bayley, H. S., and Sinclair, J. C. (1983). Energy balance and nitrogen balance in growing low birthweight infants fed human milk or formula. *Pediatr. res.* **17,** 891–898.

Whyte, R. K., Bayley, H. S., and Sinclair, J. C. (1985). Energy intake and the nature of growth. *Can. J. Physiol. Pharmacol.* **63,** 565–570.

Williamson, S., Finucane, E., Ellis, H., and Gamsu, H. R. (1978). Effects of heat treatment of human milk on absorption of nitrogen, fat, sodium, calcium, and phosphorus by preterm infants. *Arch. Dis. Child.* **53,** 555–563.

Discussion: Part IV. Special Problems Relating to the Preterm and Surgical Newborn Infant A. Infant Nutrition and Neurotransmitters

Hugo Lagercrantz
Nobel Institute for Neurophysiology
Karolinska Institutet
and
Department of Pediatrics
Karolinska Hospital
Stockholm, Sweden

The effectiveness of perinatal nutrition is mainly assessed by studying growth and weight gain. This has been the main topic at this symposium. The effects of nutrition on maturation of the liver and kidney function have also been mentioned. I would like to emphasize the possible relationship between perinatal nutrition and neural development. The idea of a relationship between nutrition and behavior is well established. "We are what we eat" was announced in food advertisements already in the late years of the nineteenth century (1). But the mediation of this relationship is not so well known, particularly in very low birth weight infants who receive fortified milk or a mixture of amino acids directly into the bloodstream. Some of these amino acids are potent neurotransmitters in the central nervous system or precursors to the monoamine transmitters (Table I). We do not really know what happens when we modify the balance of these amino acids during a critical stage of brain development.

Besides the amino acids, the lipids are also of interest in this respect; intake of choline might affect acetylcholine synthesis and the infusion of linoleic acid in Intralipid might affect prostaglandin, thromboxane, and leukotriene synthesis.

Some data are available about the relationship between nutrition and neurotransmission particularly with regard to amino acids [see reviews in Wurtman (2,3)]. Amino acids are probably the main neurotransmitters in the central nervous system (4), presumably much more abundant than most of the newly detected neuropeptides.

Tryptophan might be the most interesting amino acid in this respect, since deficiency or excess in diet has been demonstrated to affect serotonin synthesis (2) and behavior (5). Brain tryptophan levels are modified when plasma concentrations are changed, which has been demonstrated; considerably increased immunofluorescence was seen in the raphe nucleus after tryptophan administration in the rat (2). Tryptophan uptake into the brain is promoted by a high-carbohydrate and low protein diet. The increased tryptophan concentrations in the brain lead to increased serotonin synthesis. Interestingly, serotonin seems to cause a reduction of carbohydrate intake. This mechanism may prevent the bear from eating only honey, or the human from eating only cakes and sweets (2).

TABLE I

Amino Acids as Neurotransmitters in the Central Nervous System

Excitatory amino acids
Glutamic acid
Aspartic acid
Cysteic acid
Homocysteic acid
Inhibitory amino acids
GABA
Glycine
Taurine
β-Alanine
Neurotransmitter precursors
Tryptophan—serotonin
Tyrosine—catecholamines

Serotonin is probably the main neurotransmitter inducing sleep (4). It seems to increase the duration of both active and passive sleep.

Sleep patterns have actually been demonstrated to be modified by changing the amino acid composition of the diet. Yogman and Zeisel (5) gave tryptophan in concentrations similar to that in Similac formula in 10% glucose to 10 infants. The sleeping behavior was also compared after the infants received only formula. Another group of 10 babies received valine instead of tryptophan in 5% glucose, which was expected to lead to a low tryptophan uptake into the brain. Infants fed with tryptophan entered both quiet and active sleep sooner than they did when they received only formula. On the other hand, the valine group entered sleep significantly later and were more alert.

Catecholaminergic or cholinergic neurons will respond poorly if at all to an increase of available tyrosine or choline under basal conditions (2). However, when the neurons become highly activated they will be more dependent on the stores of precursors. More dopamine has been found after raising the tyrosine levels in the brain and more acetylcholine after eating choline or lecithin (3). Thus, tyrosine has been reported to reduce blood pressure in experimental hypertension by enhancing noradrenaline release from the brain stem noradrenaline neurons, which reduce sympathetic outflow and increase blood pressure in hemorrhagic shock by increasing sympathoadrenal activity. These animal studies might be relevant for very low birth weight infants with low blood pressure.

Chemical neurotransmission can probably also be affected by other types of modification of the nutritive status of the fetus or the newborn, for example, infants of diabetic mothers. Some authors have proposed that these infants have an increased sympathoadrenal activity at birth. Although we were not able to confirm this, we did find that infants of diabetic mothers have higher resting levels of catecholamine than infants with other diseases (6). Infants of diabetic mothers have been found to have lower behavioral scores such as motor and autonomic stability and social interactive/orientation items (7). These behavioral patterns were assumed to be due to interaction of insulin on serotonin synthesis.

Neurohormonal balance in the infant can also be modified by the mode of feeding. Rooting and nonnutritive sucking were found to induce a significant increase of plasma insulin levels (8,9). These hormonal changes might have a secondary effect on tryptophan uptake into the brain and serotonin synthesis.

Considerably less is known about the relationship between trace metals, neurotransmission, and behavior. Copper deficiency has been reported to lead to lower enkephalin but higher endorphin levels in the adult (9). Copper is a crucial factor for the activity of dopamine β-hydroxylase, which converts dopamine to noradrenaline. However, I have never heard about any clinical correlation to this. Disturbances of the concentrations of trace metals in the fetus and the newborn, particularly the preterm baby, might be important for the development of the central nervous system.

REFERENCES

1. E. Pollitt and M. S. Read, *Am. J. Clin. Nutr.* **42,** 348 (1985).
2. R. J. Wurtman, *Sci. Am.* **246,** 42 (1982).
3. R. J. Wurtman, *Lancet* **i,** 1145 (1983).
4. J. R. Cooper, F. E. Bloom, and R. H. Roth "The Biochemical Basis of Neuropharmacology." Oxford Univ. Press, London and New York, 1986.
5. M. W. Yogman and S. H. Zeisel, *N. Engl. J. Med.* **309,** 1147 (1983).
6. U. Broberger, U. Hansson, H. Lagercrantz, and B. Persson, *Acta Paediatr. Scand.* **73,** 620 (1984).
7. M. W. Yogman and S. H. Zeisel, *Am. J. Clin. Nutr.* **42,** 353 (1985).
8. G. Marchini, H. Lagercrantz, V. Y. Feugerberg, J. Winberg, and K. Uvnäs-Moberg, *Acta Paediatr. Scand.* (in press).
9. D. J. Rhathena, L. Recant, N. R. Voyles, K. I. Timmers, S. Reiser, J. C. Smith, Jr., and A. S. Powell, *Am. J. Clin. Nutr.* **43,** 42 (1986).

Discussion: Part IV. Special Problems Relating to the Preterm and Surgical Newborn Infant B. Application to Developing Countries

Nebiat Tafari
Department of Pediatrics and Child Health
Addis Ababa University
Addis Ababa, Ethiopia

Perinatal health in developing countries is characterized by excessive mortality. The proportion of pregnancies with unfavorable outcome tends to follow the prevalence of low birth weight (LBW), indicating that prematurity and fetal growth retardation are the main sources of variation in perinatal mortality. There are two strategies for the reduction of perinatal mortality: prevention of LBW and reduction in birth weight-specific mortality.

The most prevalent risk factors associated with LBW in developing countries are maternal undernutrition with regard to energy and protein and maternal morbidity from infections, particularly malaria. Another cause of excess fetal and neonatal mortality is bacterial infection of the fetal membranes, or chorioamnionitis. The disorder is the most important antecedent event in premature labor, accounting for as much as 14 to 40% of preterm labor (1–3).

Much of modern neonatal care is concerned with reduction of birth weight-specific mortality. Over the last three decades, an impressive catalog of technology has been developed for the diagnosis and treatment of ever-smaller babies. Many of these technologies are beyond the reach of most developing nations. Thus in the remaining decade and a half of the present century, developing countries, particularly those in sub-Saharan Africa and south Asia, must concentrate on methods for the reduction in the proportion of LBW.

The most critical factor in fetal growth appears to be the concentration of energy substrates in maternal blood and uterine blood flow. Studies on diabetic pregnancies show that fetal growth rate is sensitive to the level of glucose in maternal blood. Maternal hyperglycemia leads to excessively rapid fetal growth that is characterized by excess adipose tissue accumulation and selective organomegaly. Such growth is mediated by increased fetal insulin production in response to fetal hyperglycemia. Conversely, control of maternal hyperglycemia eliminates fetal hyperinsulinism and normalizes the rate of fetal growth. During this Symposium, evidence was presented indicating that pregnancies resulting in fetal growth retardation are associated with placental underperfusion. Studies on animal models indicate that food energy and protein restriction during pregnancy lead to reduction in the rate of expansion of blood volume in response to fetal and placental growth. The resulting maternal hypovolemia reduces uterine blood flow, particularly during the third trimester of pregnancy when rapid fetal growth normally occurs.

Our current knowledge of the energy needs during pregnancy are derived from three sources: the physiologist's estimate from theoretical calculations, observational studies on the effect of famine in previously well-nourished pregnant women, and intervention studies in which pregnant women with marginal nutrition have received dietary supplements. Birth weight is frequently used to assess the effect of variation in maternal diet. However, in both observational and intervention studies the effect of differences in diet on birth weight has not been impressive.

A new generation of studies is about to bring a radical change in our knowledge and practice regarding dietary energy requirements during pregnancy. Durnin *et al.* recently demonstrated that pregnancy does not impose as much extra energy requirement as has been suggested (4). We therefore attempted to assess the adequacy of the home diet in Addis Ababa antenatal clinic attendees (20–28 weeks gestation) by weighed inventory technique over a period of 4 consecutive days. The family food intake was then expressed as a percentage of the calculated basal metabolic rate (BMR) according to FAO/WHO/UNU methods (5). We surveyed 130 representative families with a median size of 5 persons (Table I). The median parity of the gravida in these families was 3. The dietary survey showed that the mean food energy intake was 109% of BMR with a 95% confidence interval (CI) of 99–119%. The body mass index (BMI) of the gravida at the end of the first week postpartum was 97.3% (95% CI of 95.0–99.6) and that of the husband was 83.5% (95% CI of 81.3–85.6) of the median for age and sex (6). The mean birth weight was 3252 with a 95% CI of 3174–3330. The perinatal mortality was 39 per 1000 births.

The gross deficiency in energy intake is not reflected in the nutritional status of the women at the end of pregnancy. Fetal growth has apparently progressed normally. These observations suggest that there is a homeostatic adjustment of energy requirement to energy intake (7). These homeostatic adjustments imply adaptation over a long period. Failure of these adaptive mechanisms may underlie the observed fetal growth retardation in association with maternal undernutrition. Such homeostatic mechanisms may explain why acute food deprivations produce sizable birth weight deficits, while food supplementations in chronically undernourished women do not yield the expected increase in birth weight.

Of the trace elements discussed during this session of the Symposium, zinc has received the most attention. Studies of the effect of zinc on human pregnancy have yielded conflicting results. Early reports indicated that low serum values during pregnancy were associated with abnormal labor and fetal malformations (8) and that abnormalities of labor can be corrected by administration of zinc sulfate (9). Metcoff (10) and McMicheal

TABLE I

Home Diet, Nutritional Status, and Birth Weight in Addis Ababa, 1985

Number of families	130
Median family size	5
Median parity	3
Mean dietary intake (with 95% CI)	
Energy as % BMR	108.9 (98.7–119.0)
Protein as % of requirement	121.7 (113.1–130.3)
Mean BMI as % of median (with 95% CI)	
Husband	83.5 (81.3–85.6)
Mother 1 week postpartum	97.3 (95.0–99.6)
Mean birth weight in grams (with 95% CI)	3252 (3174–3330)
Perinatal mortality (%)	3.9

[a]BMI = Body mass index (W/H^2).

et al. (11) have reported that low serum levels of zinc during pregnancy are associated with accelerated fetal growth. This inverse relationship between maternal serum zinc and fetal growth has been interpreted to indicate an efficient maternal–fetal transfer and uptake of zinc with subsequent fetal growth rate that varied directly with the amount of zinc crossing the placenta. These observational and quasi-experimental studies were followed by more studies which have yielded conflicting results. The latest studies on persons of English, Indian, and Chinese extractions show no adverse effect of zinc deficiency on the course of pregnancy and the fetus (12,13). Such negative results have persuaded some to regard all previous findings on the association of maternal zinc nutriture and fetal outcome as one of the most "bizarre diagnostic traps" seen in pregnancy (14).

The major problem in assessing the role of maternal zinc nutriture on pregnancy outcome is the lack of a sensitive and specific diagnostic method of zinc deficiency or sufficiency. The sensitivity and specificity of functional abnormalities as reflected in decreases in alkaline phosphatase, cellular immune function, taste activity, etc., have not been evaluated with appropriately designed studies. Thus, it has not been possible to identify the gravida with true zinc deficiency who may have abnormal pregnancy outcome as a result of such deficiency. Since serum values of zinc are considered to be poor indicators of the state of zinc nutriture during pregnancy, the only way of determining whether there is a zinc deficiency is to increase the amount of zinc in the diet of populations whose diets provide inadequate amounts of the trace metal and see if the supplementation produces the expected effect on fetal growth and pregnancy outcome. The identification of gravida with clinically significant zinc deficiency is of major public health importance to developing countries, since fetal growth retardation and abnormalities associated with labor and delivery are major sources of excess perinatal mortality.

While research into methods for prevention of LBW proceeds, efforts must continue to reduce the rate of death and damage among prematurely born newborns. One area of major concern has been the provision of safe food in sufficient quantities to ensure optimal growth and development. Total parenteral nutrition (TPN) has been developed to meet the nutritional needs of critically ill LBW infants and the surgical newborn. For most developing countries TPN is beyond the technological and economic base perinatal health practice. The same can be said about the fortification of human milk to meet the nutritional requirements of very LBW infants. The introduction of these forms of nutrition require careful monitoring during the period of feeding and careful long-term follow-up for possible side effects, particularly those related to the central nervous system.

Likewise, the provision of adequate levels of vitamins during TPN and early enteral feeding is of importance to avoid deficiency on the one hand and toxicity on the other. A safe level for vitamin E in very LBW infants has been determined by Dr. Green and colleagues. The same cannot be said about vitamin A. The finding that a significant amount of vitamin A may be lost on exposure to plastic tubing used in TPN and to light in nurseries underscores the technical difficulties of artificial feeding.

REFERENCES

1. Naeye, R. L., and Tafari, N. (1983). "Risk Factors in Pregancy and Diseases of the Fetus and Newborn," pp. 103–124. William & Wilkins, Baltimore, Maryland.
2. Guzick, D. S., and Winn, K. (1985). *Obstet. Gynecol.* **65,** 11.
3. Bejar, R., Curbello, V., Davis, C., and Gluck, L. (1981). *Obstet. Gynecol.* **57,** 479.
4. Durnin, J. V. G. A., McKillop, F. M., Grant, S., and Fitzgerald, G. (1985). *Lancet* **ii,** 823.
5. *W. H. O. Tech. Rep. Ser.* No. 724 (1985).
6. Crank, C. E., and Roche, A. F. (1982). *Am. J. Clin. Nutr.* **35,** 347.
7. Sukhatme, P. V., and Margen, S. (1982). *Am. J. Clin. Nutr.* **35,** 355.
8. Jameson, S. (1976). *Acta Med. Scand.* **197,** Suppl. No. 583.
9. Jameson, S. (1981). *In* "Zinc in the Environment. Part II: Health Effects" (J. O. Niragu, ed.), pp. 183–197. Wiley, New York.
10. Metcoff, J. (1980). *Early Hum. Dev.* **4,** 99.
11. McMichael, A. J., Dreosti, I. E., Gibson, G. T., Hartshorne, J. M., Buckley, R. A., and Colley, D. P. (1982). *Early Hum. Dev.* **7,** 59.
12. Campbell-Brown, M., Wnrd, R. J., Haines, A. P., North, W. R. S., Abraham, R., McFayden, I. R., Turnkund, J. R., and King, C. J. (1985). *Br. J. Obstet. Gynaecol.* **92,** 857.
13. Ghosh, A., Fong, L. Y. Y., Wan, C. W., Liang, S. T., Woo, J. S. K., and Wong, V. (1985). *Br. J. Obstet. Gynaecol.* **92,** 886.
14. Hytten, F. E. (1985). *Br. J. Obstet. Gynaecol.* **92,** 873.

Index

C

H

R

S

U

V

W

Z